久保帯人

A little while ago, I don't know what I was thinking, but I bought a suit for the first time in my life. A black suit for all occasions. But even before caring about such occasions, I realized there are no such occasions.
Tite Kubo

Bleach is author Tite Kubo's second title. Kubo made his debut with *ZOMBIE POWDER*, a four-volume series for *WEEKLY SHONEN JUMP*. To date, *BLEACH* has sold nearly 7 million volumes and has been translated into seven different languages. Beginning its serialization in 2001, Bleach is still a mainstay in the pages of *WEEKLY SHONEN JUMP*.

BLEACH
Vol. 5: RIGHT ARM OF THE GIANT
The SHONEN JUMP Graphic Novel Edition

STORY AND ART BY TITE KUBO

English Adaptation/Lance Caselman
Translation/Joe Yamazaki
Touch-Up Art & Lettering/Dave Lanphear
Cover & Interior Design/Sean Lee
Editor/Kit Fox

Managing Editor/Elizabeth Kawasaki
Director of Production/Noboru Watanabe
Editorial Director/Alvin Lu
Executive Vice President & Editor in Chief/Hyoe Narita
Sr. Director of Licensing & Acquisitions/Rika Inouye
Vice President of Sales & Marketing/Liza Coppola
Vice President of Strategic Development/Yumi Hoashi
Publisher/Seiji Horibuchi

Printed in the U.S.A.

Published by VIZ, LLC
P.O. Box 77010
San Francisco, CA 94107

SHONEN JUMP Graphic Novel Edition
10 9 8 7 6 5 4 3 2 1
First printing, January 2005

BLEACH ALL

石田雨竜
Uryû Ishida

有沢竜貴
Tatsuki Arisawa

Chad Yasutora

茶渡泰虎

STORIES

BLEACH5

RIGHT ARM OF THE GIANT

Contents

35. Will You Be My Enemy?

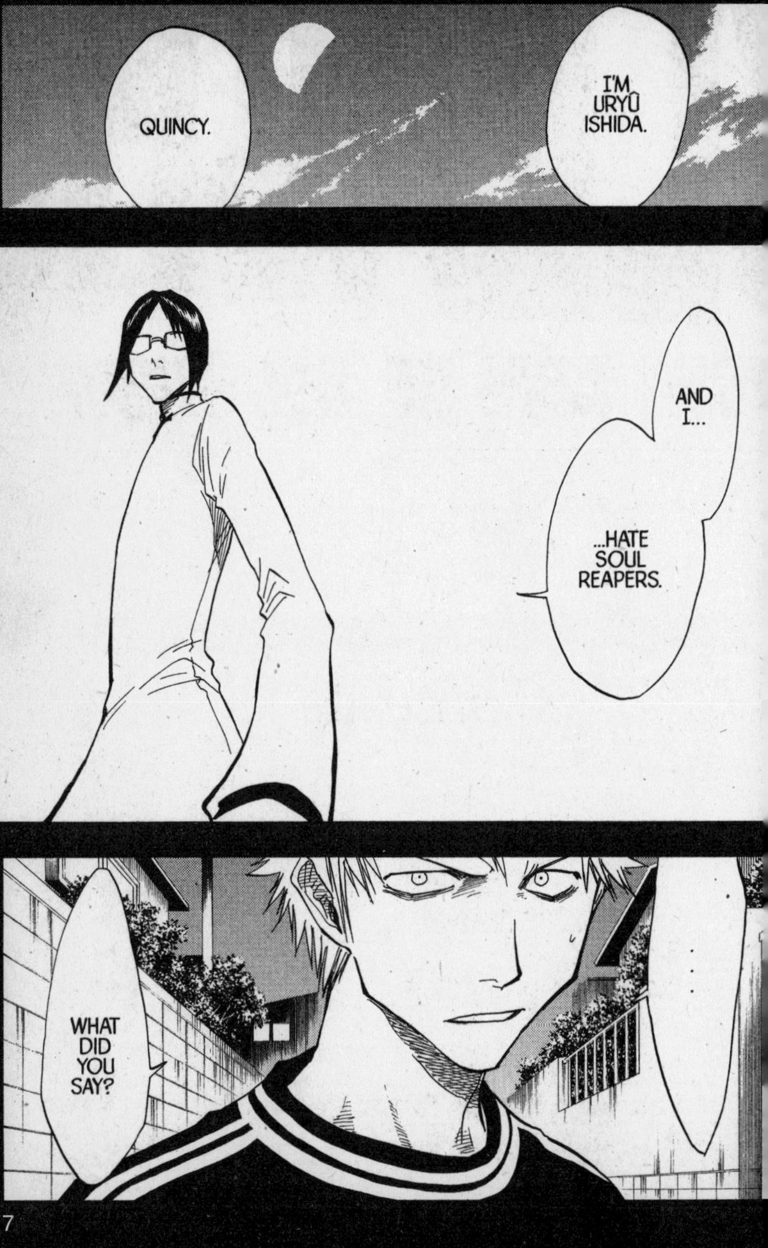
I'M URYÛ ISHIDA.
QUINCY.
AND I...
...HATE SOUL REAPERS.
.....
WHAT DID YOU SAY?

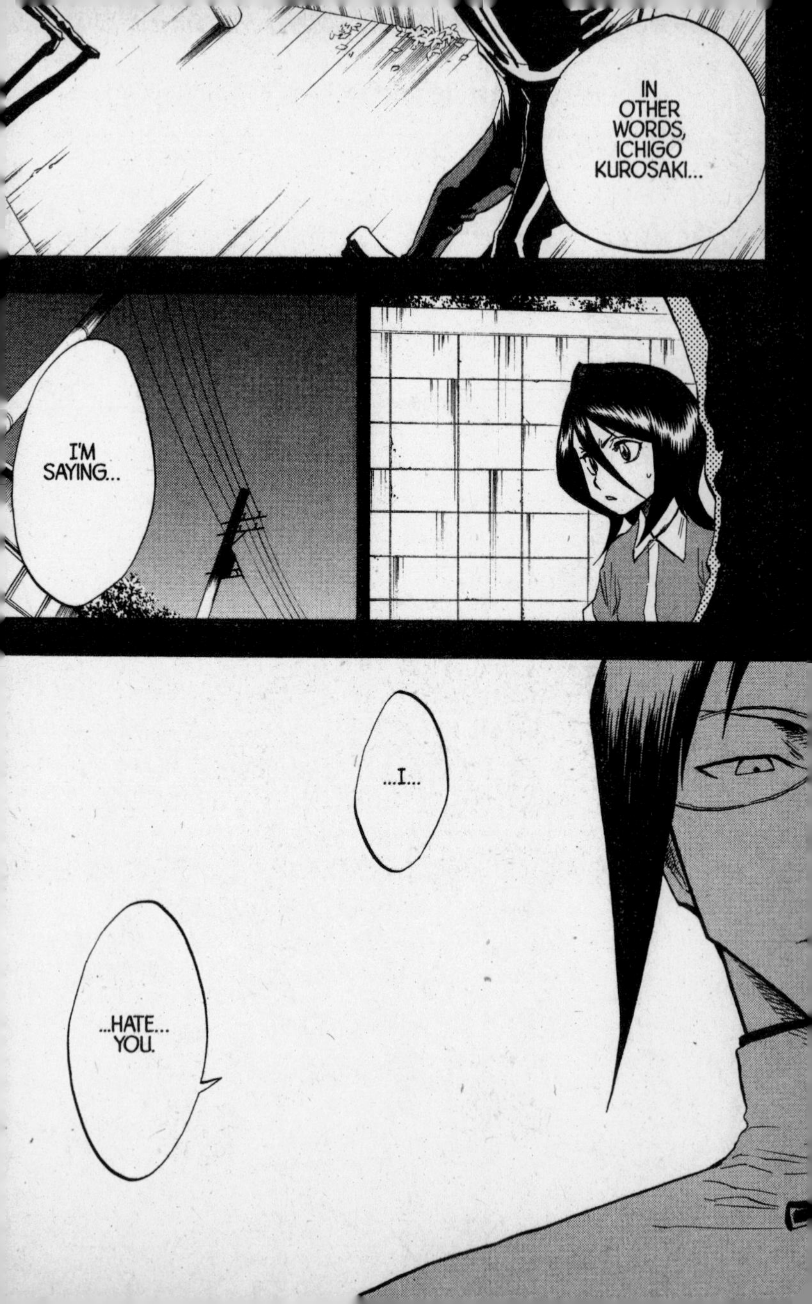
IN OTHER WORDS, ICHIGO KUROSAKI...
I'M SAYING...
...I...
...HATE... YOU.

35. Will You Be My Enemy?

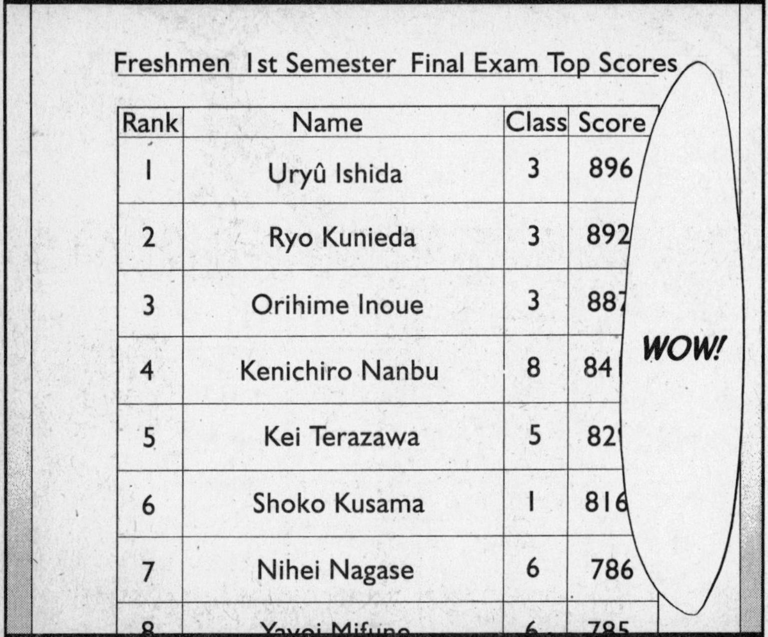
Freshmen 1st Semester Final Exam Top Scores

Rank	Name	Class	Score
1	Uryû Ishida	3	896
2	Ryo Kunieda	3	892
3	Orihime Inoue	3	887
4	Kenichiro Nanbu	8	84
5	Kei Terazawa	5	82
6	Shoko Kusama	1	816
7	Nihei Nagase	6	786
8	Yayoi Mifune	6	785

WOW!

BLEACH
ブリーチ

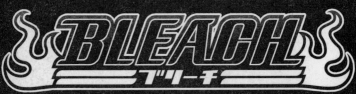

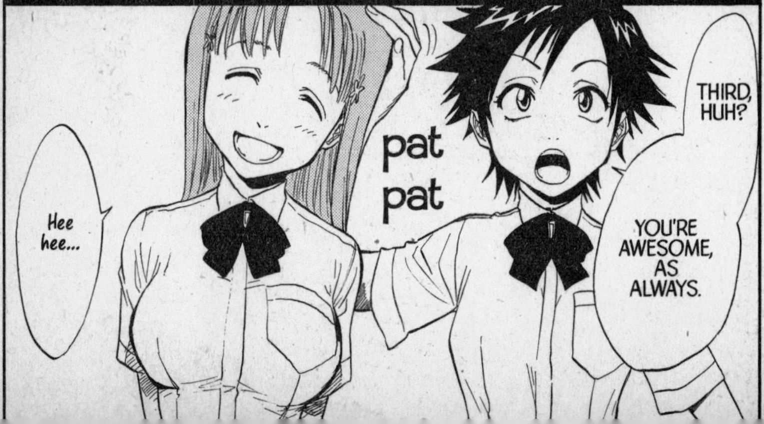
THIRD, HUH?
YOU'RE AWESOME, AS ALWAYS.
pat pat
Hee hee...

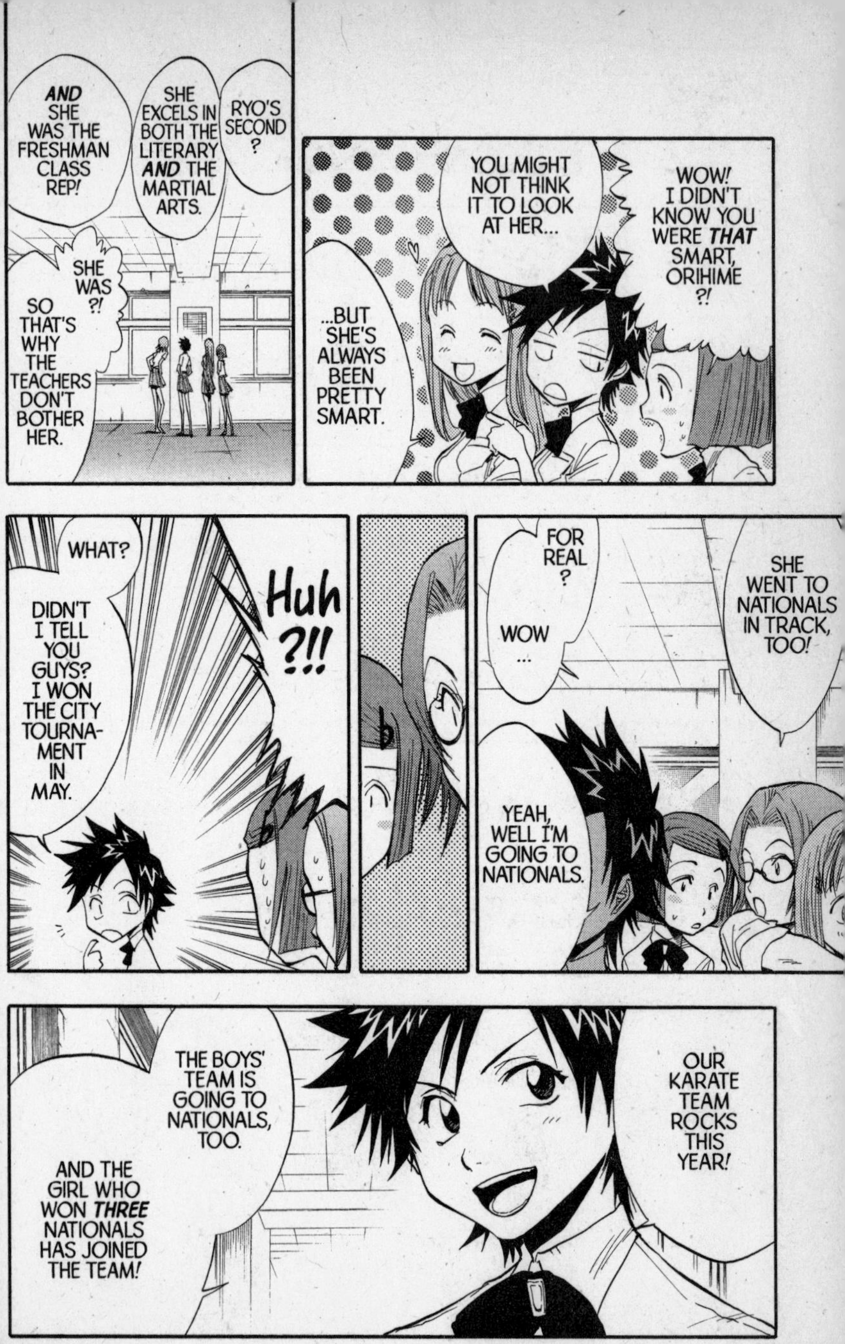
WOW! I DIDN'T KNOW YOU WERE THAT SMART, ORIHIME?!
YOU MIGHT NOT THINK IT TO LOOK AT HER...
...BUT SHE'S ALWAYS BEEN PRETTY SMART.
RYO'S SECOND?
SHE EXCELS IN BOTH THE LITERARY AND THE MARTIAL ARTS.
AND SHE WAS THE FRESHMAN CLASS REP!
SHE WAS?!
SO THAT'S WHY THE TEACHERS DON'T BOTHER HER.
SHE WENT TO NATIONALS IN TRACK, TOO!
FOR REAL?
WOW...
YEAH, WELL I'M GOING TO NATIONALS.
Huh?!!
WHAT?
DIDN'T I TELL YOU GUYS? I WON THE CITY TOURNA-MENT IN MAY.
OUR KARATE TEAM ROCKS THIS YEAR!
THE BOYS' TEAM IS GOING TO NATIONALS, TOO.
AND THE GIRL WHO WON THREE NATIONALS HAS JOINED THE TEAM!

READ THIS WAY

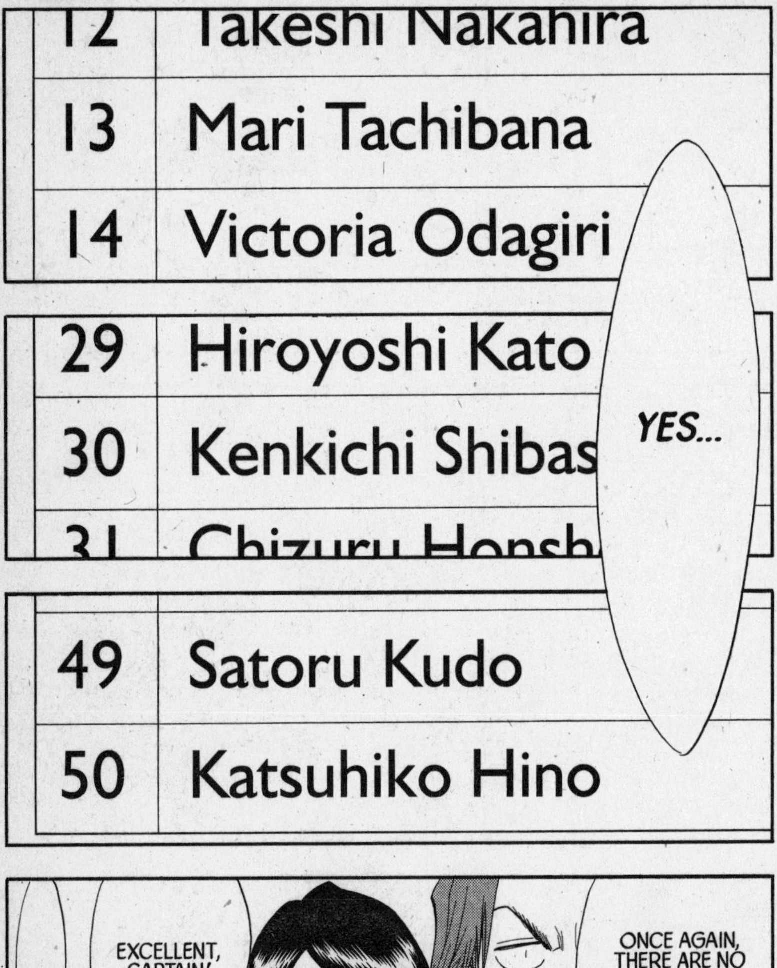

12 Takeshi Nakahira
13 Mari Tachibana
14 Victoria Odagiri
29 Hiroyoshi Kato
30 Kenkichi Shibas
YES...
49 Satoru Kudo
50 Katsuhiko Hino
ONCE AGAIN, THERE ARE NO TRAITORS AMONG US. NONE OF US HAS MADE THE TOP 50!!
EXCELLENT, CAPTAIN!
...

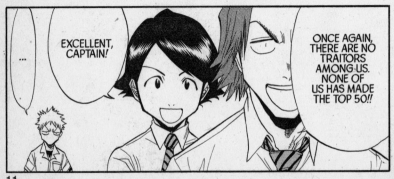

23 Ichigo Kurosaki

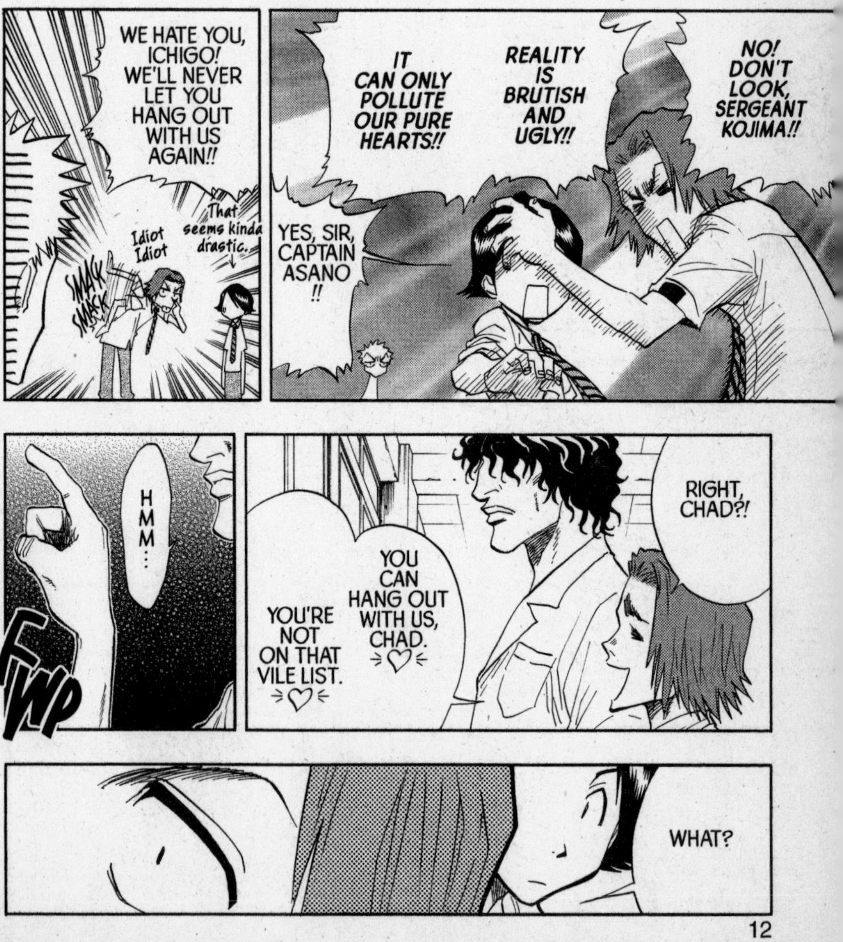

NO! DON'T LOOK, SERGEANT KOJIMA!!
REALITY IS BRUTISH AND UGLY!!
IT CAN ONLY POLLUTE OUR PURE HEARTS!!
YES, SIR, CAPTAIN ASANO!!
WE HATE YOU, ICHIGO! WE'LL NEVER LET YOU HANG OUT WITH US AGAIN!!
That seems kinda drastic.
Idiot Idiot
SMACK SMACK
RIGHT, CHAD?!
YOU CAN HANG OUT WITH US, CHAD.
YOU'RE NOT ON THAT VILE LIST.
HMM...
FWP
WHAT?

11 Chad Yasutora

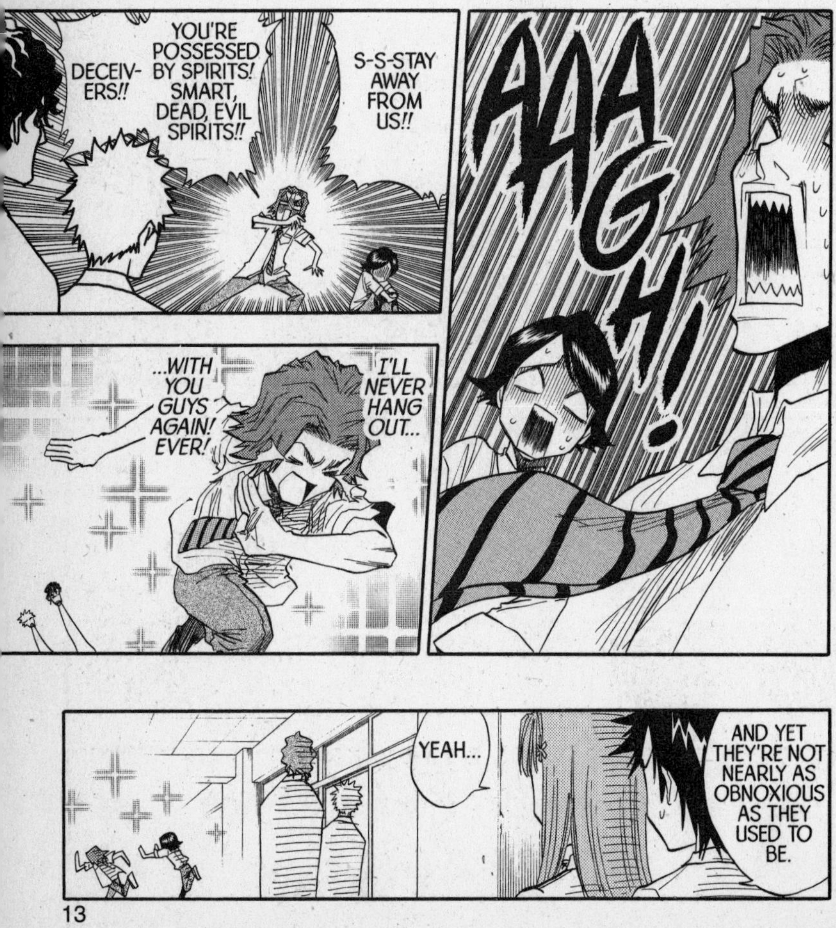
AAAGH!
S-S-STAY AWAY FROM US!!
YOU'RE POSSESSED BY SPIRITS! SMART, DEAD, EVIL SPIRITS!!
DECEIV-ERS!!
I'LL NEVER HANG OUT...
...WITH YOU GUYS AGAIN! EVER!
AND YET THEY'RE NOT NEARLY AS OBNOXIOUS AS THEY USED TO BE.
YEAH...

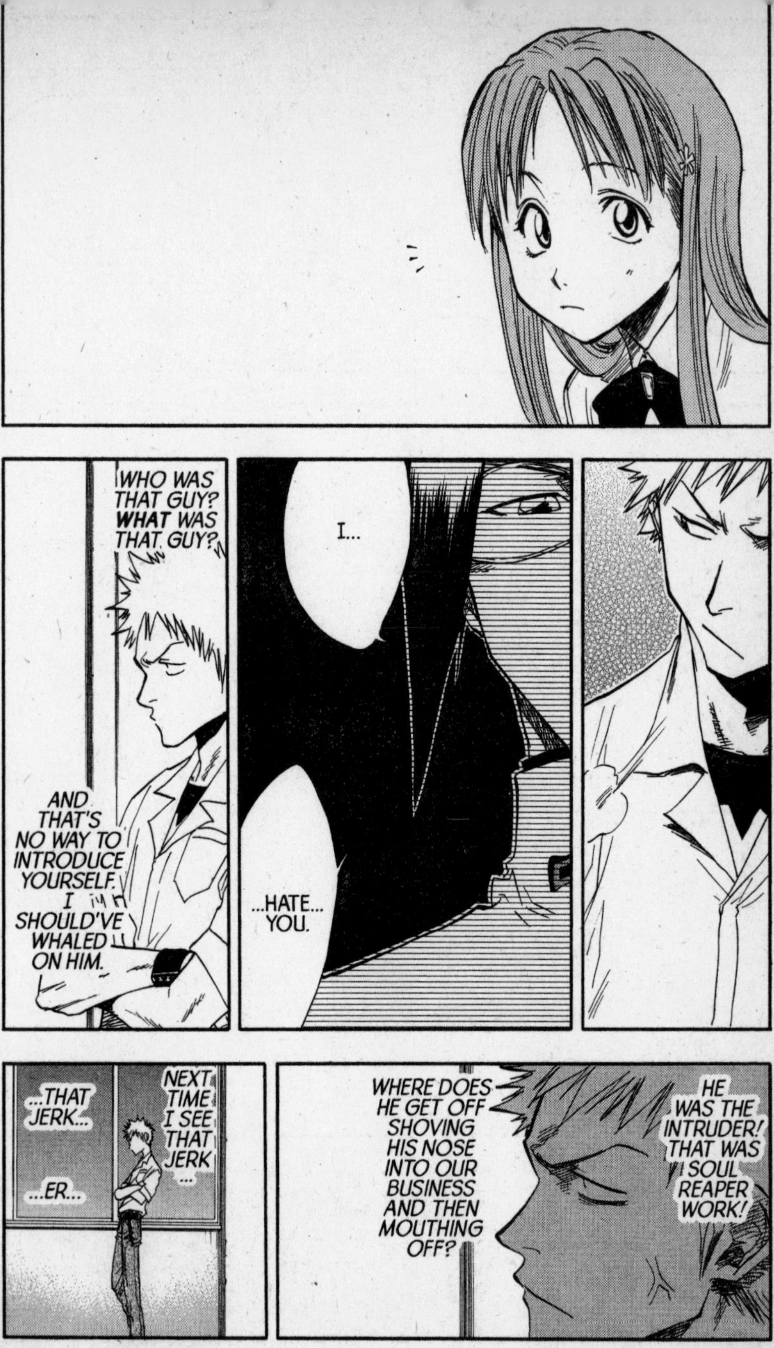
I...
...HATE... YOU.
WHO WAS THAT GUY? **WHAT** WAS THAT GUY?
AND THAT'S NO WAY TO INTRODUCE YOURSELF. I SHOULD'VE WHALED ON HIM.
HE WAS THE INTRUDER! THAT WAS SOUL REAPER WORK!
WHERE DOES HE GET OFF SHOVING HIS NOSE INTO OUR BUSINESS AND THEN MOUTHING OFF?
NEXT TIME I SEE THAT JERK...
...THAT JERK...
...ER...

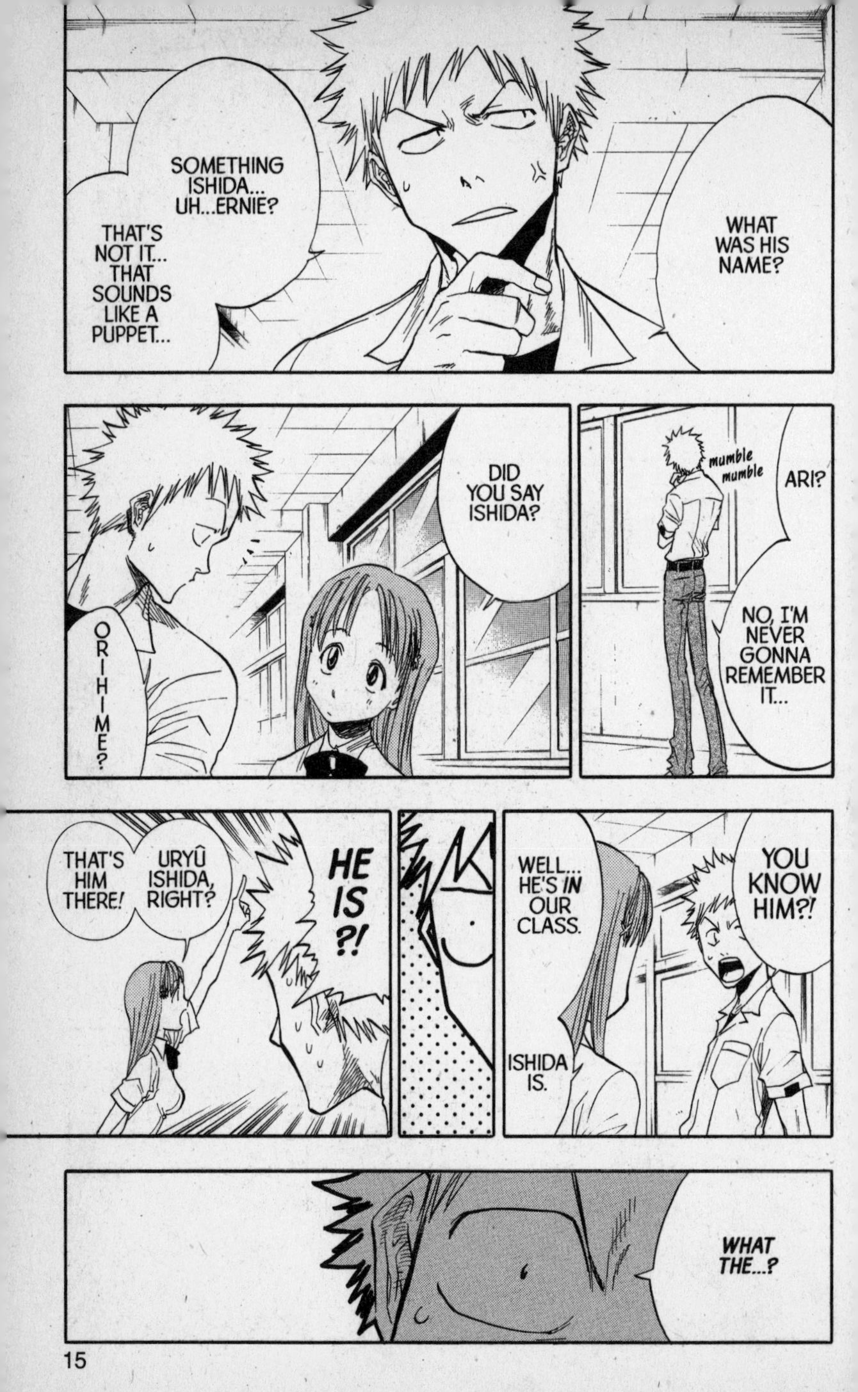
WHAT WAS HIS NAME?
SOMETHING ISHIDA... UH...ERNIE?
THAT'S NOT IT... THAT SOUNDS LIKE A PUPPET...
mumble mumble
ARI?
NO, I'M NEVER GONNA REMEMBER IT...
DID YOU SAY ISHIDA?
ORIHIME?
YOU KNOW HIM?!
WELL... HE'S *IN* OUR CLASS.
ISHIDA IS.
HE IS?!
URYÛ ISHIDA, RIGHT?
THAT'S HIM THERE!
WHAT THE...?

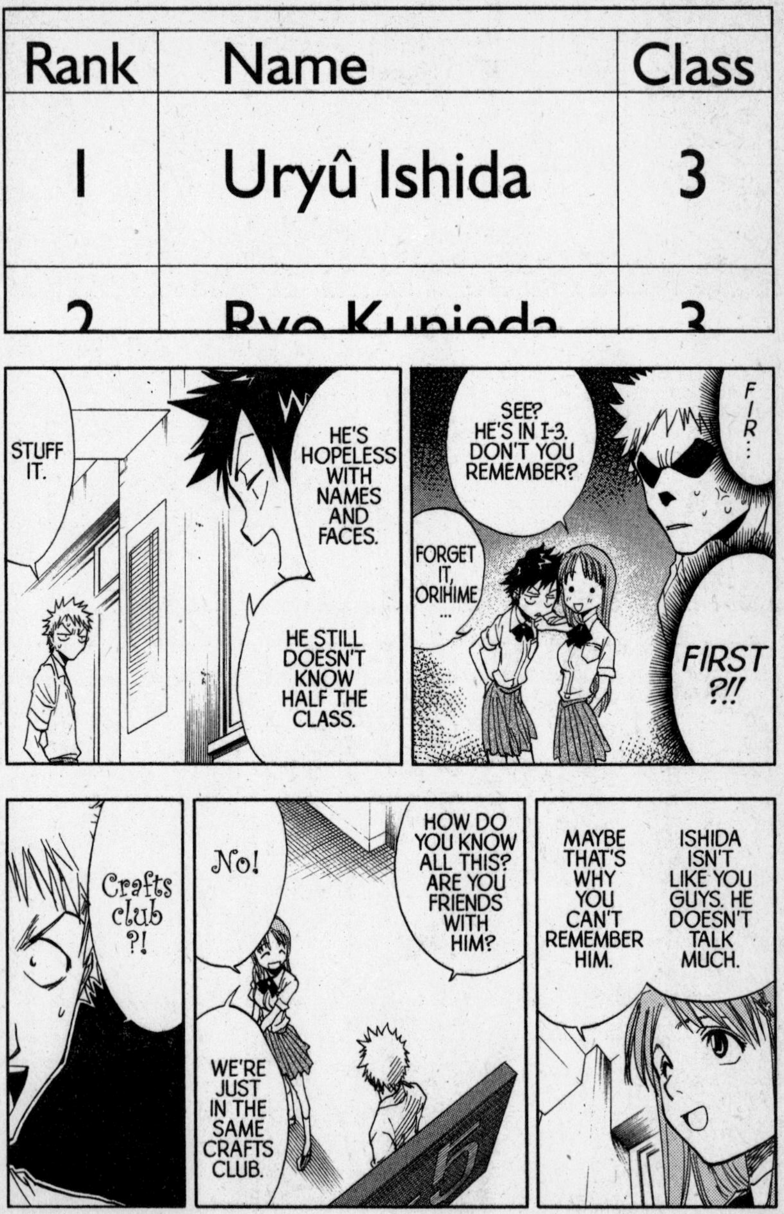

Rank
Name
Class
1
Uryû Ishida
3
2
Ryo Kunieda
3
FIR...
SEE? HE'S IN I-3. DON'T YOU REMEMBER?
FIRST ?!!
FORGET IT, ORIHIME...
HE'S HOPELESS WITH NAMES AND FACES.
STUFF IT.
HE STILL DOESN'T KNOW HALF THE CLASS.
ISHIDA ISN'T LIKE YOU GUYS. HE DOESN'T TALK MUCH.
MAYBE THAT'S WHY YOU CAN'T REMEMBER HIM.
HOW DO YOU KNOW ALL THIS? ARE YOU FRIENDS WITH HIM?
No!
WE'RE JUST IN THE SAME CRAFTS CLUB.
Crafts club ?!

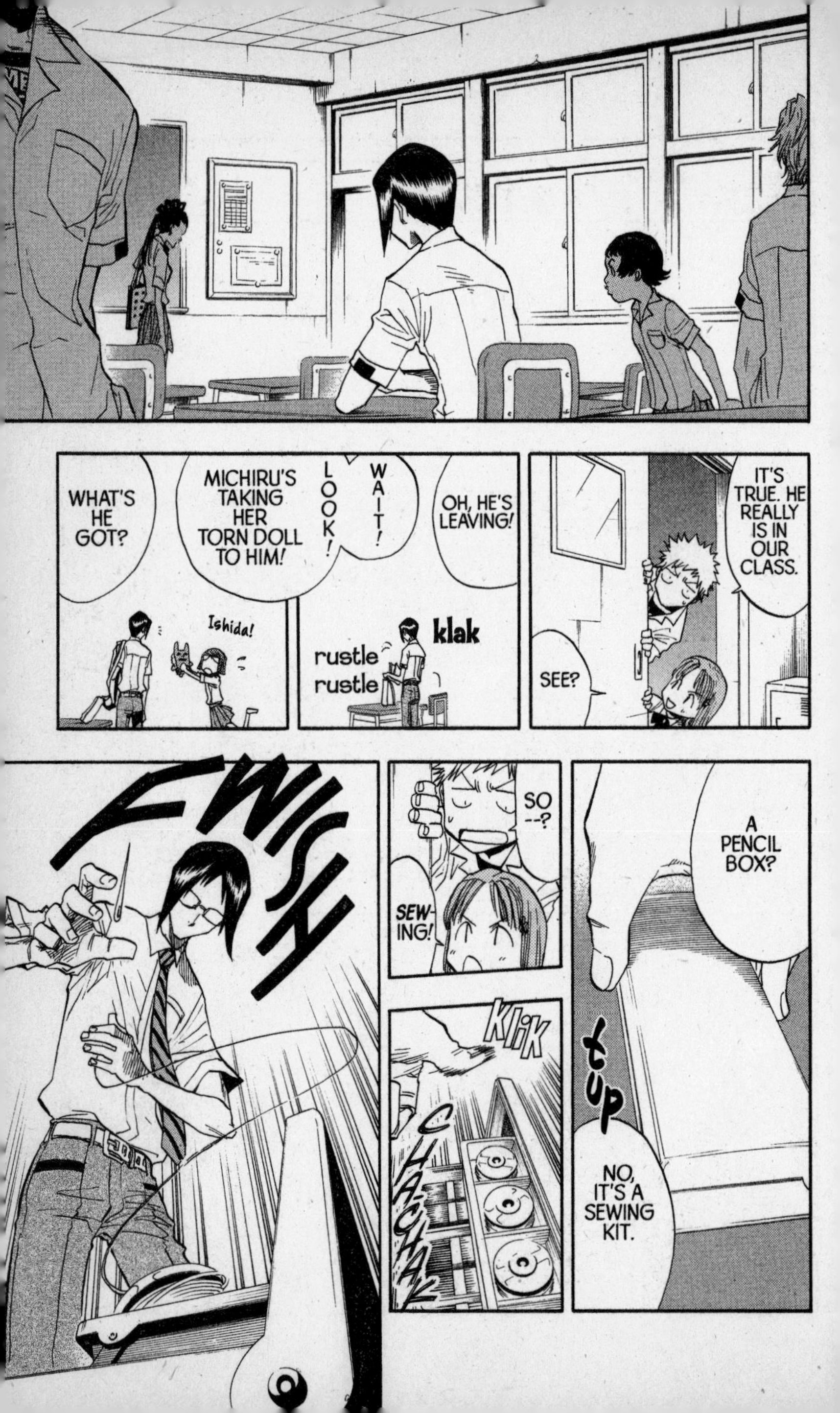
IT'S TRUE. HE REALLY IS IN OUR CLASS.
SEE?
OH, HE'S LEAVING!
WAIT!
LOOK!
klak
rustle rustle
MICHIRU'S TAKING HER TORN DOLL TO HIM!
WHAT'S HE GOT?
Ishida!
A PENCIL BOX?
tup
NO, IT'S A SEWING KIT.
SO --?
SEW-ING!
Klik
CHACHAK
FWISH

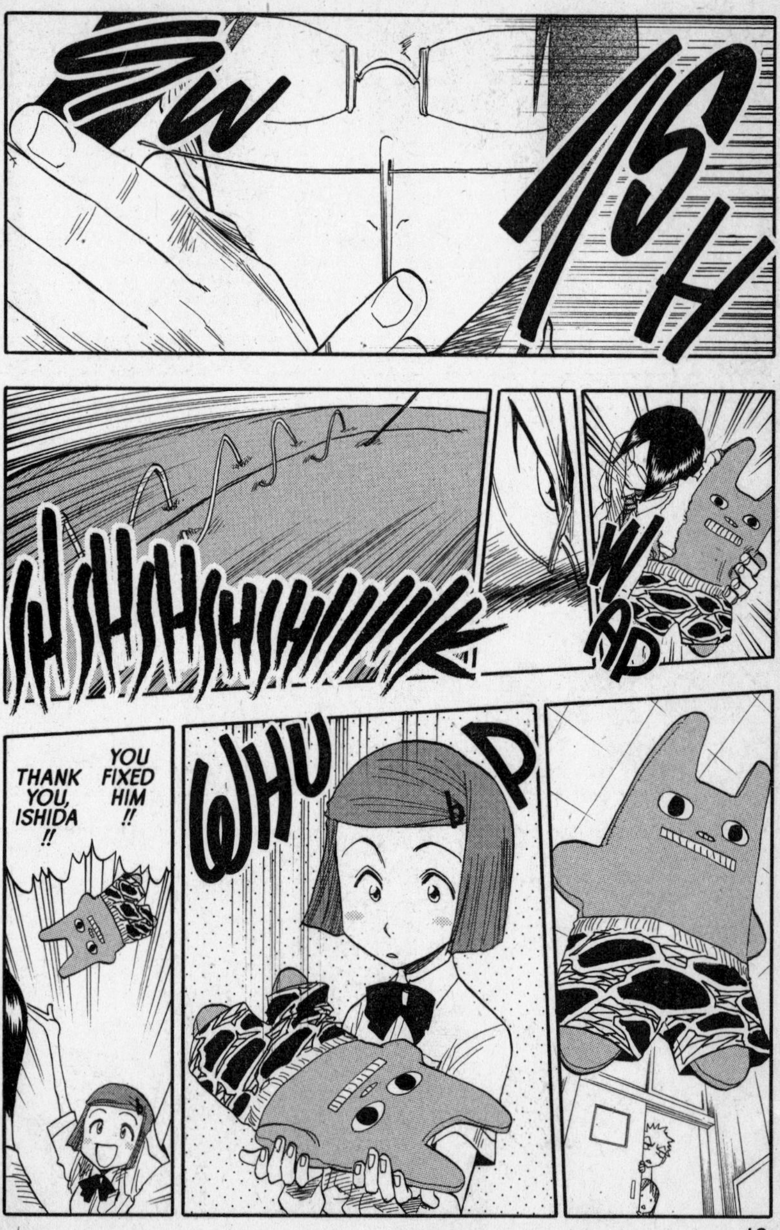
SWISH
SHSHSHSHSHIIIIIK
WAD
WHUP
YOU FIXED HIM !!
THANK YOU, ISHIDA !!

READ THIS WAY

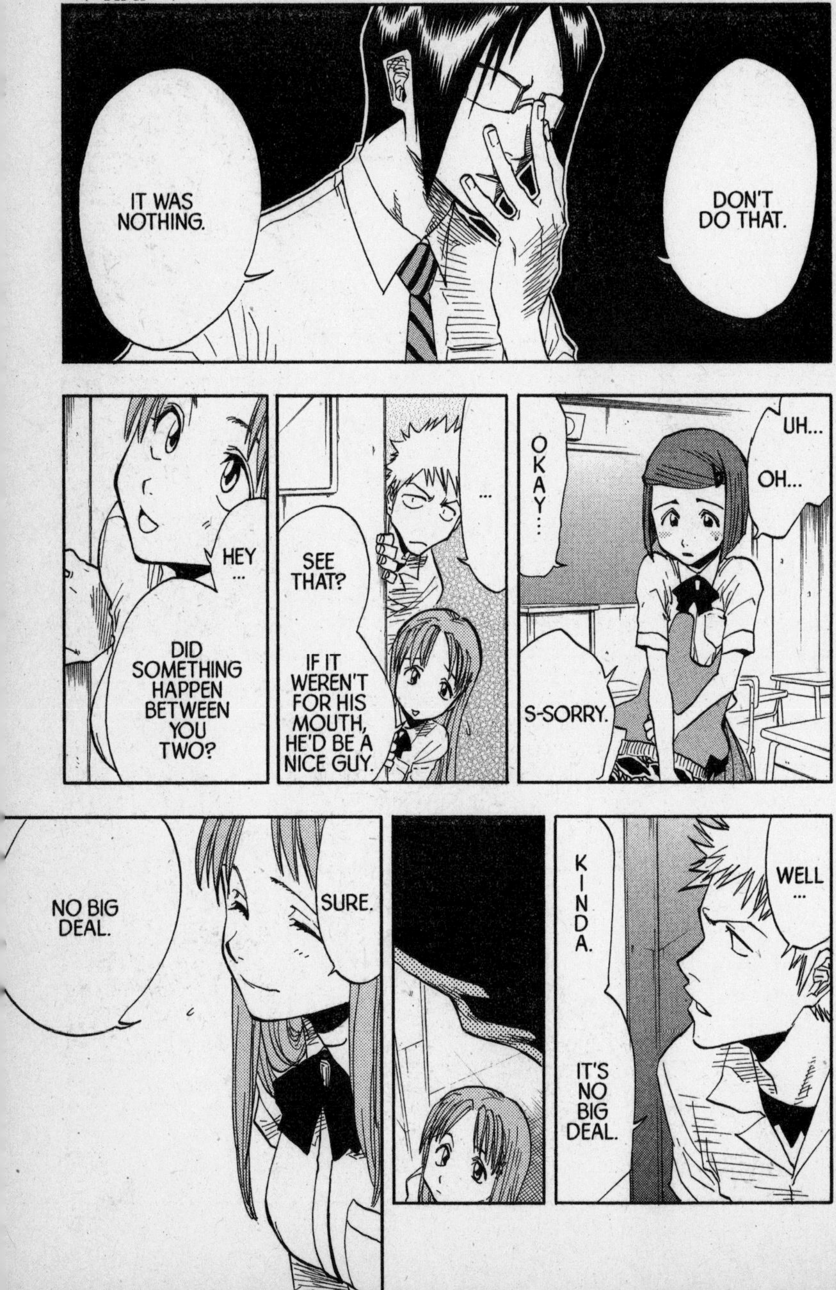
DON'T DO THAT.
IT WAS NOTHING.
UH...
OH...
OKAY...
S-SORRY.
...
SEE THAT?
IF IT WEREN'T FOR HIS MOUTH, HE'D BE A NICE GUY.
HEY...
DID SOMETHING HAPPEN BETWEEN YOU TWO?
WELL...
KINDA.
IT'S NO BIG DEAL.
SURE.
NO BIG DEAL.

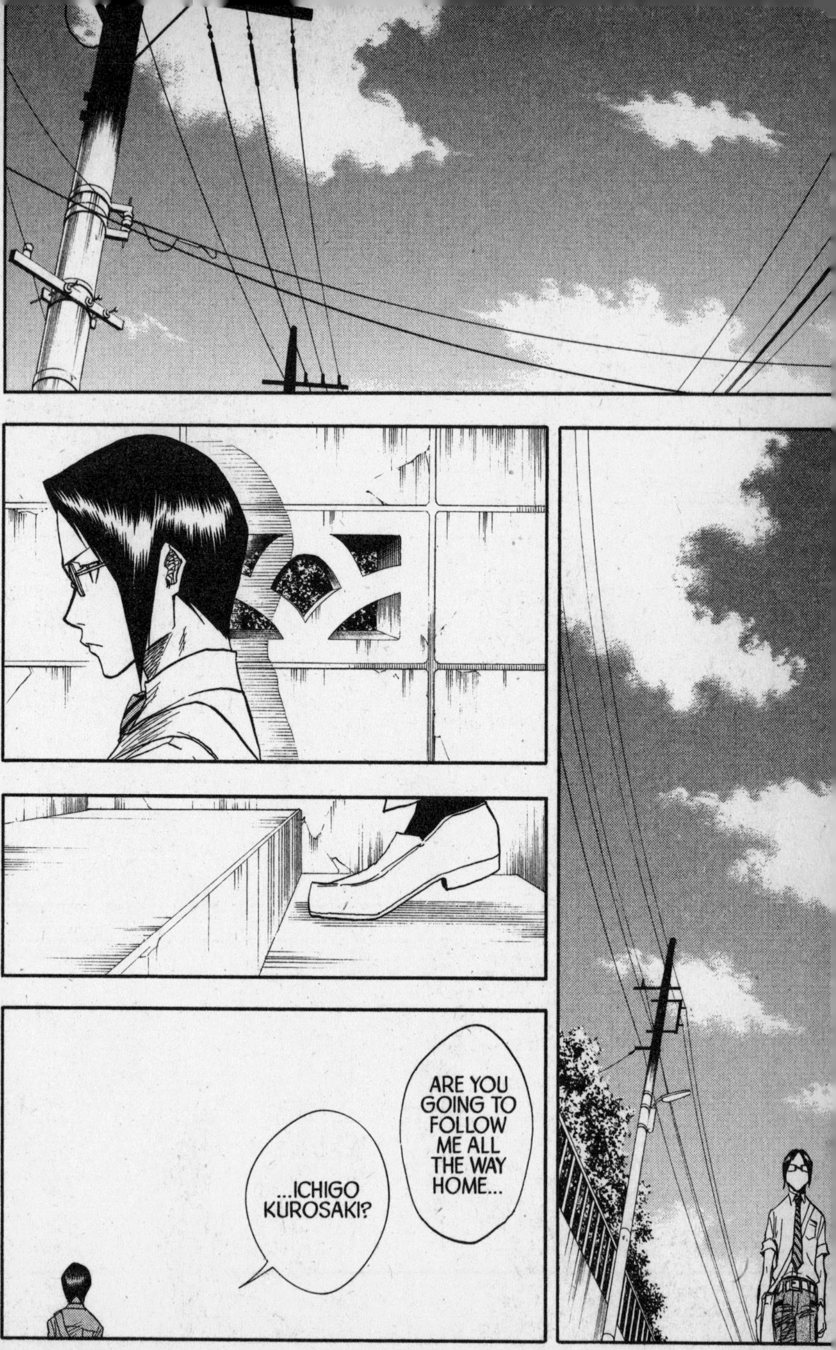
ARE YOU GOING TO FOLLOW ME ALL THE WAY HOME...
...ICHIGO KUROSAKI?

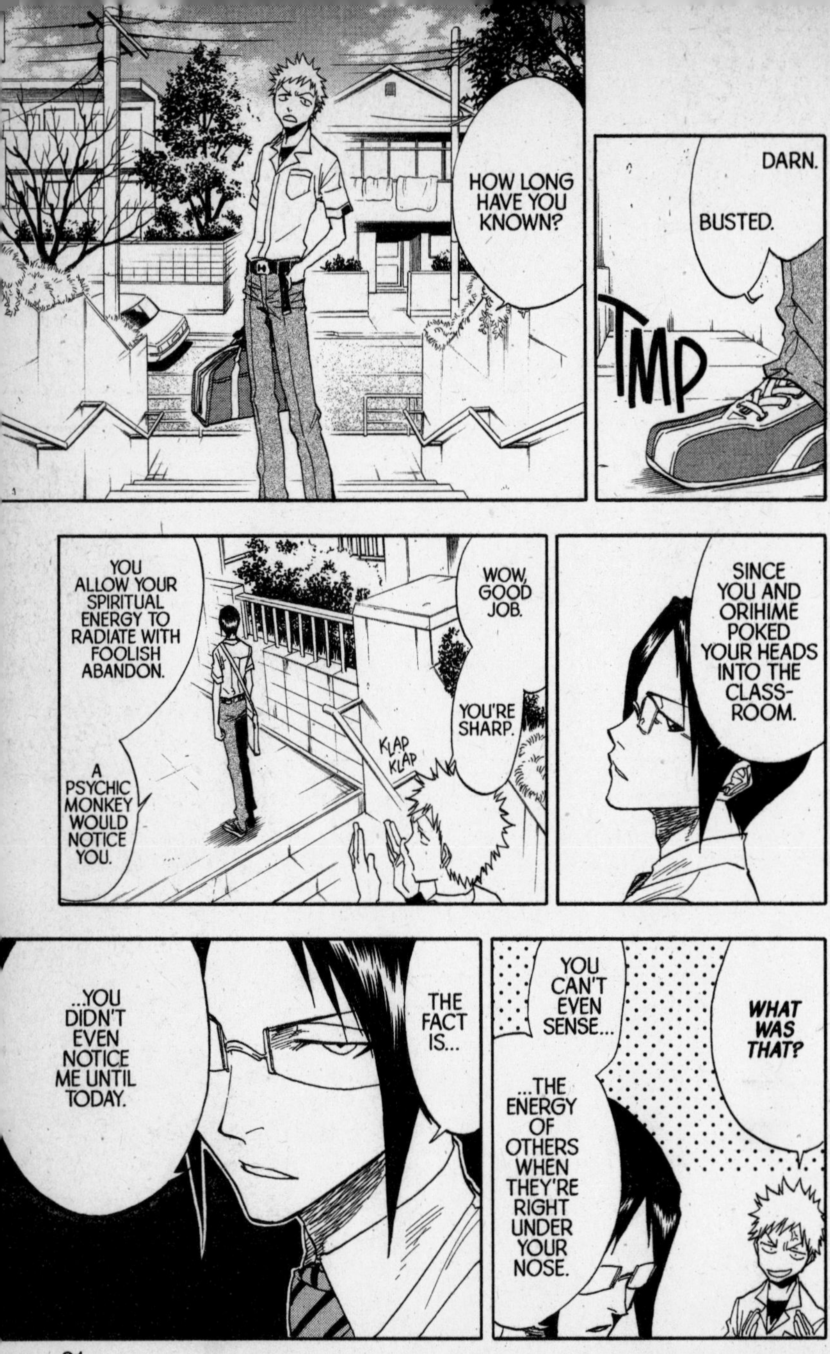
DARN.
BUSTED.
TMP
HOW LONG HAVE YOU KNOWN?
SINCE YOU AND ORIHIME POKED YOUR HEADS INTO THE CLASS-ROOM.
WOW, GOOD JOB.
YOU'RE SHARP.
KLAP KLAP
YOU ALLOW YOUR SPIRITUAL ENERGY TO RADIATE WITH FOOLISH ABANDON.
A PSYCHIC MONKEY WOULD NOTICE YOU.
WHAT WAS THAT?
YOU CAN'T EVEN SENSE...
...THE ENERGY OF OTHERS WHEN THEY'RE RIGHT UNDER YOUR NOSE.
THE FACT IS...
...YOU DIDN'T EVEN NOTICE ME UNTIL TODAY.

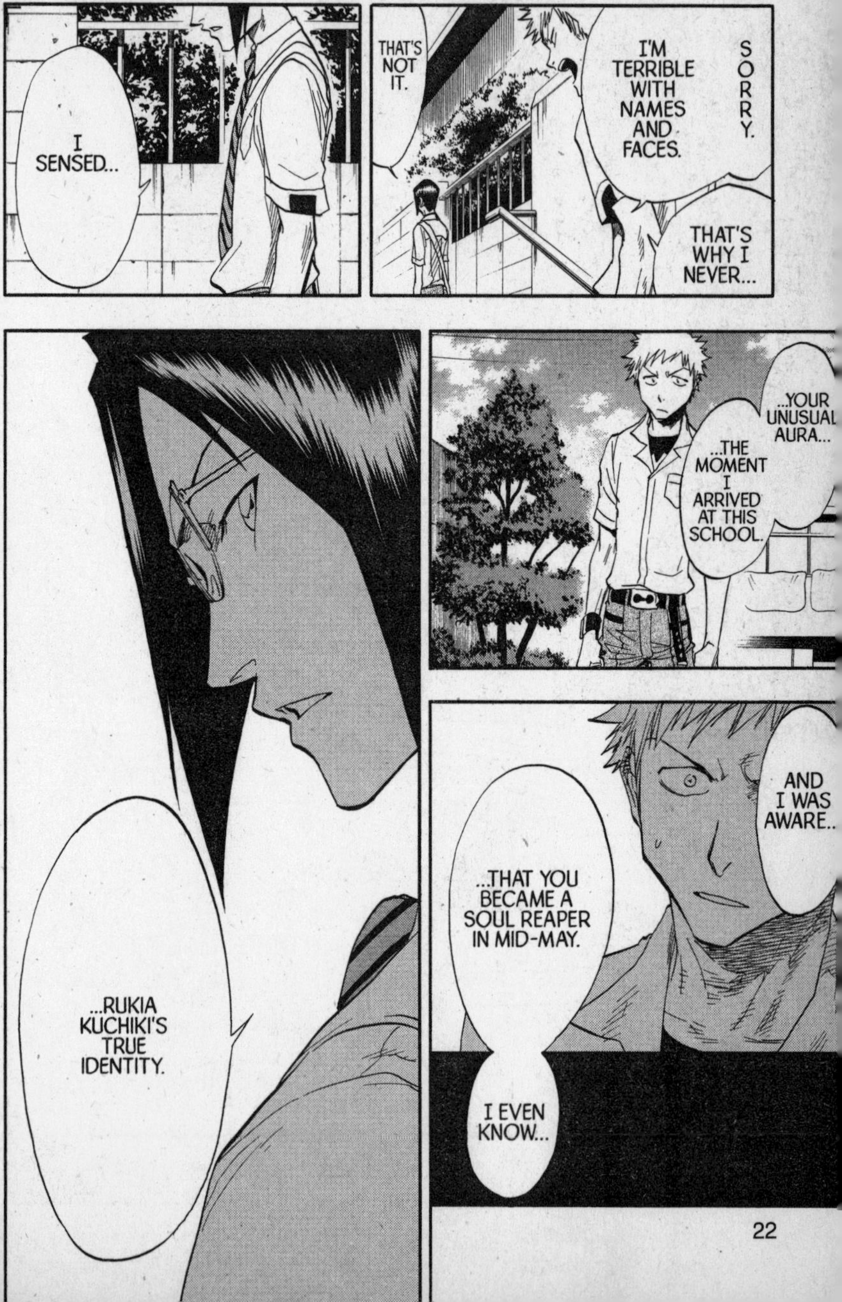
SORRY.
I'M TERRIBLE WITH NAMES AND FACES.
THAT'S WHY I NEVER...
THAT'S NOT IT.
I SENSED...
...YOUR UNUSUAL AURA...
...THE MOMENT I ARRIVED AT THIS SCHOOL.
AND I WAS AWARE...
...THAT YOU BECAME A SOUL REAPER IN MID-MAY.
I EVEN KNOW...
...RUKIA KUCHIKI'S TRUE IDENTITY.

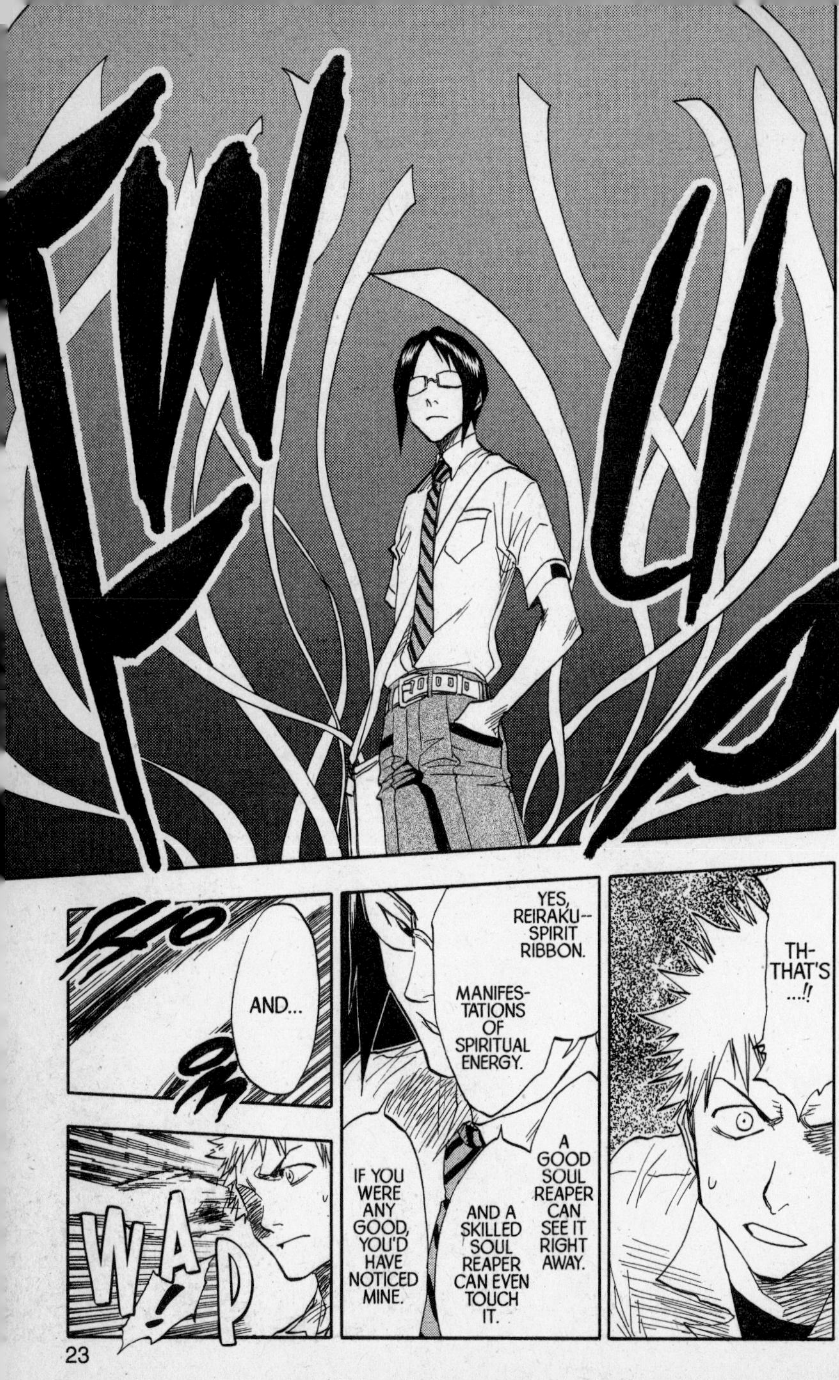
FWUP
TH-THAT'S ...!!
YES, REIRAKU--SPIRIT RIBBON.
MANIFESTATIONS OF SPIRITUAL ENERGY.
A GOOD SOUL REAPER CAN SEE IT RIGHT AWAY.
AND A SKILLED SOUL REAPER CAN EVEN TOUCH IT.
IF YOU WERE ANY GOOD, YOU'D HAVE NOTICED MINE.
SHOOM
AND...
WAP!

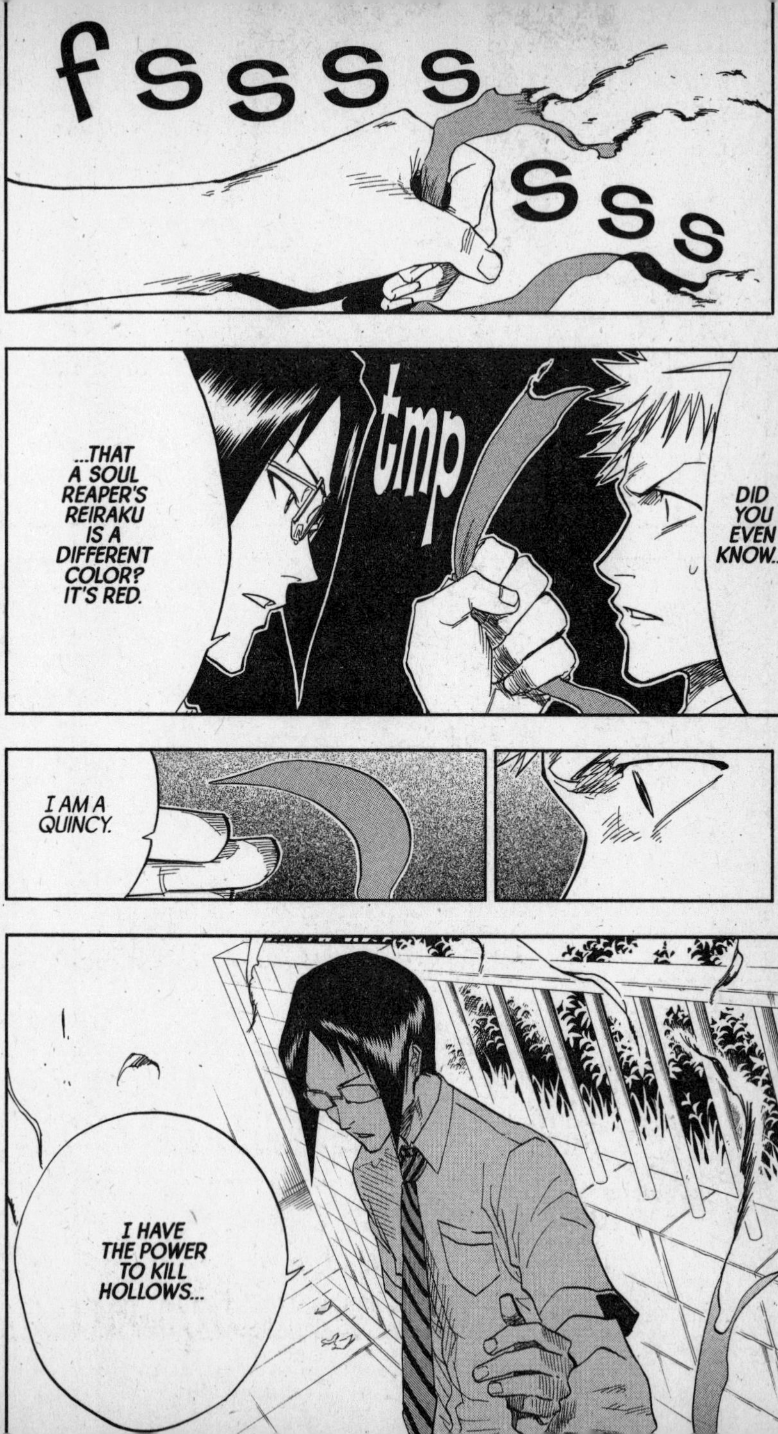
fssss
sss
DID YOU EVEN KNOW...
tmp
...THAT A SOUL REAPER'S REIRAKU IS A DIFFERENT COLOR? IT'S RED.
I AM A QUINCY.
!
I HAVE THE POWER TO KILL HOLLOWS...

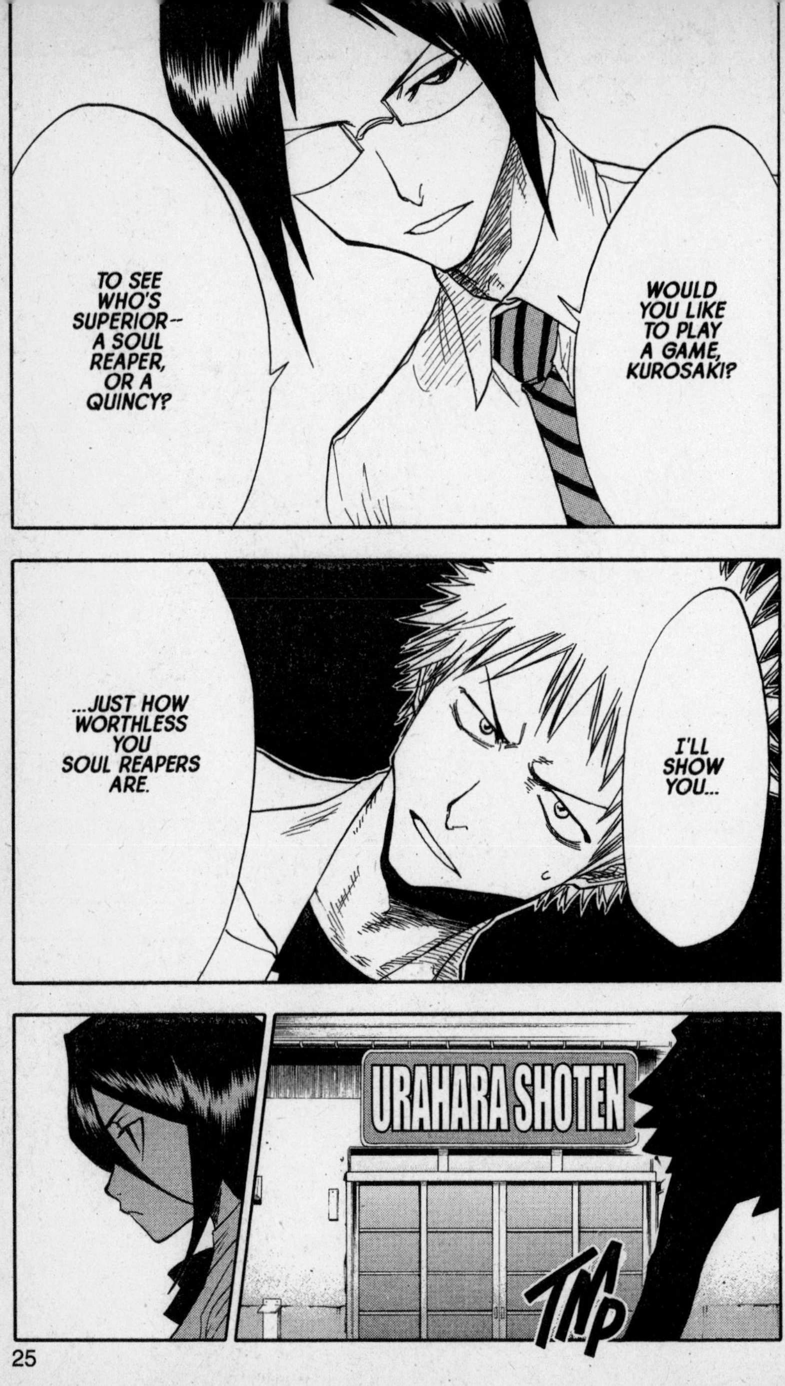
WOULD YOU LIKE TO PLAY A GAME, KUROSAKI?
TO SEE WHO'S SUPERIOR-- A SOUL REAPER, OR A QUINCY?
I'LL SHOW YOU...
...JUST HOW WORTHLESS YOU SOUL REAPERS ARE.
URAHARA SHOTEN
TMP

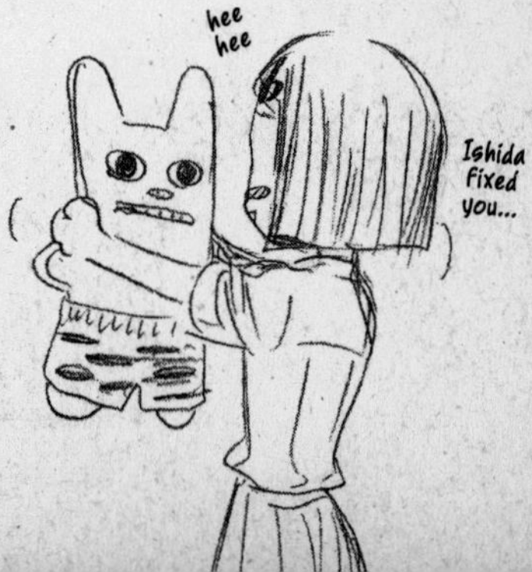
hee hee
Ishida fixed you...

36. They Died For Vengeance

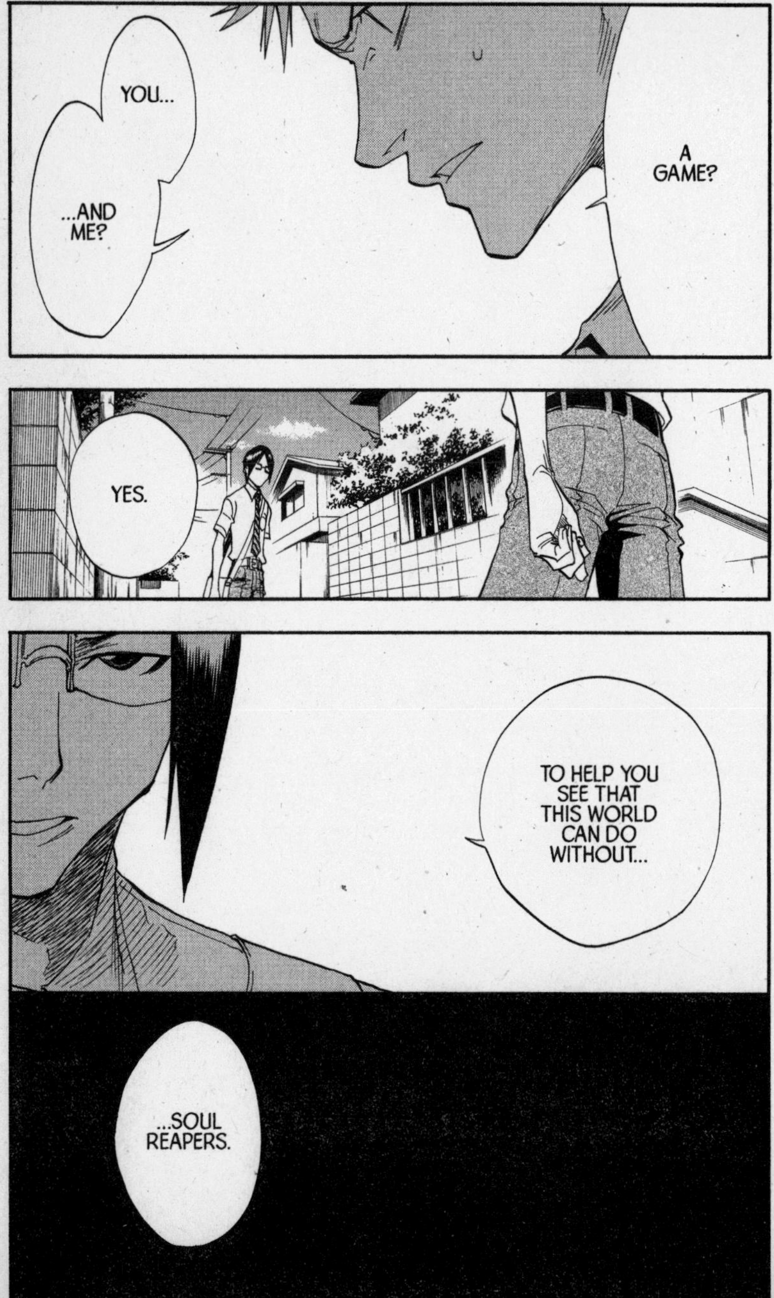
A GAME?
YOU... ...AND ME?
YES.
TO HELP YOU SEE THAT THIS WORLD CAN DO WITHOUT...
...SOUL REAPERS.

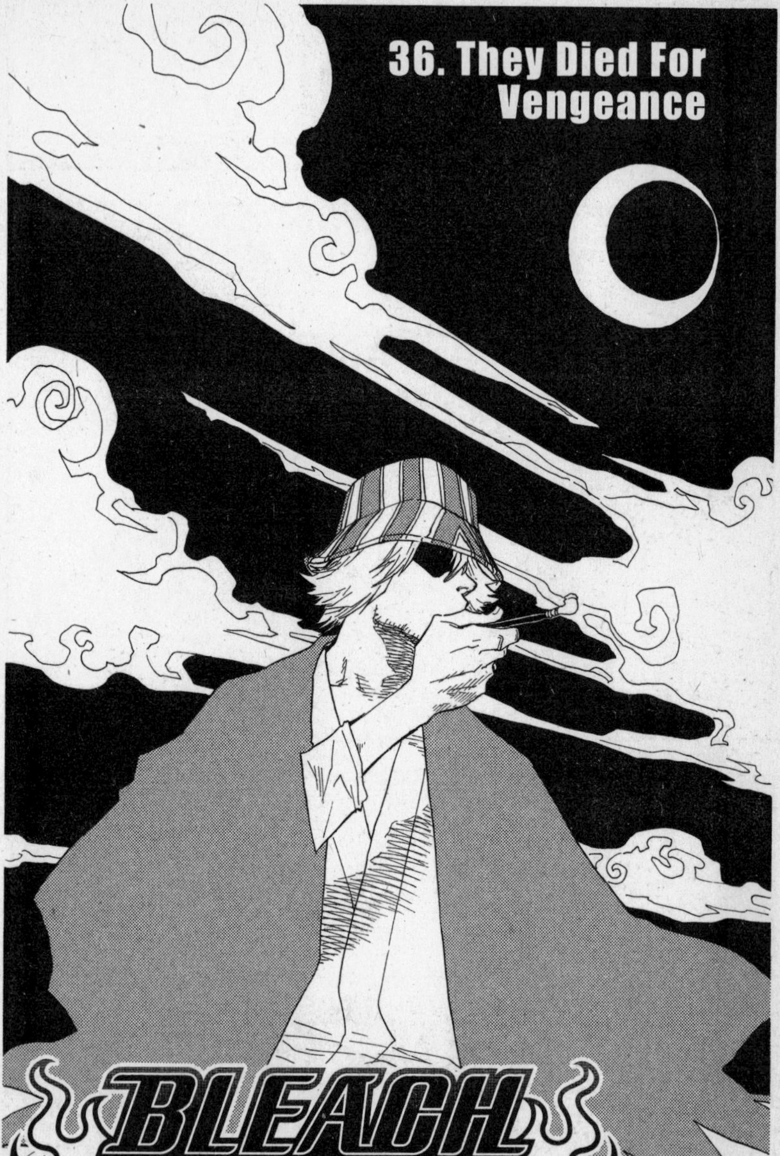
36. They Died For Vengeance
BLEACH
ブリーチ

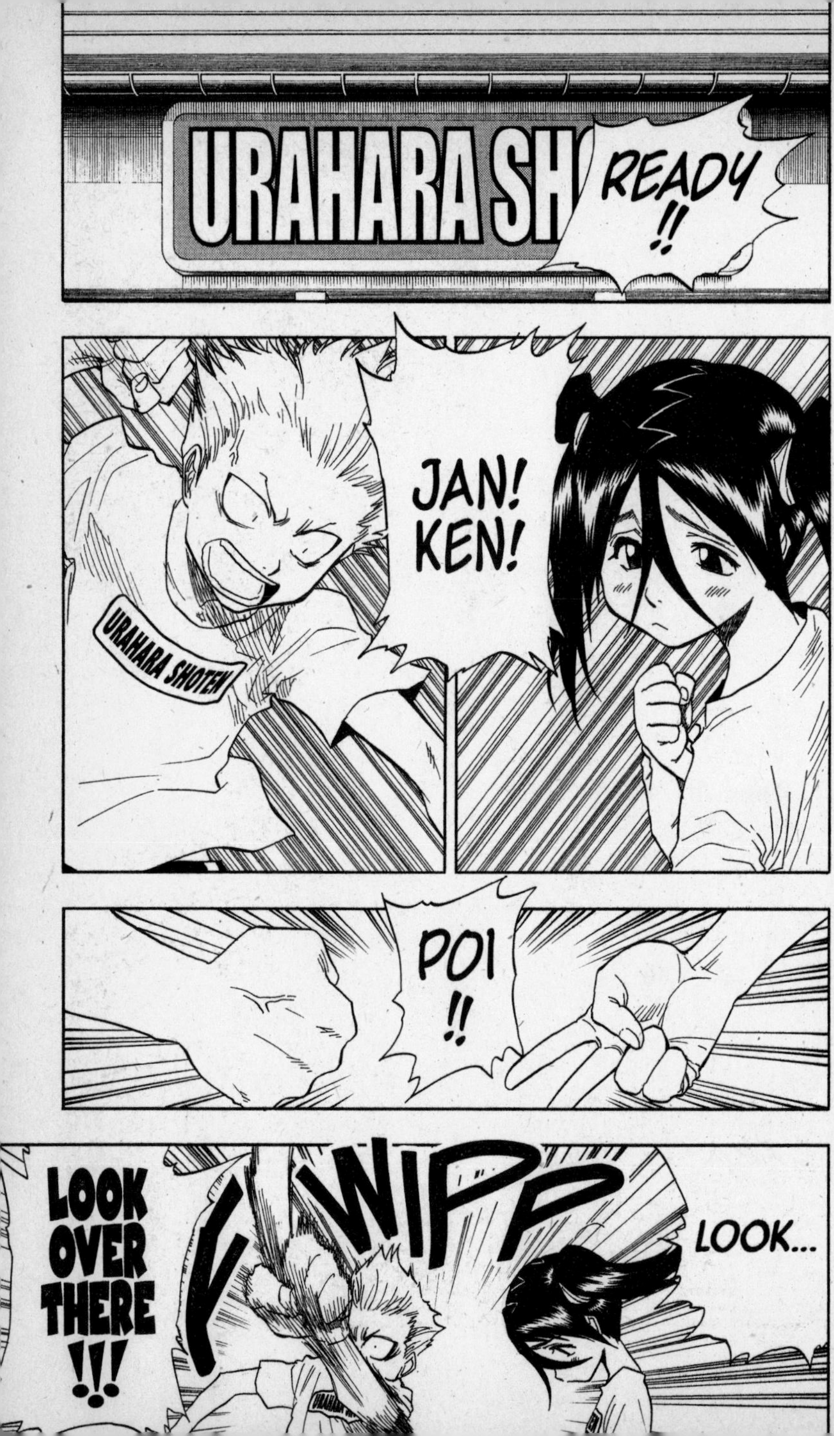

URAHARA SH
READY !!
JAN! KEN!
URAHARA SHOTEN
POI !!
LOOK...
WIPP
LOOK OVER THERE !!!

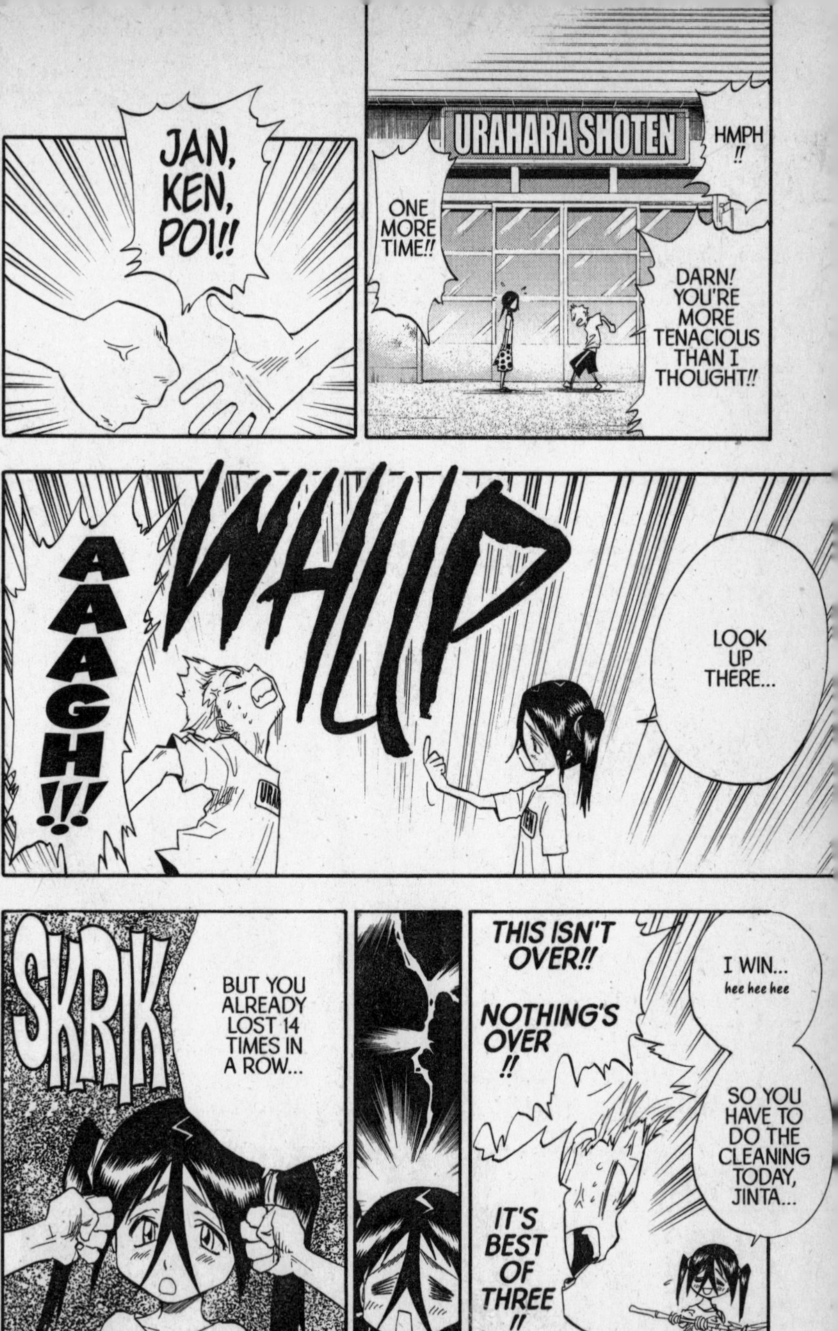
HMPH!!
URAHARA SHOTEN
DARN! YOU'RE MORE TENACIOUS THAN I THOUGHT!!
ONE MORE TIME!!
JAN, KEN, POI!!
LOOK UP THERE...
WHIP
AAAGH!!!
I WIN... hee hee hee
SO YOU HAVE TO DO THE CLEANING TODAY, JINTA...
THIS ISN'T OVER!!
NOTHING'S OVER!!
IT'S BEST OF THREE!!
SKRIK
BUT YOU ALREADY LOST 14 TIMES IN A ROW...

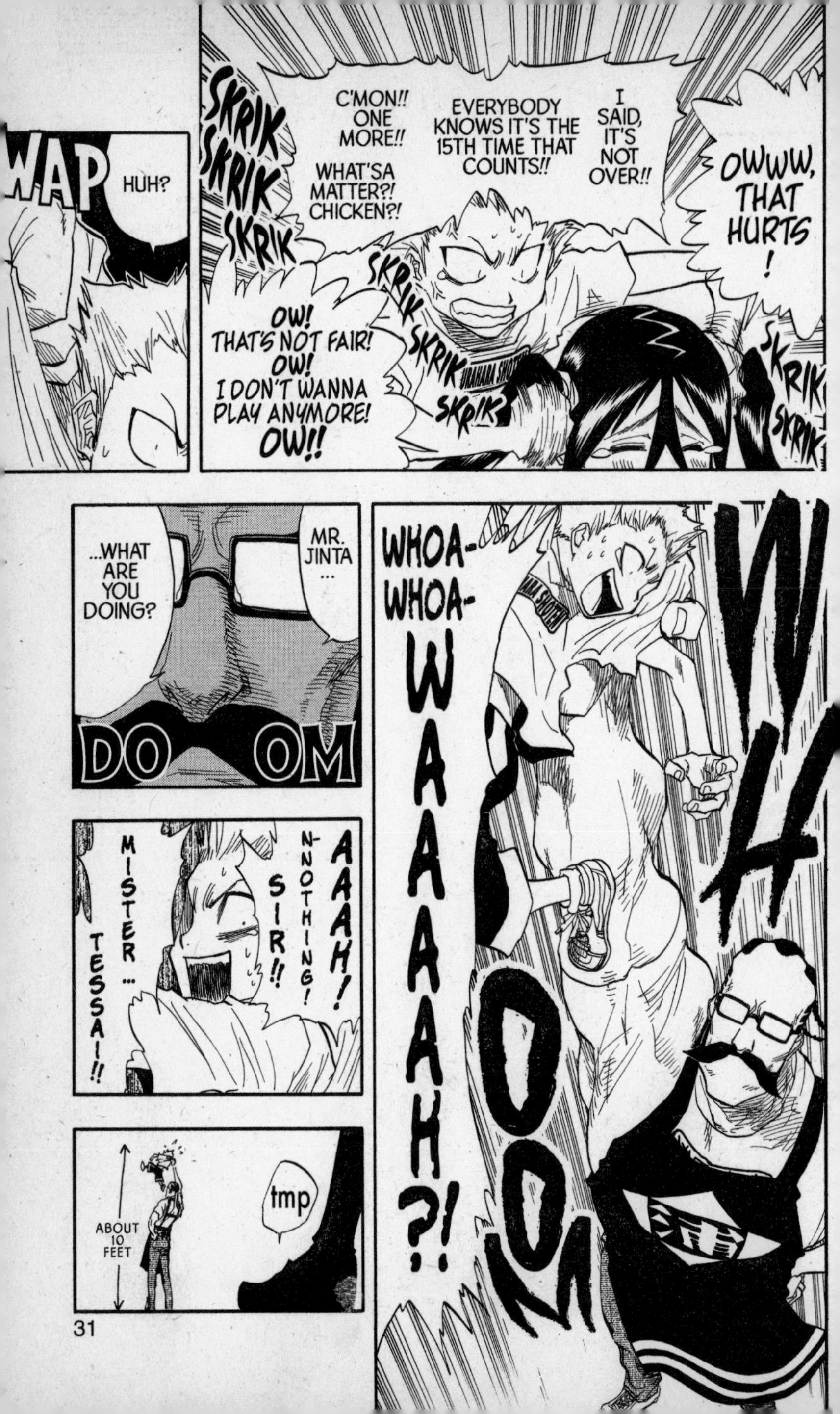
OWWW, THAT HURTS!
I SAID, IT'S NOT OVER!!
EVERYBODY KNOWS IT'S THE 15TH TIME THAT COUNTS!!
C'MON!! ONE MORE!!
WHAT'SA MATTER?! CHICKEN?!
SKRIK SKRIK SKRIK
SKRIK
SKRIK
SKRIK
SKRIK SKRIK
URAHARA SHOTEN
OW! THAT'S NOT FAIR! OW! I DON'T WANNA PLAY ANYMORE! OW!!
WAP
HUH?
WHOA-WHOA-WAAAAAAH?!
DOOM
MR. JINTA...
...WHAT ARE YOU DOING?
DO OM
AAAAH!
N-NNOTHING! SIR!!
MISTER... TESSAI!!
tmp
ABOUT 10 FEET

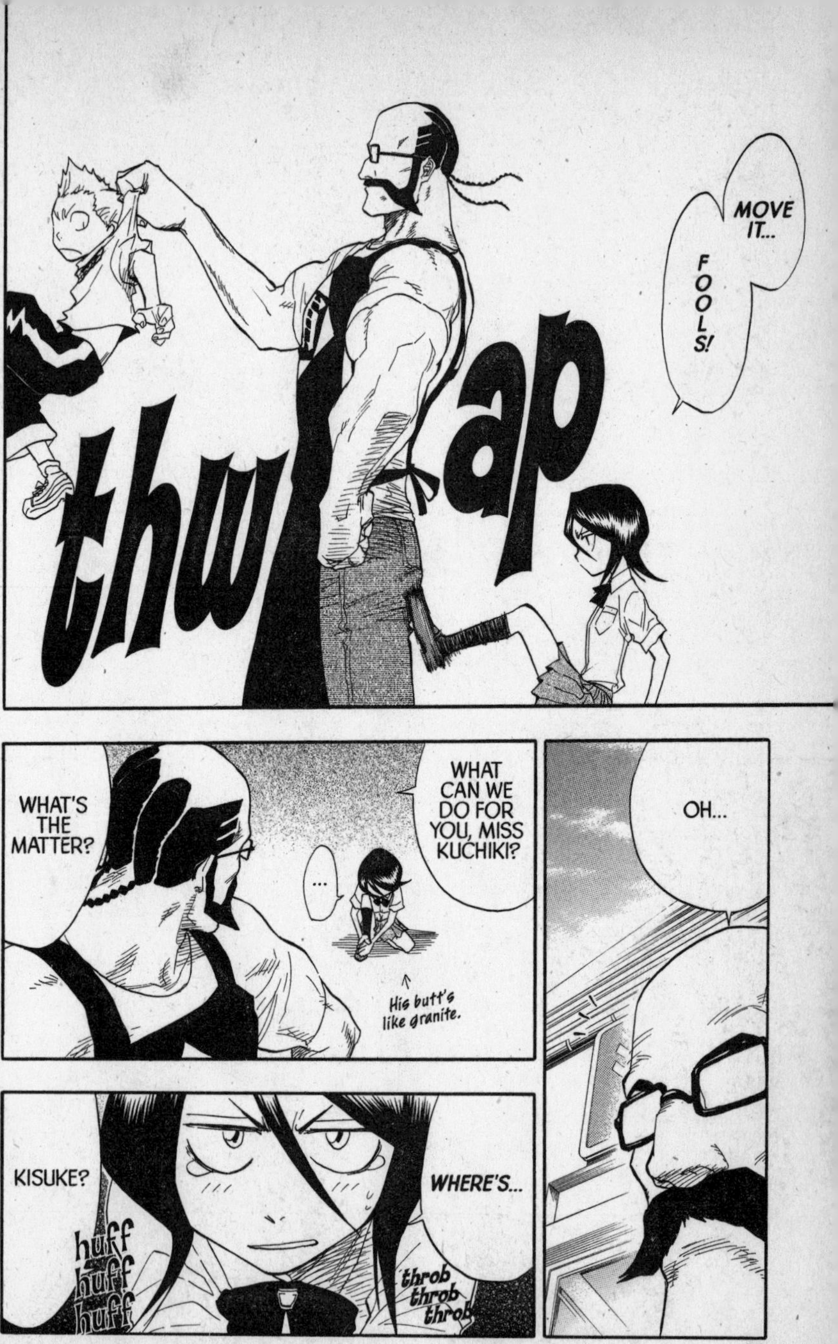
MOVE IT... FOOLS!
thwap
OH...
WHAT CAN WE DO FOR YOU, MISS KUCHIKI?
WHAT'S THE MATTER?
...
His butt's like granite.
WHERE'S...
KISUKE?
throb throb throb
huff huff huff

READ THIS WAY

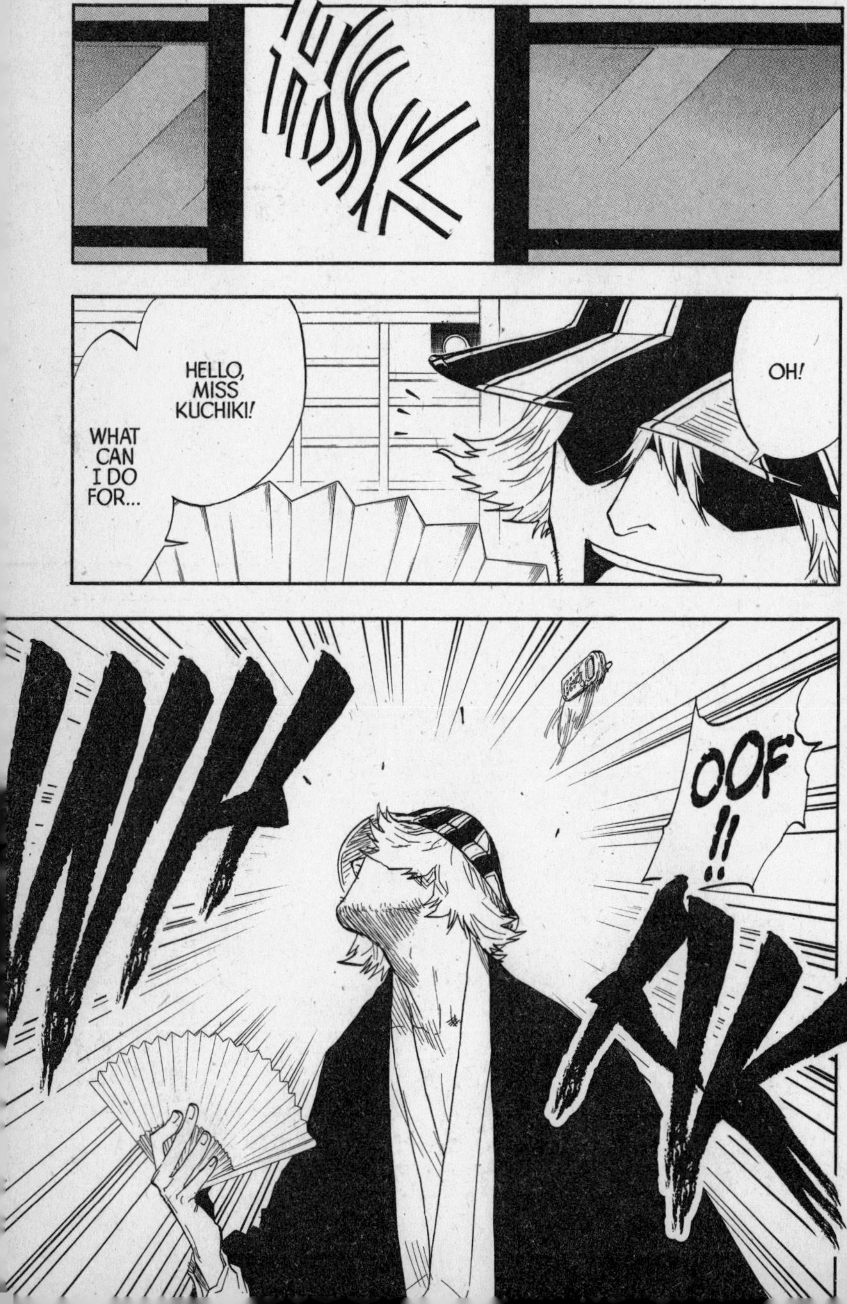
OH!
HELLO, MISS KUCHIKI!
WHAT CAN I DO FOR...
OOF !!

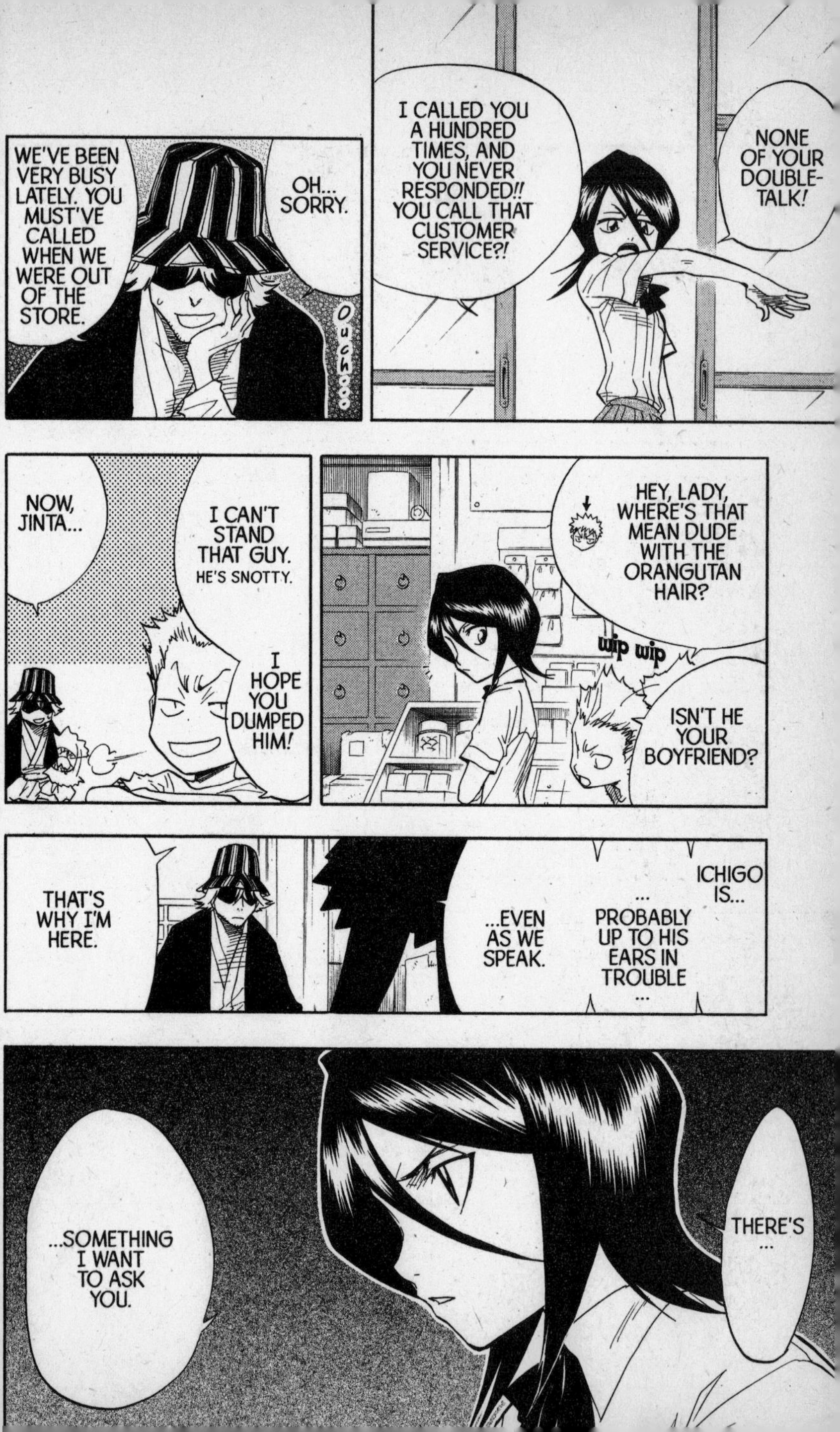
NONE OF YOUR DOUBLE-TALK!
I CALLED YOU A HUNDRED TIMES, AND YOU NEVER RESPONDED!! YOU CALL THAT CUSTOMER SERVICE?!
OH... SORRY.
WE'VE BEEN VERY BUSY LATELY. YOU MUST'VE CALLED WHEN WE WERE OUT OF THE STORE.
Ouchooo
HEY, LADY, WHERE'S THAT MEAN DUDE WITH THE ORANGUTAN HAIR?
wip wip
ISN'T HE YOUR BOYFRIEND?
I CAN'T STAND THAT GUY. HE'S SNOTTY.
I HOPE YOU DUMPED HIM!
NOW, JINTA...
ICHIGO IS...
... PROBABLY UP TO HIS EARS IN TROUBLE ...
...EVEN AS WE SPEAK.
THAT'S WHY I'M HERE.
THERE'S ...
...SOMETHING I WANT TO ASK YOU.

READ THIS WAY

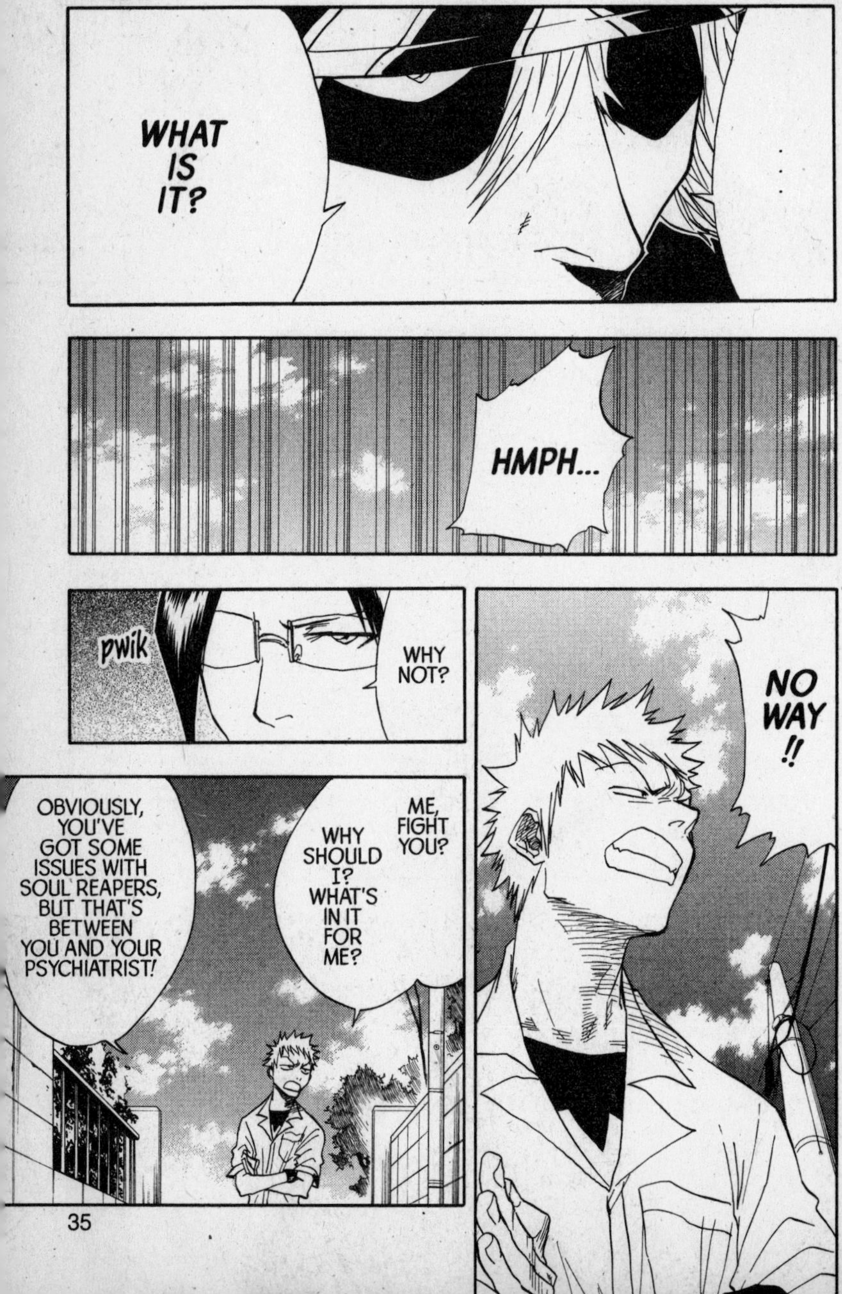
WHAT IS IT?
HMPH...
NO WAY!!
pwik
WHY NOT?
ME, FIGHT YOU?
WHY SHOULD I? WHAT'S IN IT FOR ME?
OBVIOUSLY, YOU'VE GOT SOME ISSUES WITH SOUL REAPERS, BUT THAT'S BETWEEN YOU AND YOUR PSYCHIATRIST!

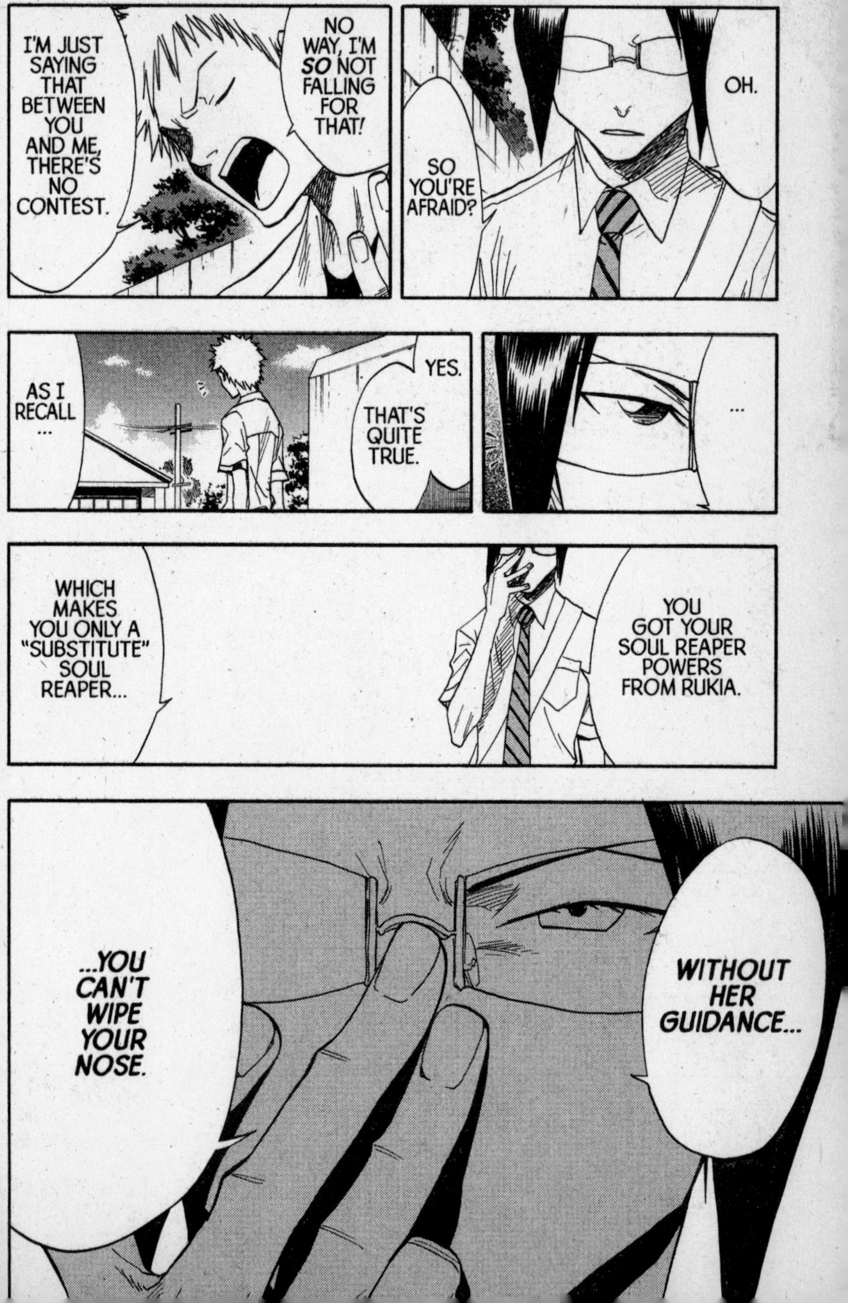
OH.
SO YOU'RE AFRAID?
NO WAY, I'M SO NOT FALLING FOR THAT!
I'M JUST SAYING THAT BETWEEN YOU AND ME, THERE'S NO CONTEST.
...
YES.
THAT'S QUITE TRUE.
AS I RECALL ...
YOU GOT YOUR SOUL REAPER POWERS FROM RUKIA.
WHICH MAKES YOU ONLY A "SUBSTITUTE" SOUL REAPER...
WITHOUT HER GUIDANCE...
...YOU CAN'T WIPE YOUR NOSE.

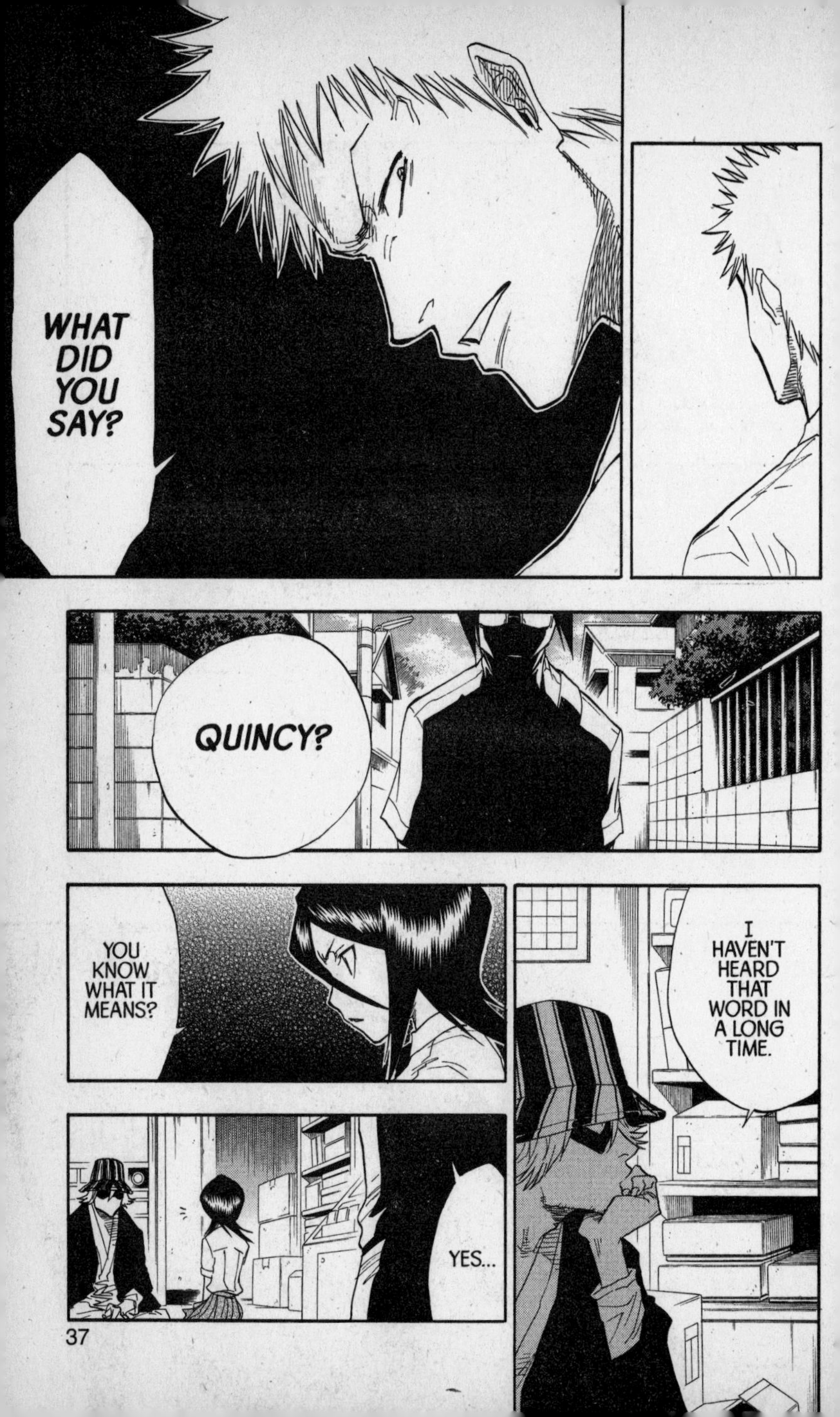
WHAT DID YOU SAY?
QUINCY?
I HAVEN'T HEARD THAT WORD IN A LONG TIME.
YOU KNOW WHAT IT MEANS?
YES...

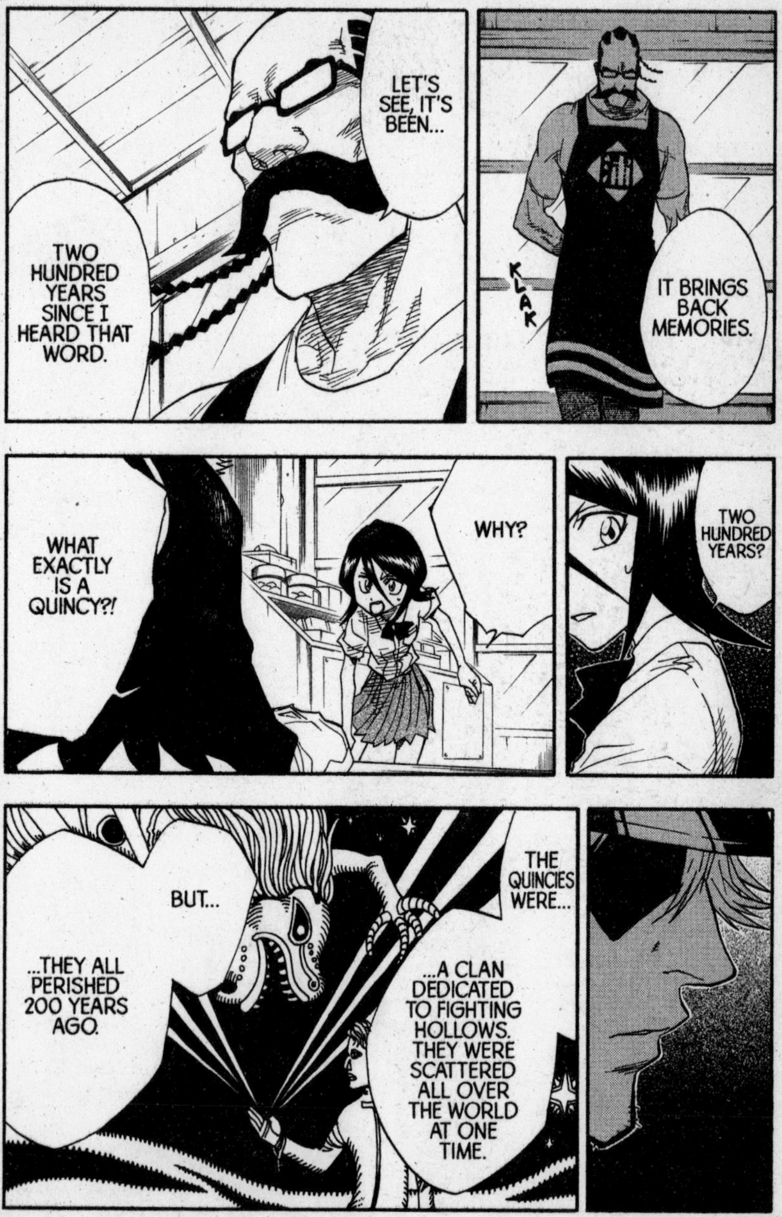
IT BRINGS BACK MEMORIES.
KLAK
LET'S SEE, IT'S BEEN...
TWO HUNDRED YEARS SINCE I HEARD THAT WORD.
TWO HUNDRED YEARS?
WHY?
WHAT EXACTLY IS A QUINCY?!
THE QUINCIES WERE...
...A CLAN DEDICATED TO FIGHTING HOLLOWS. THEY WERE SCATTERED ALL OVER THE WORLD AT ONE TIME.
BUT...
...THEY ALL PERISHED 200 YEARS AGO.

READ THIS WAY

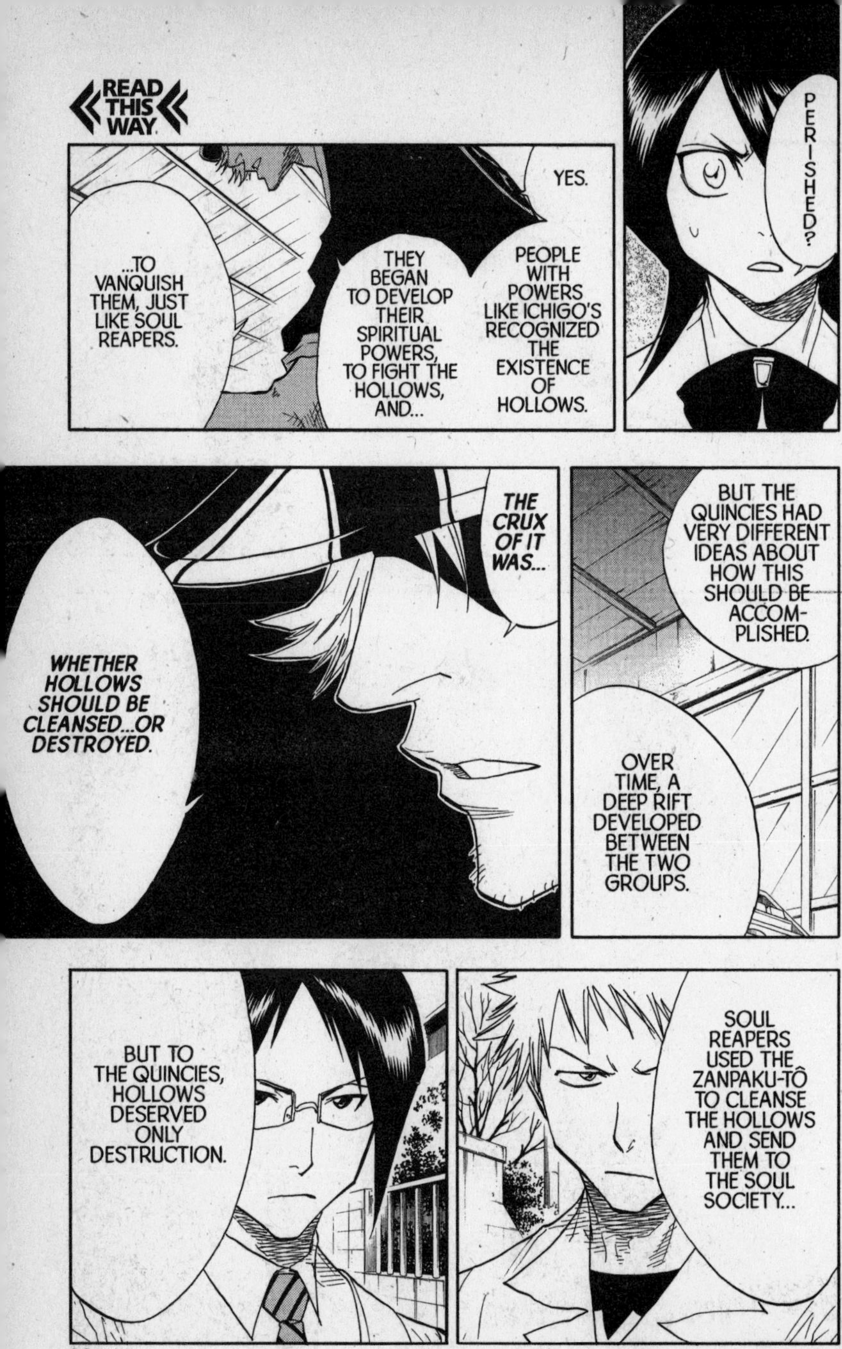

PERISHED?
YES.
PEOPLE WITH POWERS LIKE ICHIGO'S RECOGNIZED THE EXISTENCE OF HOLLOWS.
THEY BEGAN TO DEVELOP THEIR SPIRITUAL POWERS, TO FIGHT THE HOLLOWS, AND...
...TO VANQUISH THEM, JUST LIKE SOUL REAPERS.
BUT THE QUINCIES HAD VERY DIFFERENT IDEAS ABOUT HOW THIS SHOULD BE ACCOM-PLISHED.
OVER TIME, A DEEP RIFT DEVELOPED BETWEEN THE TWO GROUPS.
THE CRUX OF IT WAS...
WHETHER HOLLOWS SHOULD BE CLEANSED...OR DESTROYED.
SOUL REAPERS USED THE ZANPAKU-TÔ TO CLEANSE THE HOLLOWS AND SEND THEM TO THE SOUL SOCIETY...
BUT TO THE QUINCIES, HOLLOWS DESERVED ONLY DESTRUCTION.

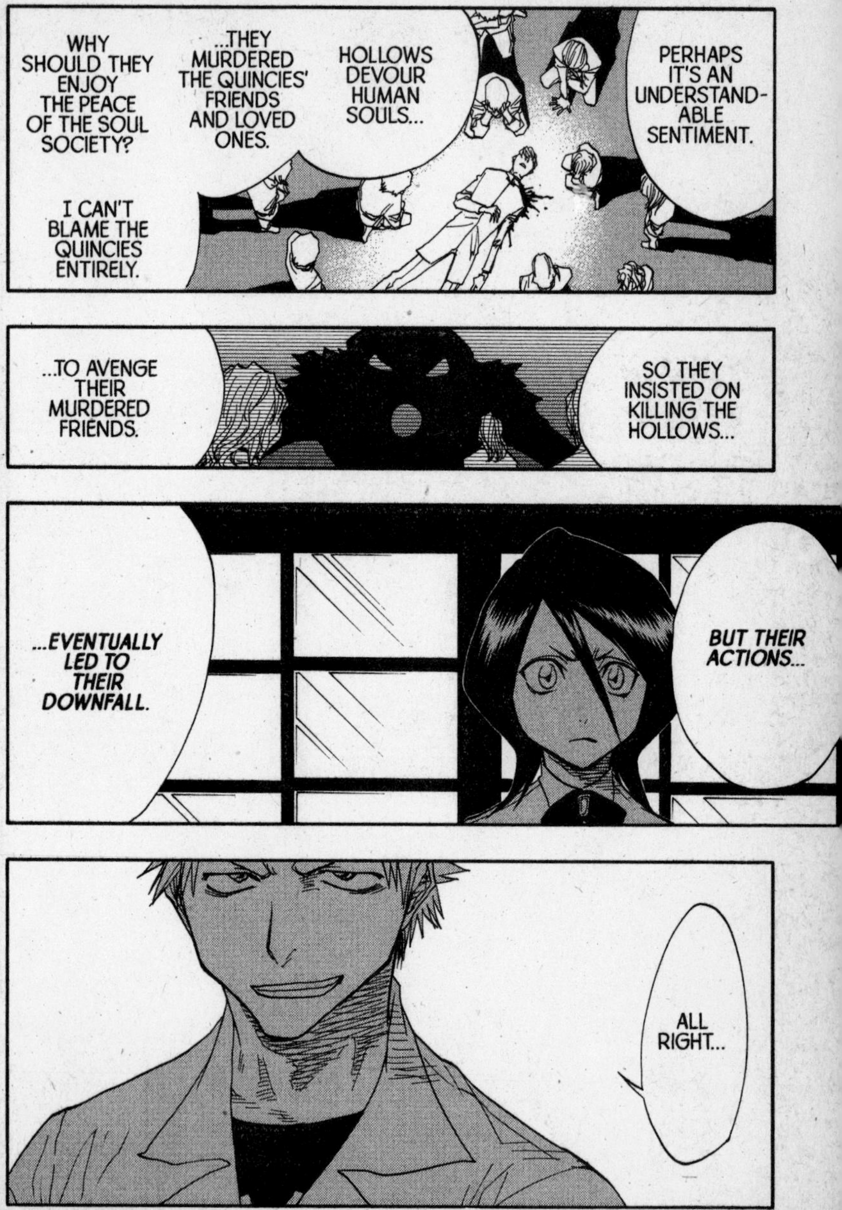

PERHAPS IT'S AN UNDERSTAND-ABLE SENTIMENT.
HOLLOWS DEVOUR HUMAN SOULS...
...THEY MURDERED THE QUINCIES' FRIENDS AND LOVED ONES.
WHY SHOULD THEY ENJOY THE PEACE OF THE SOUL SOCIETY?
I CAN'T BLAME THE QUINCIES ENTIRELY.
SO THEY INSISTED ON KILLING THE HOLLOWS...
...TO AVENGE THEIR MURDERED FRIENDS.
BUT THEIR ACTIONS...
...EVENTUALLY LED TO THEIR DOWNFALL.
ALL RIGHT...

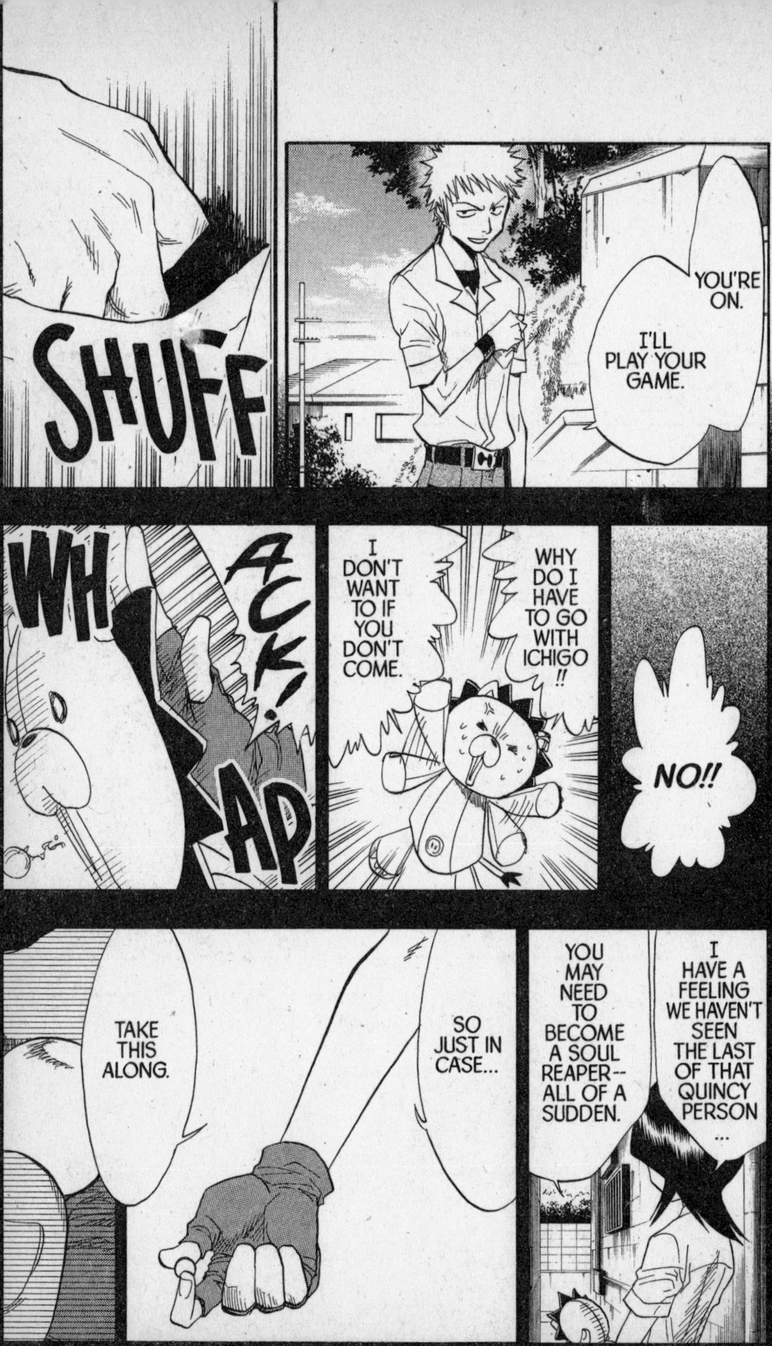
YOU'RE ON.
I'LL PLAY YOUR GAME.
SHUFF
NO!!
WHY DO I HAVE TO GO WITH ICHIGO!!
I DON'T WANT TO IF YOU DON'T COME.
ACK!
WHAP
I HAVE A FEELING WE HAVEN'T SEEN THE LAST OF THAT QUINCY PERSON...
YOU MAY NEED TO BECOME A SOUL REAPER--ALL OF A SUDDEN.
SO JUST IN CASE...
TAKE THIS ALONG.

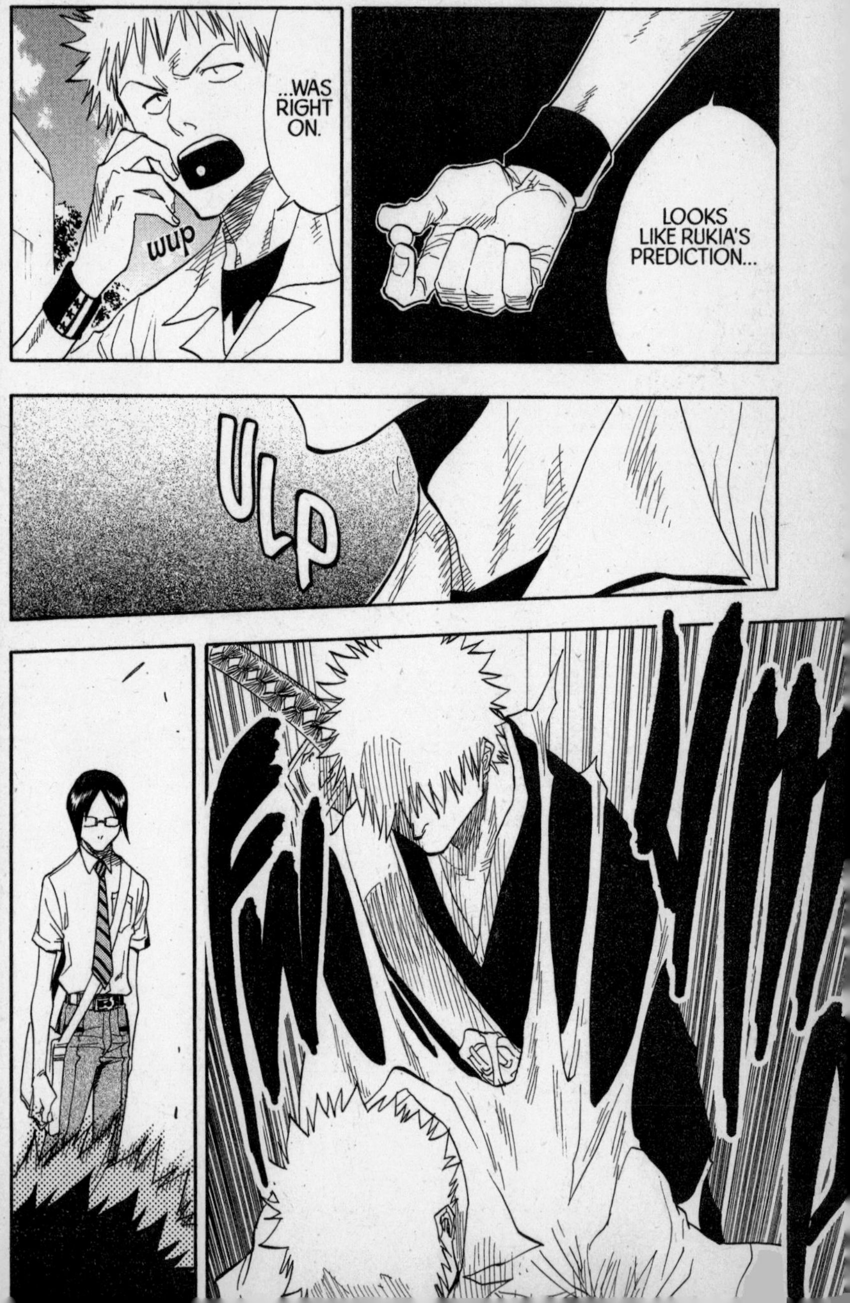
LOOKS LIKE RUKIA'S PREDICTION...
...WAS RIGHT ON.
wup
ULP

READ THIS WAY

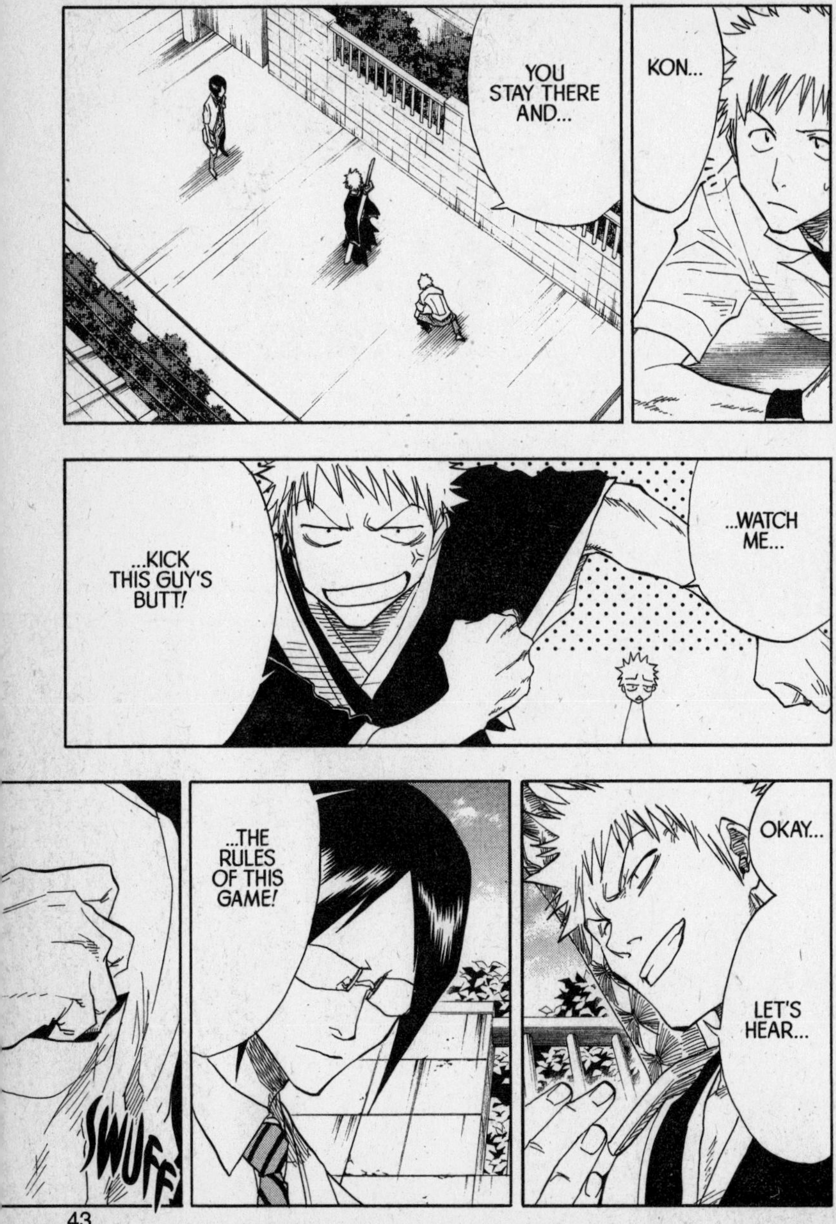

KON...
YOU STAY THERE AND...
...WATCH ME...
...KICK THIS GUY'S BUTT!
OKAY...
LET'S HEAR...
...THE RULES OF THIS GAME!
SWUFF

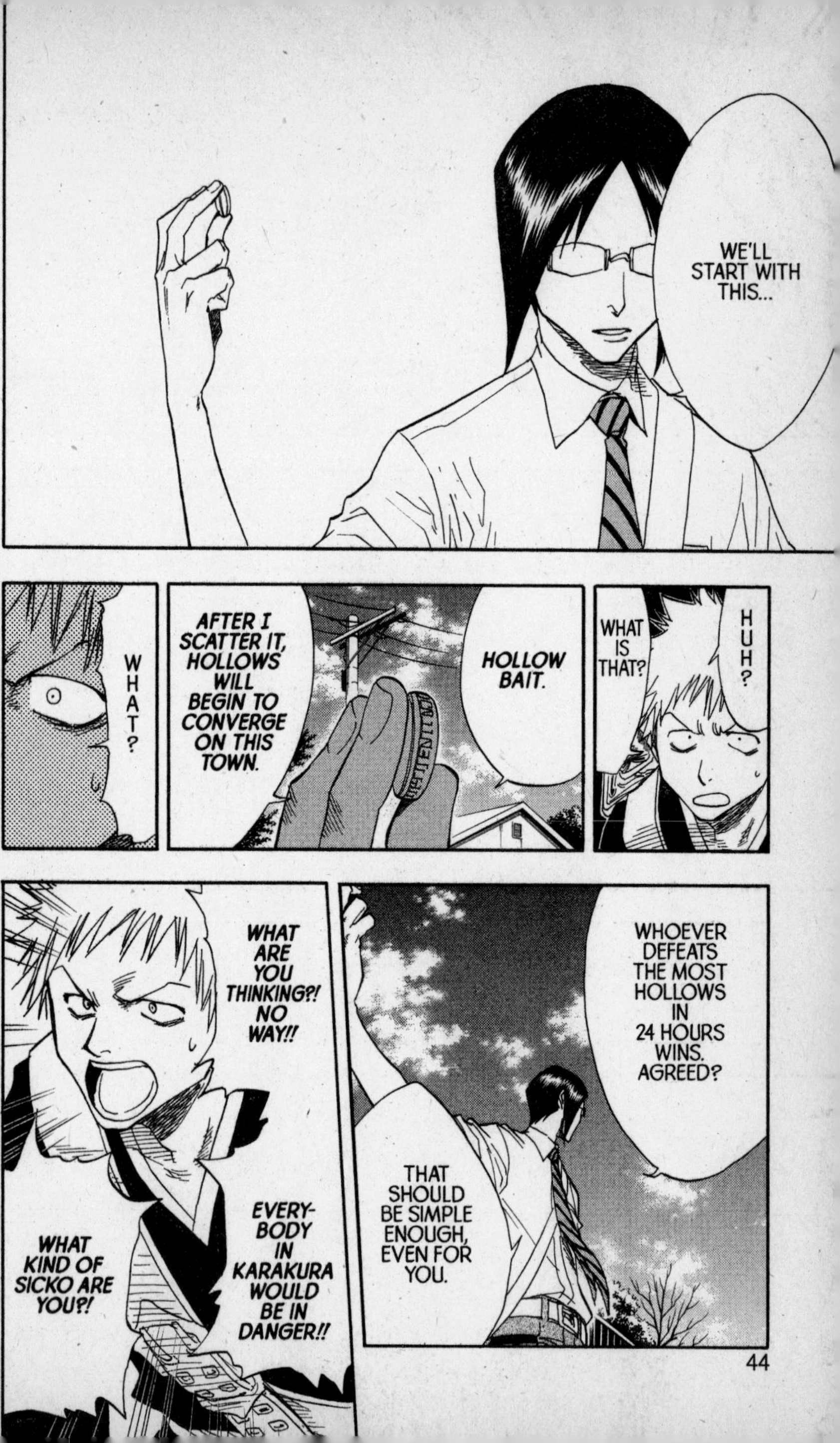
WE'LL START WITH THIS...
HUH?
WHAT IS THAT?
HOLLOW BAIT.
AFTER I SCATTER IT, HOLLOWS WILL BEGIN TO CONVERGE ON THIS TOWN.
WHAT?
WHOEVER DEFEATS THE MOST HOLLOWS IN 24 HOURS WINS. AGREED?
THAT SHOULD BE SIMPLE ENOUGH, EVEN FOR YOU.
WHAT ARE YOU THINKING?! NO WAY!!
EVERY-BODY IN KARAKURA WOULD BE IN DANGER!!
WHAT KIND OF SICKO ARE YOU?!

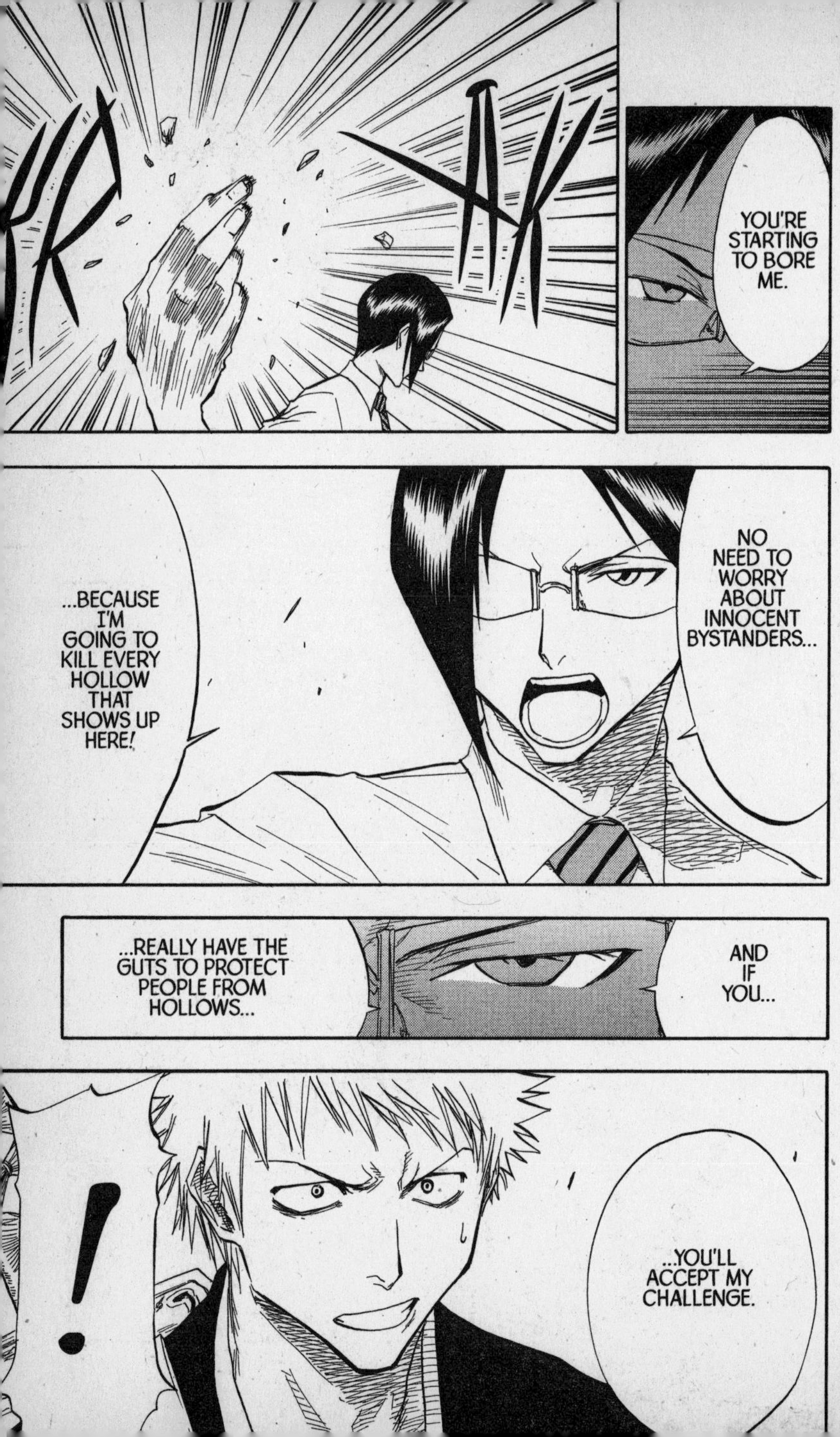

YOU'RE STARTING TO BORE ME.
NO NEED TO WORRY ABOUT INNOCENT BYSTANDERS...
...BECAUSE I'M GOING TO KILL EVERY HOLLOW THAT SHOWS UP HERE!
AND IF YOU...
...REALLY HAVE THE GUTS TO PROTECT PEOPLE FROM HOLLOWS...
...YOU'LL ACCEPT MY CHALLENGE.
!

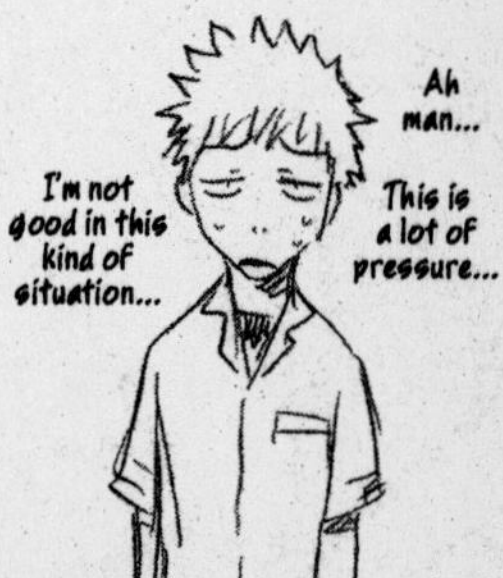
Ah man...
This is a lot of pressure...
I'm not good in this kind of situation...

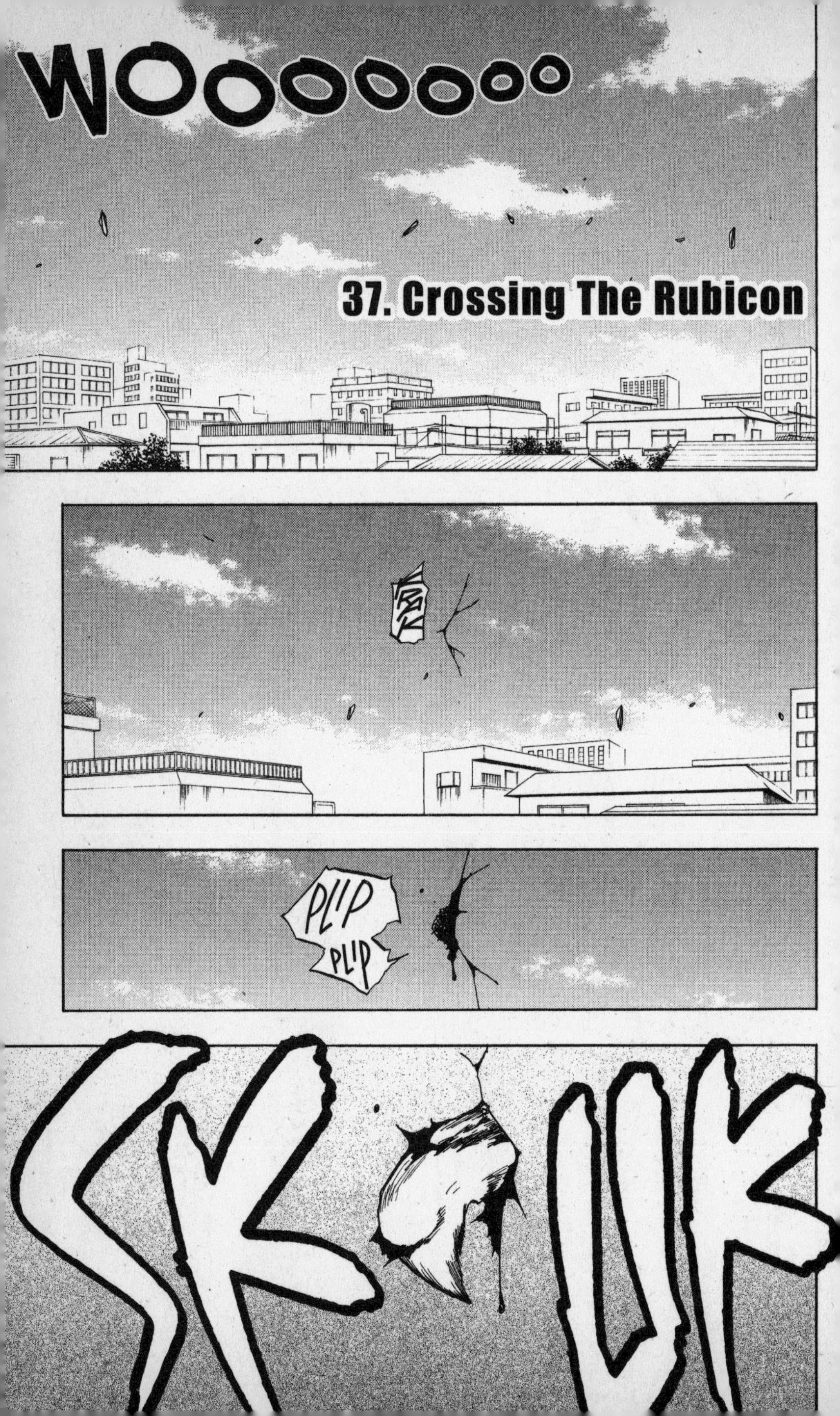
WOOOOOOO
37. Crossing The Rubicon
PLIP
PLIP
SK UK

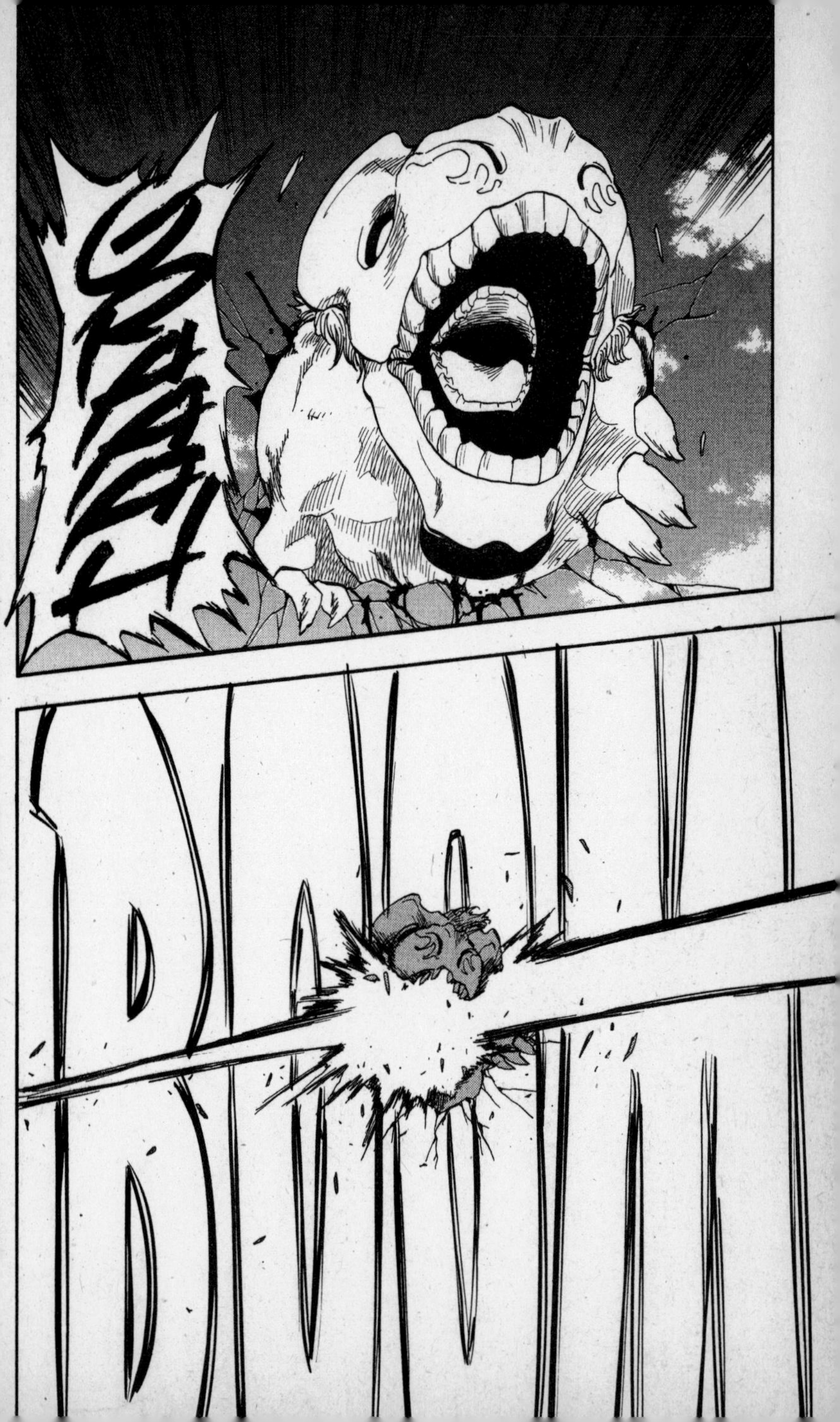

READ THIS WAY

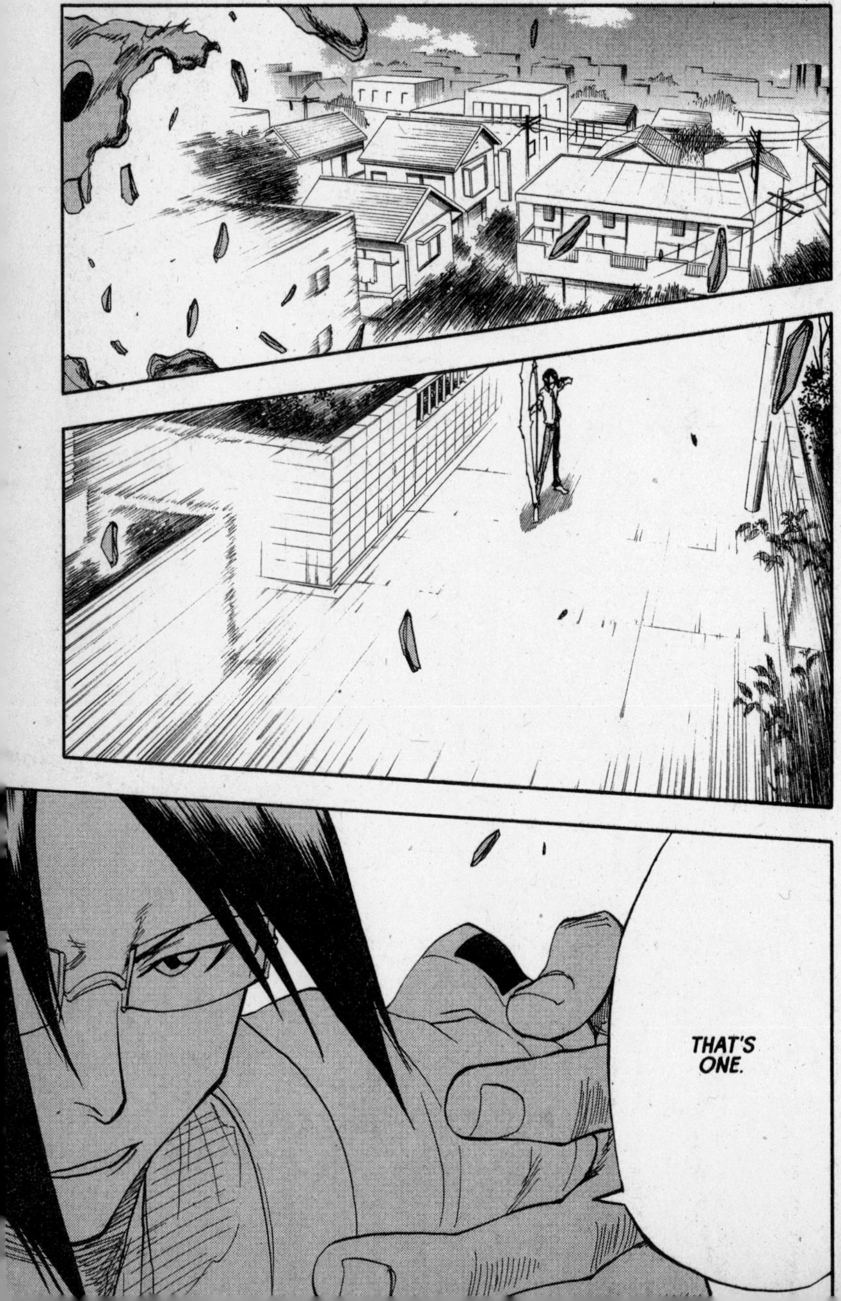
THAT'S ONE.

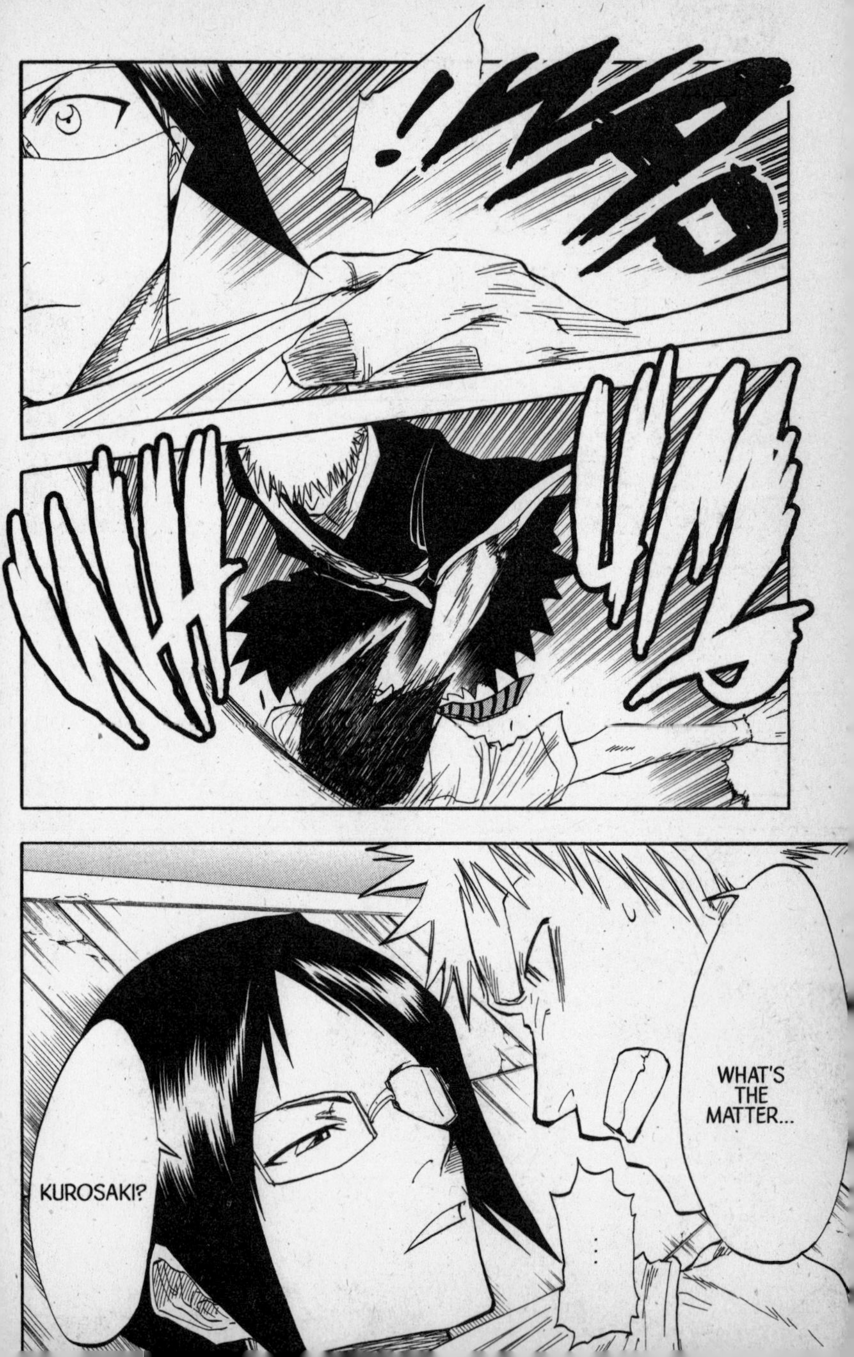
WHAT'S THE MATTER...
KUROSAKI?

READ THIS WAY

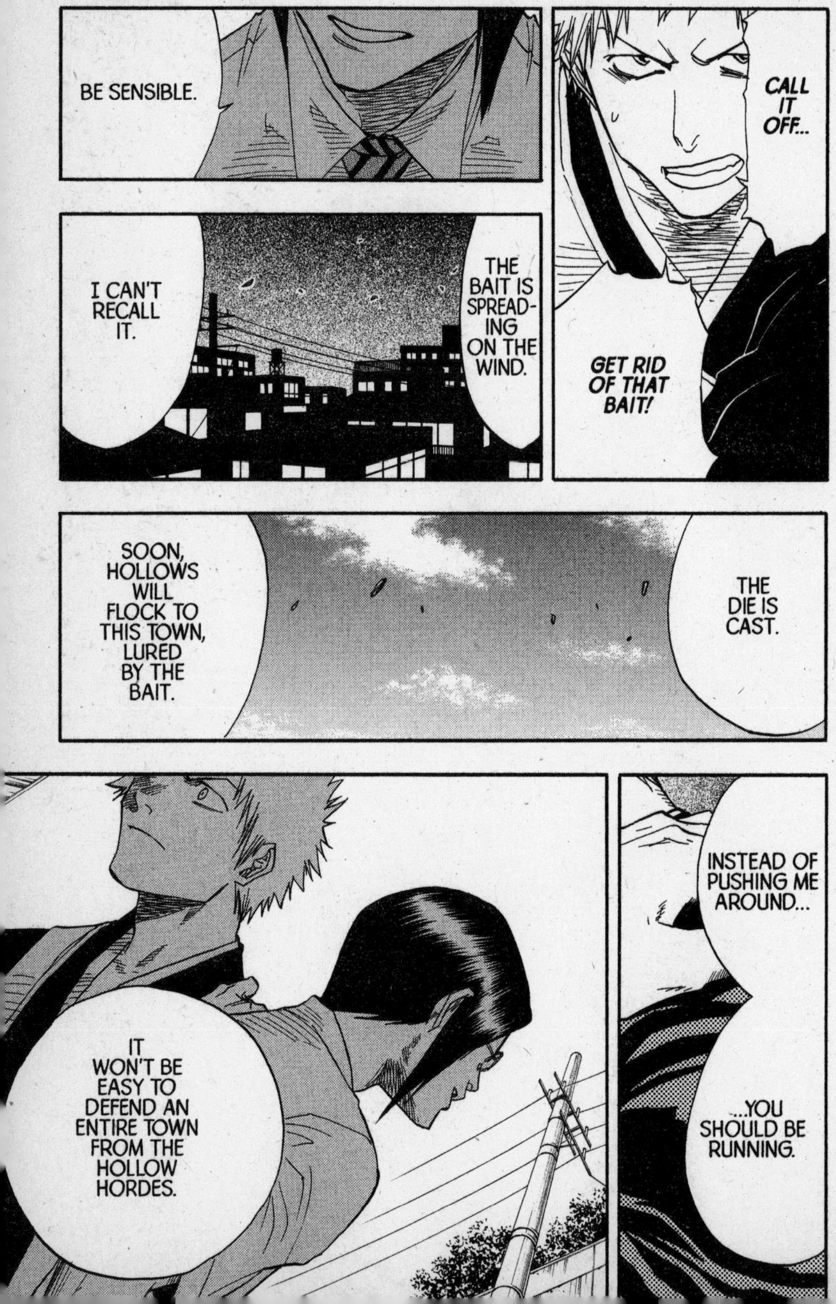
CALL IT OFF...
GET RID OF THAT BAIT!
BE SENSIBLE.
THE BAIT IS SPREAD-ING ON THE WIND.
I CAN'T RECALL IT.
THE DIE IS CAST.
SOON, HOLLOWS WILL FLOCK TO THIS TOWN, LURED BY THE BAIT.
INSTEAD OF PUSHING ME AROUND...
...YOU SHOULD BE RUNNING.
IT WON'T BE EASY TO DEFEND AN ENTIRE TOWN FROM THE HOLLOW HORDES.

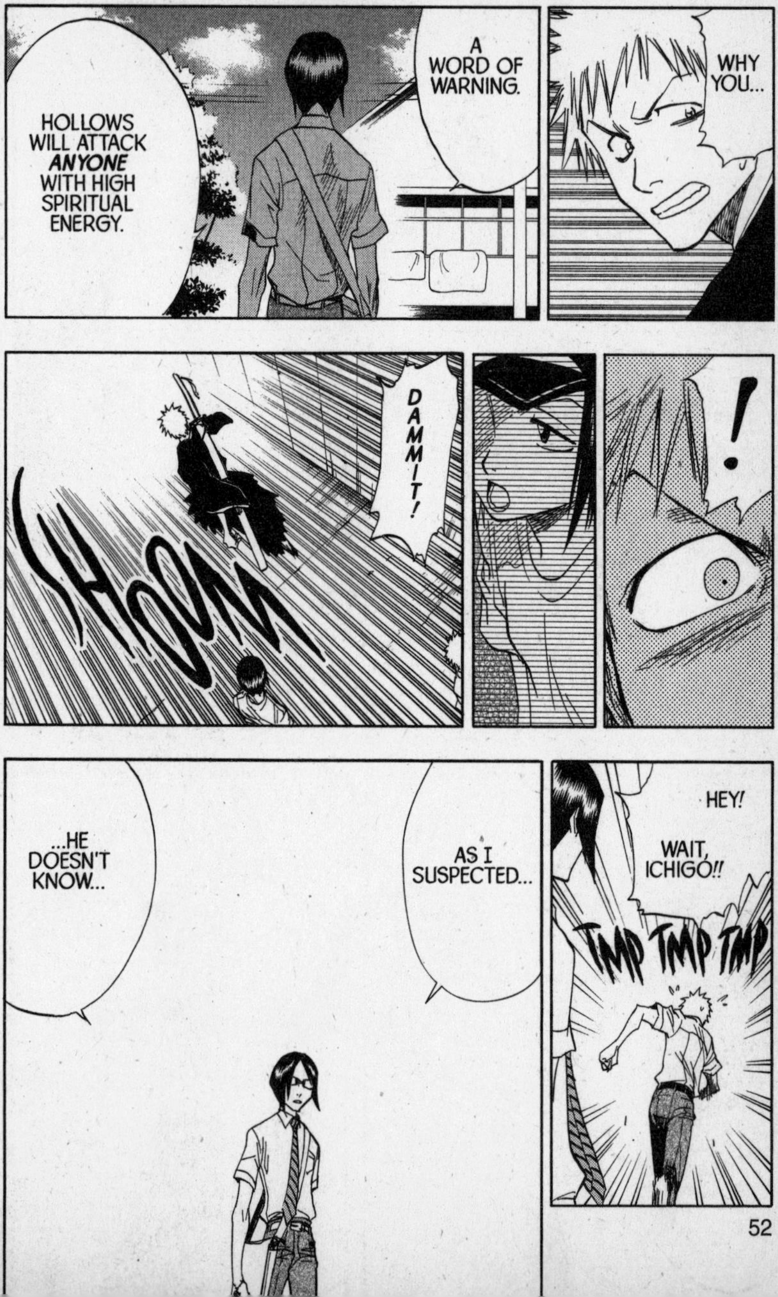
WHY YOU...
A WORD OF WARNING.
HOLLOWS WILL ATTACK *ANYONE* WITH HIGH SPIRITUAL ENERGY.
!
DAMMIT!
SHOOM
HEY!
WAIT, ICHIGO!!
TMP TMP TMP
AS I SUSPECTED...
...HE DOESN'T KNOW...

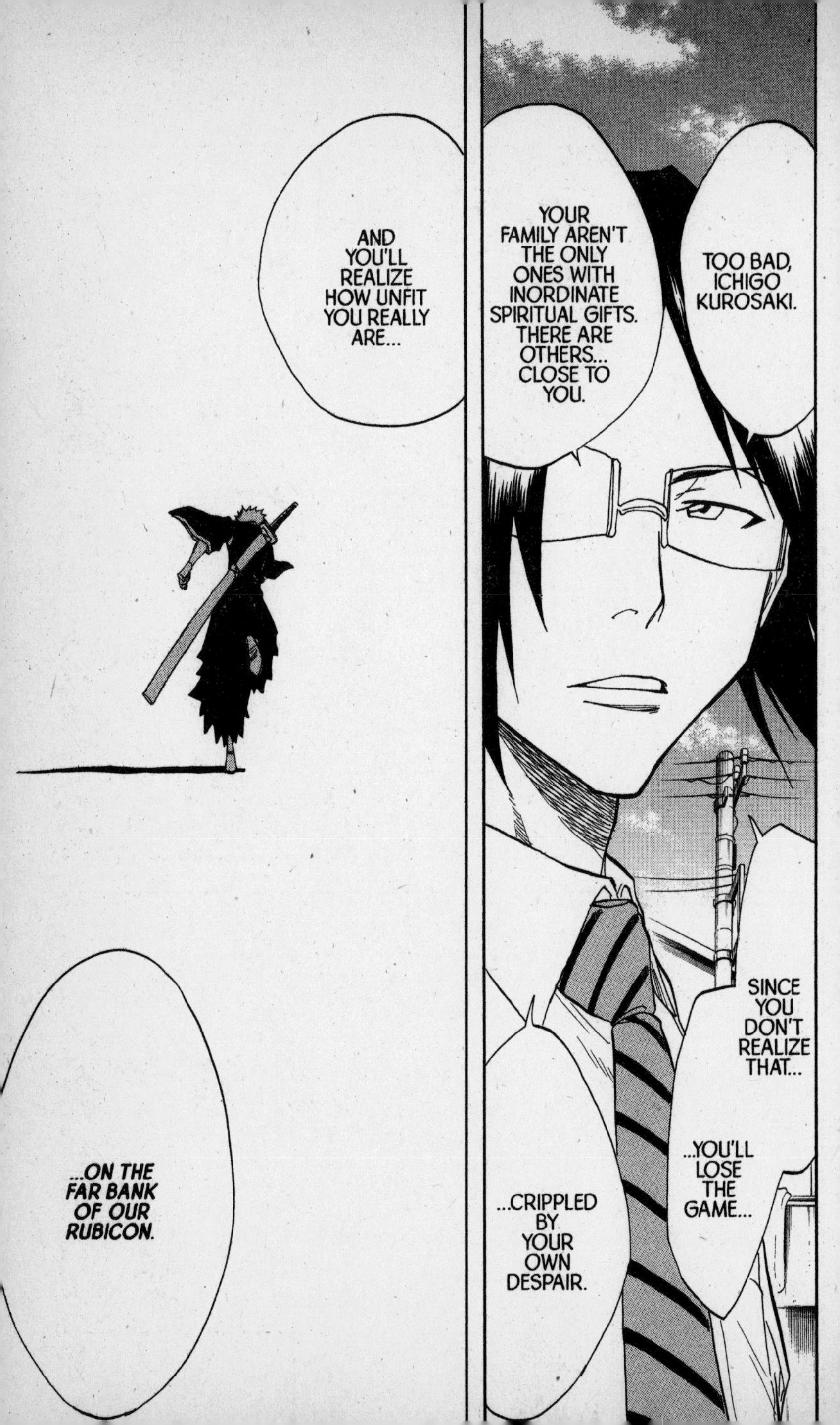
TOO BAD, ICHIGO KUROSAKI.
YOUR FAMILY AREN'T THE ONLY ONES WITH INORDINATE SPIRITUAL GIFTS. THERE ARE OTHERS... CLOSE TO YOU.
SINCE YOU DON'T REALIZE THAT...
...YOU'LL LOSE THE GAME...
...CRIPPLED BY YOUR OWN DESPAIR.
AND YOU'LL REALIZE HOW UNFIT YOU REALLY ARE...
...ON THE FAR BANK OF OUR RUBICON.

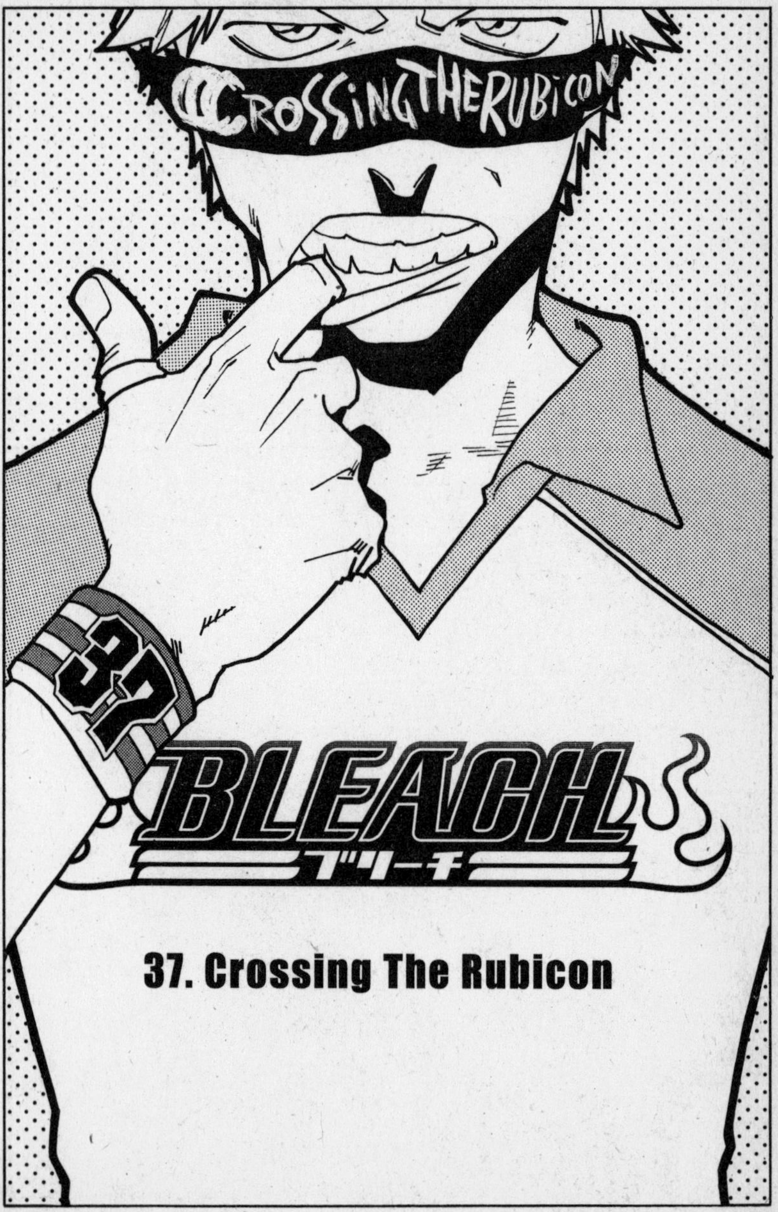
CROSSING THE RUBICON
37
BLEACH
ブリーチ
37. Crossing The Rubicon

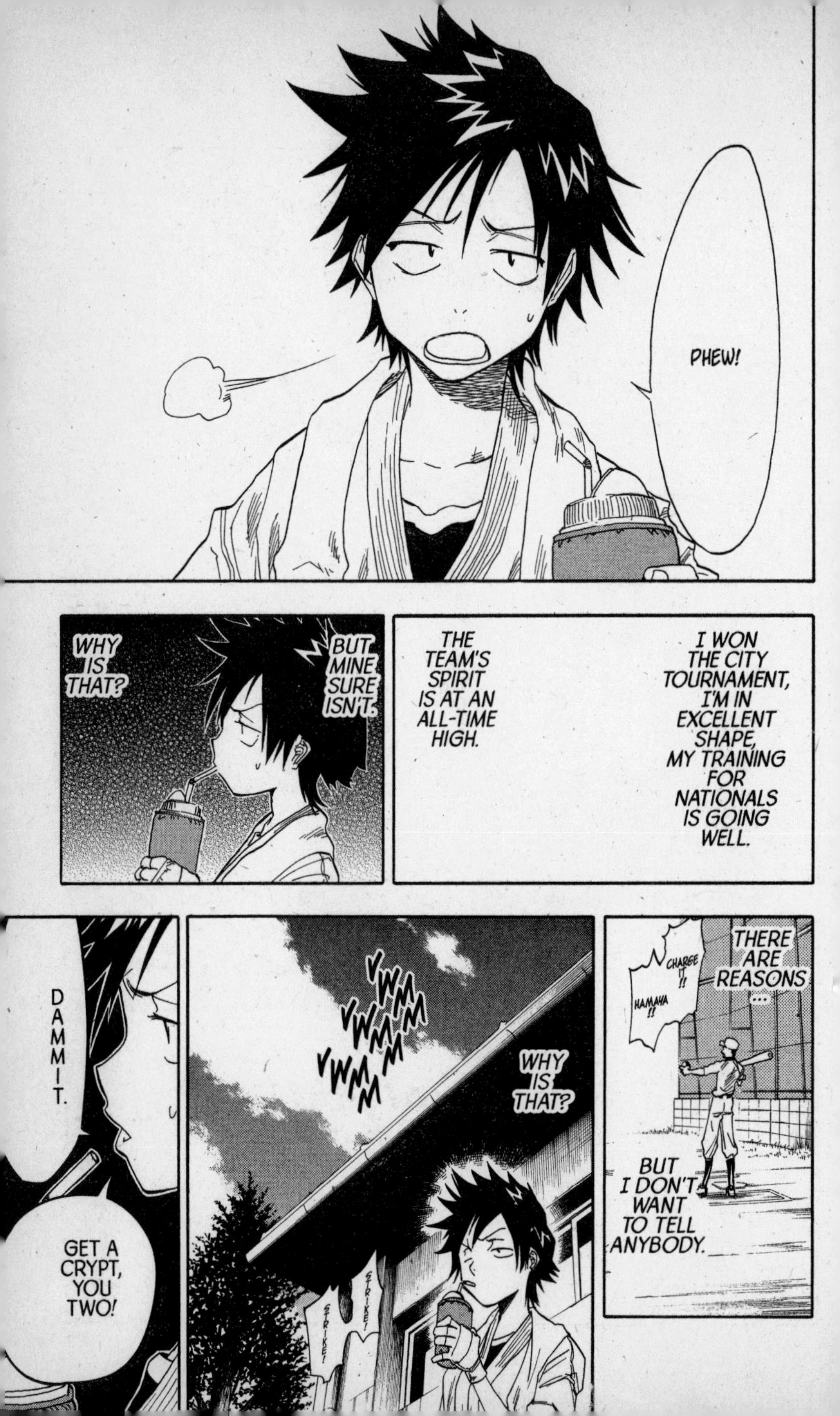
PHEW!
I WON THE CITY TOURNAMENT, I'M IN EXCELLENT SHAPE, MY TRAINING FOR NATIONALS IS GOING WELL.
THE TEAM'S SPIRIT IS AT AN ALL-TIME HIGH.
BUT MINE SURE ISN'T.
WHY IS THAT?
THERE ARE REASONS...
CHARGE IT!!
HAMAYA!!
BUT I DON'T WANT TO TELL ANYBODY.
WHY IS THAT?
VWMM
VWMM
VWMM
STRIKE!
STRIKE!
DAMMIT.
GET A CRYPT, YOU TWO!

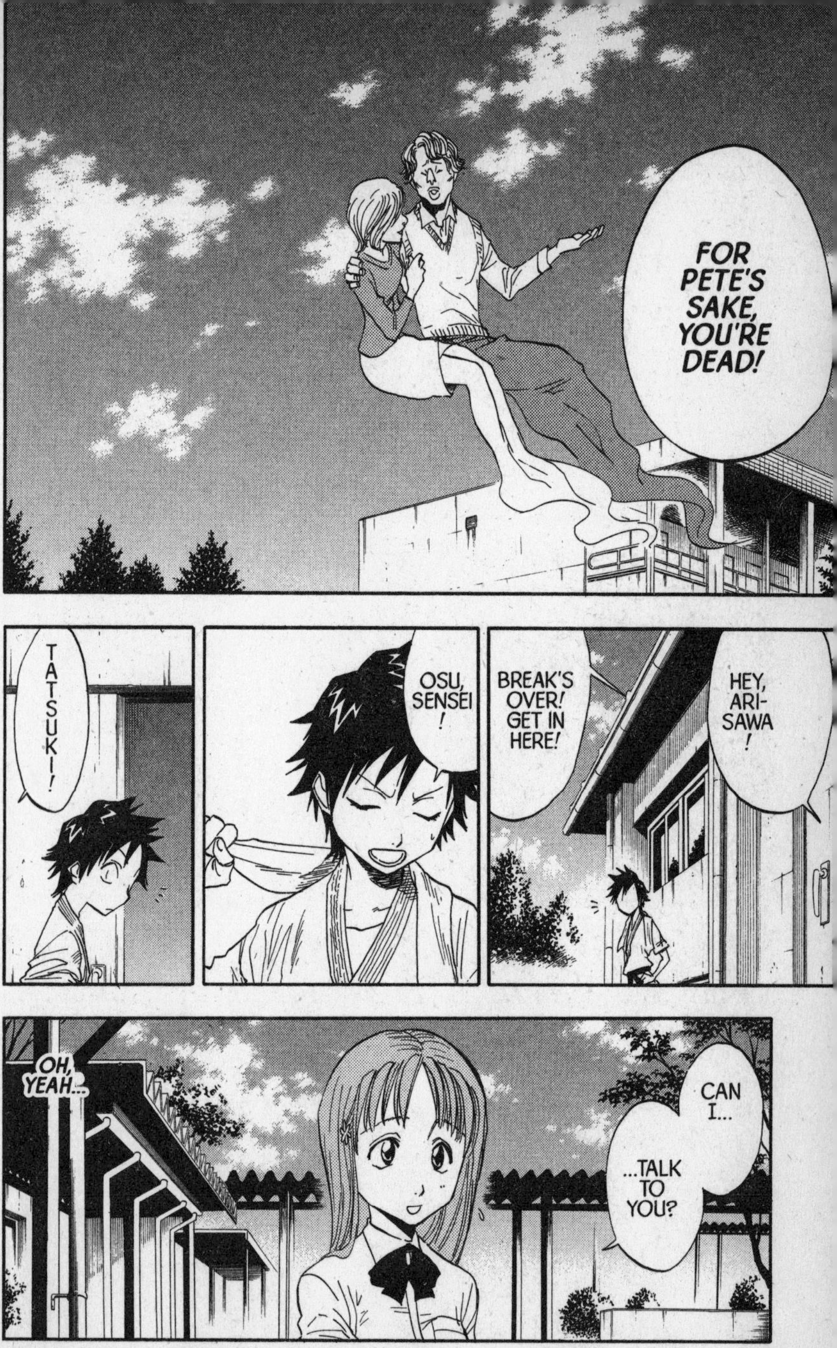
FOR PETE'S SAKE, YOU'RE DEAD!
HEY, ARI-SAWA!
BREAK'S OVER! GET IN HERE!
OSU, SENSEI!
TATSUKI!
CAN I...
...TALK TO YOU?
OH, YEAH...

READ THIS WAY

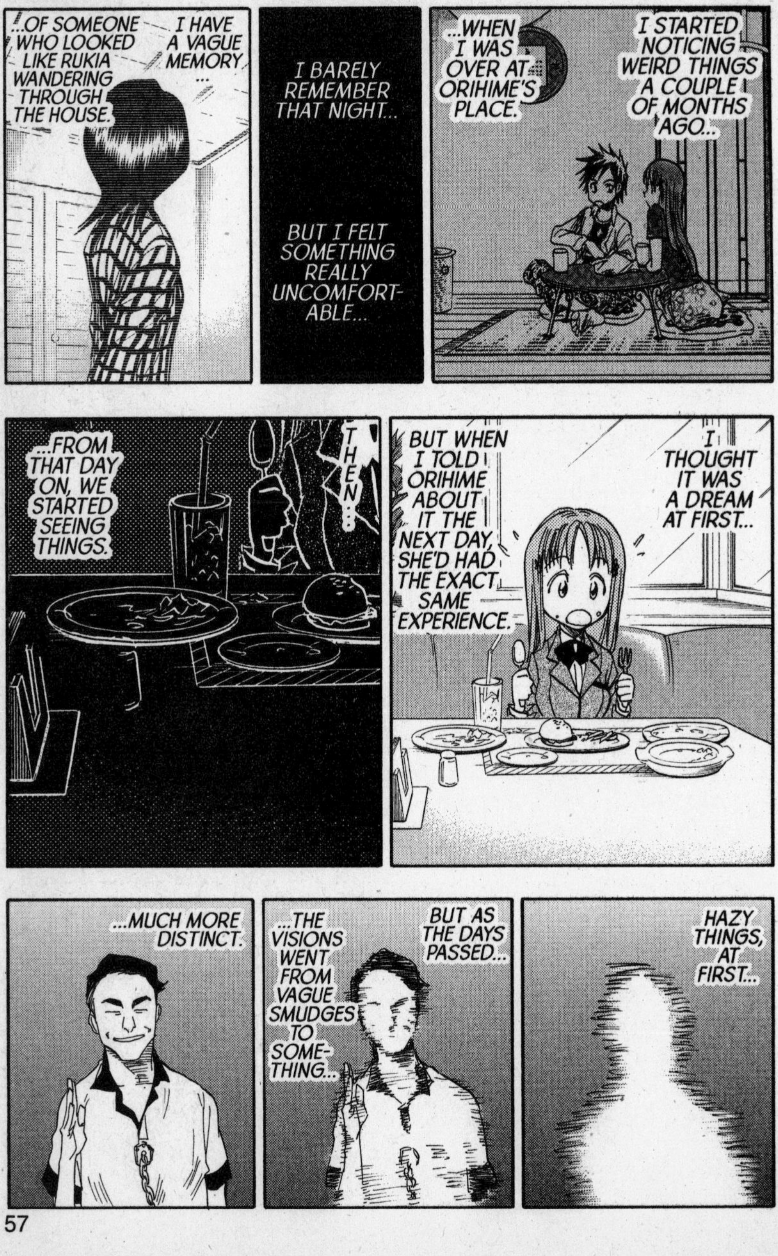

I STARTED NOTICING WEIRD THINGS A COUPLE OF MONTHS AGO...
...WHEN I WAS OVER AT ORIHIME'S PLACE.
I BARELY REMEMBER THAT NIGHT...
BUT I FELT SOMETHING REALLY UNCOMFORTABLE...
I HAVE A VAGUE MEMORY...
...OF SOMEONE WHO LOOKED LIKE RUKIA WANDERING THROUGH THE HOUSE.
I THOUGHT IT WAS A DREAM AT FIRST...
BUT WHEN I TOLD ORIHIME ABOUT IT THE NEXT DAY, SHE'D HAD THE EXACT SAME EXPERIENCE.
THEN...
...FROM THAT DAY ON, WE STARTED SEEING THINGS.
HAZY THINGS, AT FIRST...
BUT AS THE DAYS PASSED...
...THE VISIONS WENT FROM VAGUE SMUDGES TO SOMETHING...
...MUCH MORE DISTINCT.

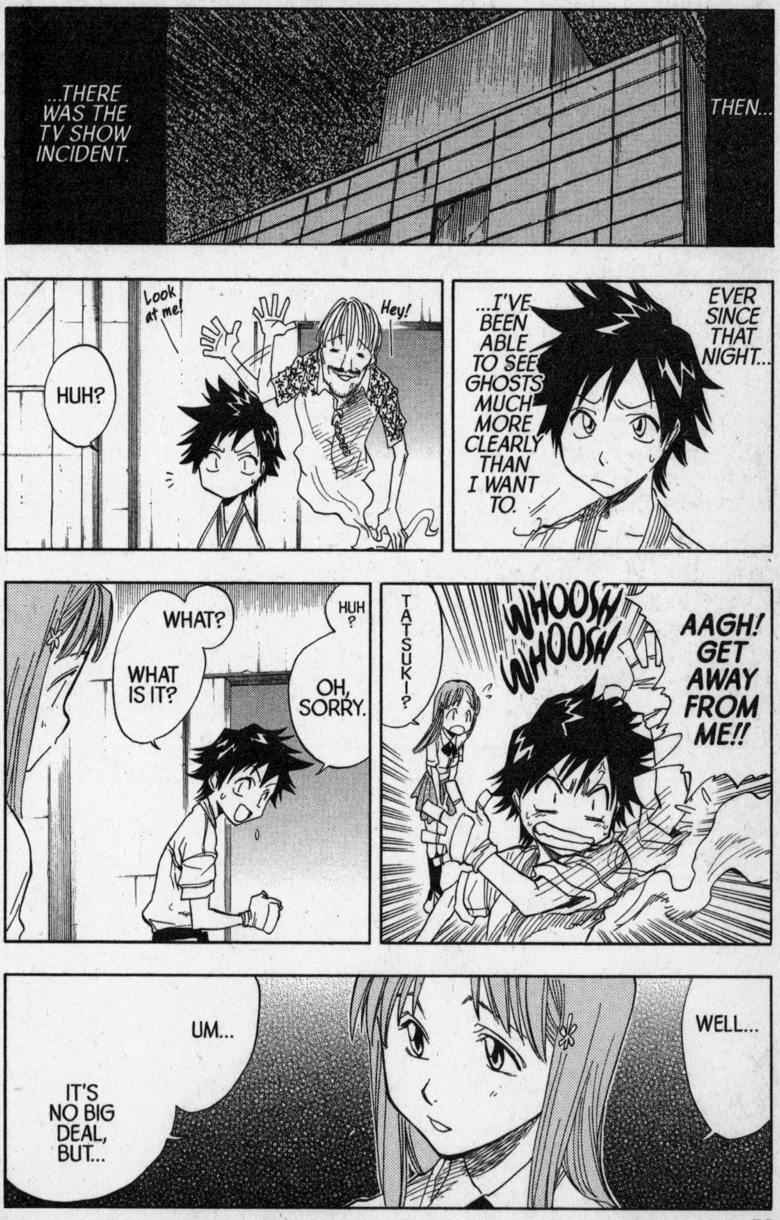
THEN...
...THERE WAS THE TV SHOW INCIDENT.
EVER SINCE THAT NIGHT...
...I'VE BEEN ABLE TO SEE GHOSTS MUCH MORE CLEARLY THAN I WANT TO.
Hey!
Look at me!
HUH?
AAGH! GET AWAY FROM ME!!
WHOOSH WHOOSH
TATSUKI!?
HUH?
OH, SORRY.
WHAT?
WHAT IS IT?
WELL...
UM...
IT'S NO BIG DEAL, BUT...

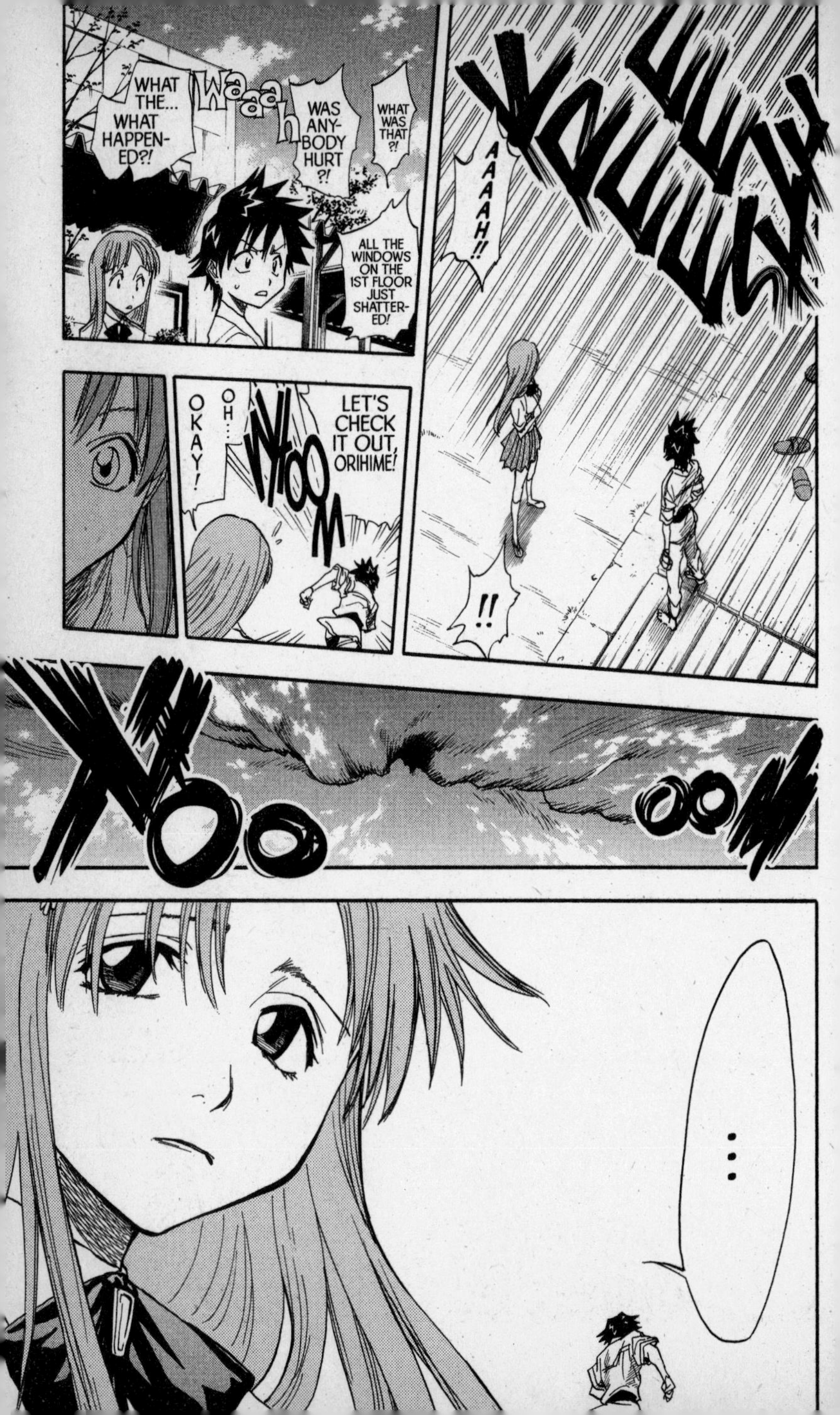
AAAAAH!!
!!
WHAT WAS THAT?!
WAS ANYBODY HURT?!
Waaaah
WHAT THE... WHAT HAPPENED?!
ALL THE WINDOWS ON THE 1ST FLOOR JUST SHATTERED!
LET'S CHECK IT OUT, ORIHIME!
OH...
OKAY!
...

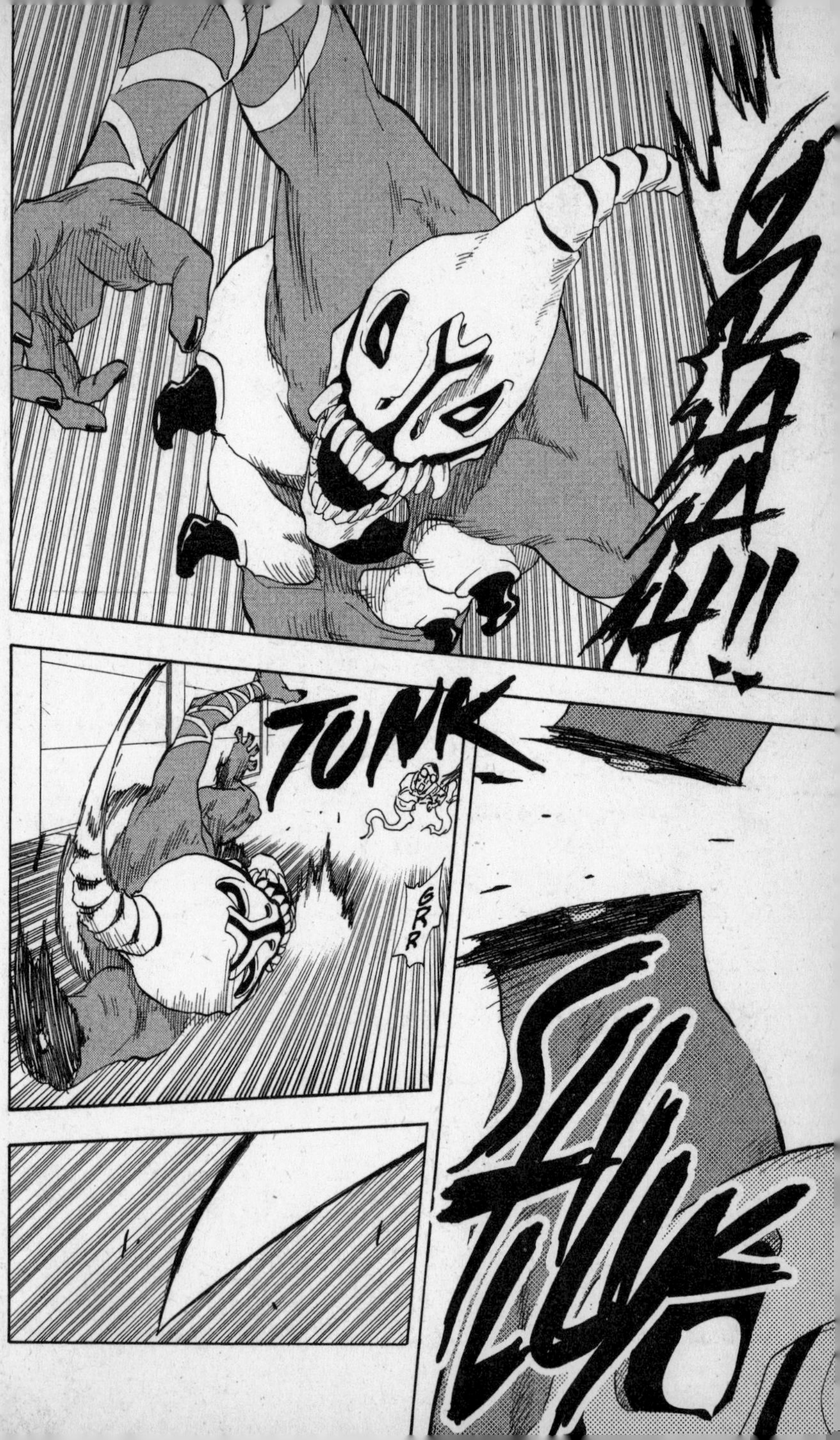

NNGOAAAAAH!!
TONK
GRR
SHK

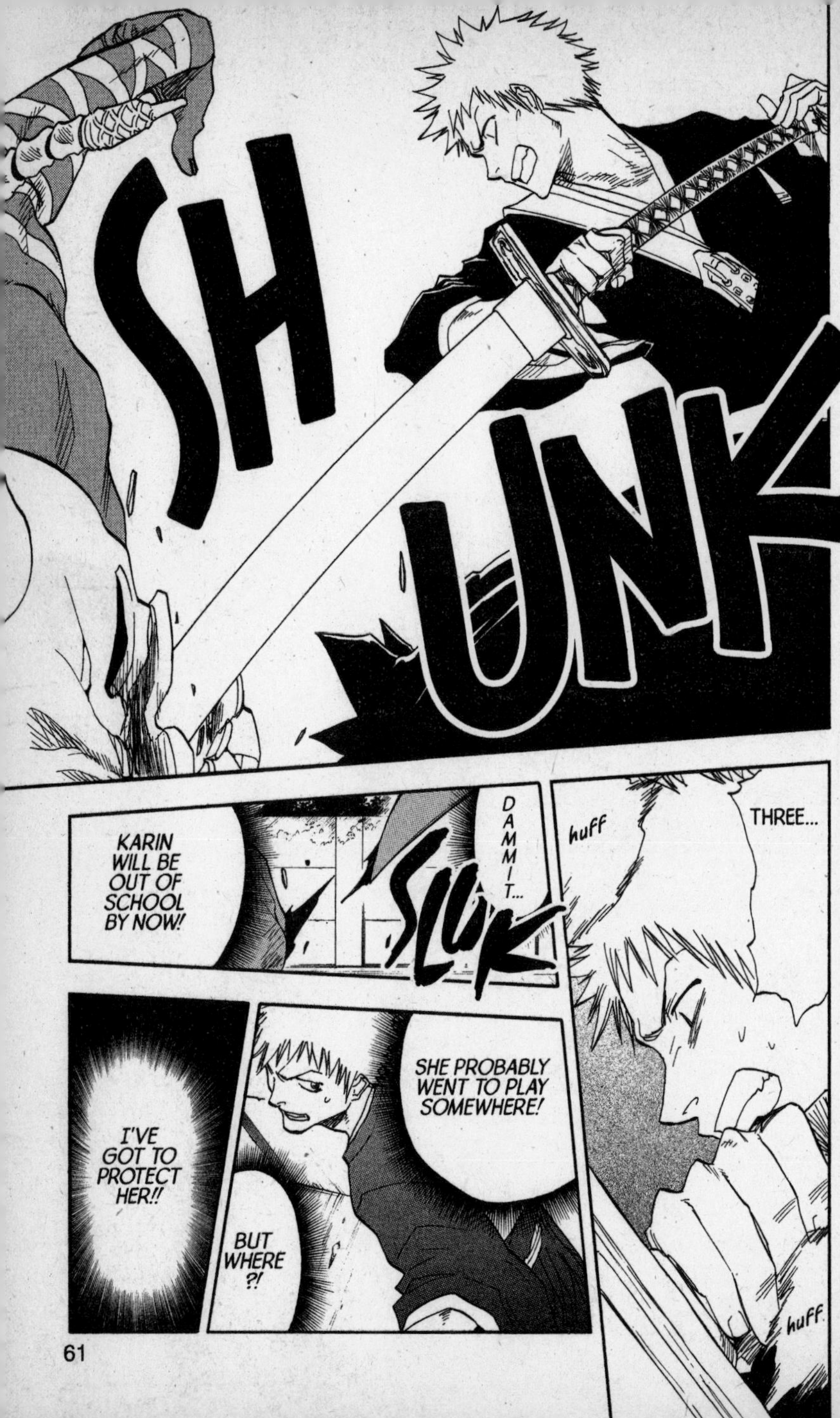
SH
UNK
THREE...
huff
huff
DAMMIT...
SLUK
KARIN WILL BE OUT OF SCHOOL BY NOW!
SHE PROBABLY WENT TO PLAY SOMEWHERE!
BUT WHERE?!
I'VE GOT TO PROTECT HER!!

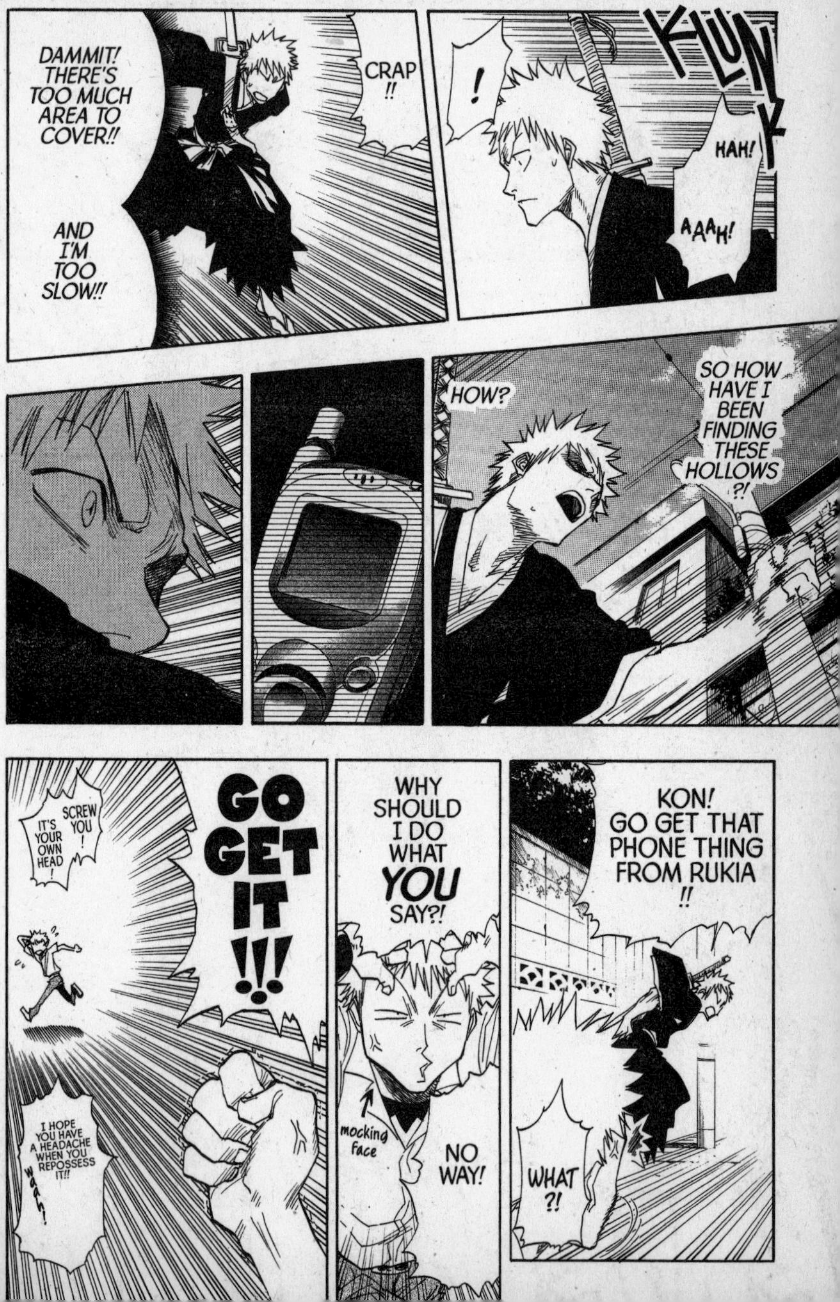
KLUNK
!
HAH!
AAAH!
CRAP!!
DAMMIT! THERE'S TOO MUCH AREA TO COVER!!
AND I'M TOO SLOW!!
SO HOW HAVE I BEEN FINDING THESE HOLLOWS?!
HOW?
KON! GO GET THAT PHONE THING FROM RUKIA!!
WHAT?!
WHY SHOULD I DO WHAT YOU SAY?!
mocking face
NO WAY!
GO GET IT!!!
SCREW YOU!
IT'S YOUR OWN HEAD!
I HOPE YOU HAVE A HEADACHE WHEN YOU REPOSSESS IT!!
waah!

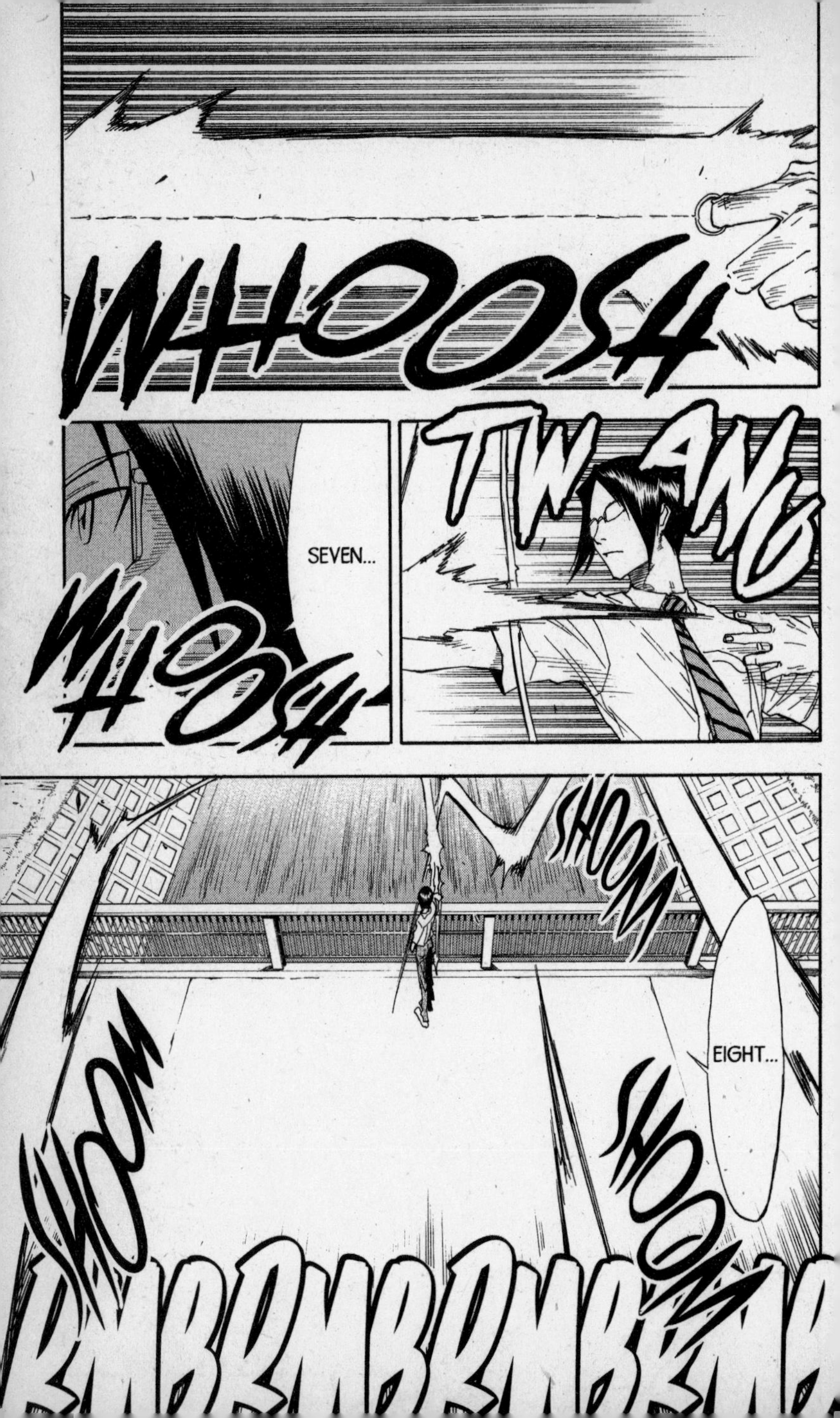
WHOOSH
TWANG
SEVEN...
WHOOSH
SHOOM
EIGHT...
SHOOM
SHOOM

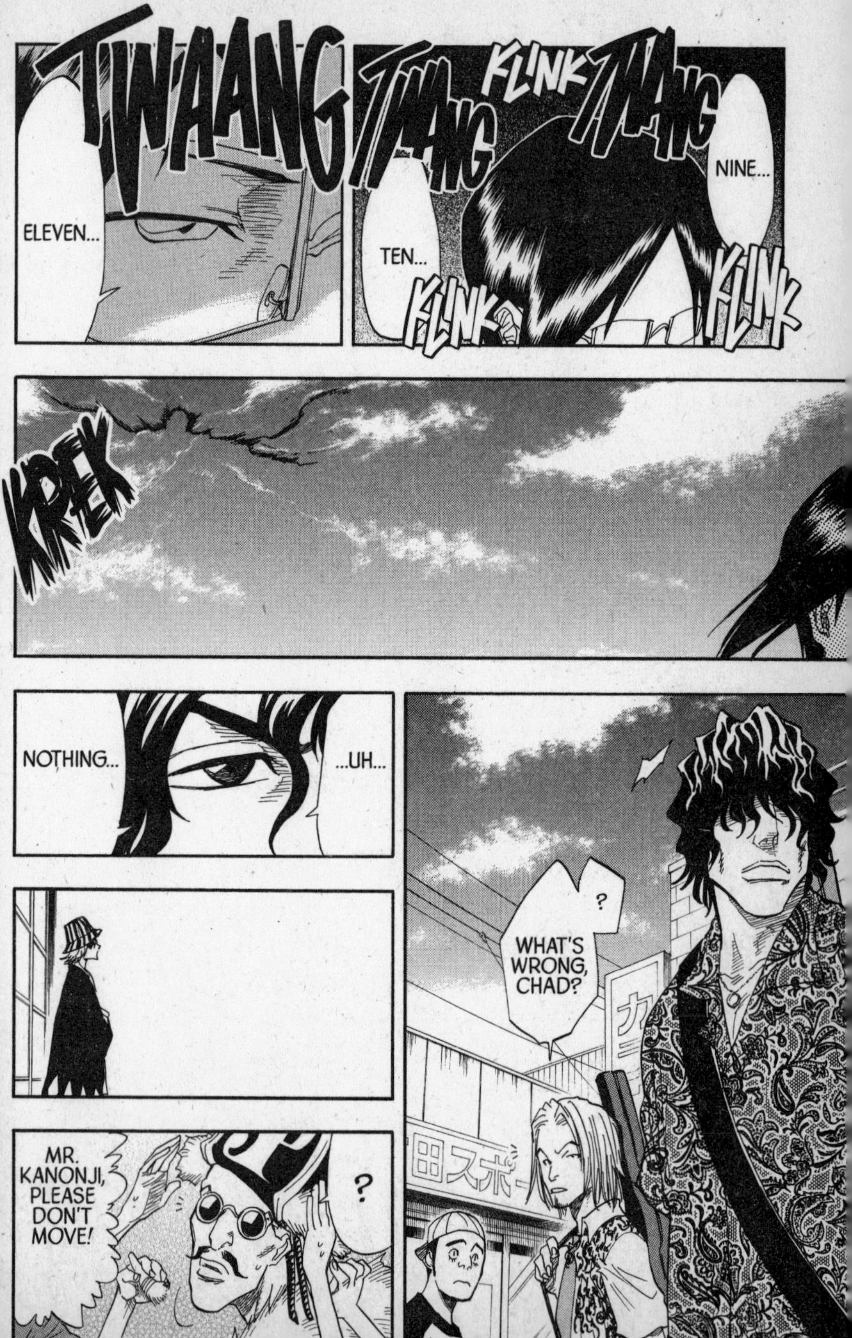
TWANG
KLINK
TWANG
NINE...
KLINK
TEN...
KLINK
TWAANG
ELEVEN...
KREEK
?
WHAT'S WRONG, CHAD?
...UH...
NOTHING...
MR. KANONJI, PLEASE DON'T MOVE!
?

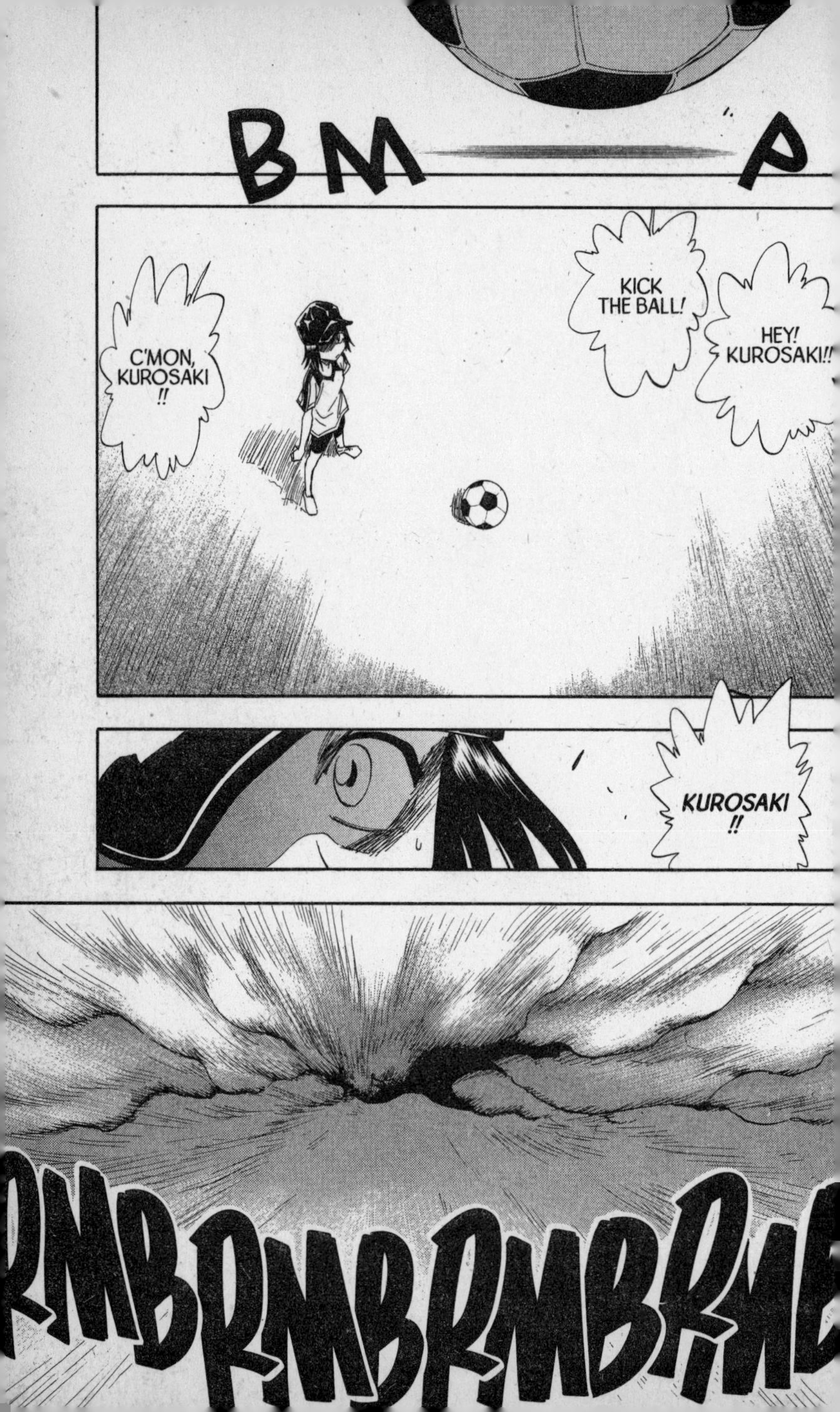
BM P
HEY! KUROSAKI!!
KICK THE BALL!
C'MON, KUROSAKI !!
KUROSAKI !!
RMBRMBRMBRMBRMB

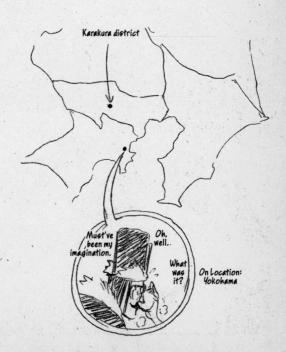

Karakura district

Must've been my imagination.

Oh, well..

What was it?

On Location: Yokohama

38. BENT

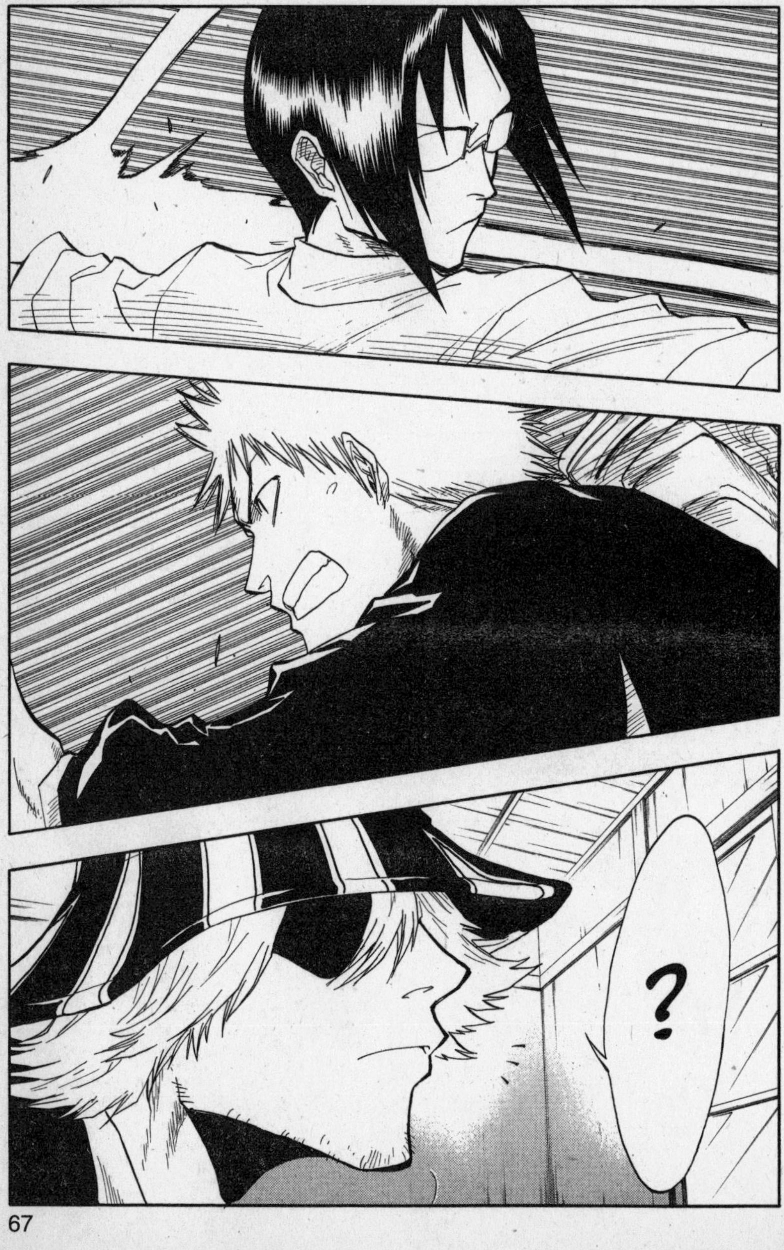
?

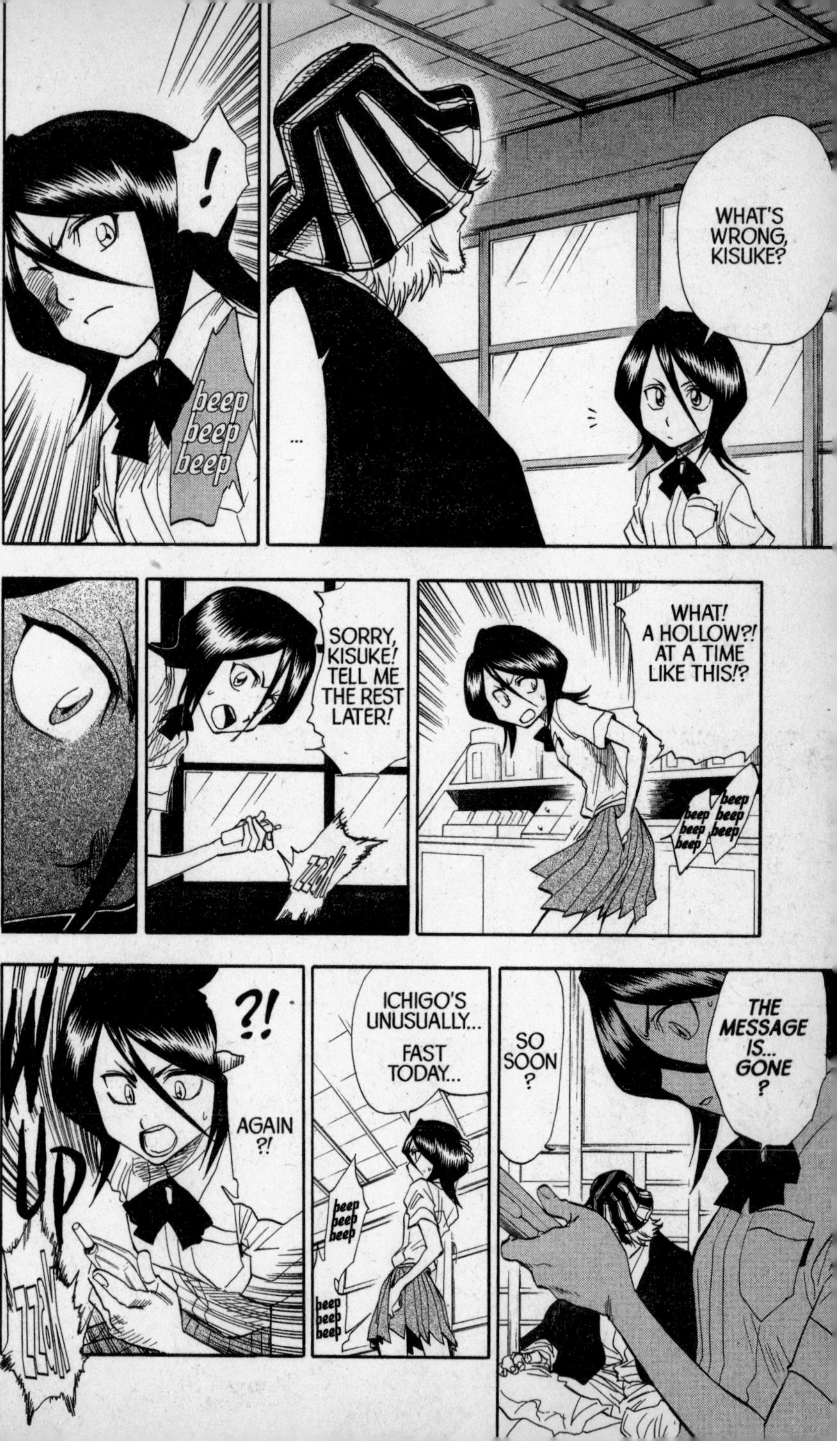
WHAT'S WRONG, KISUKE?
...
!
beep beep beep
WHAT! A HOLLOW?! AT A TIME LIKE THIS!?
beep beep beep
beep beep beep
SORRY, KISUKE! TELL ME THE REST LATER!
THE MESSAGE IS... GONE?
SO SOON?
ICHIGO'S UNUSUALLY... FAST TODAY...
beep beep beep
beep beep beep
?!
AGAIN?!

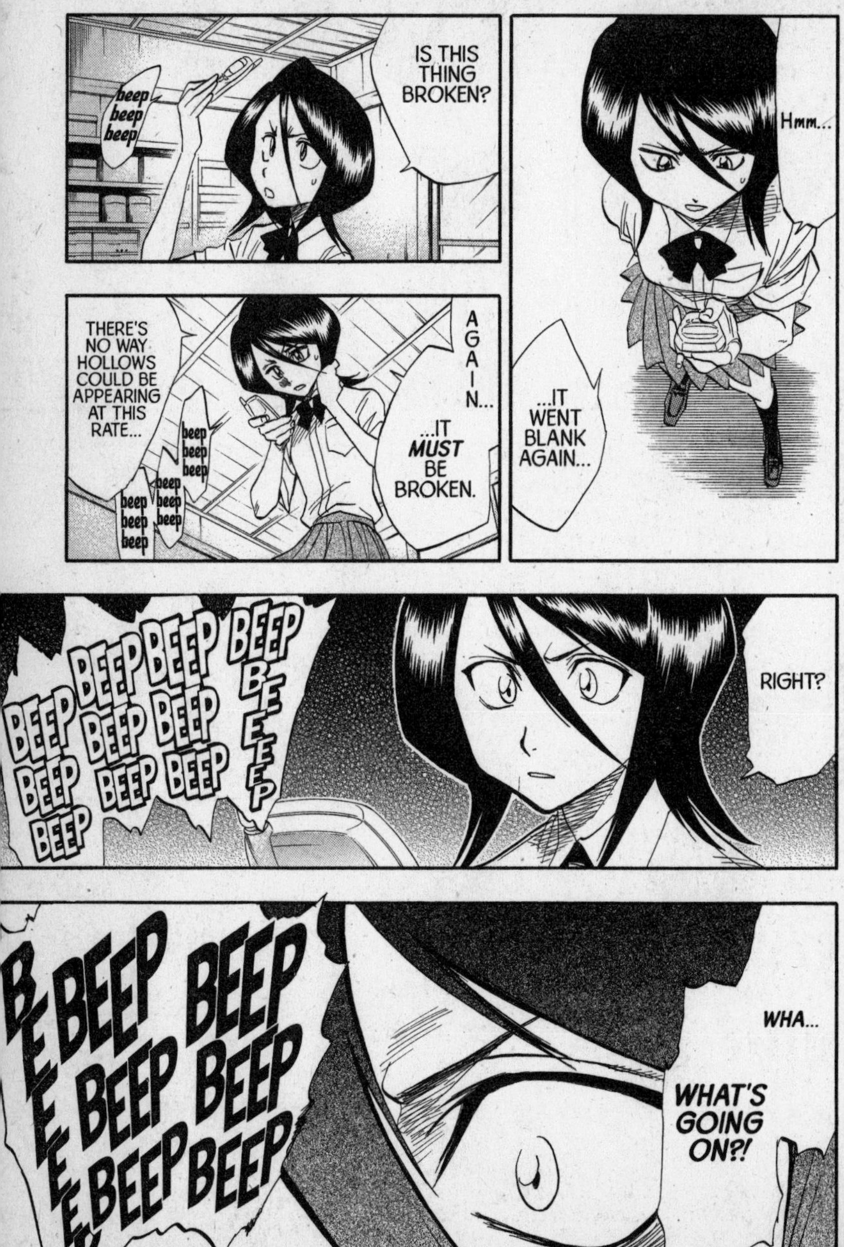

Hmm...
...IT WENT BLANK AGAIN...
IS THIS THING BROKEN?
beep beep beep
AGAIN...
...IT *MUST* BE BROKEN.
THERE'S NO WAY HOLLOWS COULD BE APPEARING AT THIS RATE...
beep beep beep
beep beep beep
beep beep beep
RIGHT?
BEEP BEEP BEEP BEEP BEEEEP
BEEP BEEP BEEP BEEP BEEP BEEP BEEP BEEP BEEP
WHA...
WHAT'S GOING ON?!
BEEP BEEP BEEP BEEP BEEP BEEP BEEEEEP

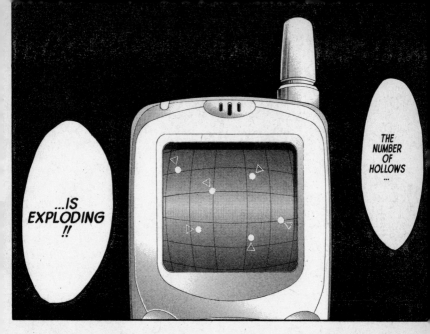

THE NUMBER OF HOLLOWS ...

...IS EXPLODING !!

70

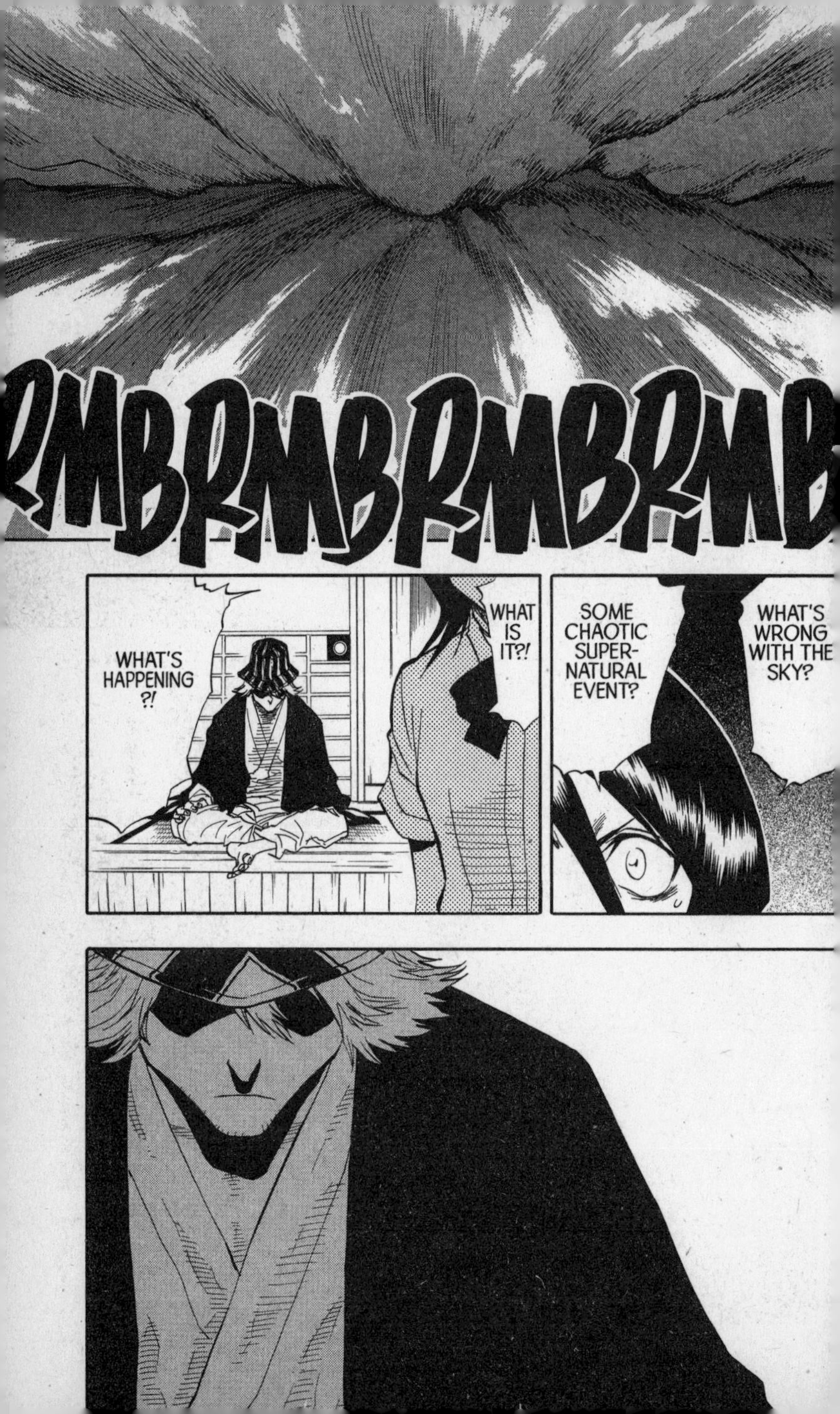
RMBRMBRMBRMB
WHAT'S WRONG WITH THE SKY?
SOME CHAOTIC SUPER-NATURAL EVENT?
WHAT IS IT?!
WHAT'S HAPPENING?!

38. BENT

BLEACH

ブリーチ

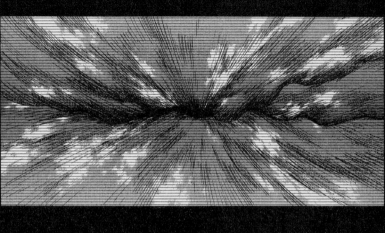

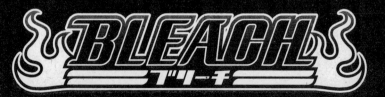

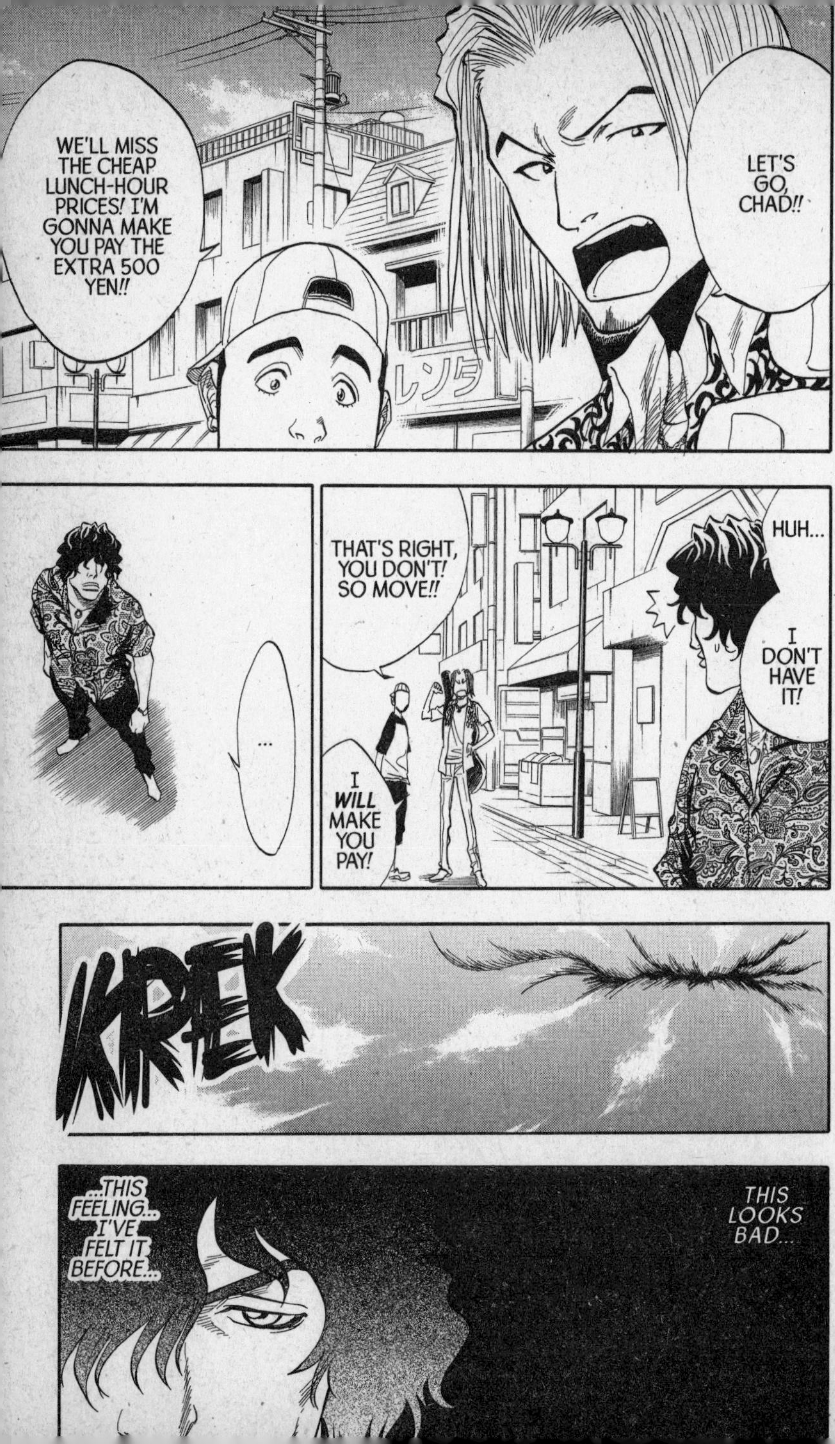
LET'S GO, CHAD!!
WE'LL MISS THE CHEAP LUNCH-HOUR PRICES! I'M GONNA MAKE YOU PAY THE EXTRA 500 YEN!!
HUH...
I DON'T HAVE IT!
THAT'S RIGHT, YOU DON'T! SO MOVE!!
I *WILL* MAKE YOU PAY!
...
KREK
THIS LOOKS BAD...
...THIS FEELING... I'VE FELT IT BEFORE...

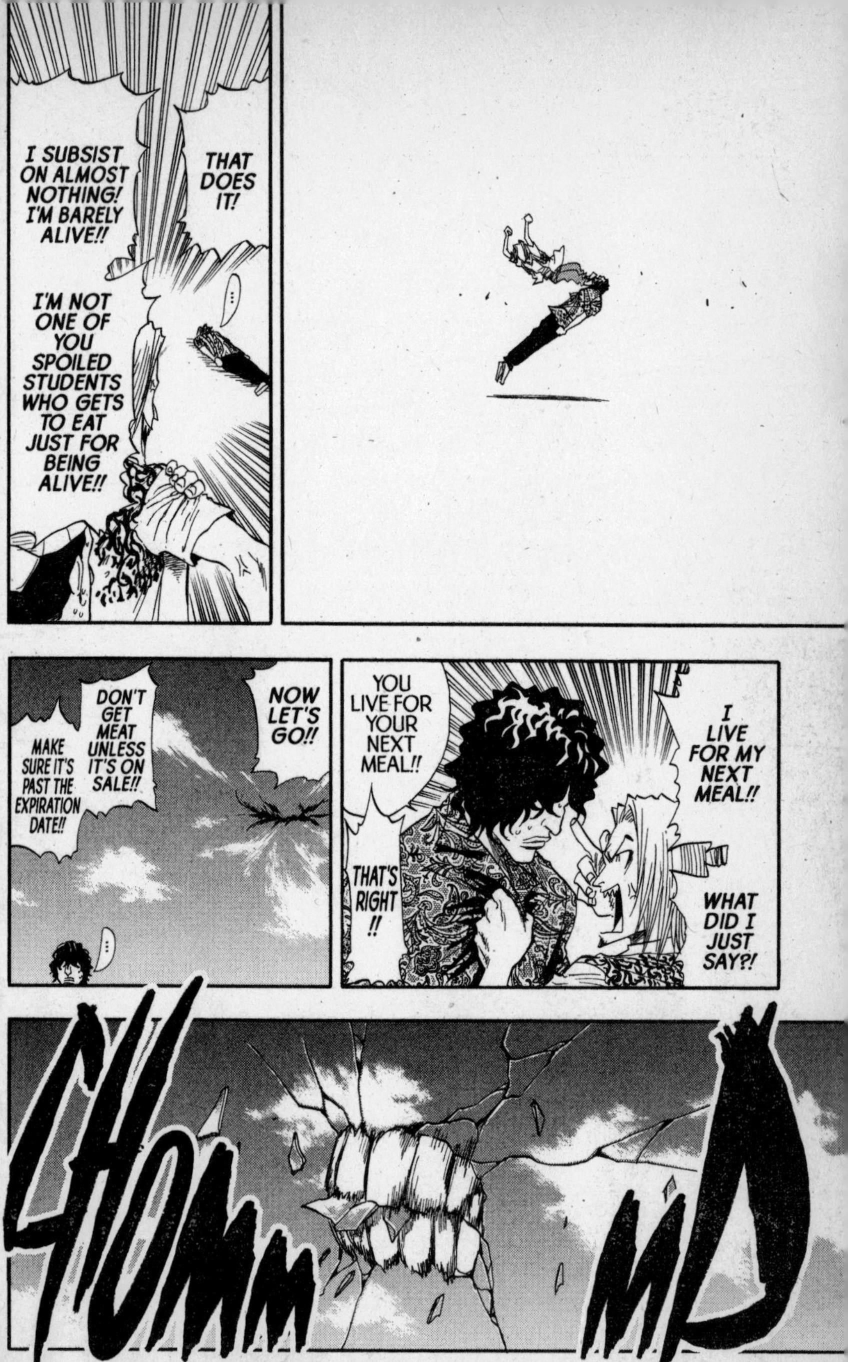
THAT DOES IT!
I SUBSIST ON ALMOST NOTHING! I'M BARELY ALIVE!!
I'M NOT ONE OF YOU SPOILED STUDENTS WHO GETS TO EAT JUST FOR BEING ALIVE!!
...
I LIVE FOR MY NEXT MEAL!!
YOU LIVE FOR YOUR NEXT MEAL!!
THAT'S RIGHT!!
WHAT DID I JUST SAY?!
NOW LET'S GO!!
DON'T GET MEAT UNLESS IT'S ON SALE!!
MAKE SURE IT'S PAST THE EXPIRATION DATE!!
...
CHOMMMMP

READ THIS WAY

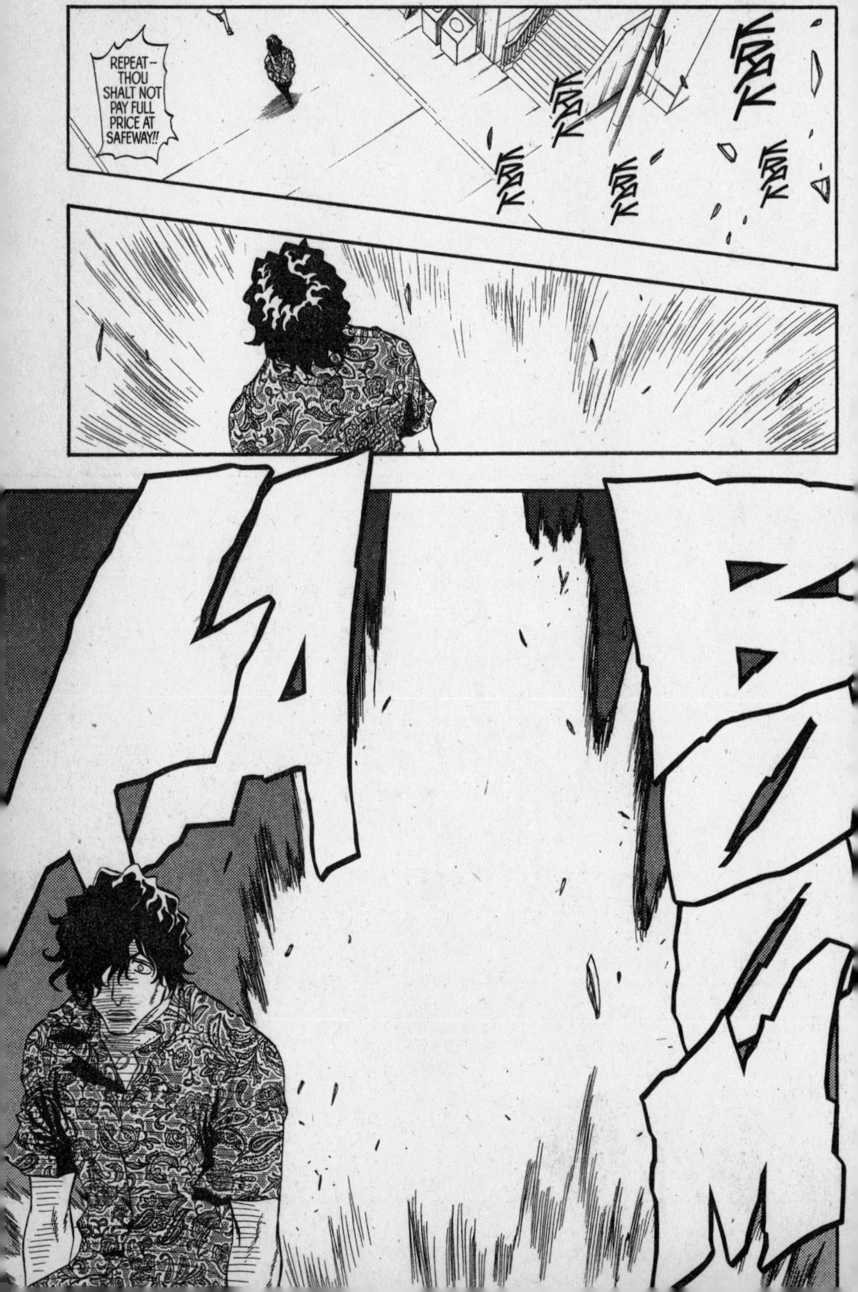
REPEAT--THOU SHALT NOT PAY FULL PRICE AT SAFEWAY!!

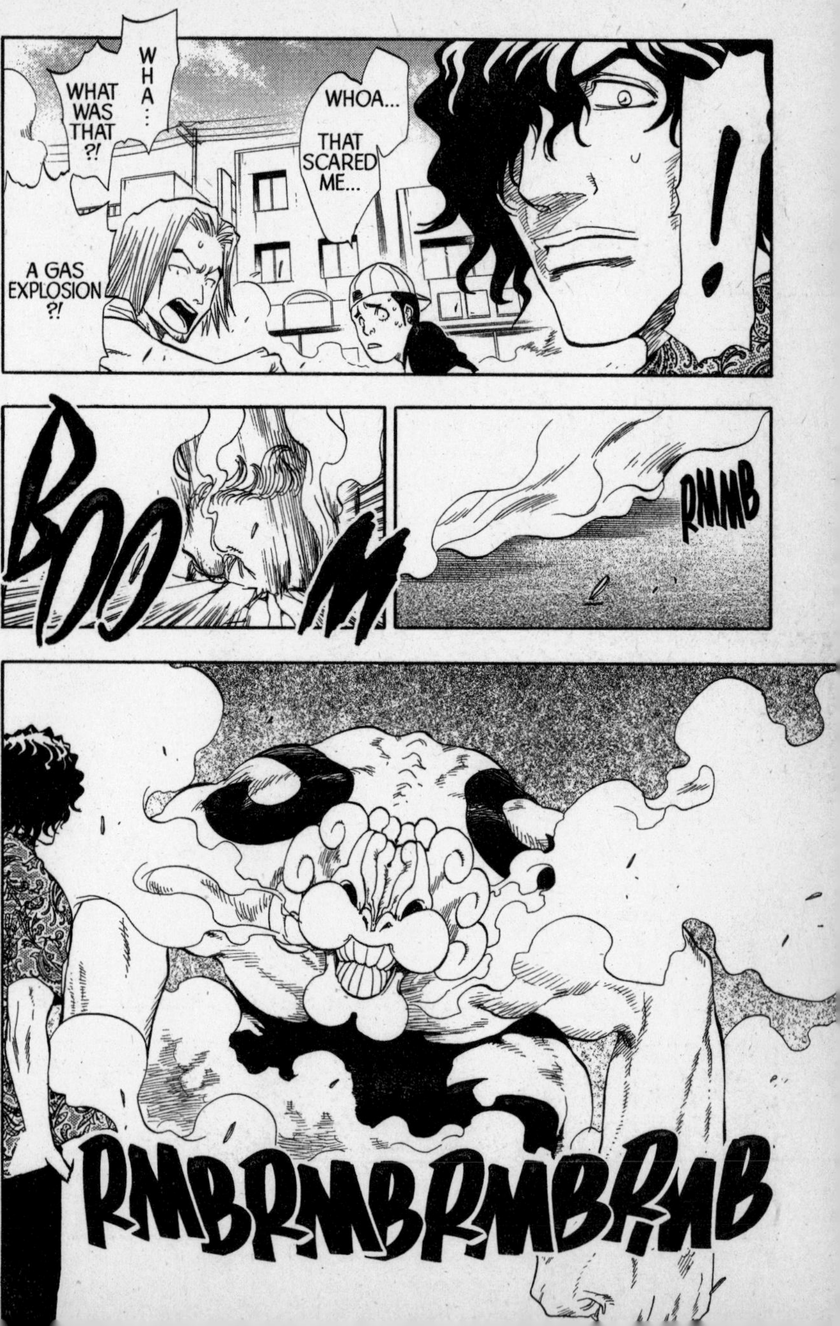
!
WHOA...
THAT SCARED ME...
WHA...
WHAT WAS THAT ?!
A GAS EXPLOSION ?!
RMMB
BOOM
RMBRMBRMBRMB

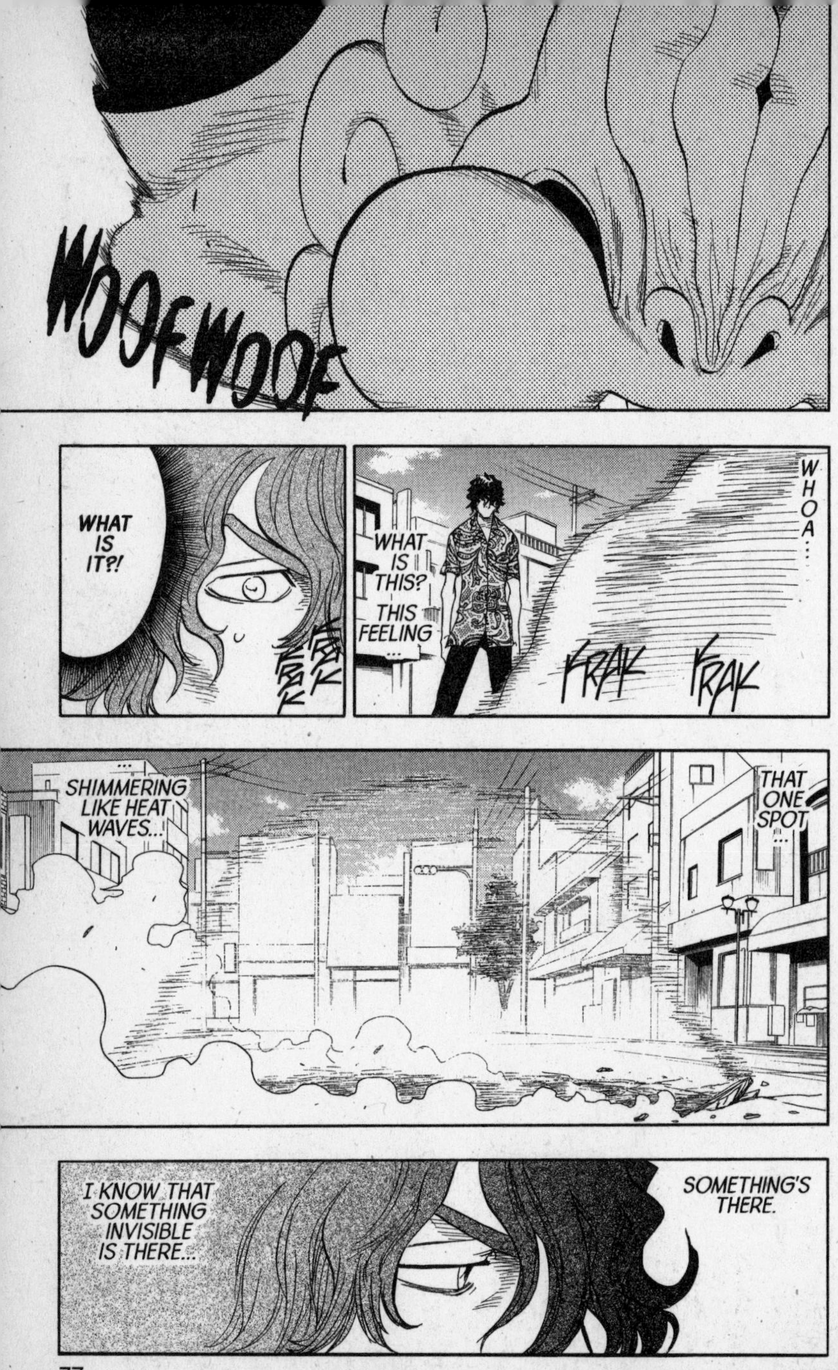
WOOF WOOF
WHOA...
WHAT IS THIS? THIS FEELING...
KRAK KRAK
WHAT IS IT?!
KRAK KRAK
THAT ONE SPOT...
...SHIMMERING LIKE HEAT WAVES...
SOMETHING'S THERE.
I KNOW THAT SOMETHING INVISIBLE IS THERE...

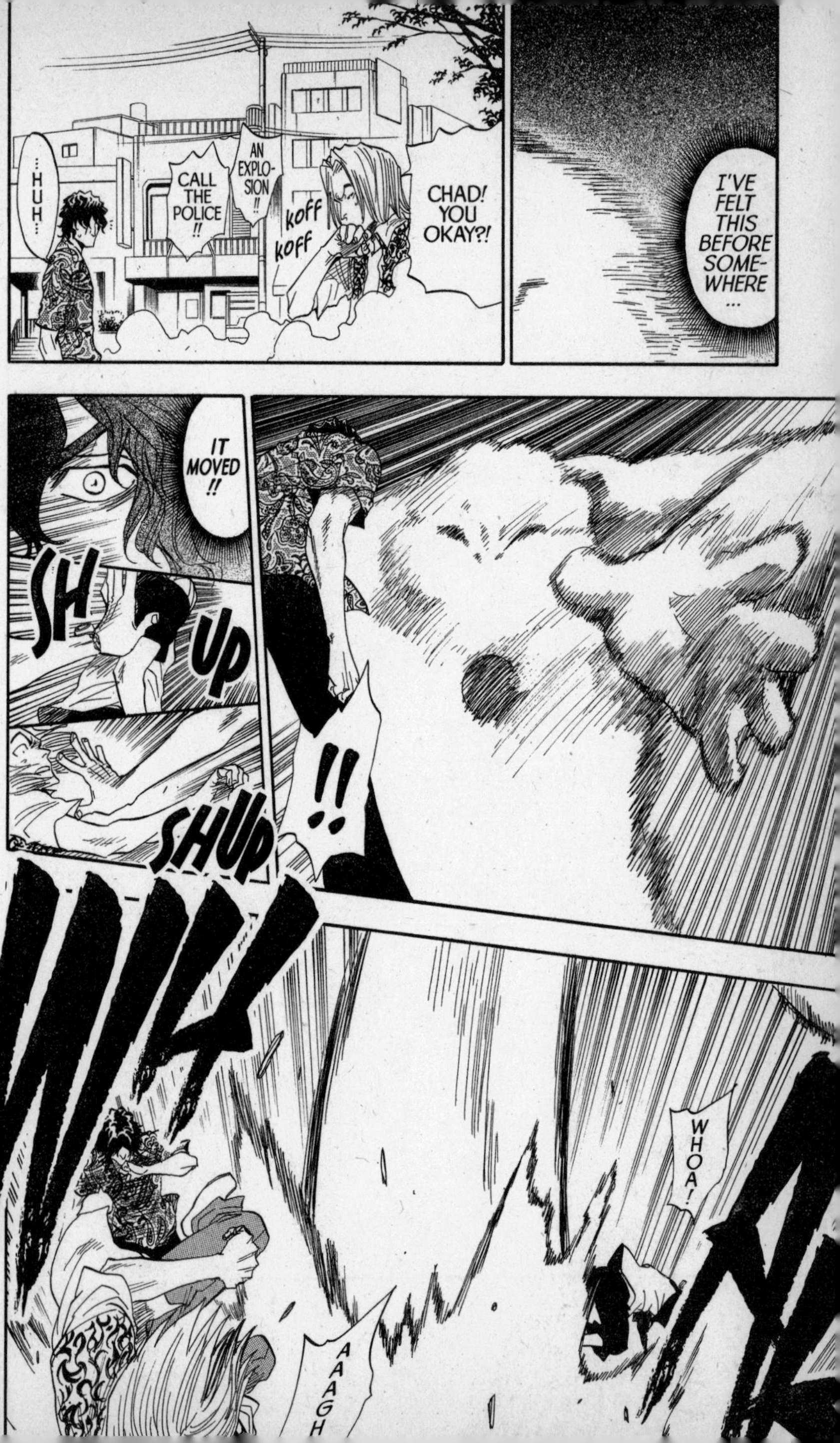
I'VE FELT THIS BEFORE SOME-WHERE ...
CHAD! YOU OKAY?!
koff koff
AN EXPLO-SION!!
CALL THE POLICE!!
...HUH...
!!
IT MOVED!!
SH UP
SHUP
WHOA!
AAAGH

READ THIS WAY

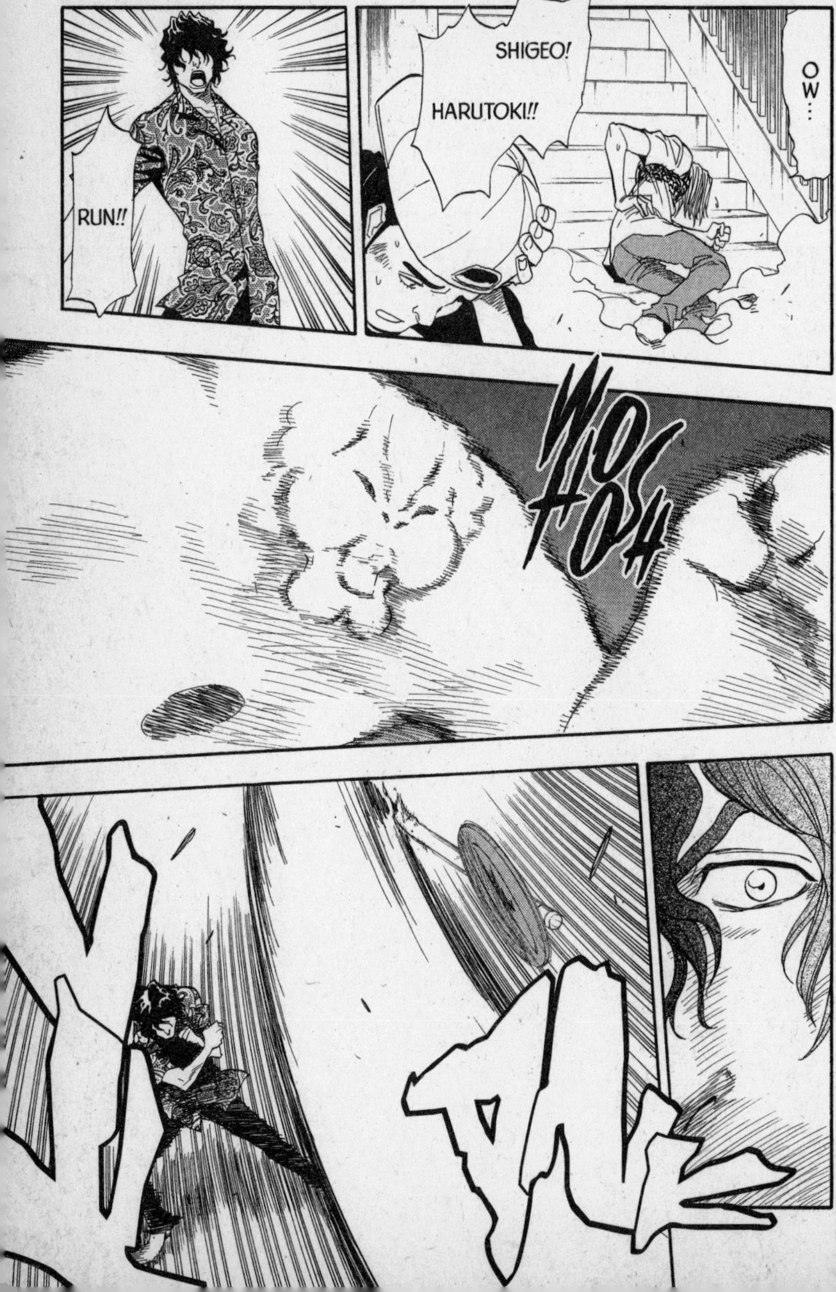
OW...
SHIGEO!
HARUTOKI!!
RUN!!
WHOOSH

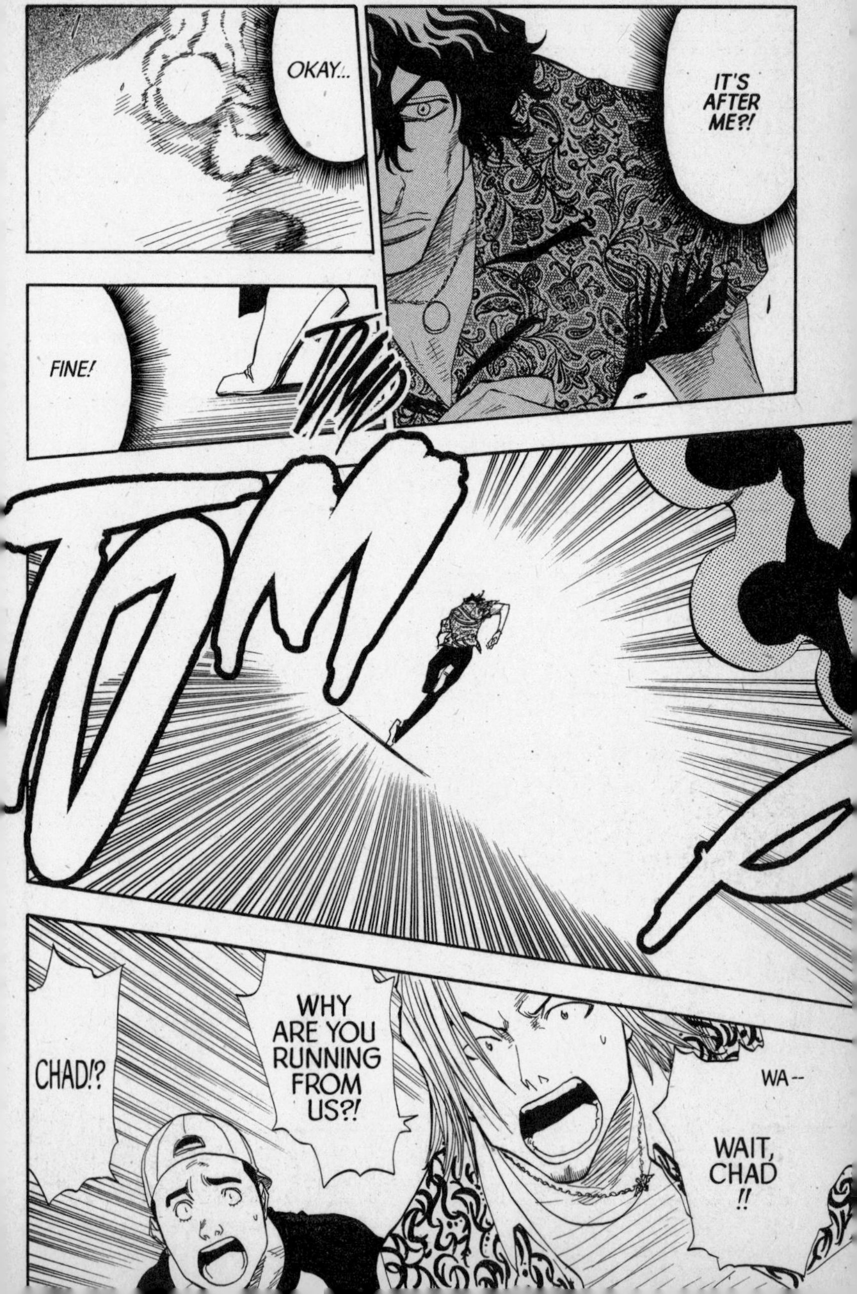
IT'S AFTER ME?!
OKAY...
FINE!
WA--
WAIT, CHAD !!
WHY ARE YOU RUNNING FROM US?!
CHAD!?

READ THIS WAY

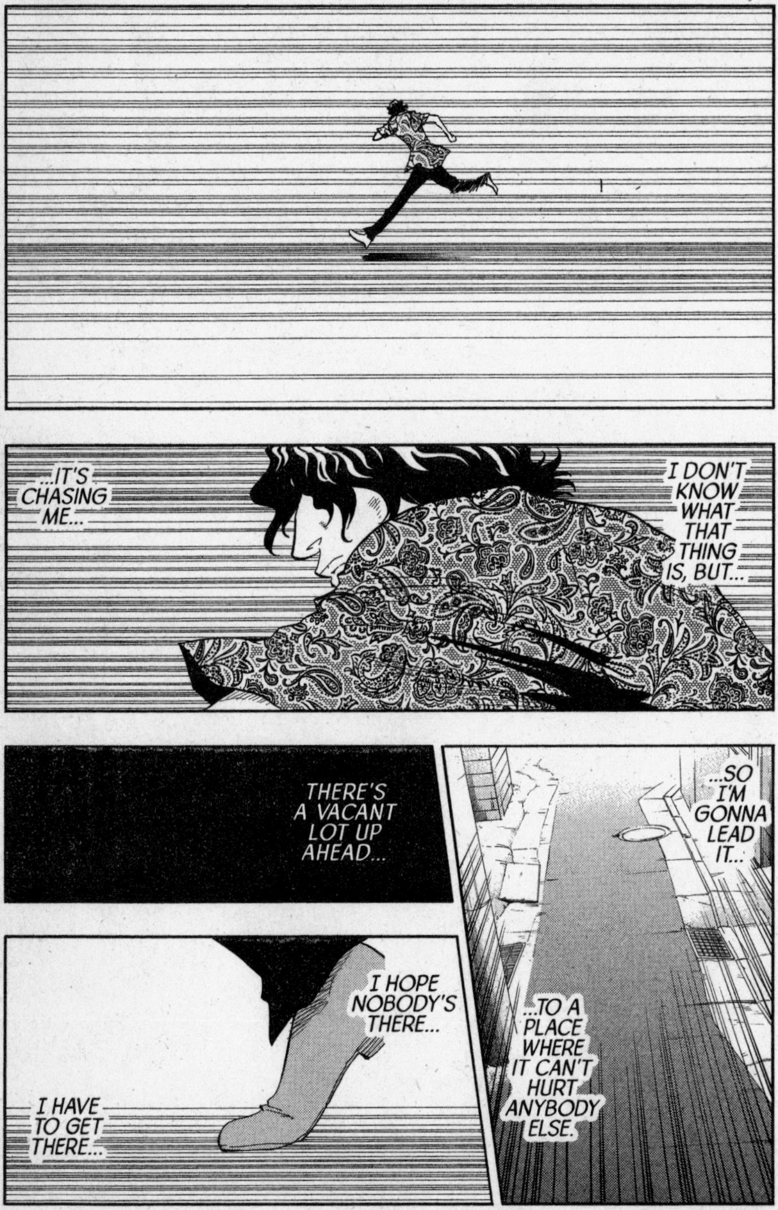

I DON'T KNOW WHAT THAT THING IS, BUT...
...IT'S CHASING ME...
...SO I'M GONNA LEAD IT...
...TO A PLACE WHERE IT CAN'T HURT ANYBODY ELSE.
THERE'S A VACANT LOT UP AHEAD...
I HOPE NOBODY'S THERE...
I HAVE TO GET THERE...

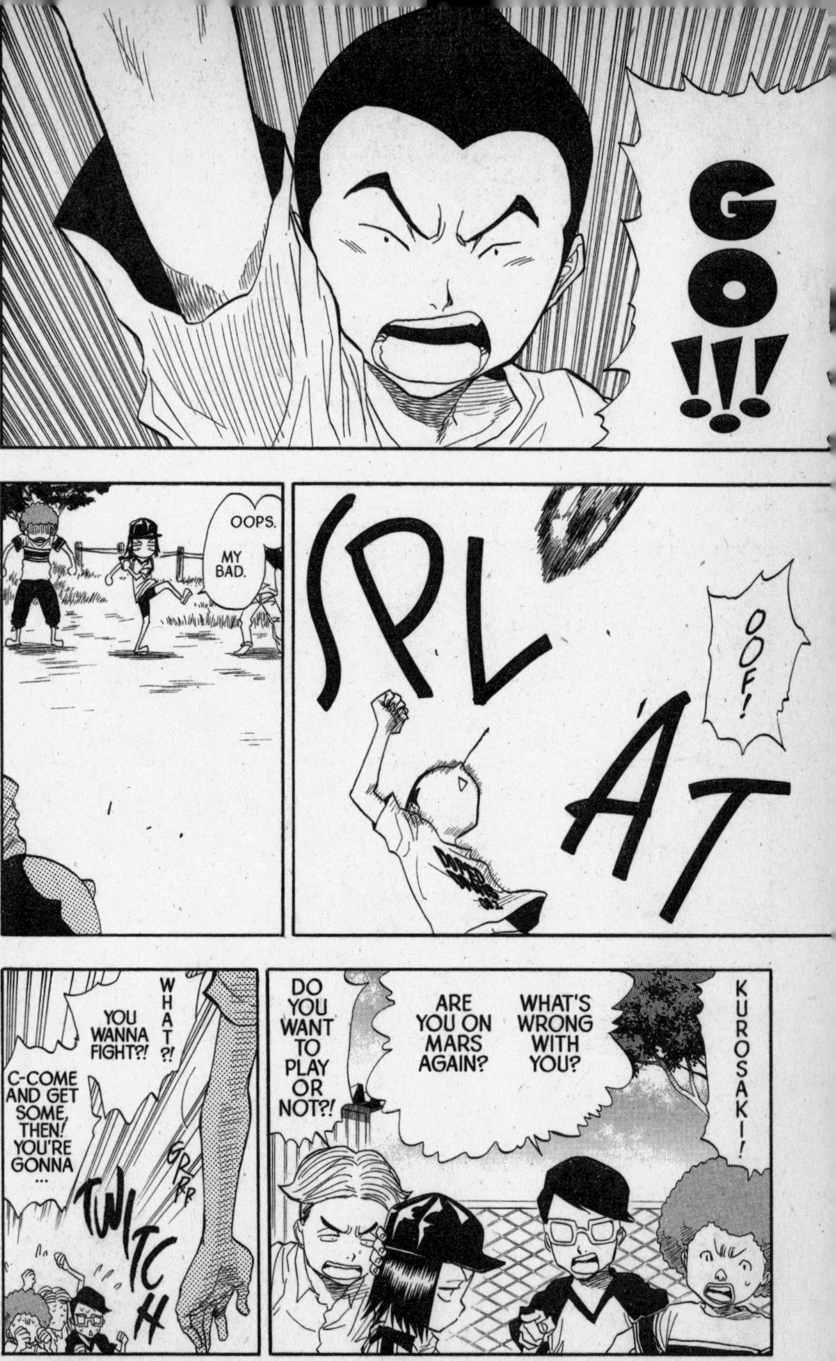
GO!!!
SPLAT
OOF!
OOPS.
MY BAD.
KUROSAKI!
WHAT'S WRONG WITH YOU?
ARE YOU ON MARS AGAIN?
DO YOU WANT TO PLAY OR NOT?!
WHAT?!
YOU WANNA FIGHT?!
GRRR
TWITCH
C-COME AND GET SOME, THEN! YOU'RE GONNA ...

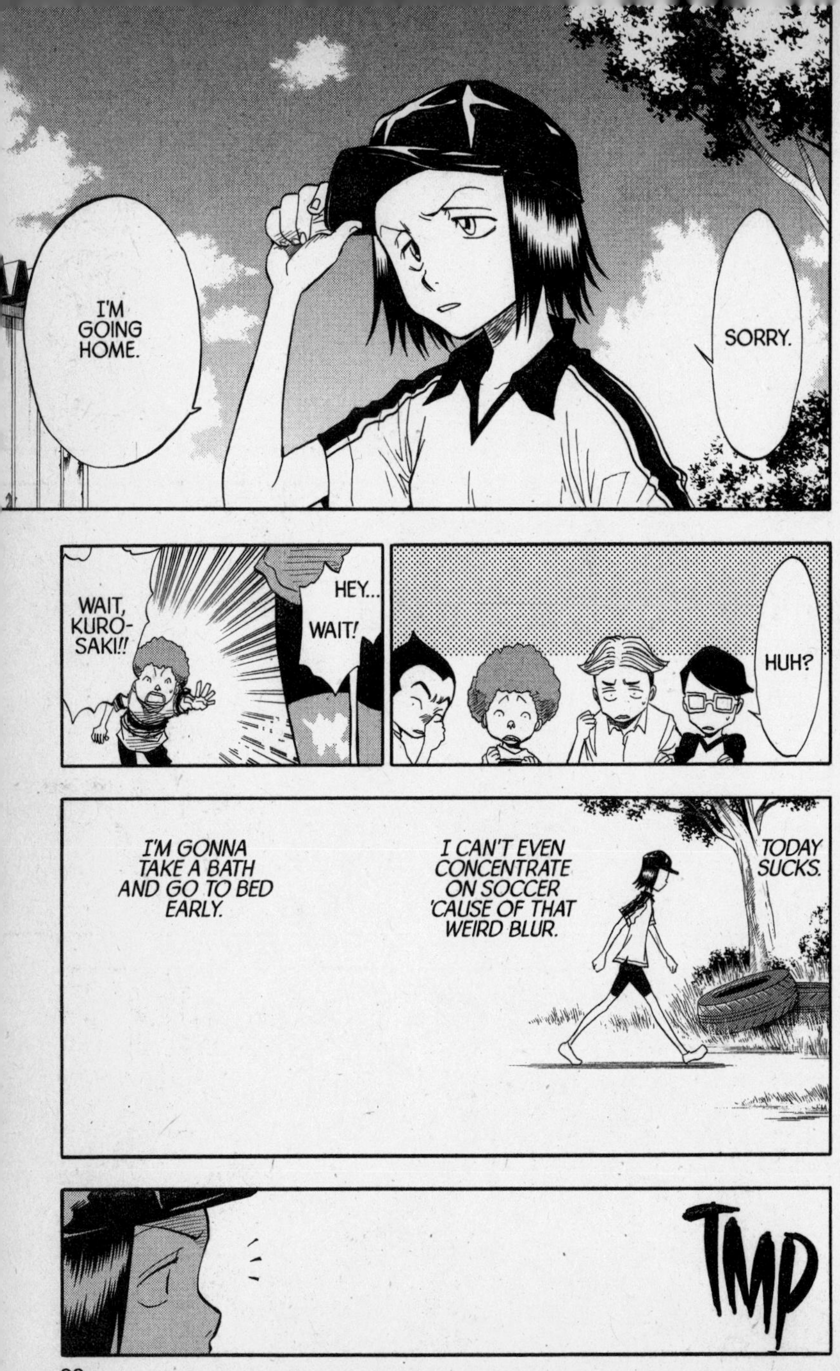
SORRY.
I'M GOING HOME.
HUH?
HEY...
WAIT!
WAIT, KURO-SAKI!!
TODAY SUCKS.
I CAN'T EVEN CONCENTRATE ON SOCCER 'CAUSE OF THAT WEIRD BLUR.
I'M GONNA TAKE A BATH AND GO TO BED EARLY.
TMP

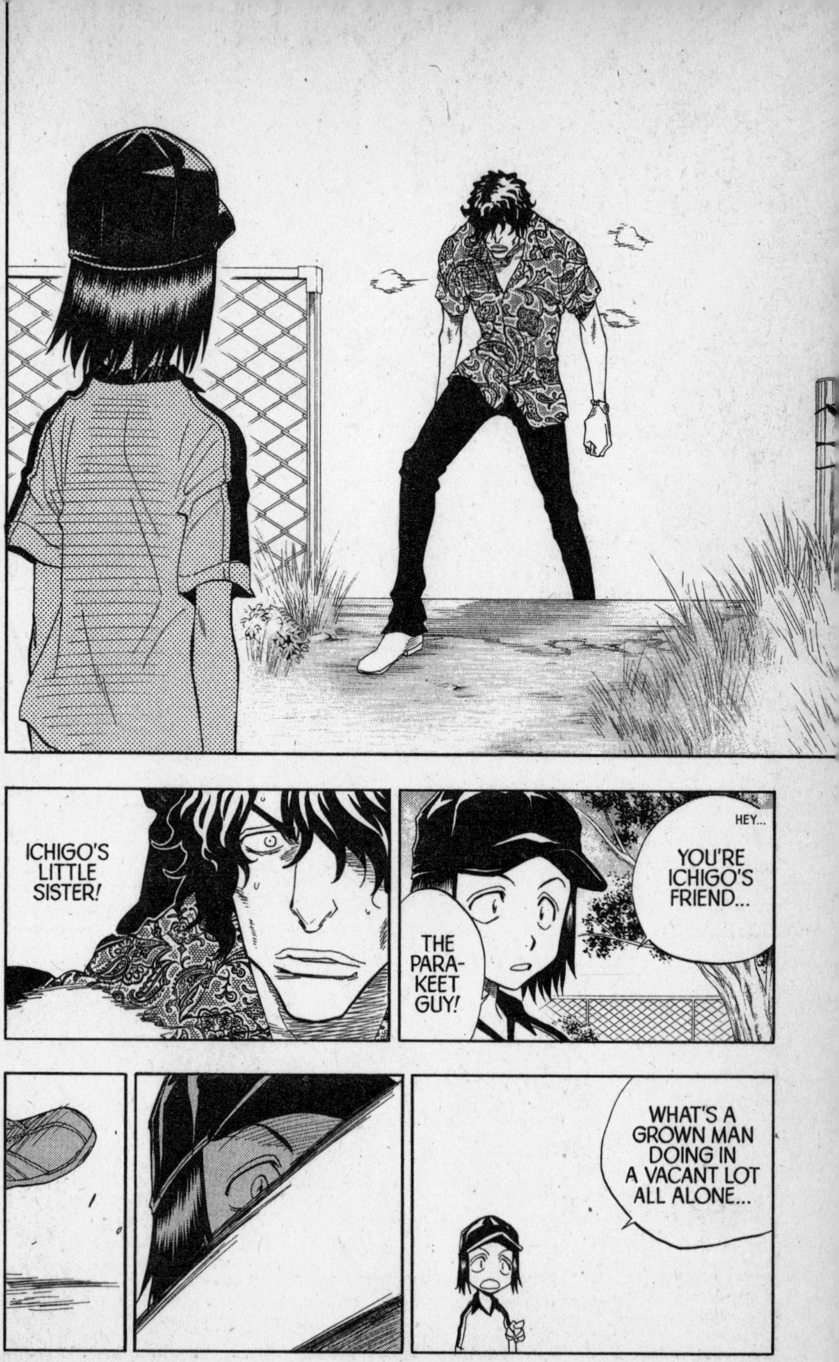
HEY...
YOU'RE ICHIGO'S FRIEND...
THE PARA-KEET GUY!
ICHIGO'S LITTLE SISTER!
WHAT'S A GROWN MAN DOING IN A VACANT LOT ALL ALONE...

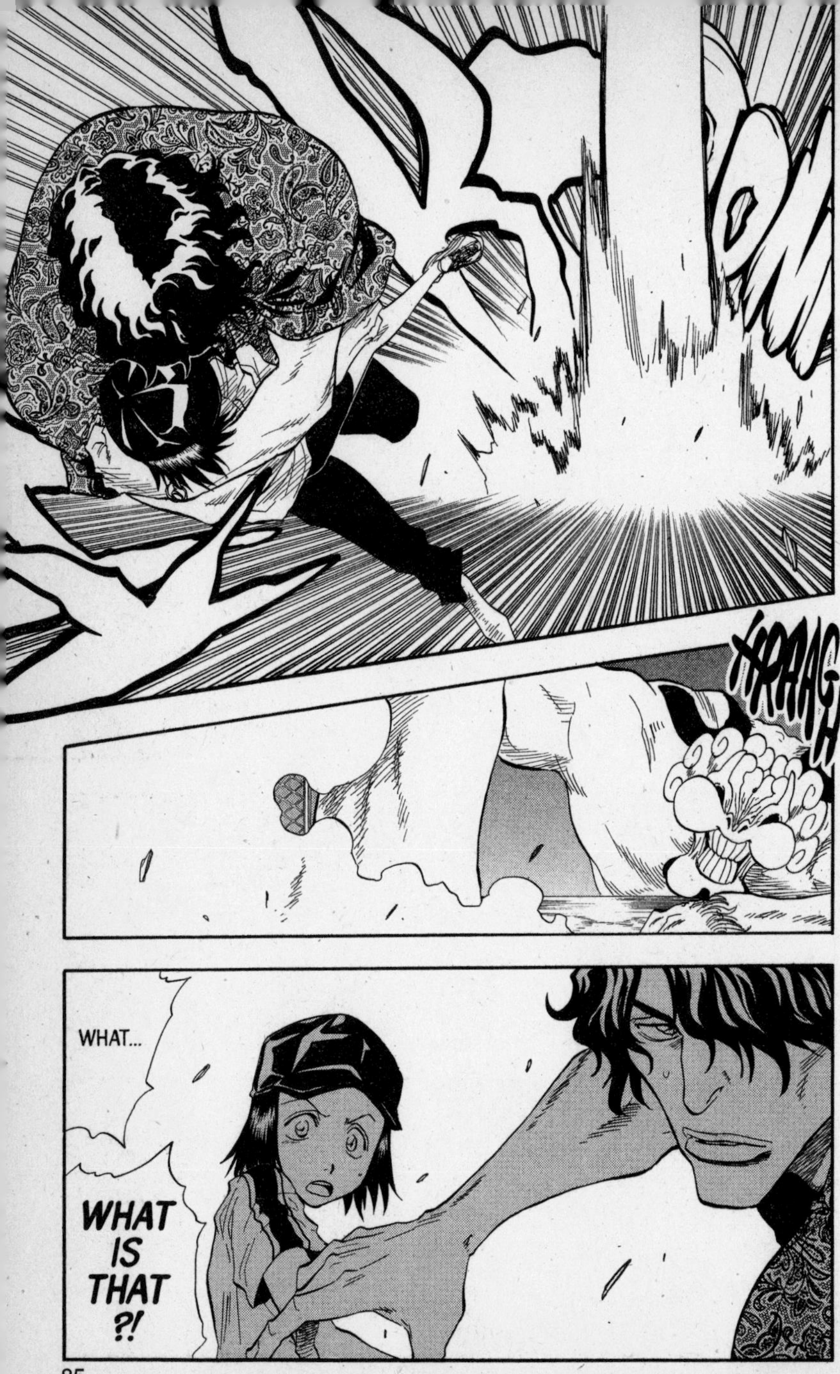
HRAAGH
WHAT...
WHAT IS THAT ?!

KARIN'S FRIENDS

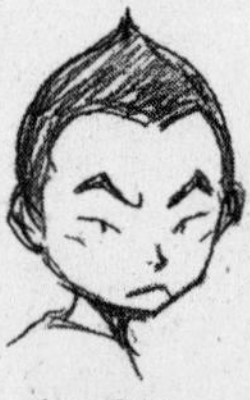

Heita Tôjôin
A.K.A.
"Pinta"
Despite having an upper-class last name, he's as poor as poor gets.

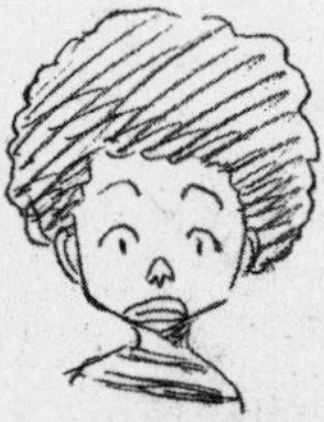

Kei Uehara
A.K.A.
"Donny"
"Donny," 'cause he looks like Donald Duck.

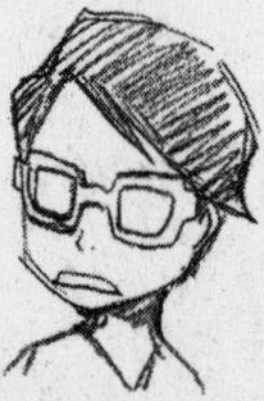

Kazuya Usaka
A.K.A.
"Usaka"
Wears glasses, but isn't smart.

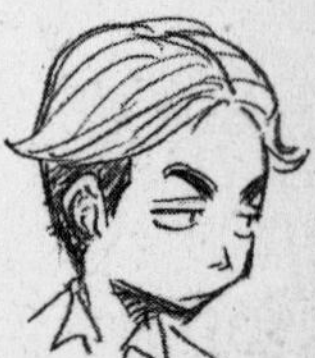

Ryôhei Toba
A.K.A.
"Ryôhei"
The Nastiest.

39. Right Arm of the Giant

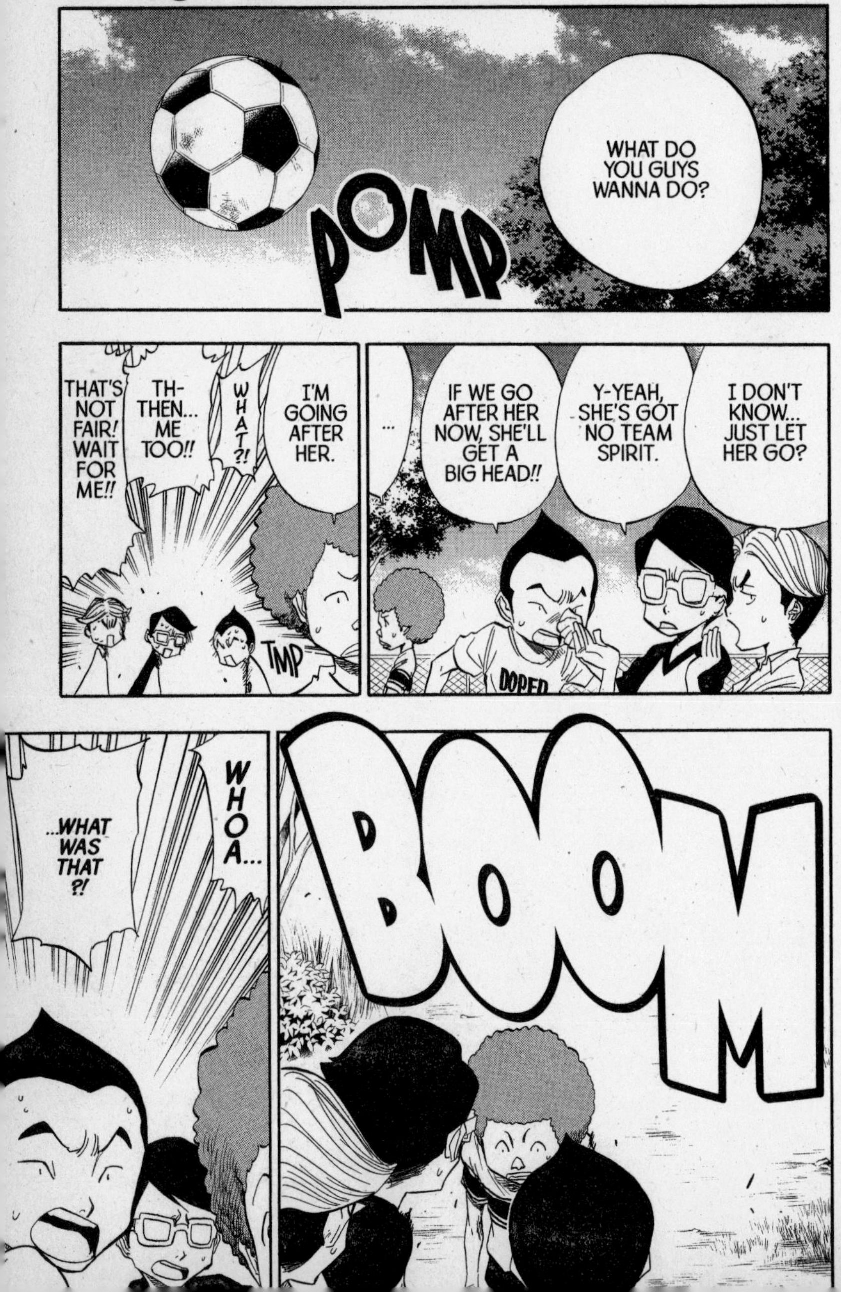
WHAT DO YOU GUYS WANNA DO?
POMP
I DON'T KNOW... JUST LET HER GO?
Y-YEAH, SHE'S GOT NO TEAM SPIRIT.
IF WE GO AFTER HER NOW, SHE'LL GET A BIG HEAD!!
...
I'M GOING AFTER HER.
WHAT?!
TH-THEN... ME TOO!!
THAT'S NOT FAIR! WAIT FOR ME!!
TMP
BOOM
WHOA...
...WHAT WAS THAT?!

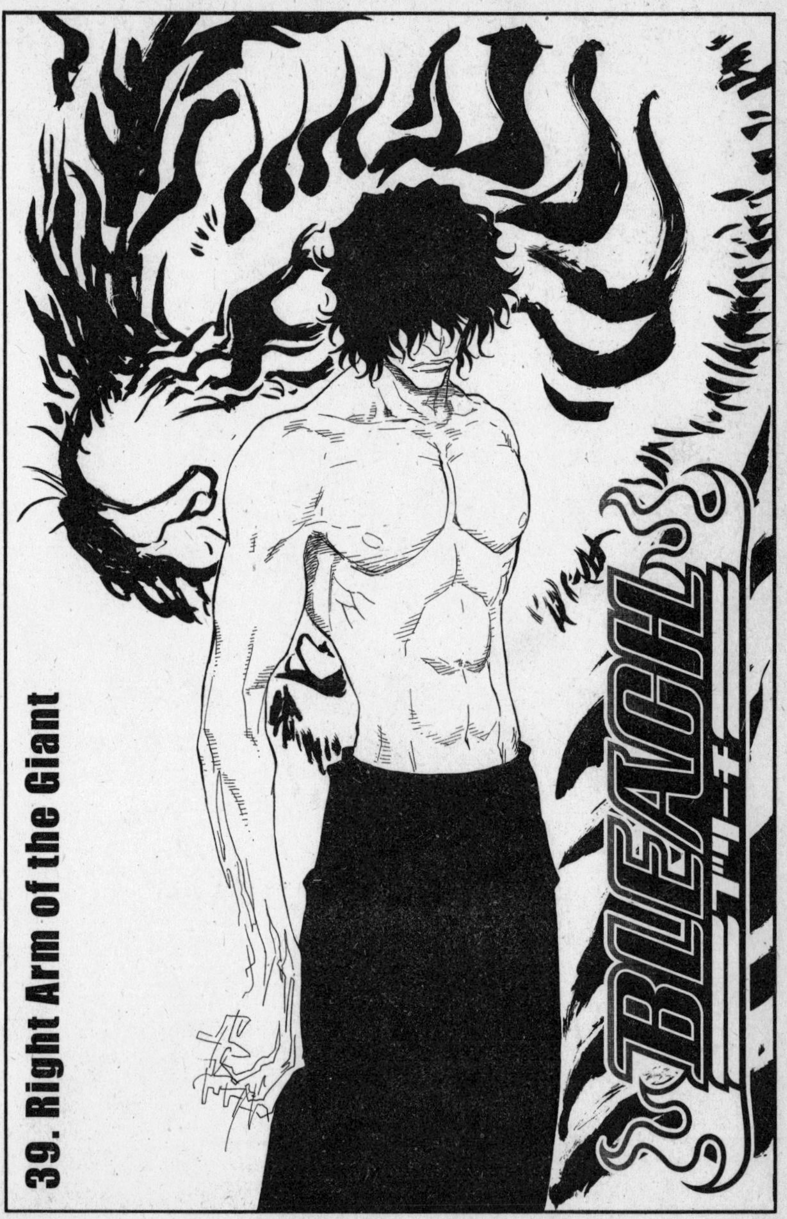
39. Right Arm of the Giant
BLEACH
ブリーチ

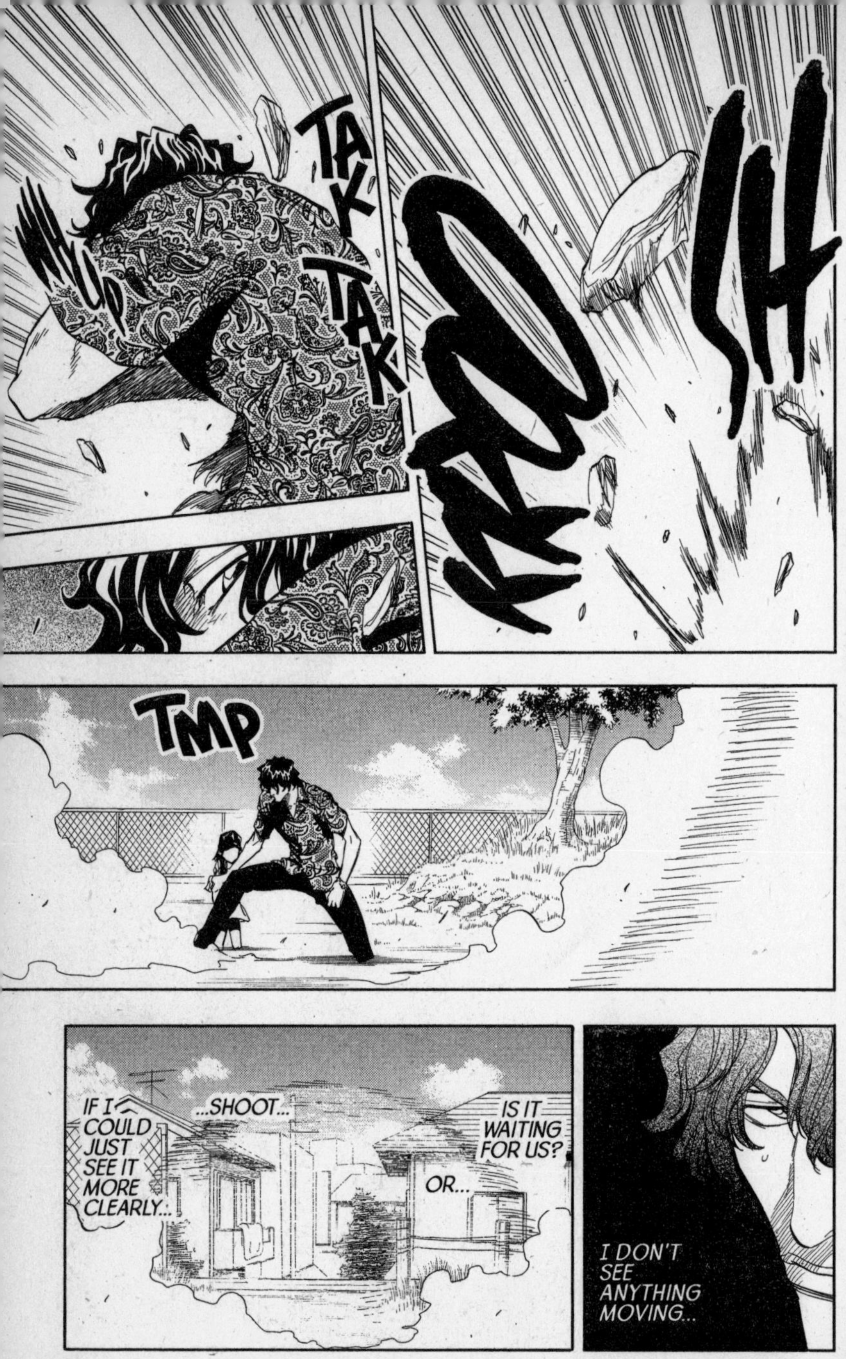
WHUP
TAK TAK TAK
TMP
I DON'T SEE ANYTHING MOVING...
IS IT WAITING FOR US?
OR...
...SHOOT...
IF I COULD JUST SEE IT MORE CLEARLY...

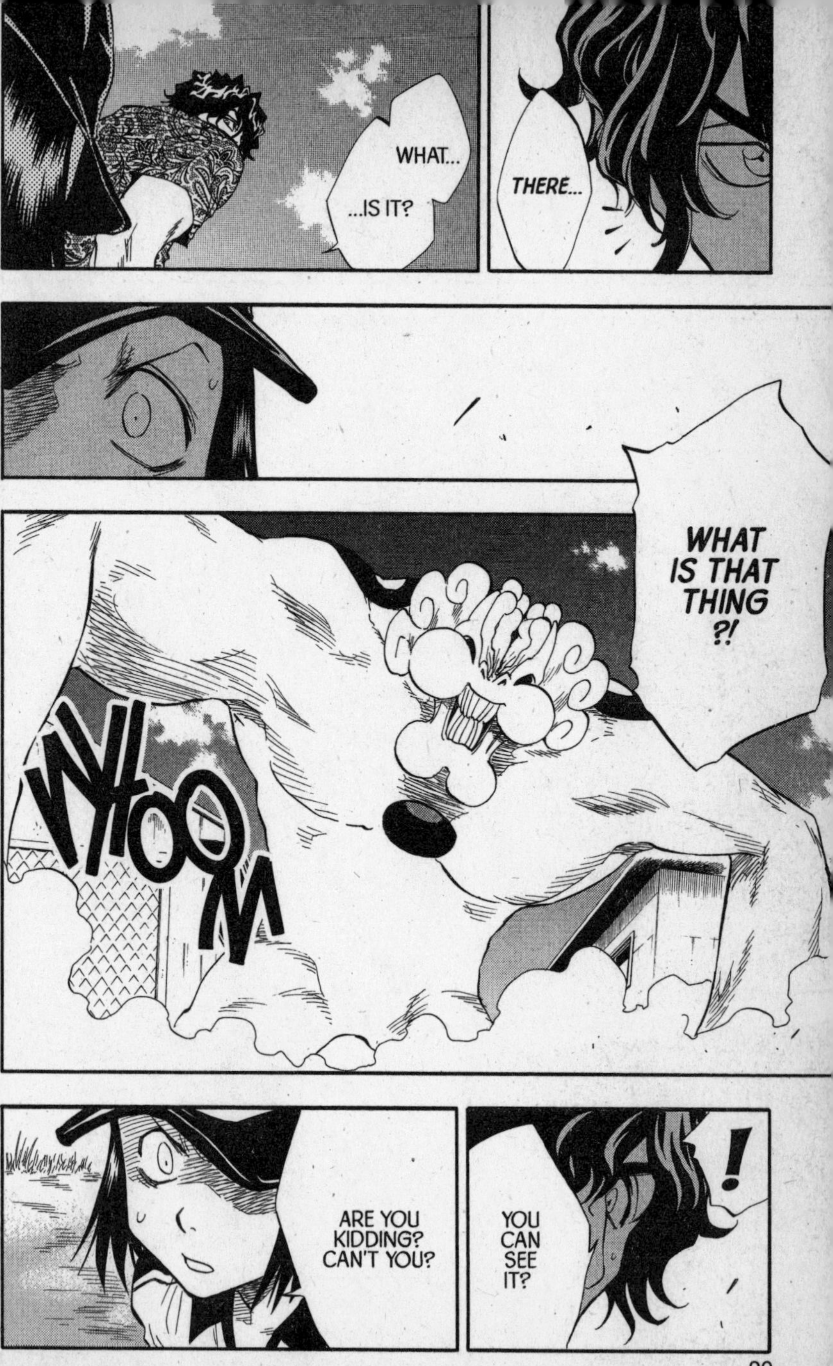
THERE...
WHAT... ...IS IT?
WHAT IS THAT THING?!
WHOOM
!
YOU CAN SEE IT?
ARE YOU KIDDING? CAN'T YOU?

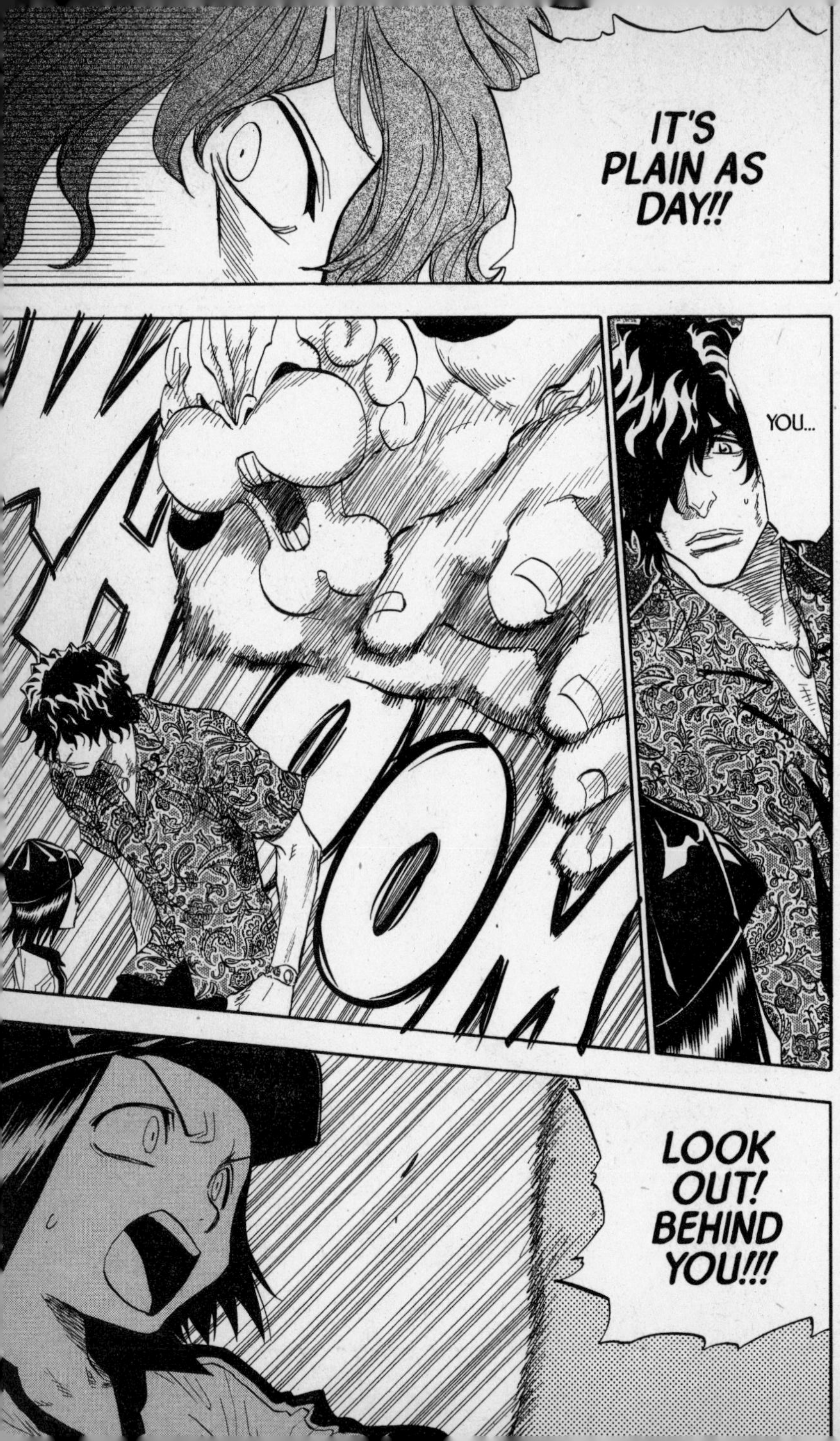
IT'S PLAIN AS DAY!!
YOU...
LOOK OUT! BEHIND YOU!!!

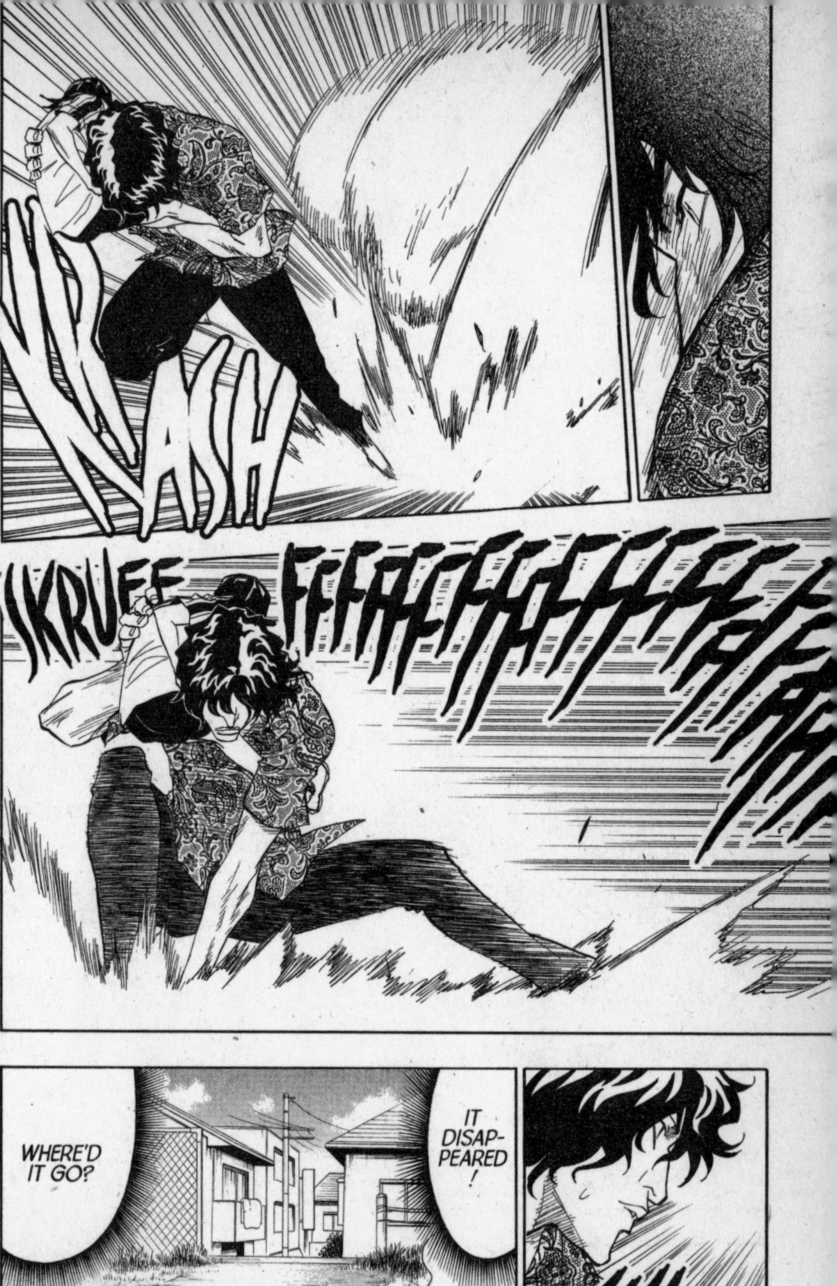
WASH
SKRUFFFFFFFFFFFFFFFFFF
WIP
IT DISAPPEARED!
WHERE'D IT GO?

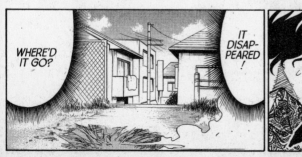

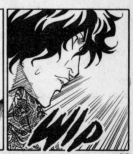

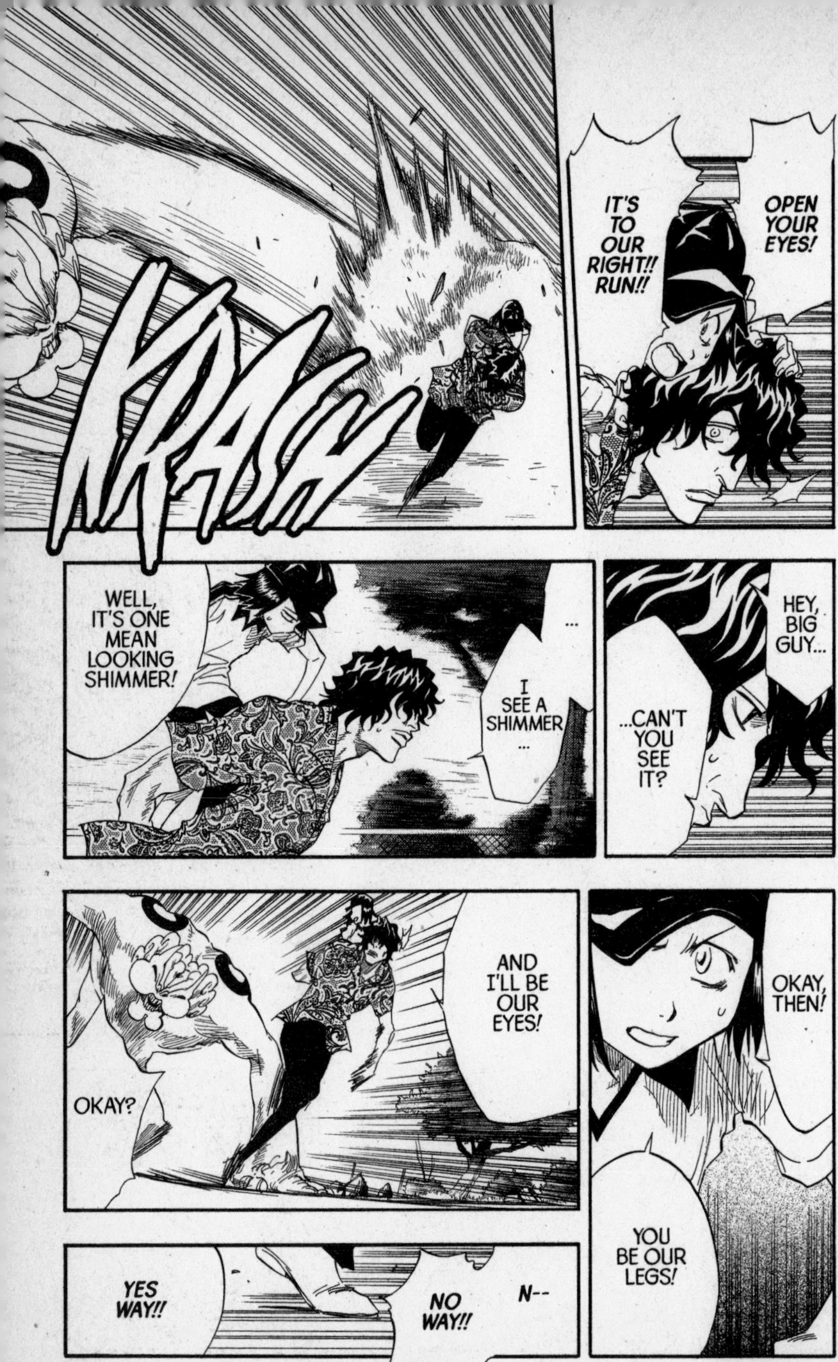
OPEN YOUR EYES!
IT'S TO OUR RIGHT!! RUN!!
KRASH
HEY, BIG GUY...
...CAN'T YOU SEE IT?
...
I SEE A SHIMMER...
WELL, IT'S ONE MEAN LOOKING SHIMMER!
OKAY, THEN!
YOU BE OUR LEGS!
AND I'LL BE OUR EYES!
OKAY?
N--
NO WAY!!
YES WAY!!

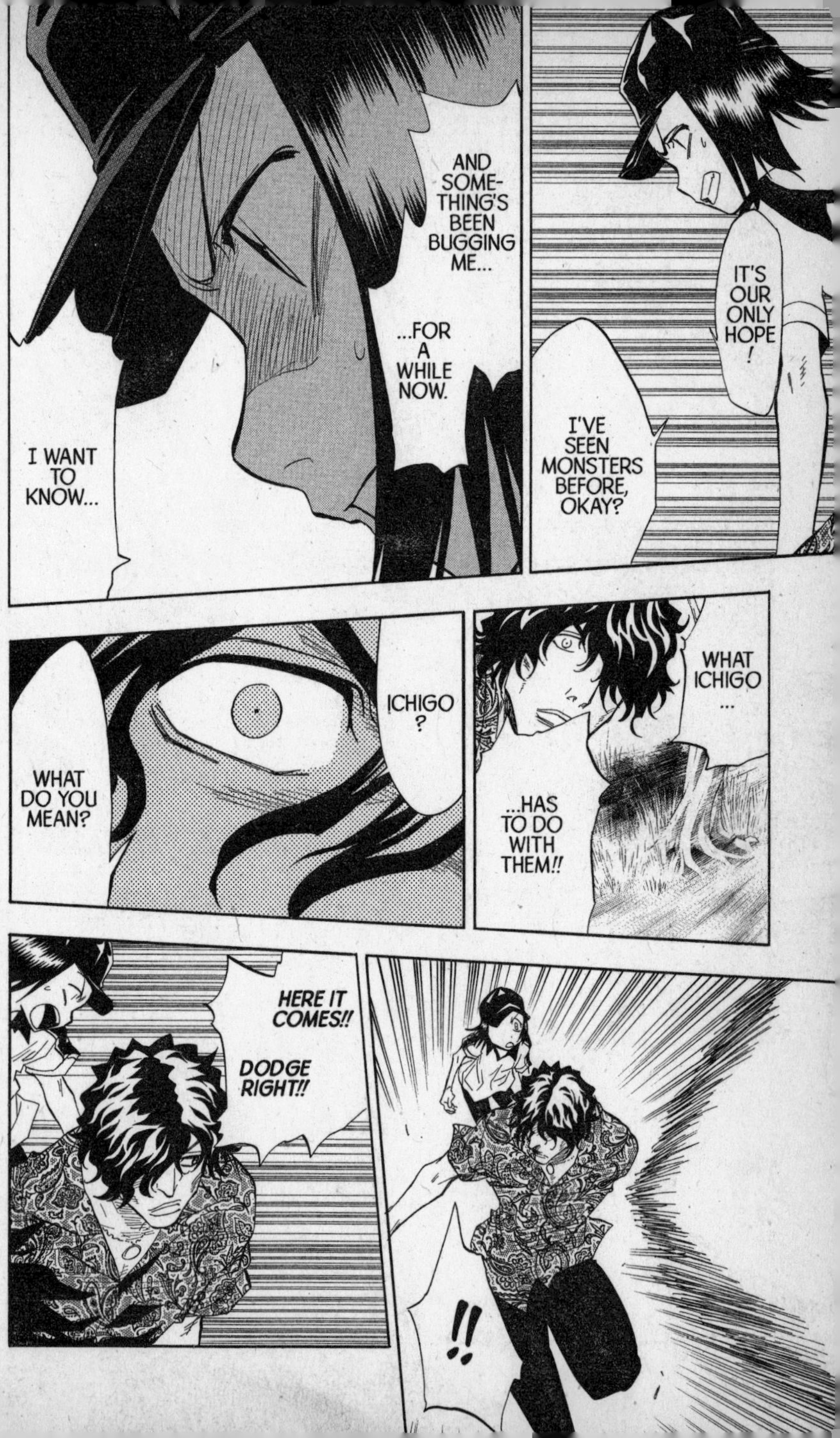
IT'S OUR ONLY HOPE!
I'VE SEEN MONSTERS BEFORE, OKAY?
AND SOMETHING'S BEEN BUGGING ME...
...FOR A WHILE NOW.
I WANT TO KNOW...
WHAT ICHIGO...
...HAS TO DO WITH THEM!!
ICHIGO?
WHAT DO YOU MEAN?
!!
HERE IT COMES!!
DODGE RIGHT!!

READ THIS WAY

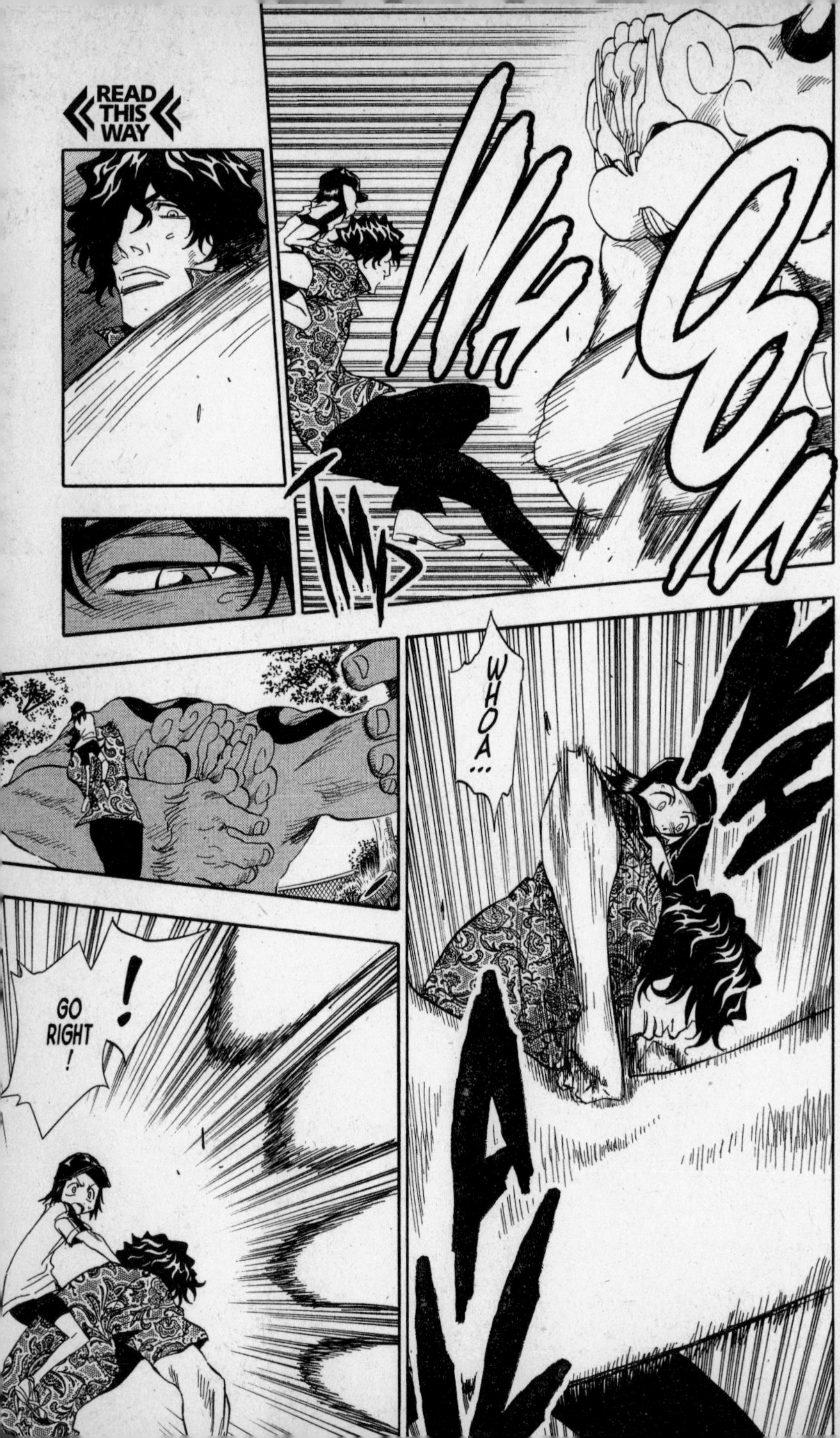
TMP
WHOA...
!
GO RIGHT!

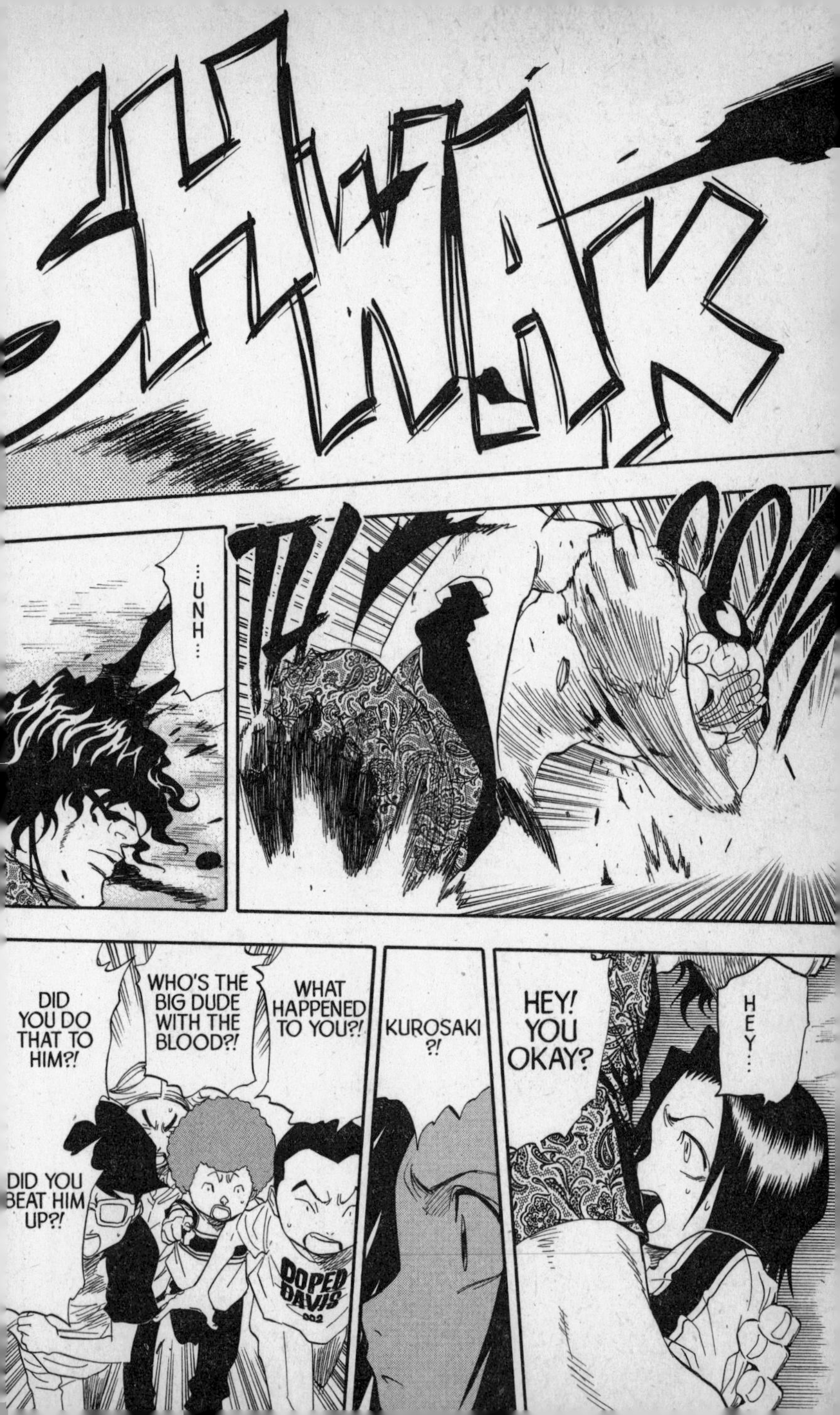
...UNH...
HEY...
HEY! YOU OKAY?
KUROSAKI?!
WHAT HAPPENED TO YOU?!
WHO'S THE BIG DUDE WITH THE BLOOD?!
DID YOU DO THAT TO HIM?!
DID YOU BEAT HIM UP?!

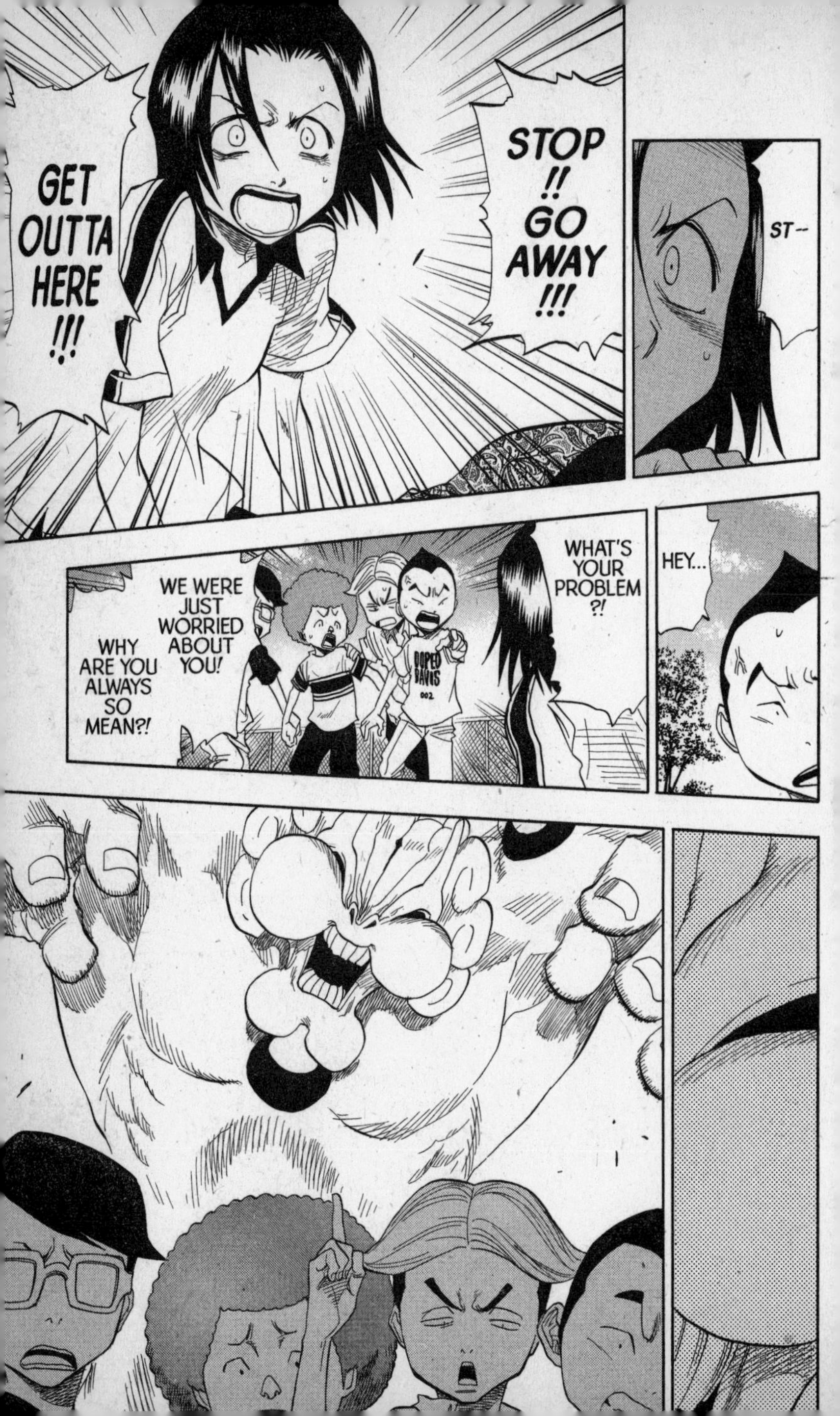
ST--
STOP!! GO AWAY!!!
GET OUTTA HERE!!!
HEY...
WHAT'S YOUR PROBLEM?!
WE WERE JUST WORRIED ABOUT YOU!
WHY ARE YOU ALWAYS SO MEAN?!
DOPED DAVIS 002

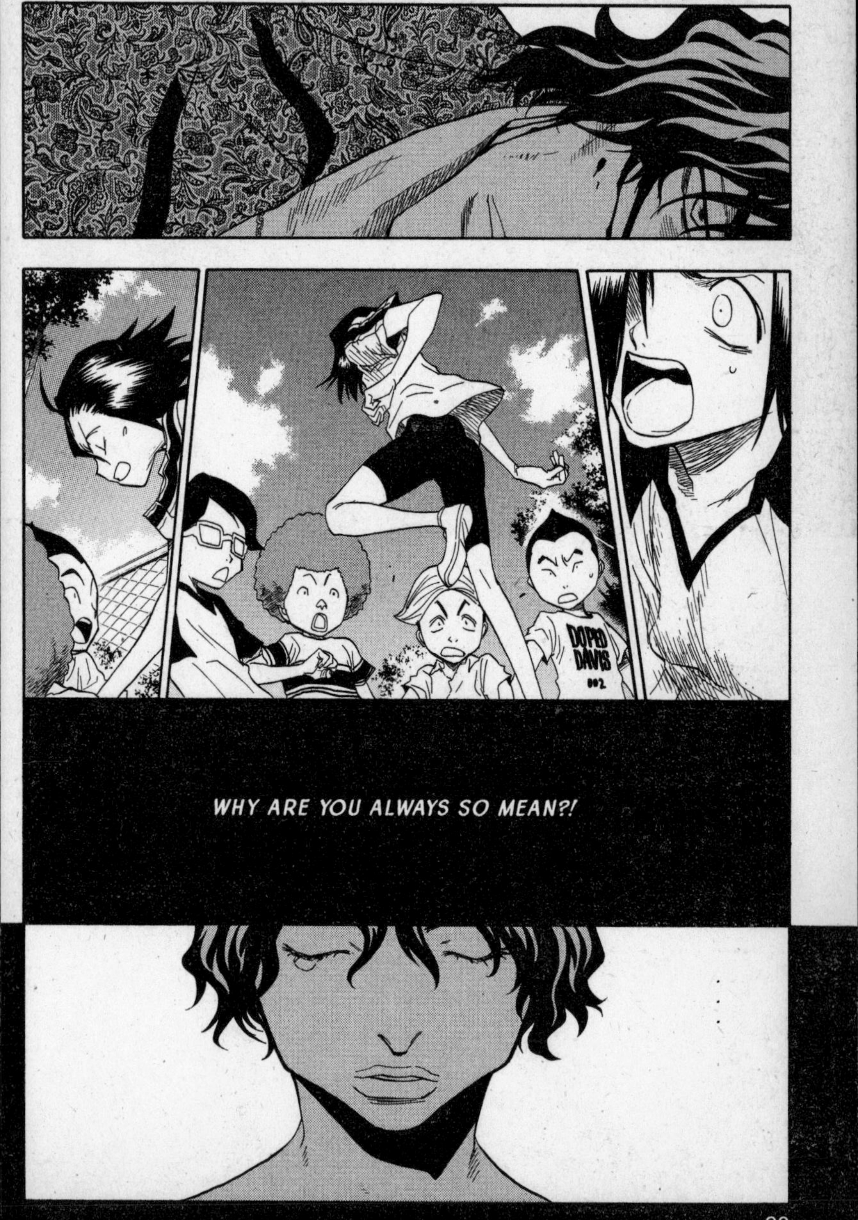
WHY ARE YOU ALWAYS SO MEAN?!

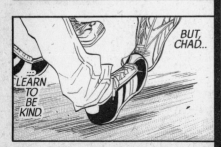

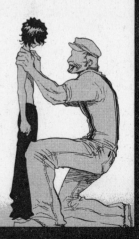

READ THIS WAY

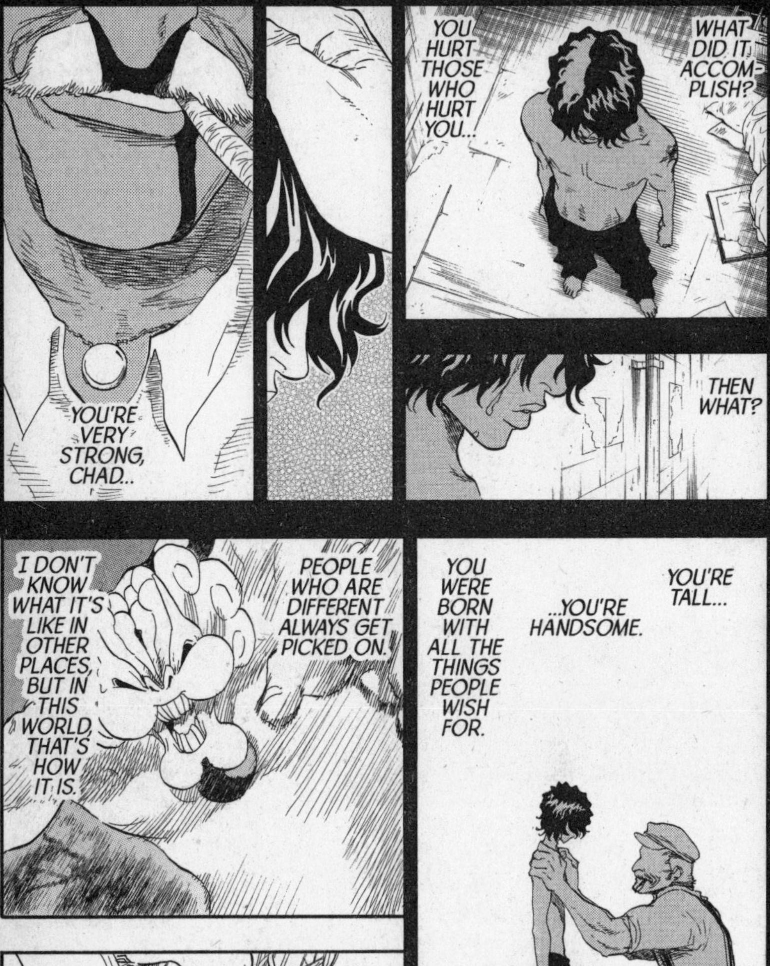

WHAT DID IT ACCOMPLISH?
YOU HURT THOSE WHO HURT YOU...
THEN WHAT?
YOU'RE VERY STRONG, CHAD...
YOU'RE TALL...
...YOU'RE HANDSOME.
YOU WERE BORN WITH ALL THE THINGS PEOPLE WISH FOR.
PEOPLE WHO ARE DIFFERENT ALWAYS GET PICKED ON.
I DON'T KNOW WHAT IT'S LIKE IN OTHER PLACES, BUT IN THIS WORLD, THAT'S HOW IT IS.
BUT, CHAD...
...LEARN TO BE KIND.

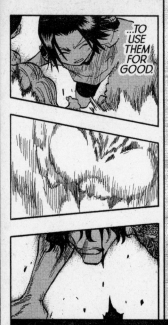

YOU'VE GOT BIG, STRONG FISTS.
YOU NEED TO LEARN...
...TO USE THEM FOR GOOD.
I KNOW, ABUELO...
...THAT MY BIG FISTS AREN'T FOR HURTING PEOPLE.

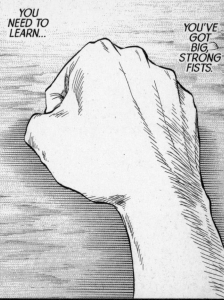

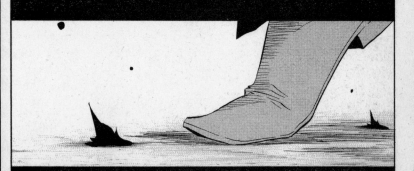

THEY ARE FOR PROTECTING MY MIGHTY BODY.

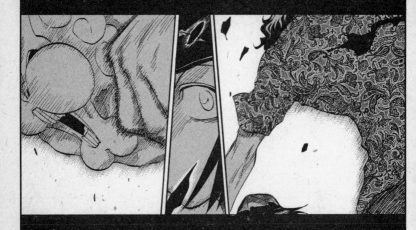

I KNOW THAT NOW.

I'VE LEARNED MY LESSON.

PLEASE...

SO...

GIVE
ME
THE
POWER.

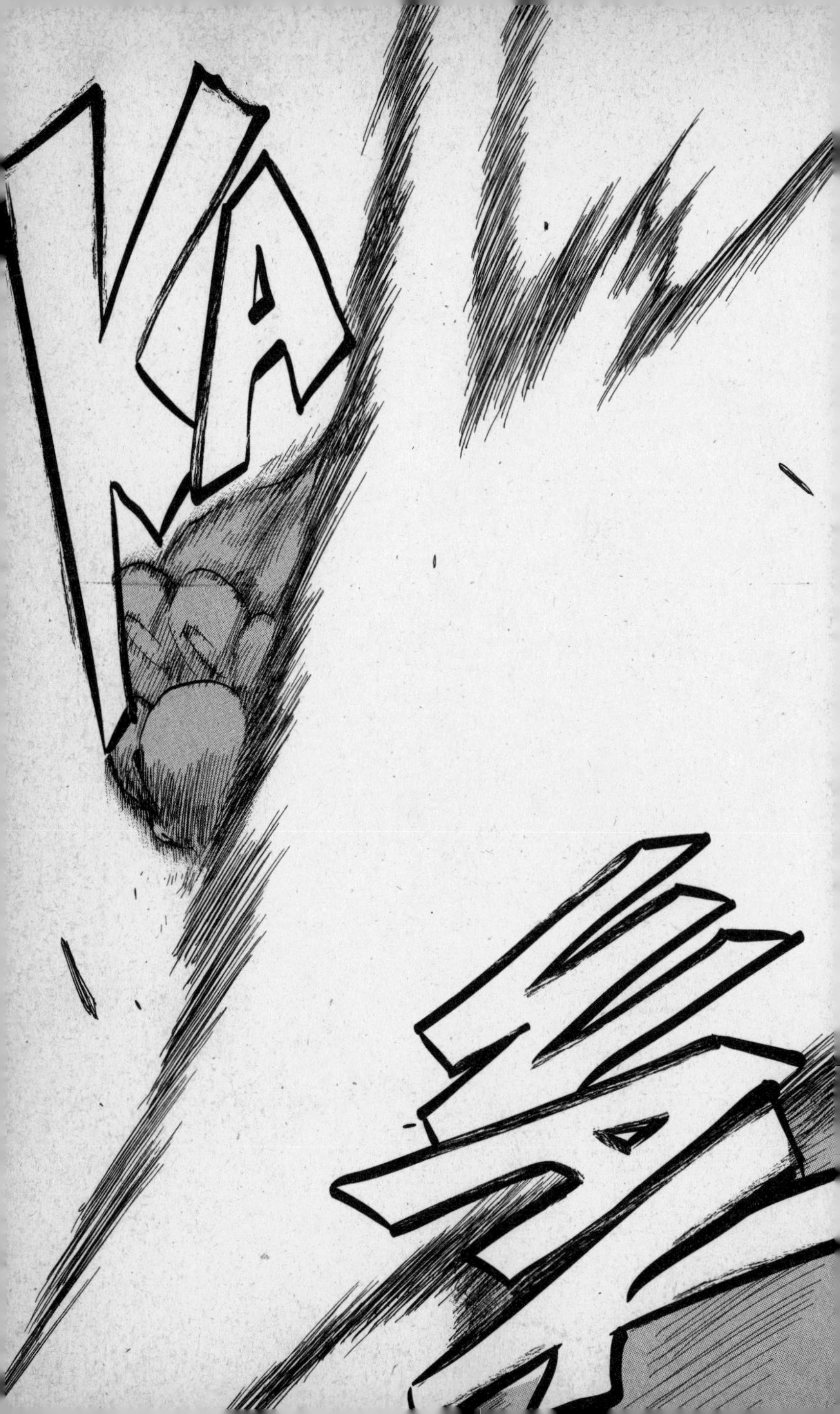

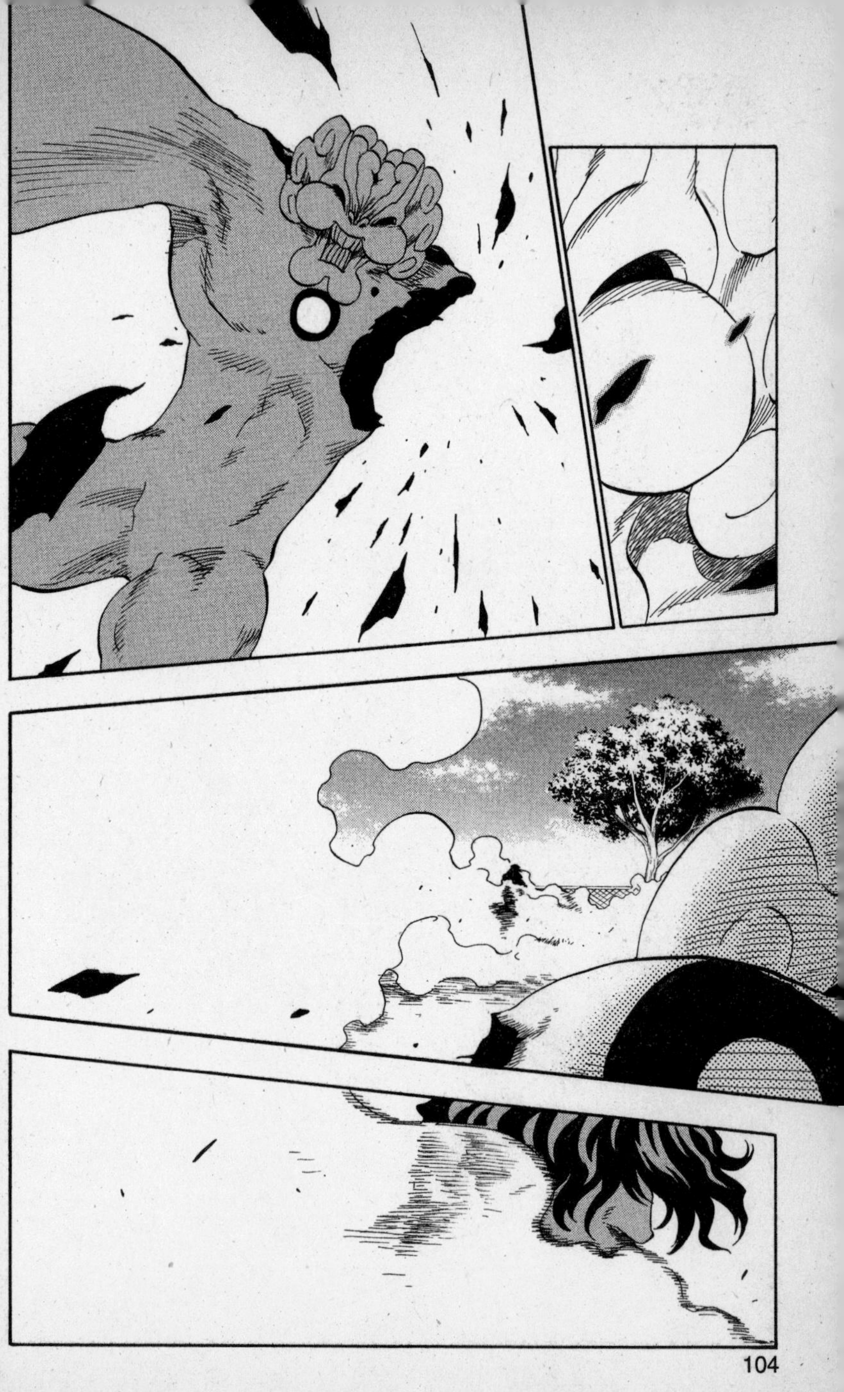

READ THIS WAY

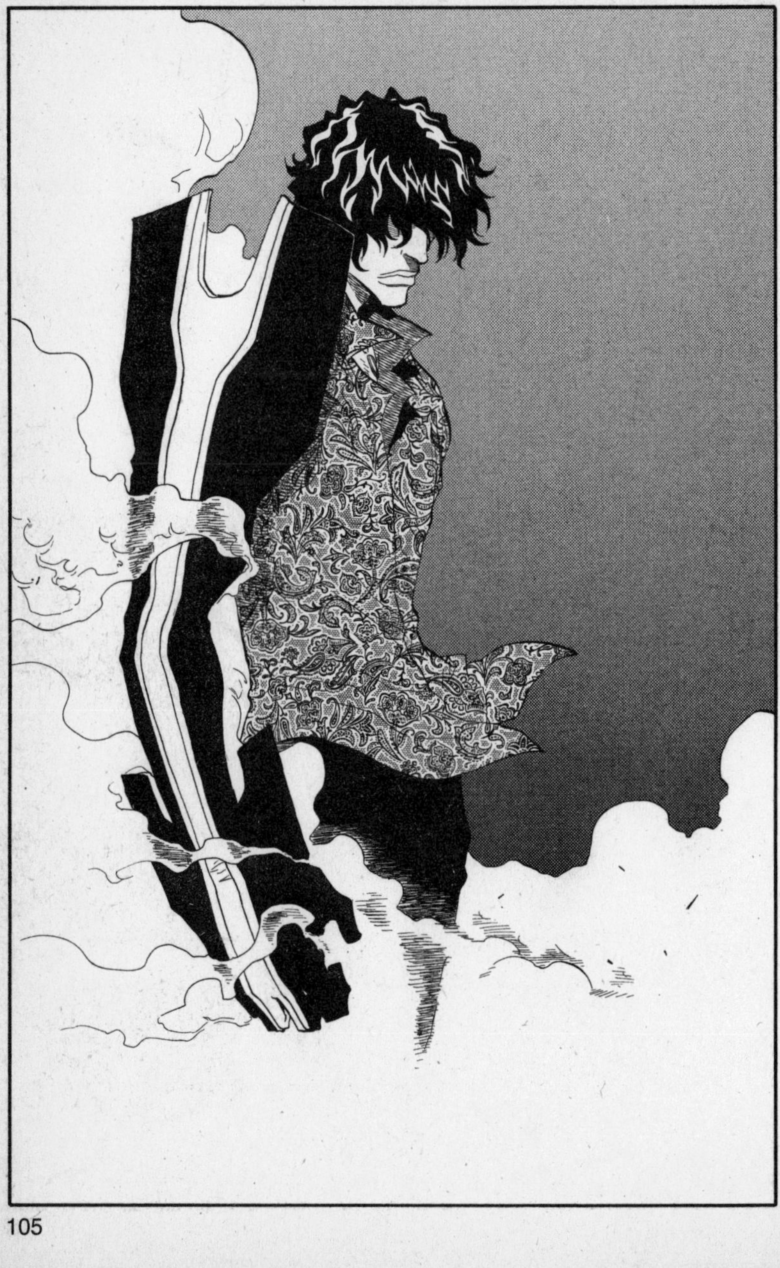

Please...
Give me the power.

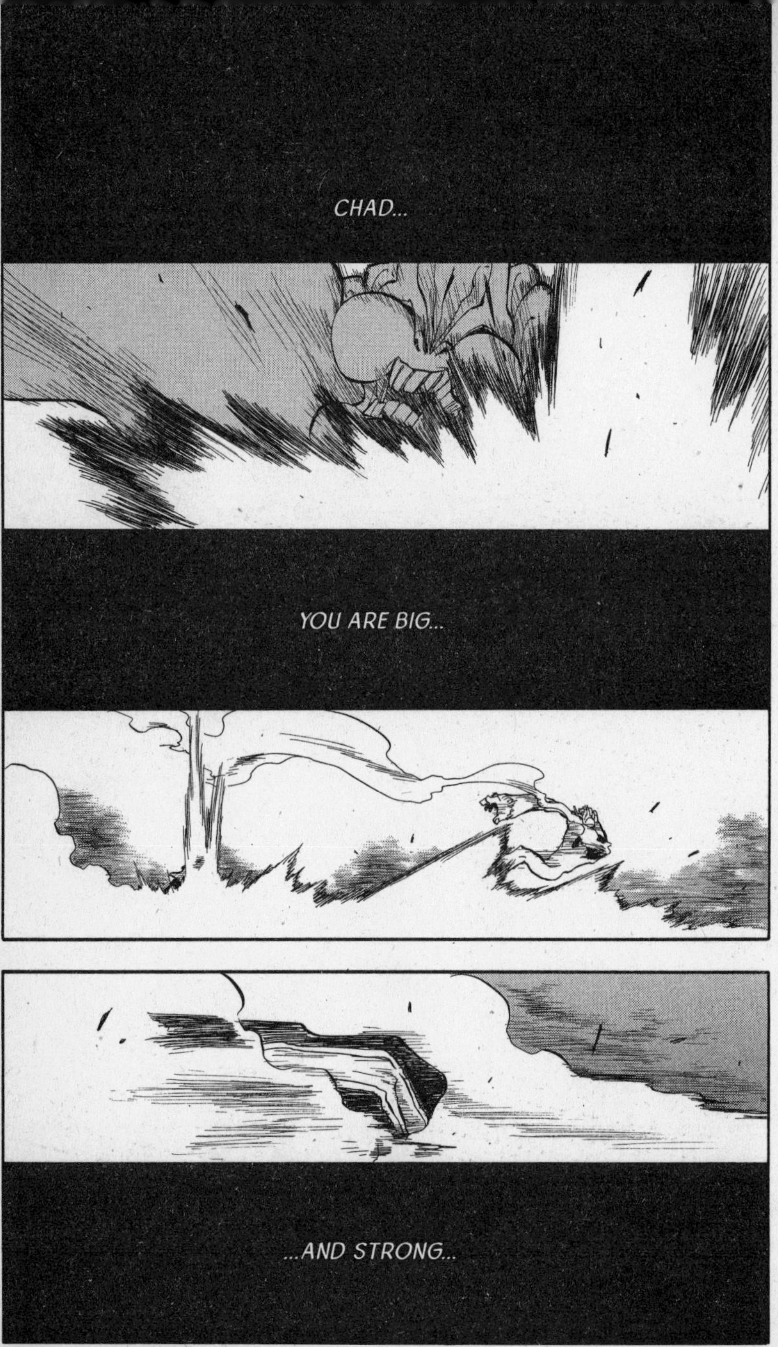
CHAD...
YOU ARE BIG...
...AND STRONG...

40. Grow?

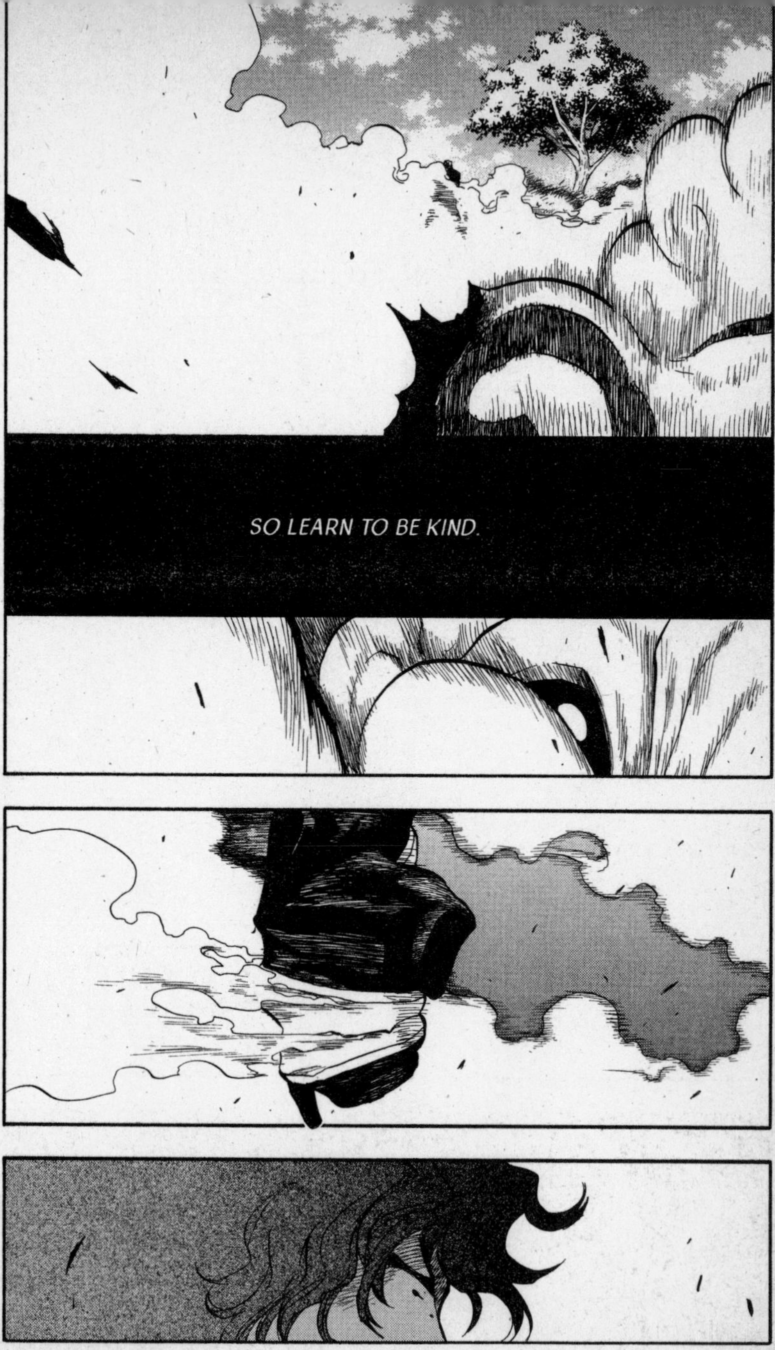
SO LEARN TO BE KIND.

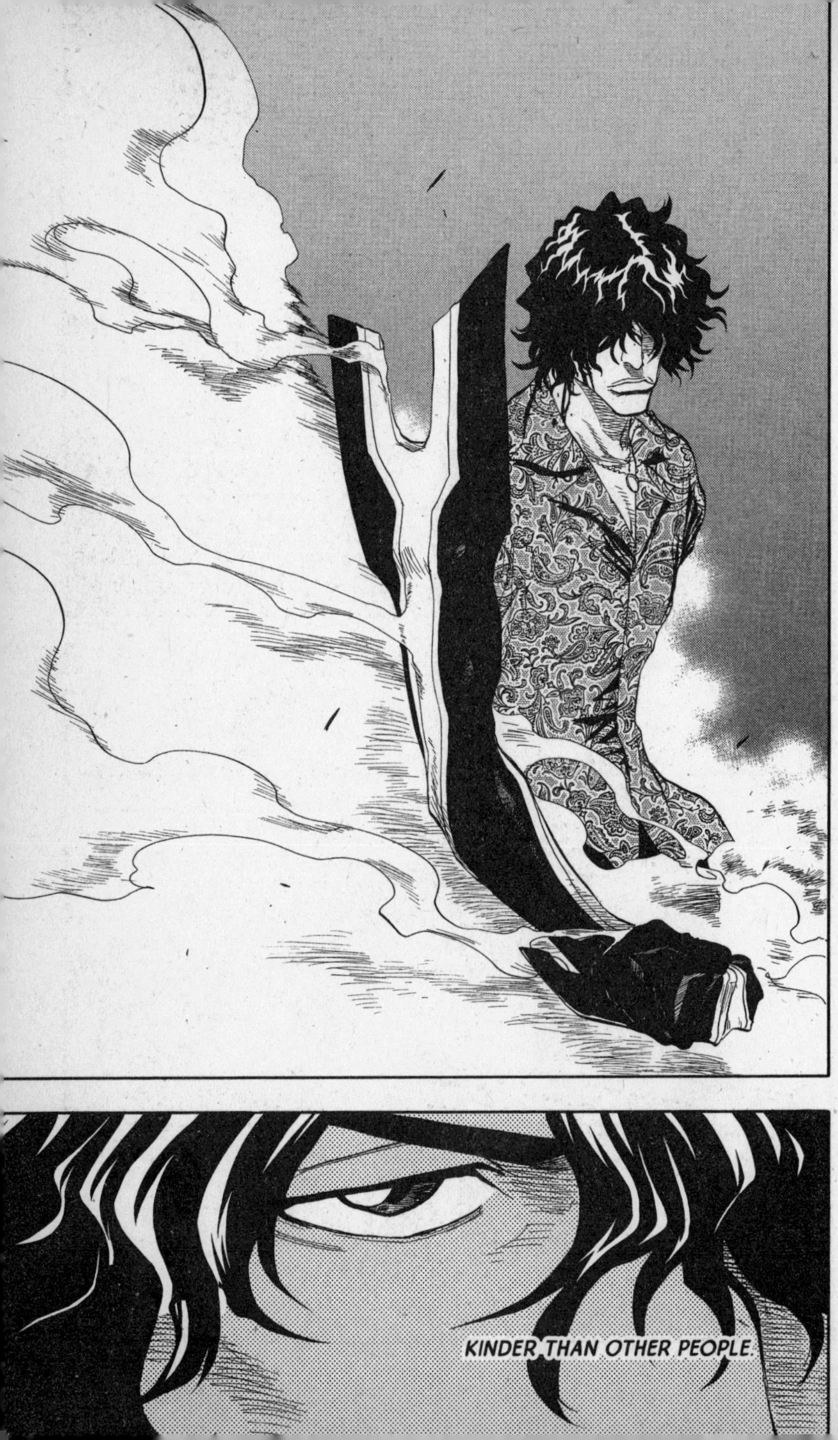
KINDER THAN OTHER PEOPLE.

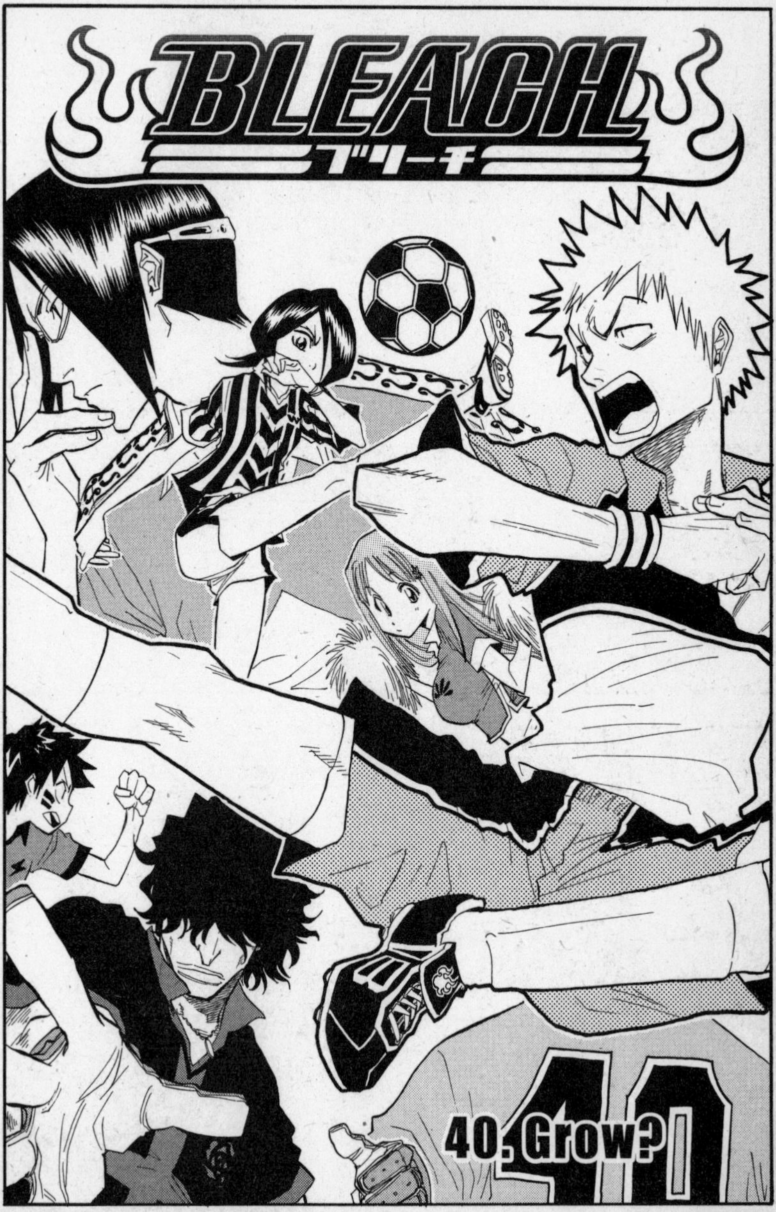
BLEACH
ブリーチ
40. Grow?

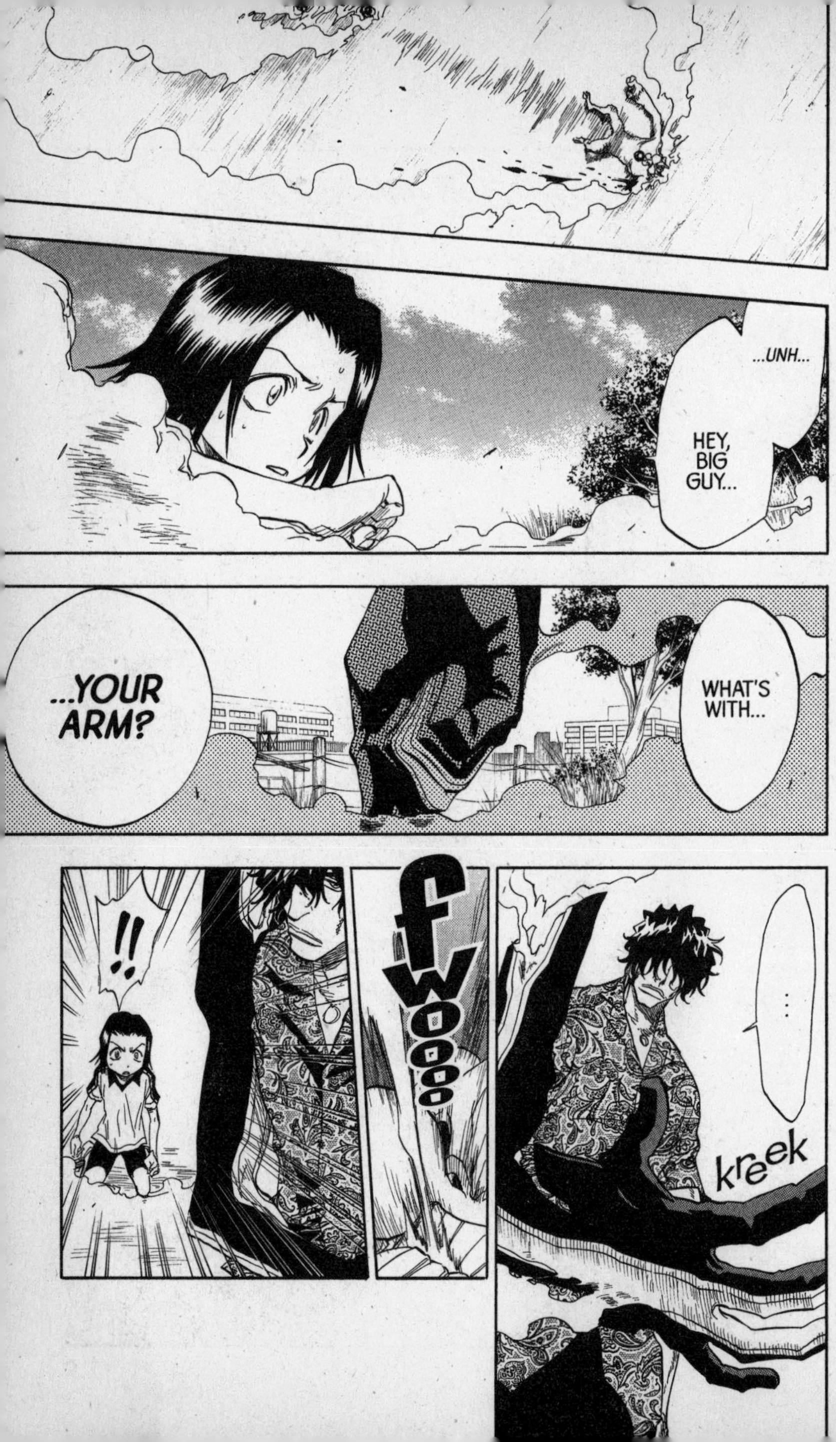

...UNH...
HEY, BIG GUY...
WHAT'S WITH...
...YOUR ARM?
...
kreek
fwoooo
!!

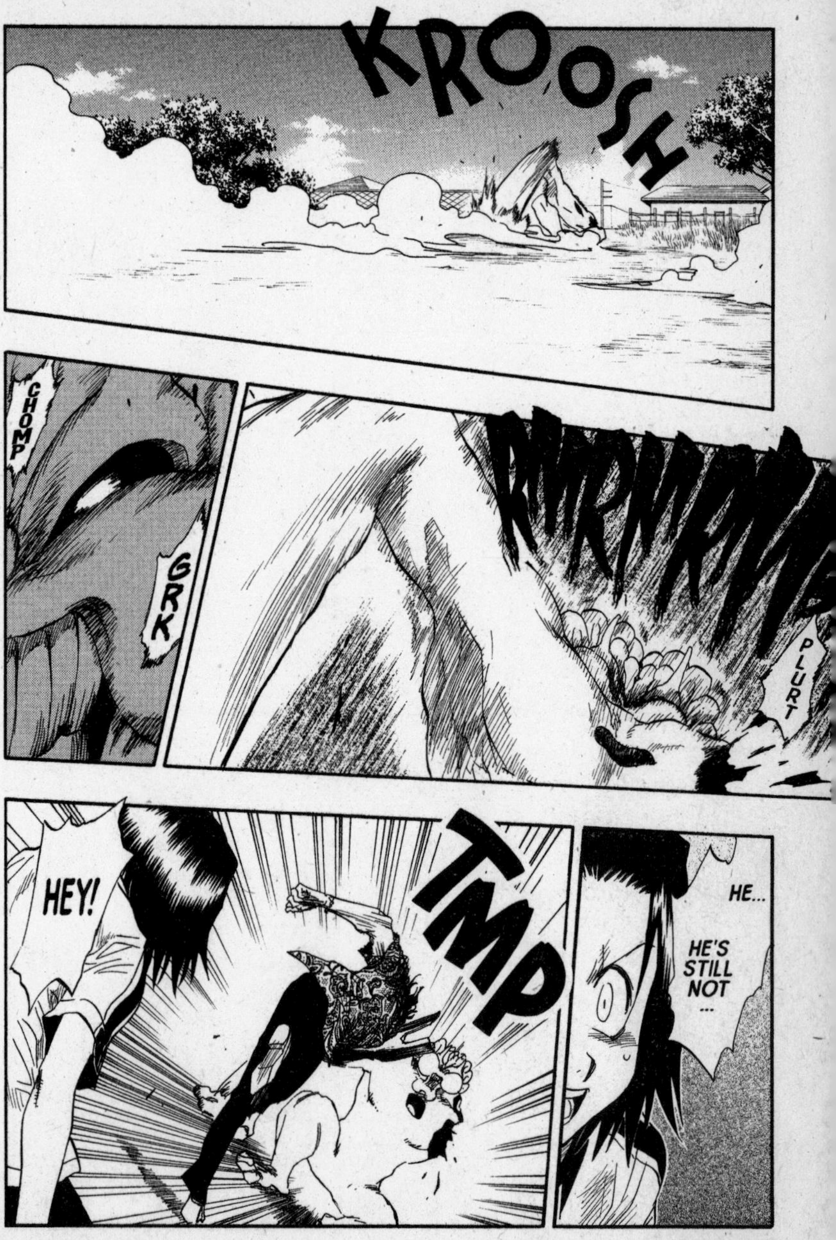
KROOSH
PLURT
CHOMP
GRK
HE...
HE'S STILL NOT ...
TMP
HEY!

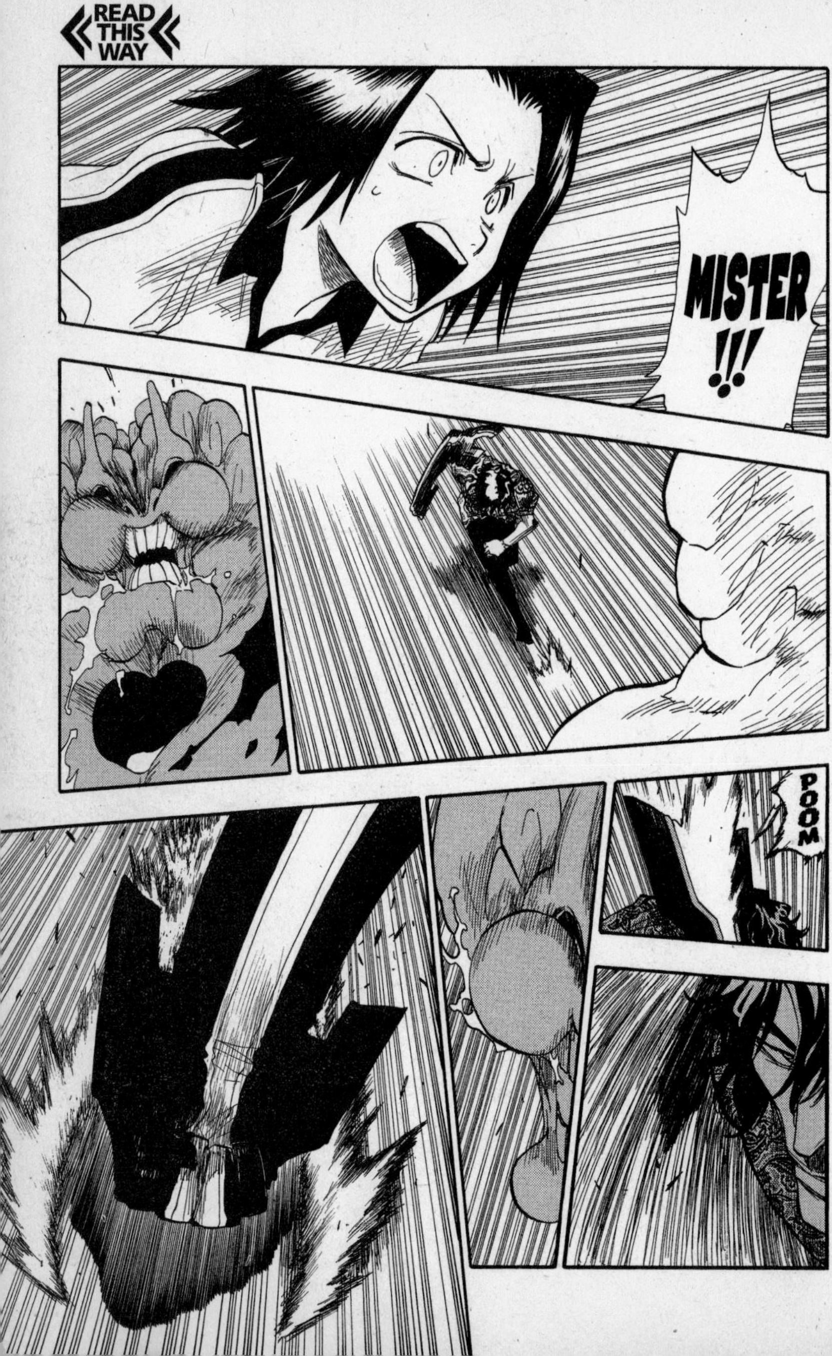
READ THIS WAY
MISTER !!!
POOM

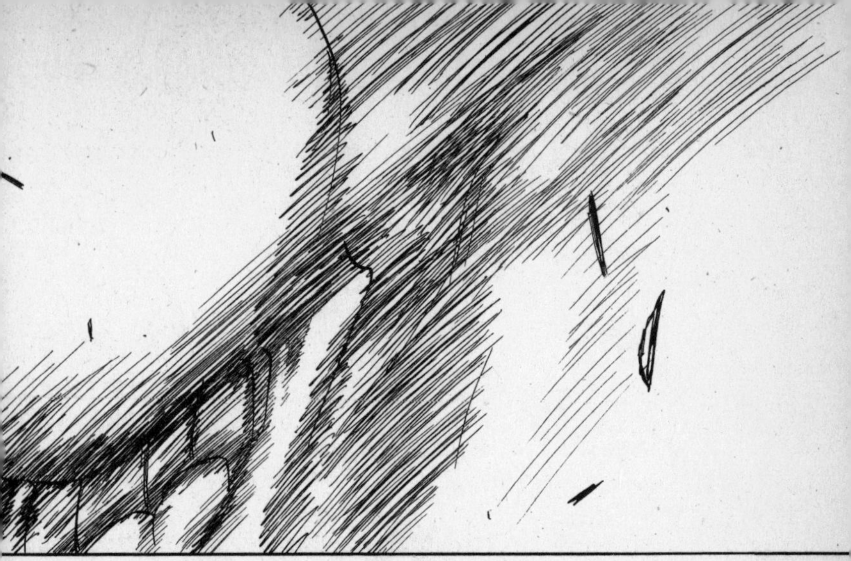

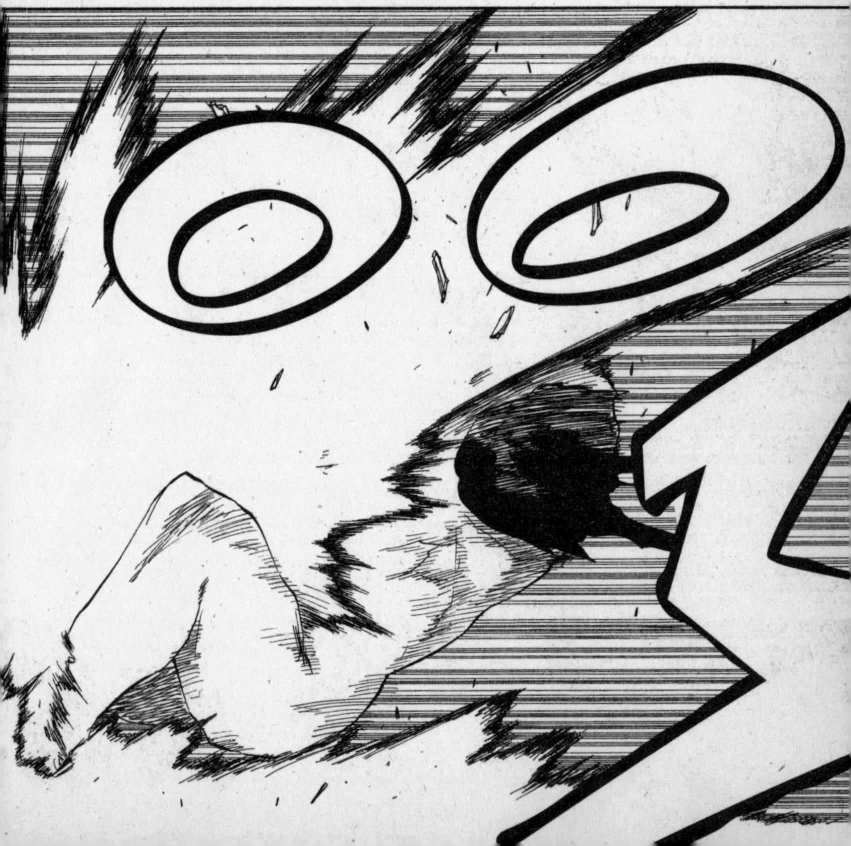
OO

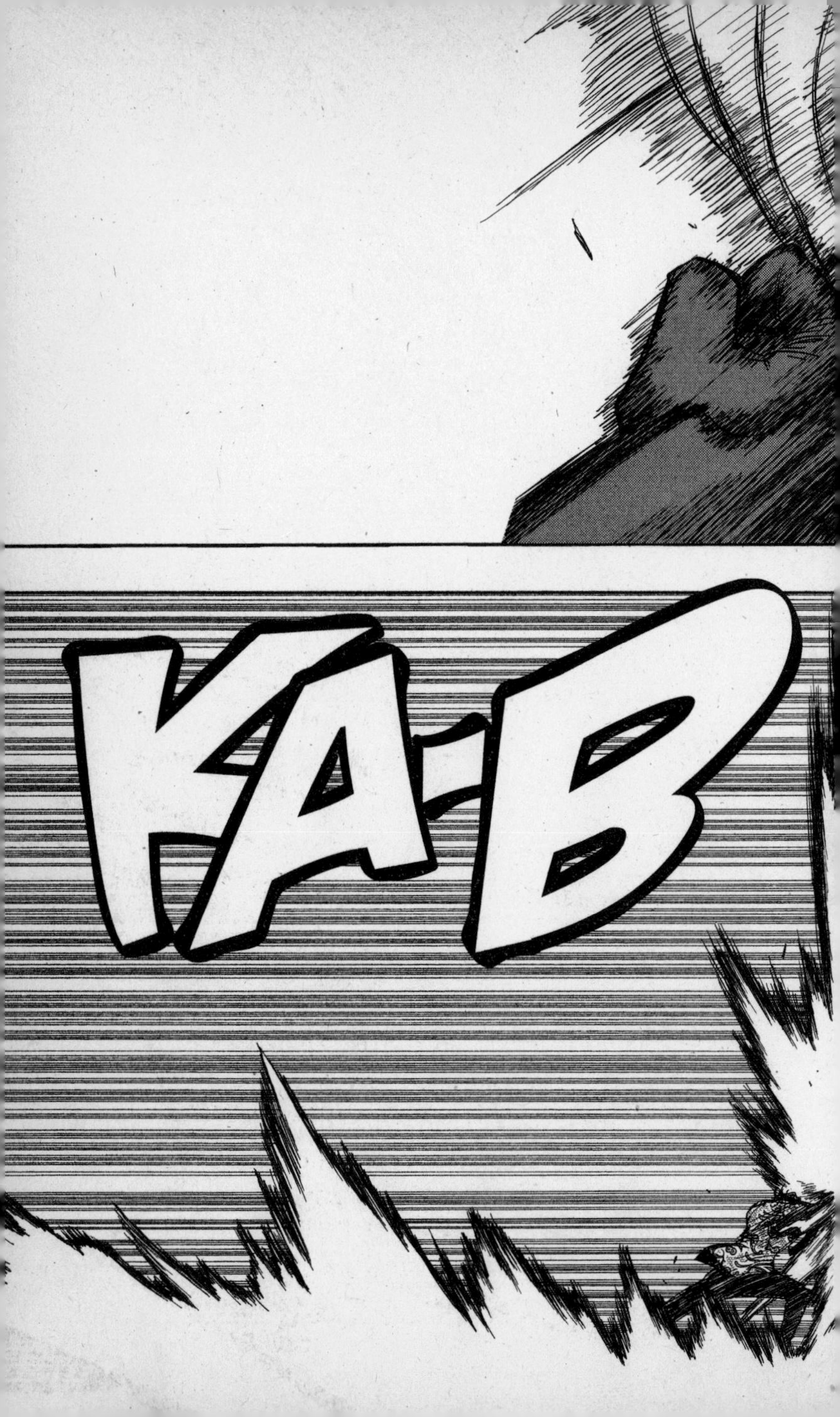
KA-B

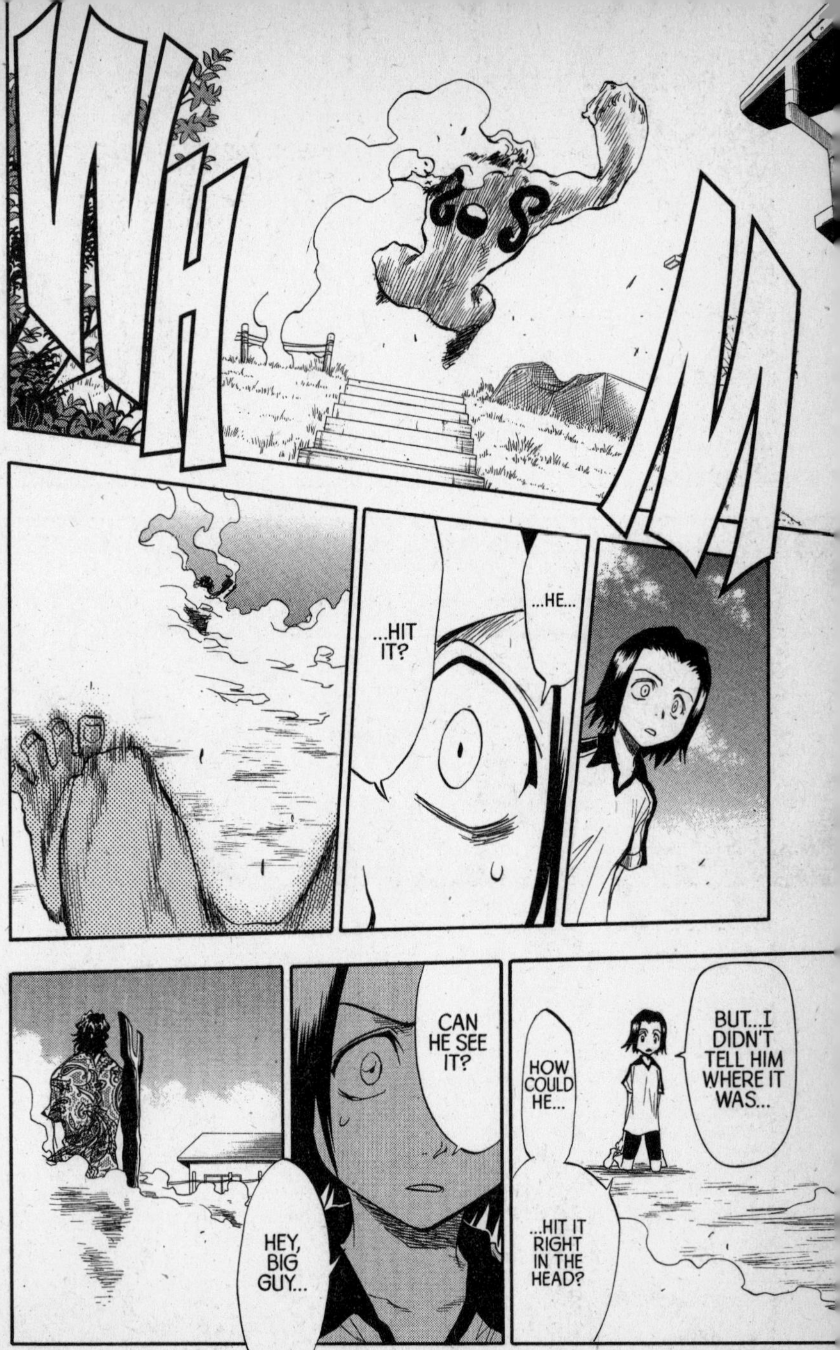
WHAM
...HE...
...HIT IT?
BUT...I DIDN'T TELL HIM WHERE IT WAS...
HOW COULD HE...
...HIT IT RIGHT IN THE HEAD?
CAN HE SEE IT?
HEY, BIG GUY...

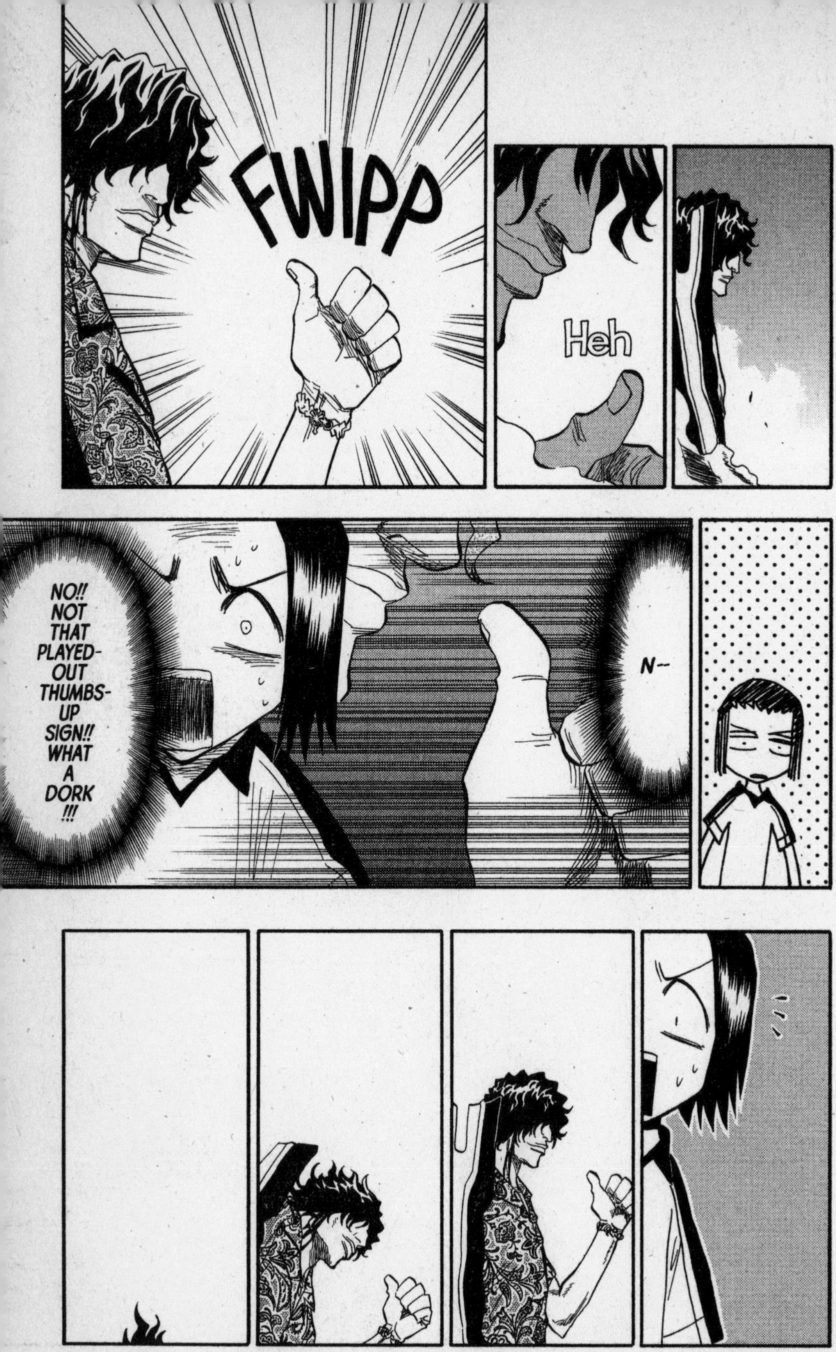
Heh
FWIPP
N--
NO!! NOT THAT PLAYED-OUT THUMBS-UP SIGN!! WHAT A DORK!!!

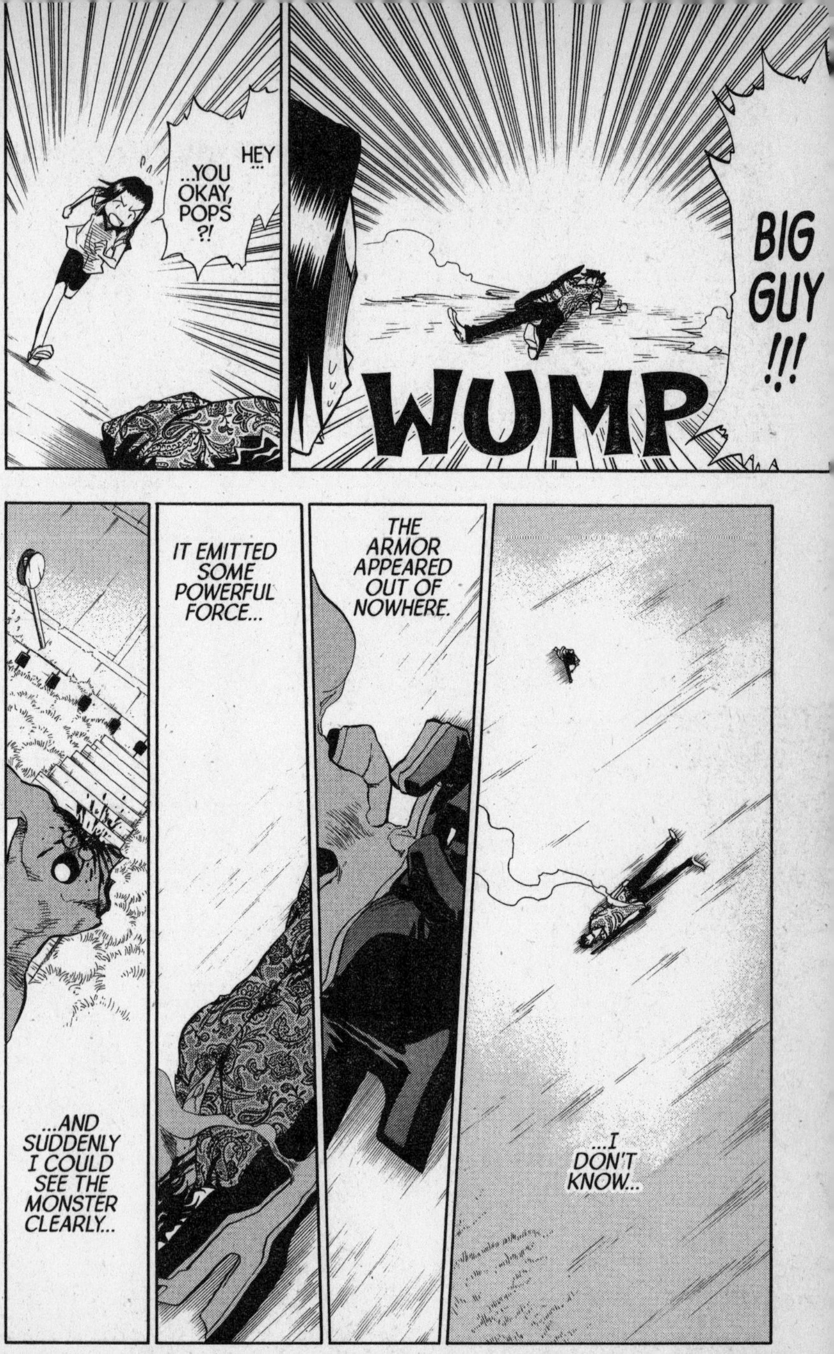
BIG GUY !!!
WUMP
HEY... ...YOU OKAY, POPS ?!
...I DON'T KNOW...
THE ARMOR APPEARED OUT OF NOWHERE.
IT EMITTED SOME POWERFUL FORCE...
...AND SUDDENLY I COULD SEE THE MONSTER CLEARLY...

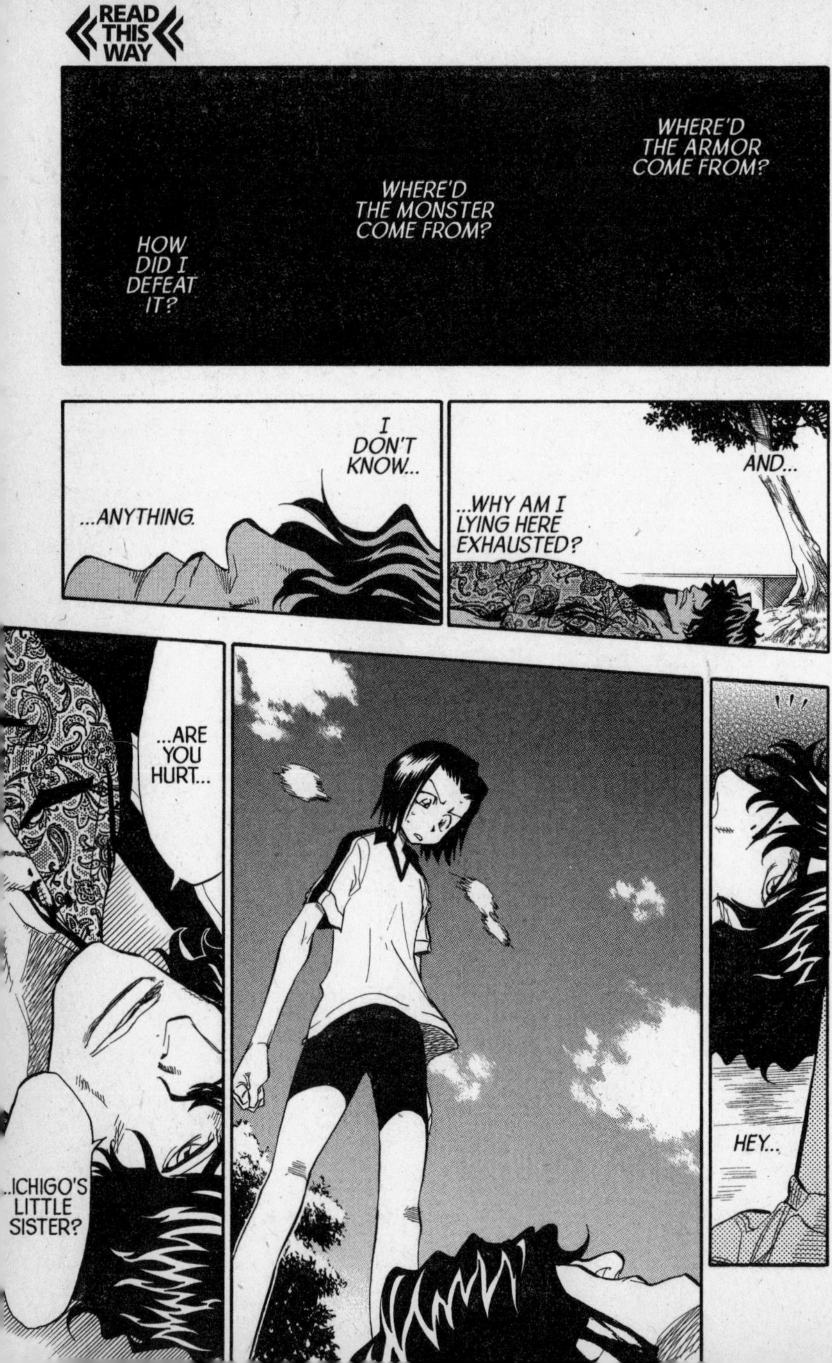

READ THIS WAY
WHERE'D THE ARMOR COME FROM?
WHERE'D THE MONSTER COME FROM?
HOW DID I DEFEAT IT?
AND...
...WHY AM I LYING HERE EXHAUSTED?
I DON'T KNOW...
...ANYTHING.
HEY...
...ARE YOU HURT...
..ICHIGO'S LITTLE SISTER?

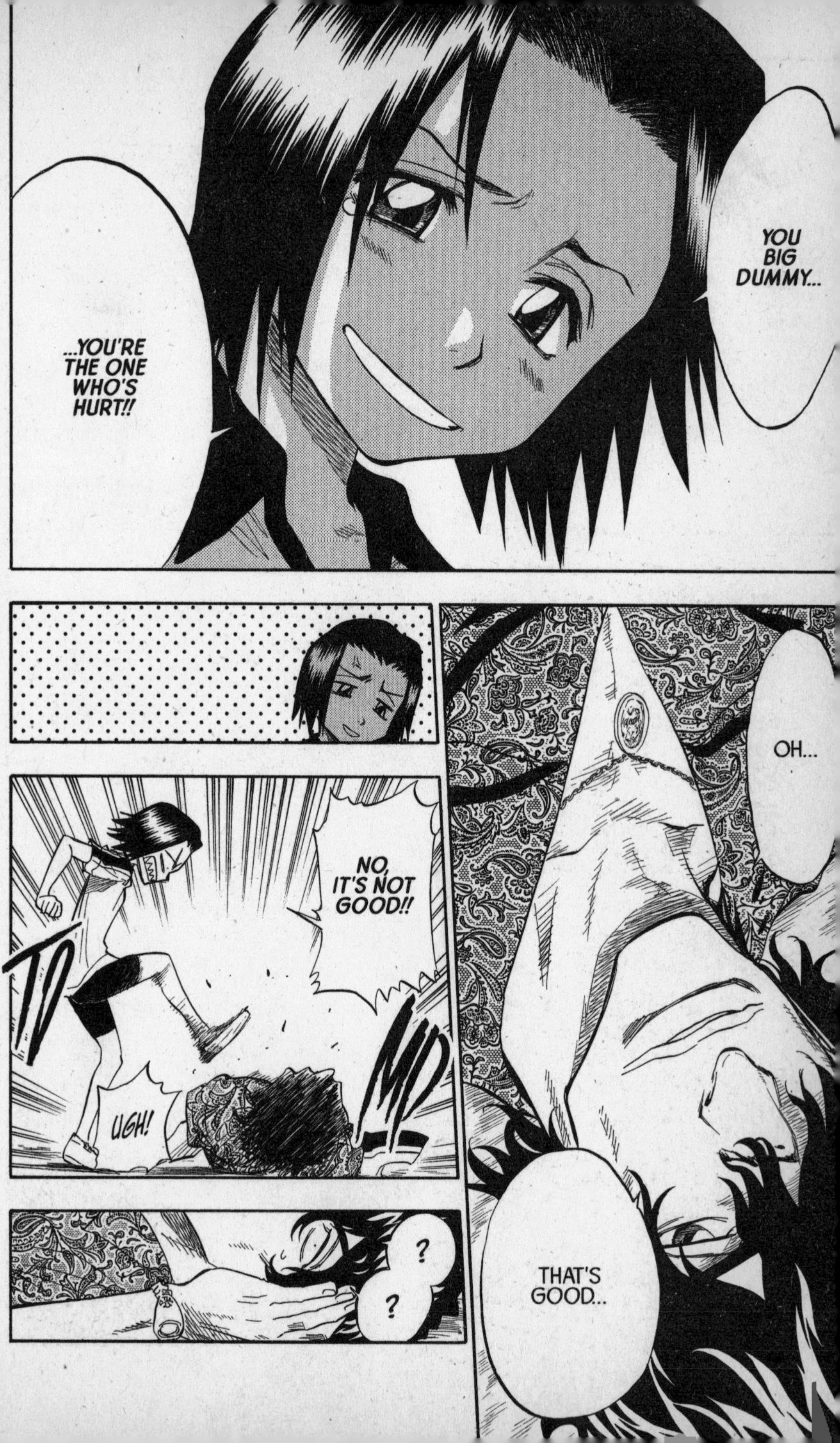
YOU BIG DUMMY...
...YOU'RE THE ONE WHO'S HURT!!
OH...
THAT'S GOOD...
NO, IT'S NOT GOOD!!
UGH!
?
?

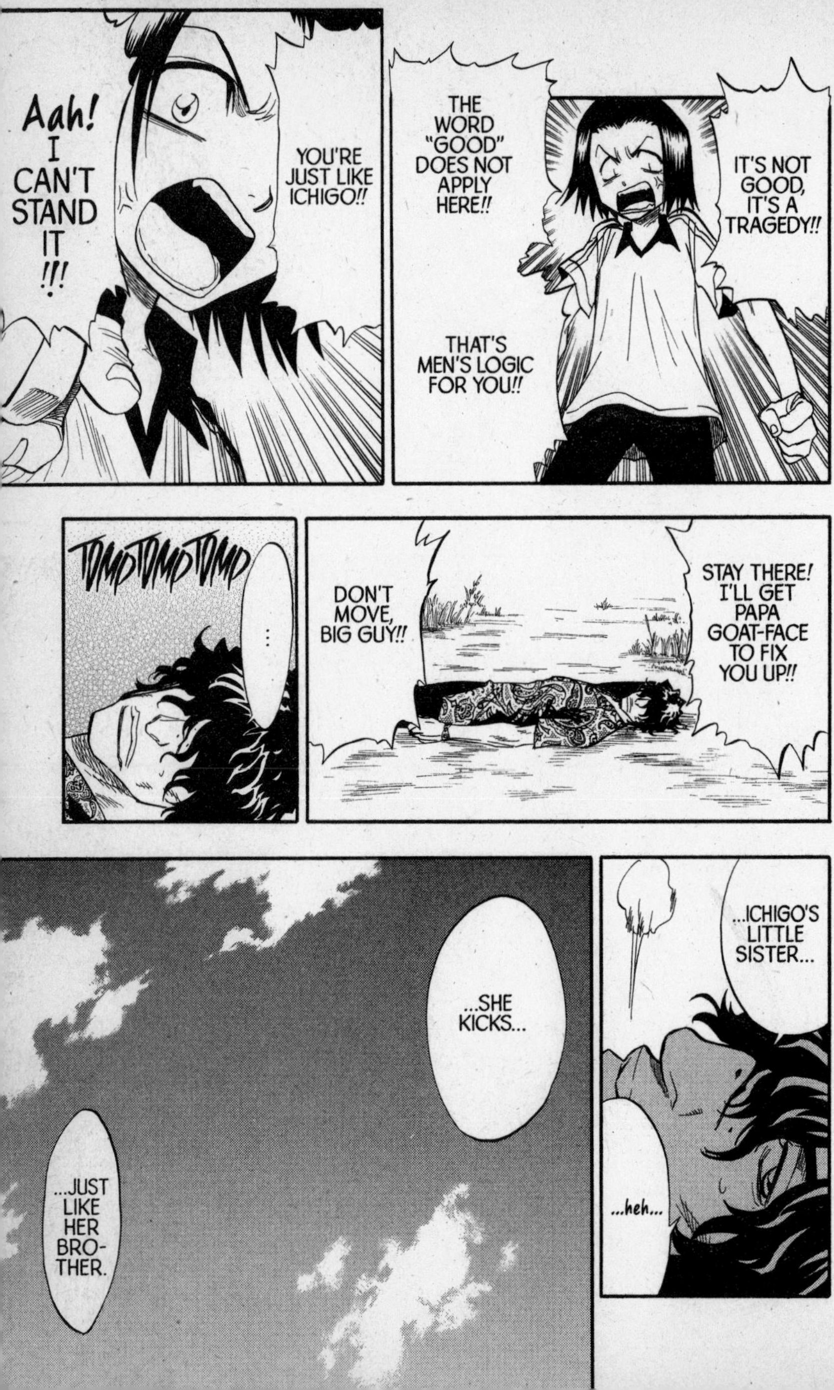
IT'S NOT GOOD, IT'S A TRAGEDY!!
THE WORD "GOOD" DOES NOT APPLY HERE!!
THAT'S MEN'S LOGIC FOR YOU!!
YOU'RE JUST LIKE ICHIGO!!
Aah! I CAN'T STAND IT !!!
STAY THERE! I'LL GET PAPA GOAT-FACE TO FIX YOU UP!!
DON'T MOVE, BIG GUY!!
TOMP TOMP TOMP
...
...ICHIGO'S LITTLE SISTER...
...heh...
...SHE KICKS...
...JUST LIKE HER BRO-THER.

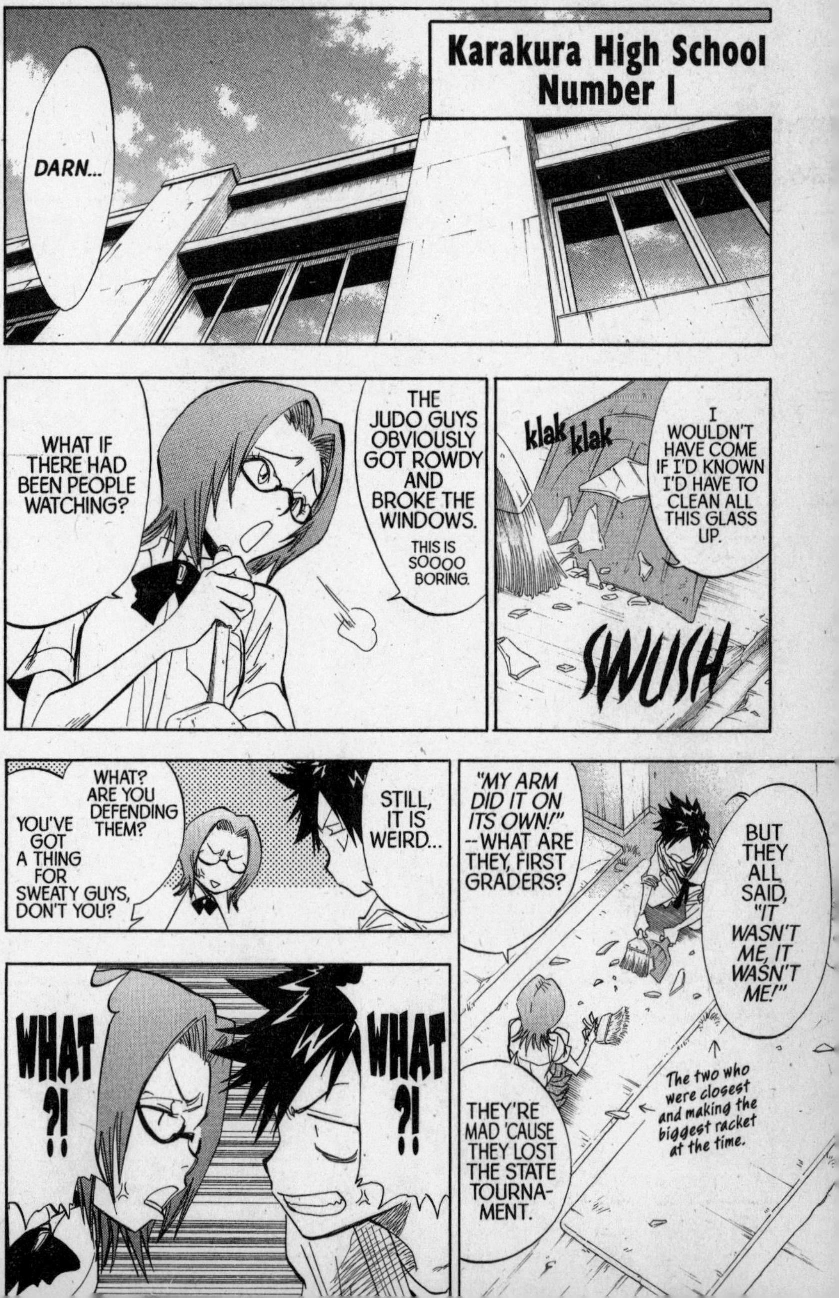
Karakura High School Number 1
DARN...
I WOULDN'T HAVE COME IF I'D KNOWN I'D HAVE TO CLEAN ALL THIS GLASS UP.
klak klak
SWUSH
THE JUDO GUYS OBVIOUSLY GOT ROWDY AND BROKE THE WINDOWS.
THIS IS SOOOO BORING.
WHAT IF THERE HAD BEEN PEOPLE WATCHING?
BUT THEY ALL SAID, "IT WASN'T ME, IT WASN'T ME!"
"MY ARM DID IT ON ITS OWN!" --WHAT ARE THEY, FIRST GRADERS?
The two who were closest and making the biggest racket at the time.
THEY'RE MAD 'CAUSE THEY LOST THE STATE TOURNAMENT.
STILL, IT IS WEIRD...
WHAT? ARE YOU DEFENDING THEM?
YOU'VE GOT A THING FOR SWEATY GUYS, DON'T YOU?
WHAT?!
WHAT?!

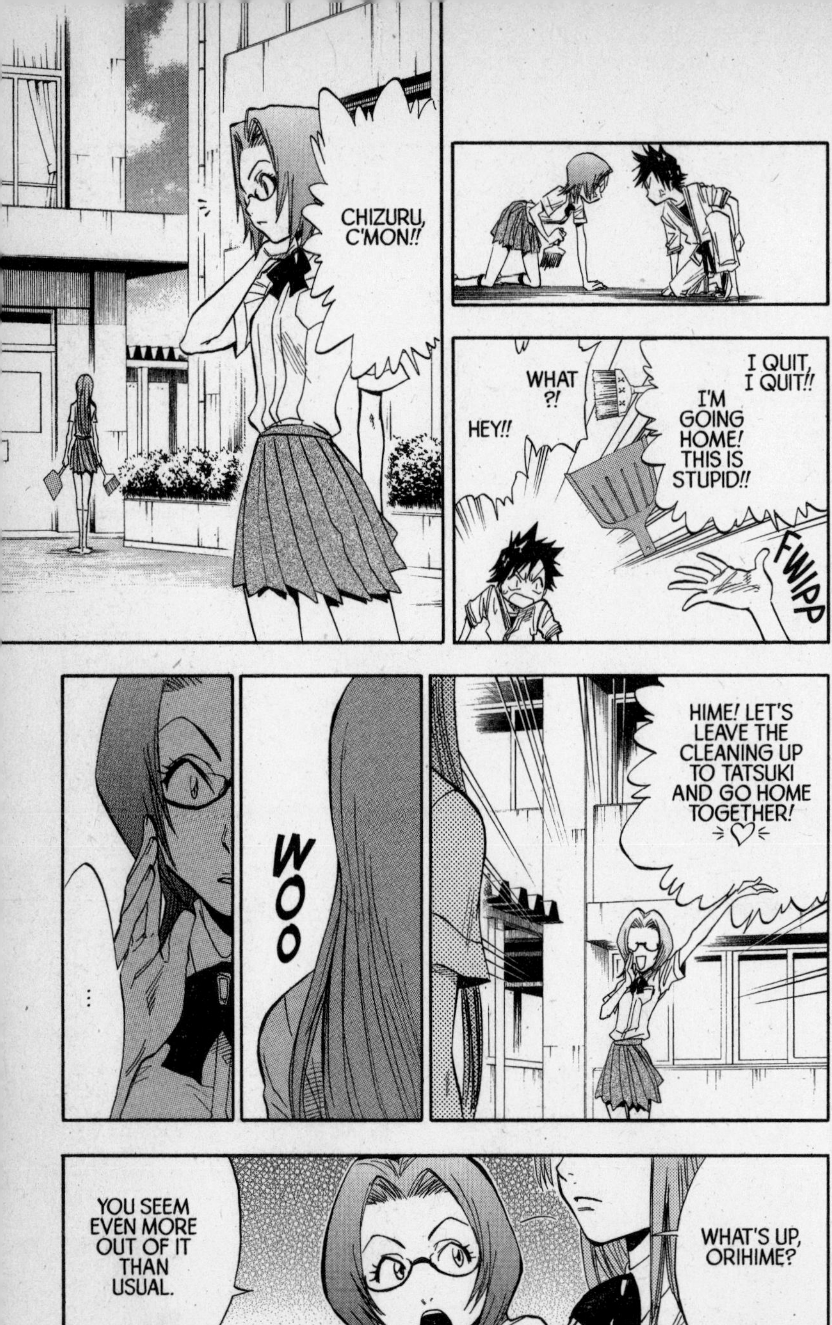
I QUIT, I QUIT!!
I'M GOING HOME! THIS IS STUPID!!
FWIPP
WHAT?!
HEY!!
CHIZURU, C'MON!!
HIME! LET'S LEAVE THE CLEANING UP TO TATSUKI AND GO HOME TOGETHER! ♡
WOO
...
WHAT'S UP, ORIHIME?
YOU SEEM EVEN MORE OUT OF IT THAN USUAL.

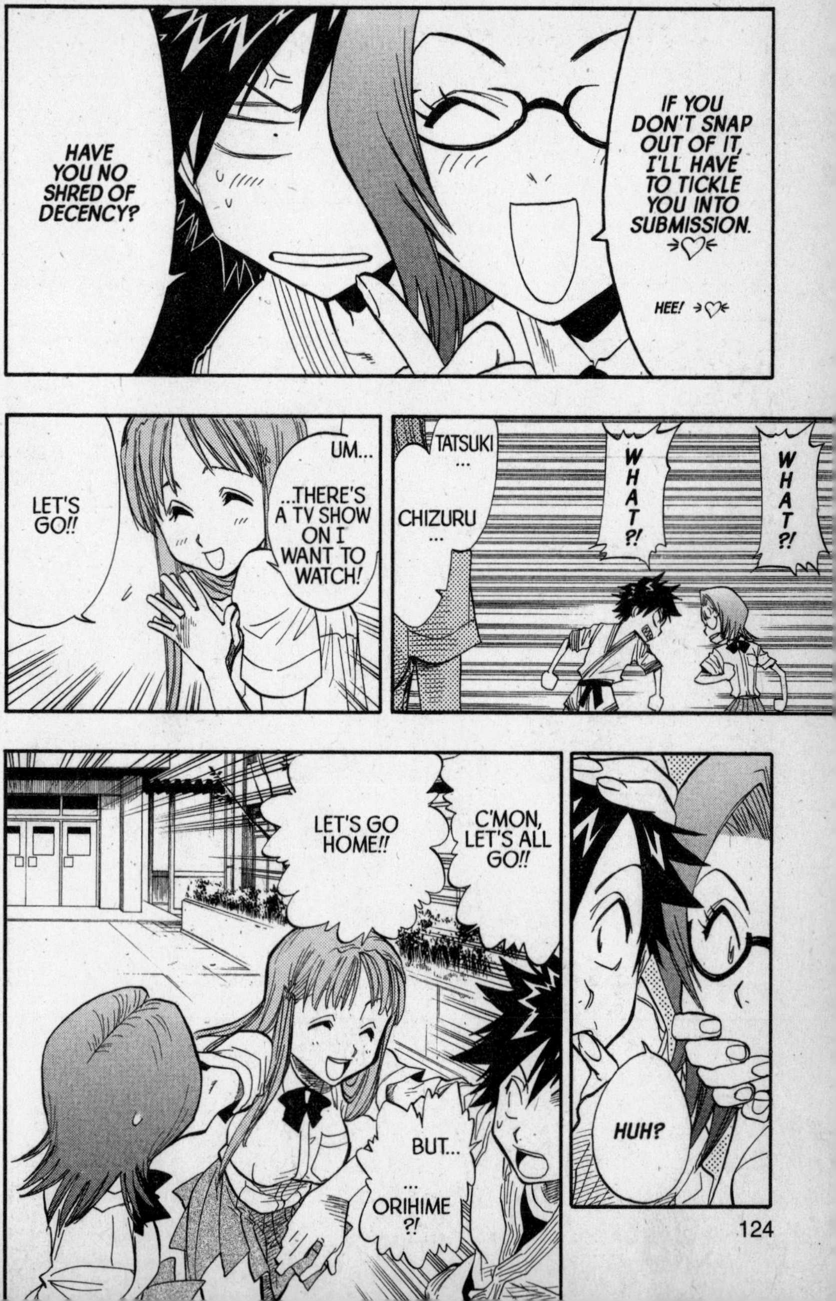
IF YOU DON'T SNAP OUT OF IT, I'LL HAVE TO TICKLE YOU INTO SUBMISSION. ♡
HEE! ♡
HAVE YOU NO SHRED OF DECENCY?
WHAT?!
WHAT?!
TATSUKI ...
CHIZURU ...
UM...
...THERE'S A TV SHOW ON I WANT TO WATCH!
LET'S GO!!
HUH?
C'MON, LET'S ALL GO!!
LET'S GO HOME!!
BUT...
... ORIHIME ?!

READ THIS WAY

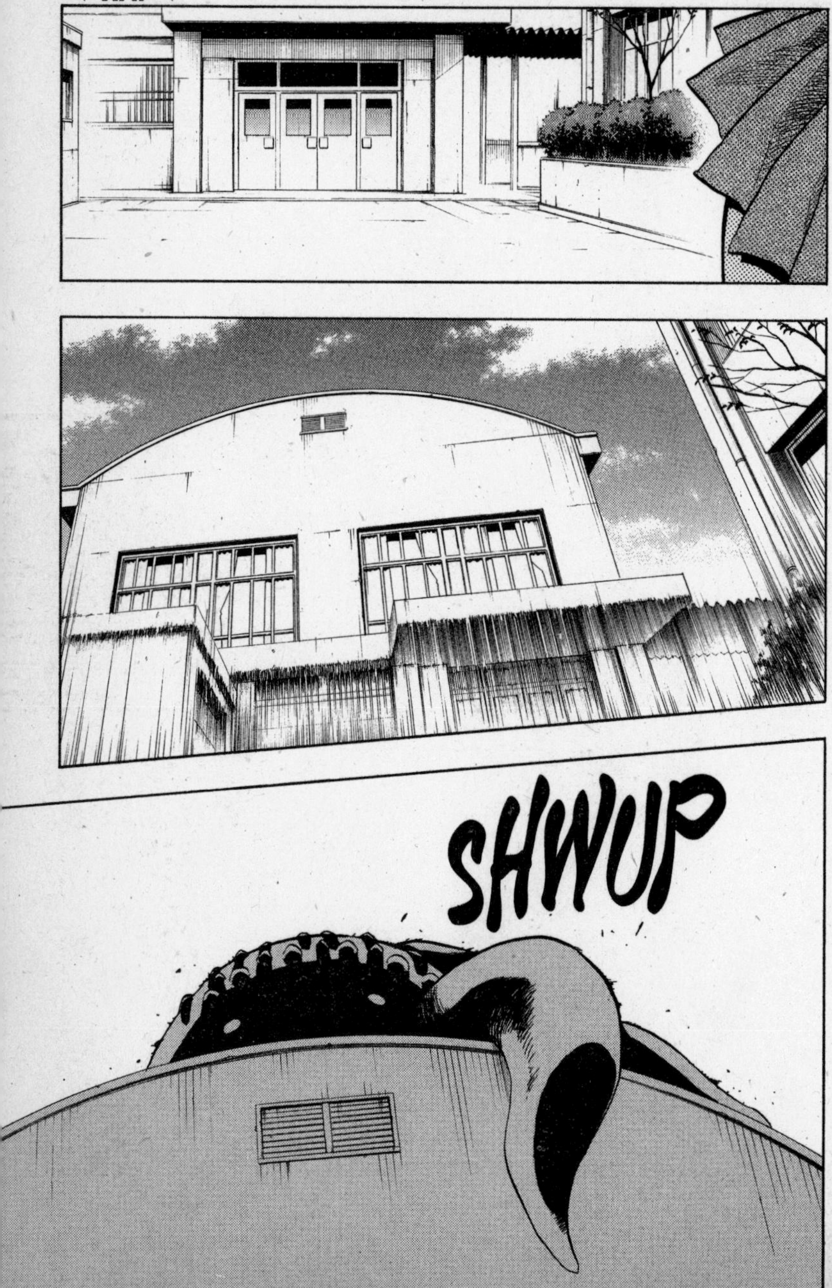
SHWUP

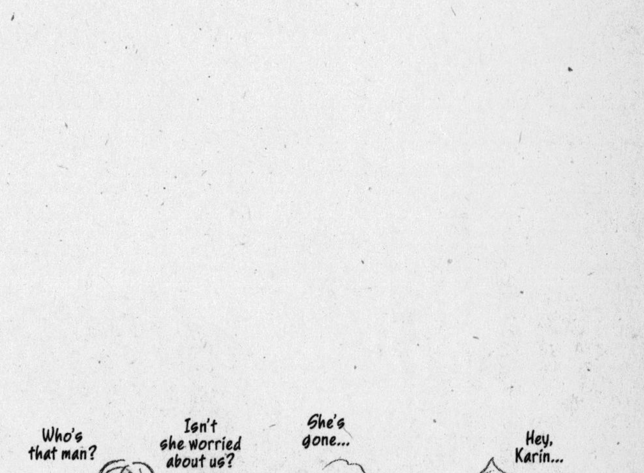
Hey, Karin...
She's gone...
Isn't she worried about us?
Who's that man?

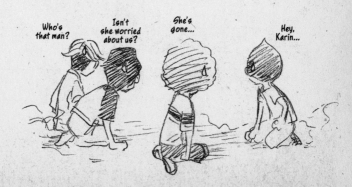

41. Princess & Dragon

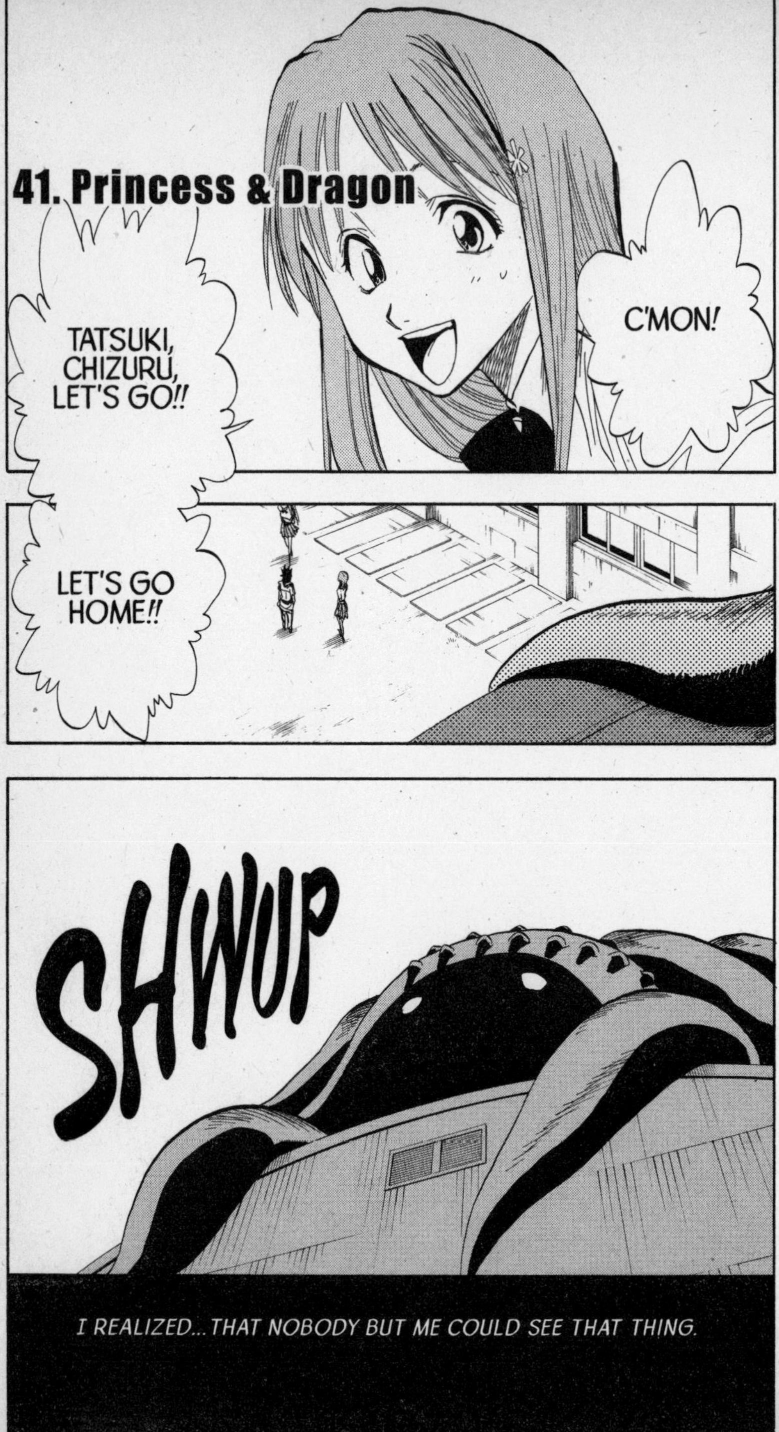
C'MON!
TATSUKI, CHIZURU, LET'S GO!!
LET'S GO HOME!!
SHWUP
I REALIZED... THAT NOBODY BUT ME COULD SEE THAT THING.

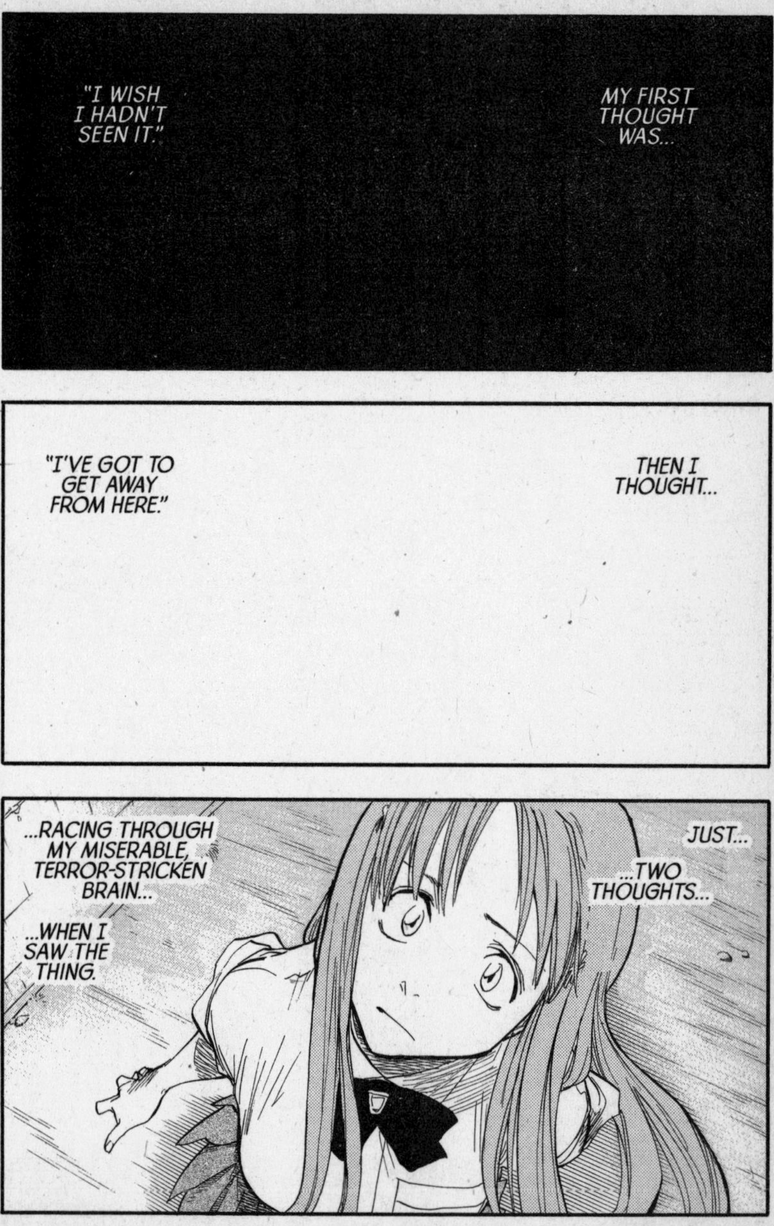
MY FIRST THOUGHT WAS...
"I WISH I HADN'T SEEN IT."
THEN I THOUGHT...
"I'VE GOT TO GET AWAY FROM HERE."
JUST...
...TWO THOUGHTS...
...RACING THROUGH MY MISERABLE, TERROR-STRICKEN BRAIN...
...WHEN I SAW THE THING.

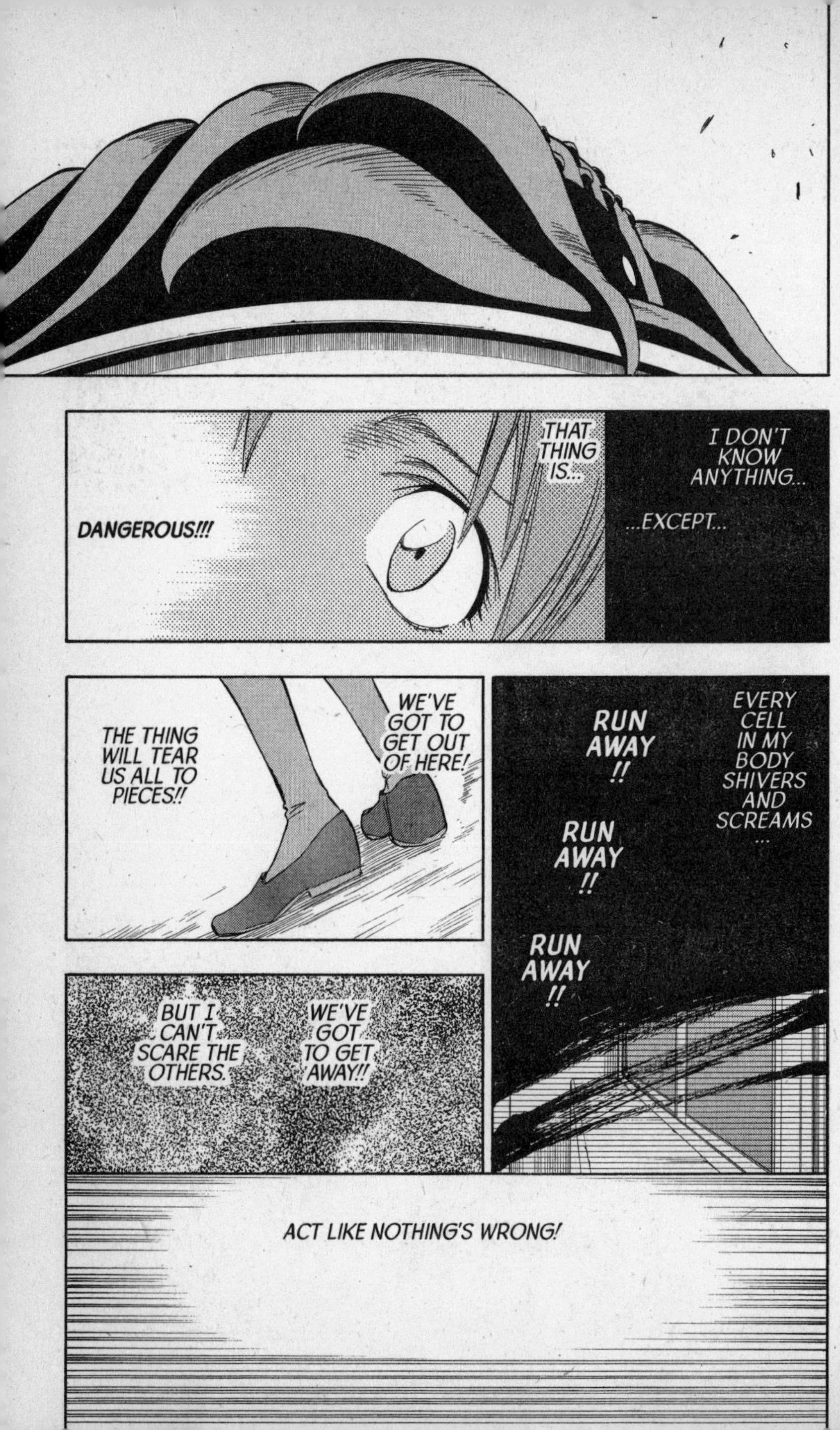
I DON'T KNOW ANYTHING...
...EXCEPT...
THAT THING IS...
DANGEROUS!!!
EVERY CELL IN MY BODY SHIVERS AND SCREAMS ...
RUN AWAY !!
RUN AWAY !!
RUN AWAY !!
WE'VE GOT TO GET OUT OF HERE!
THE THING WILL TEAR US ALL TO PIECES!!
WE'VE GOT TO GET AWAY!!
BUT I CAN'T SCARE THE OTHERS.
ACT LIKE NOTHING'S WRONG!

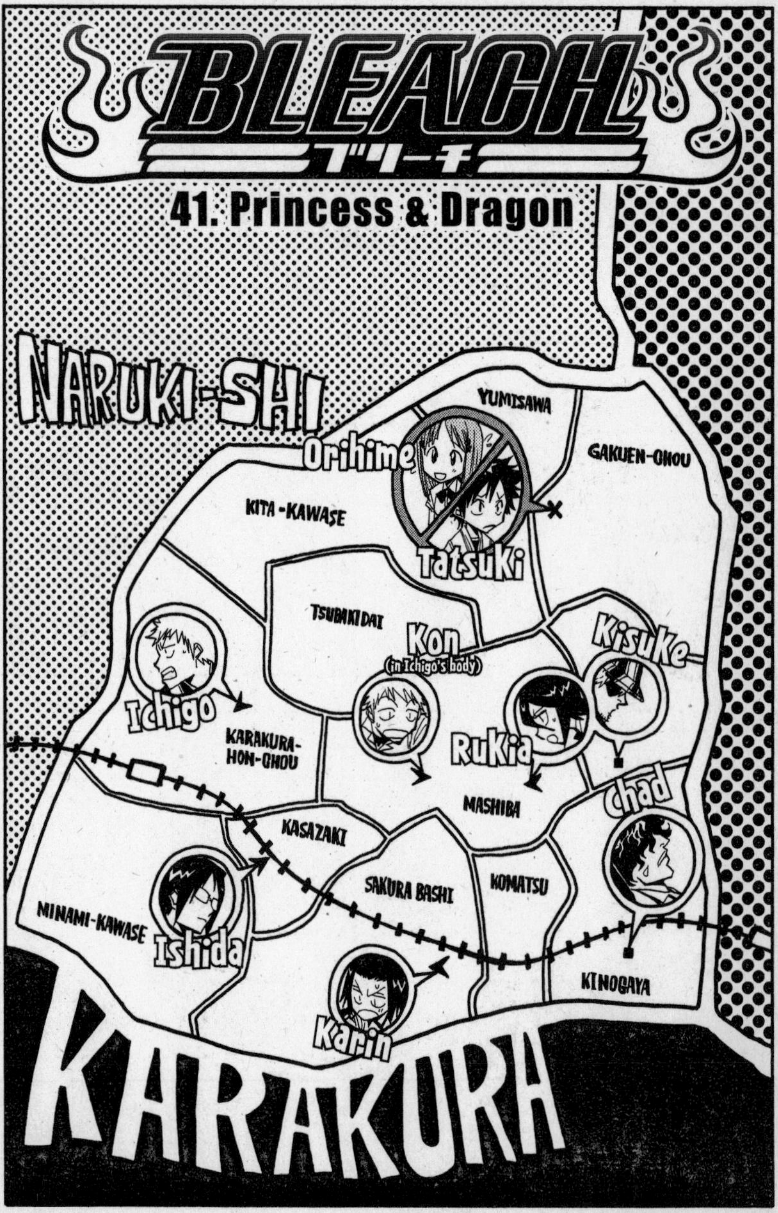
BLEACH
ブリーチ
41. Princess & Dragon
NARUKI-SHI
YUMISAWA
Orihime
GAKUEN-CHOU
KITA-KAWASE
Tatsuki
TSUBAKIDAI
Kon
(in Ichigo's body)
Kisuke
Ichigo
KARAKURA-
HON-CHOU
Rukia
MASHIBA
Chad
KASAZAKI
SAKURA BASHI
KOMATSU
MINAMI-KAWASE
Ishida
KINOGAYA
Karin
KARAKURA

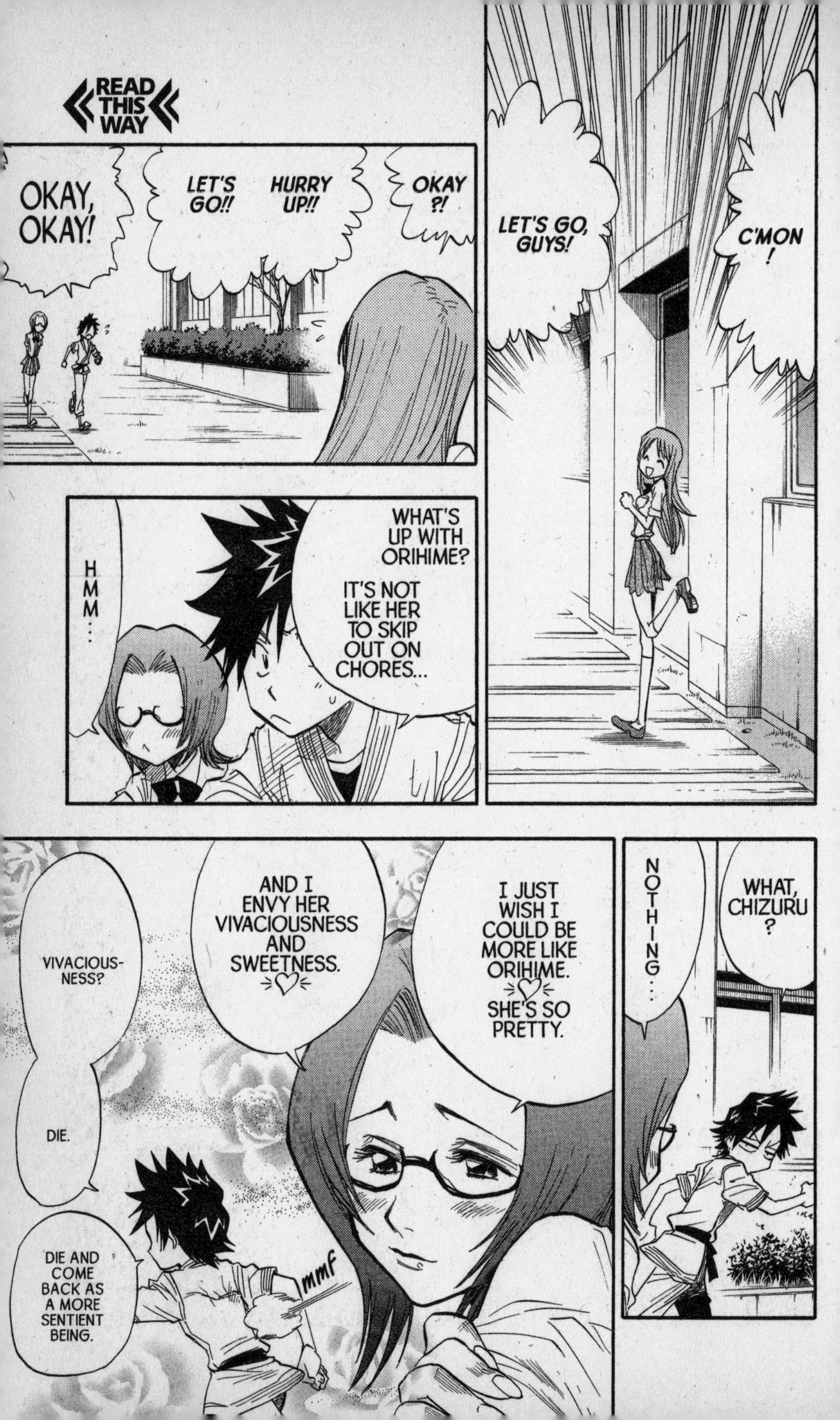
READ THIS WAY
C'MON!
LET'S GO, GUYS!
OKAY ?!
HURRY UP!!
LET'S GO!!
OKAY, OKAY!
WHAT'S UP WITH ORIHIME? IT'S NOT LIKE HER TO SKIP OUT ON CHORES...
HMM...
WHAT, CHIZURU?
NOTHING...
I JUST WISH I COULD BE MORE LIKE ORIHIME. ♡ SHE'S SO PRETTY.
AND I ENVY HER VIVACIOUSNESS AND SWEETNESS. ♡
VIVACIOUS-NESS?
DIE.
mmf
DIE AND COME BACK AS A MORE SENTIENT BEING.

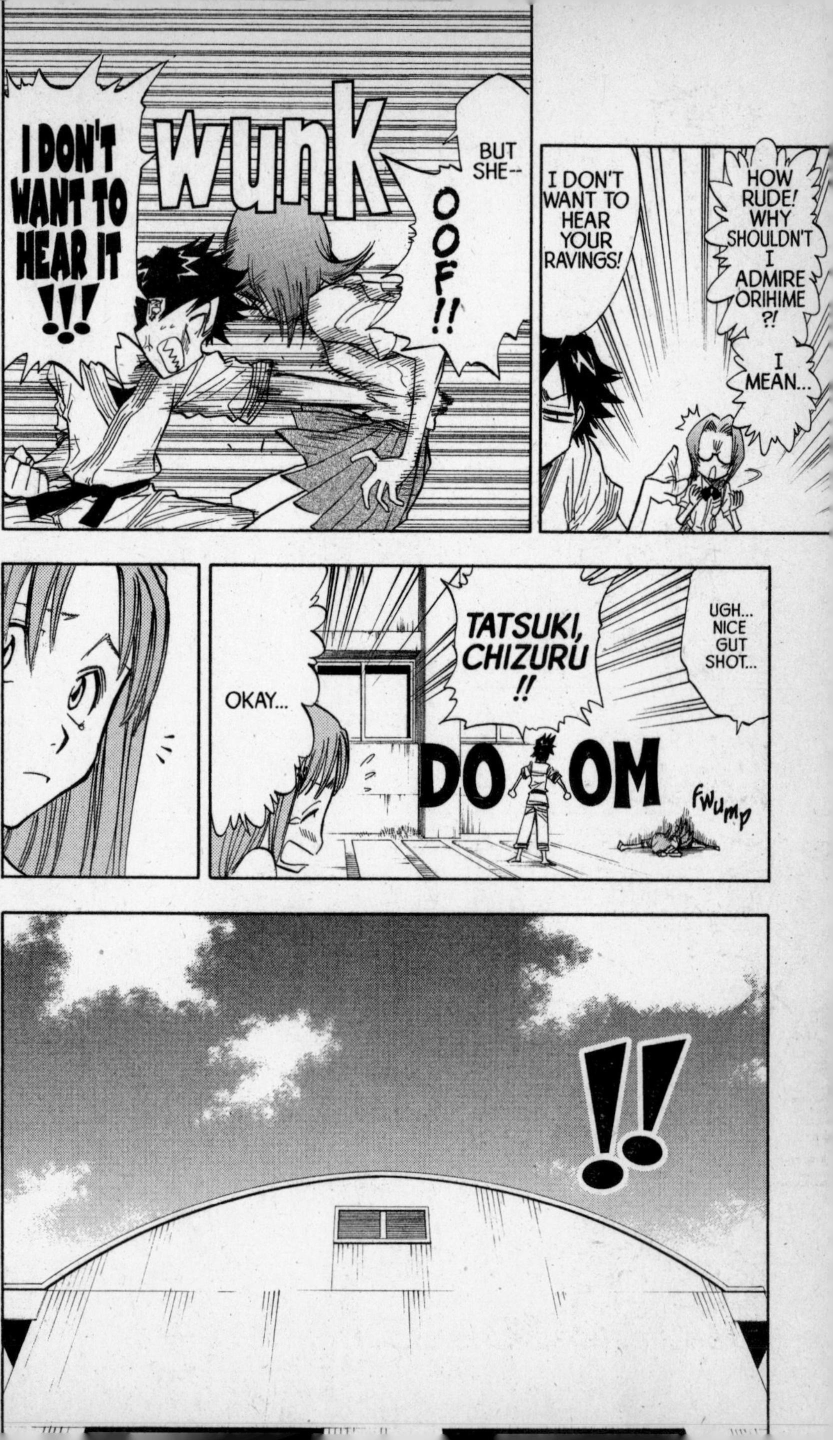
HOW RUDE! WHY SHOULDN'T I ADMIRE ORIHIME?!
I MEAN...
I DON'T WANT TO HEAR YOUR RAVINGS!
BUT SHE--
OOF!!
WUNK
I DON'T WANT TO HEAR IT!!!
UGH... NICE GUT SHOT...
TATSUKI, CHIZURU!!
DOOM
FWUMP
OKAY...
!!

READ THIS WAY

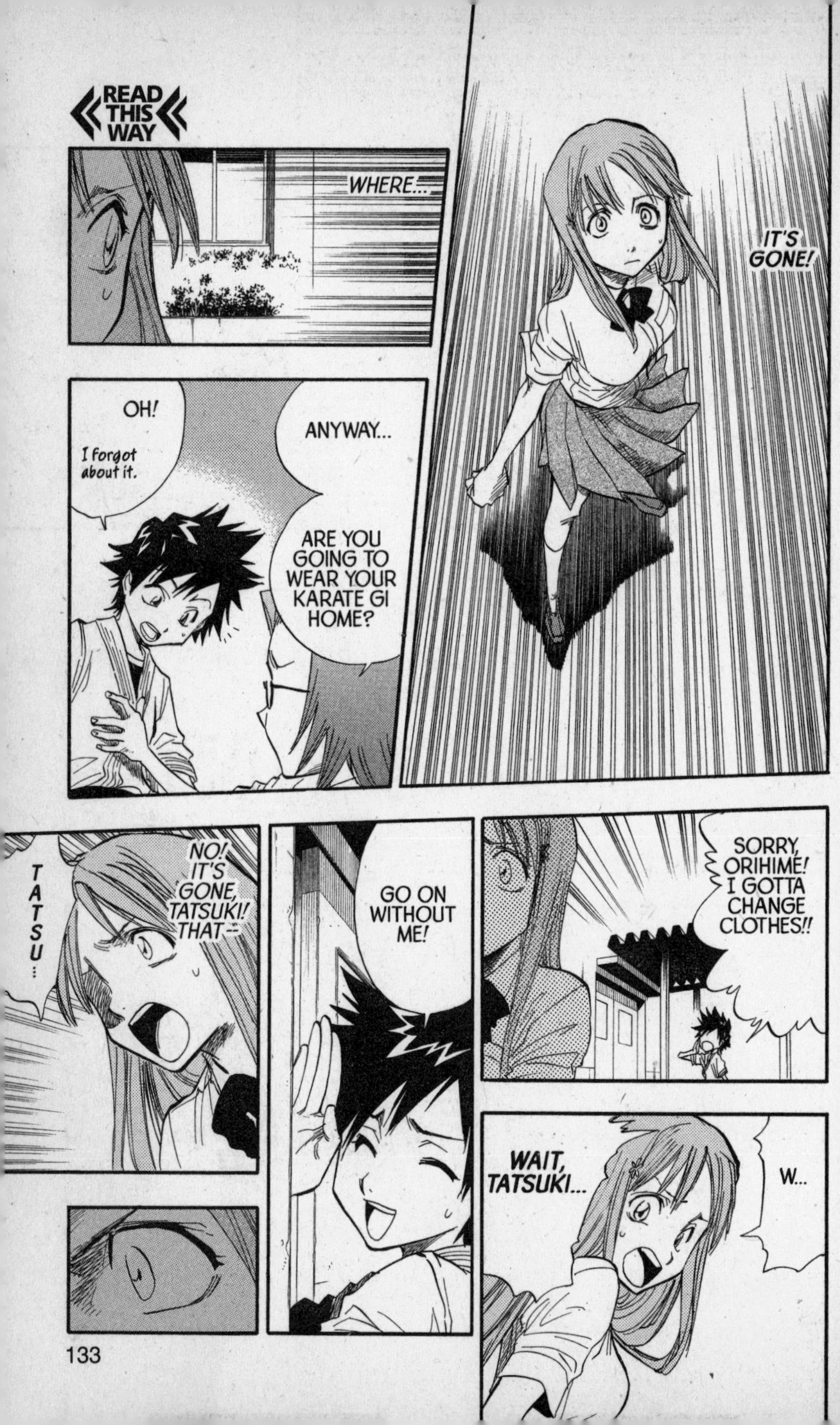
IT'S GONE!
WHERE...
ANYWAY...
ARE YOU GOING TO WEAR YOUR KARATE GI HOME?
OH!
I forgot about it.
SORRY, ORIHIME! I GOTTA CHANGE CLOTHES!!
W...
WAIT, TATSUKI...
GO ON WITHOUT ME!
NO! IT'S GONE, TATSUKI! THAT--
TATSU...

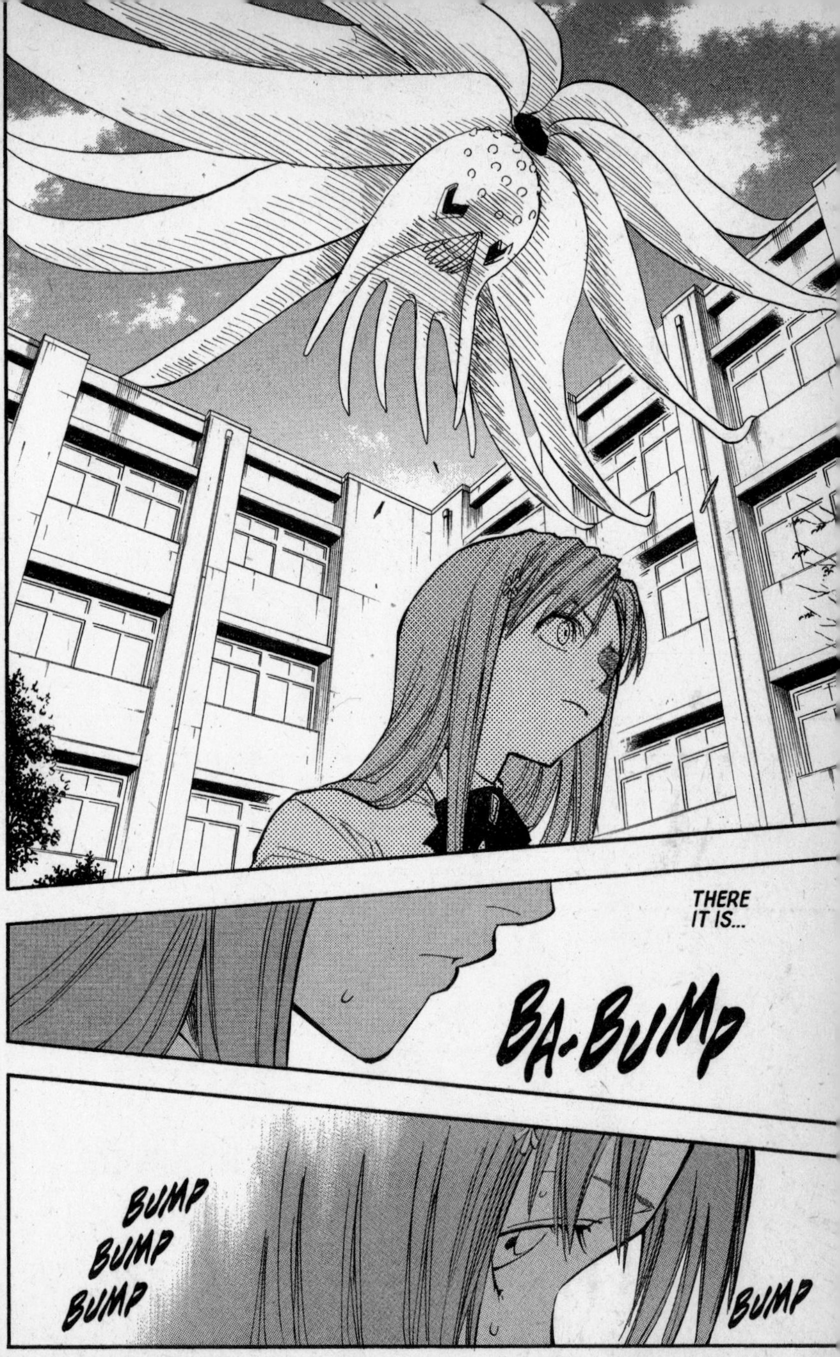
THERE IT IS...
BA-BUMP
BUMP
BUMP
BUMP
BUMP

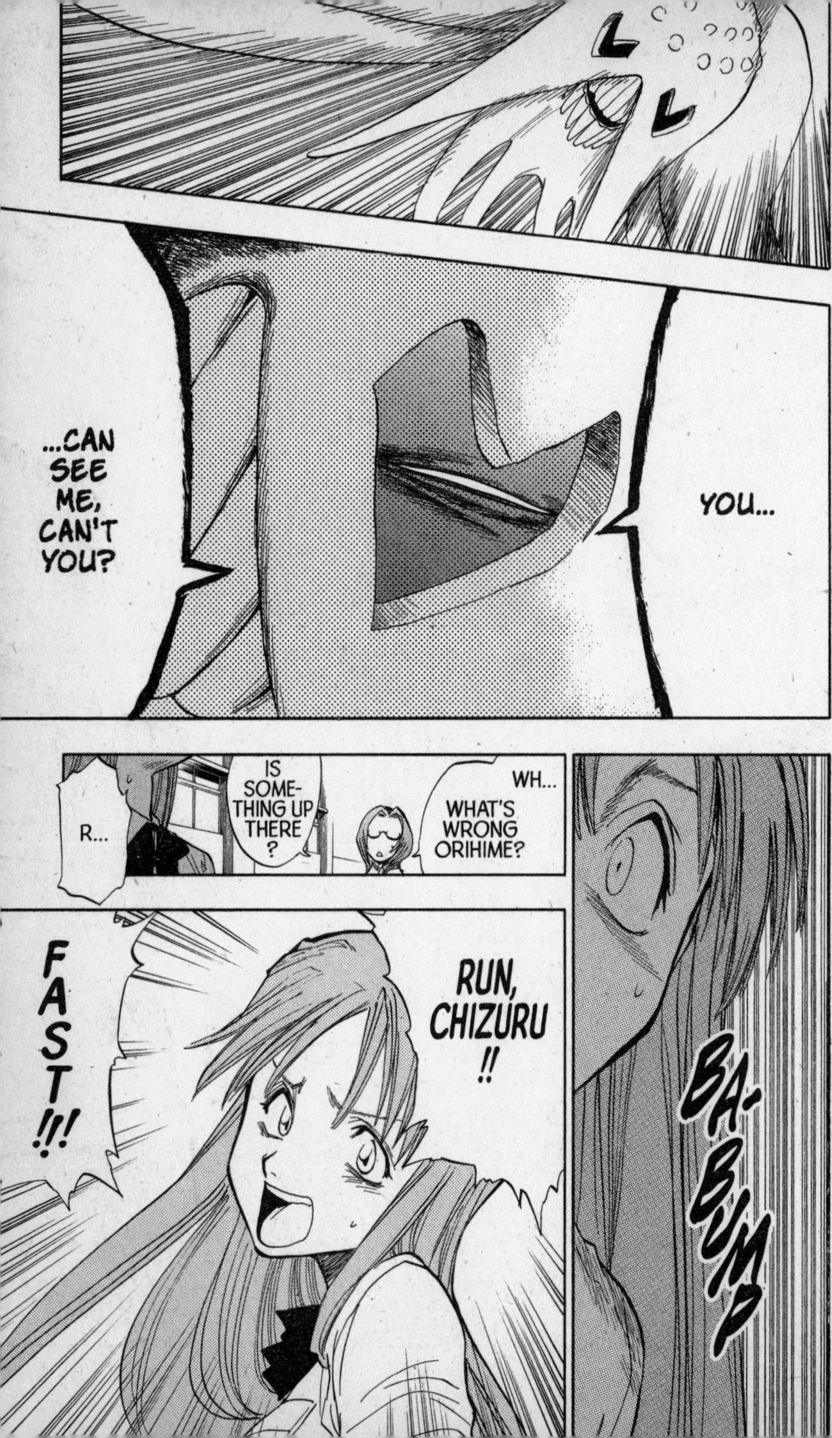
YOU...
...CAN SEE ME, CAN'T YOU?
BA-BUMP
WH... WHAT'S WRONG ORIHIME?
IS SOME-THING UP THERE?
R...
RUN, CHIZURU!!
FAST!!!

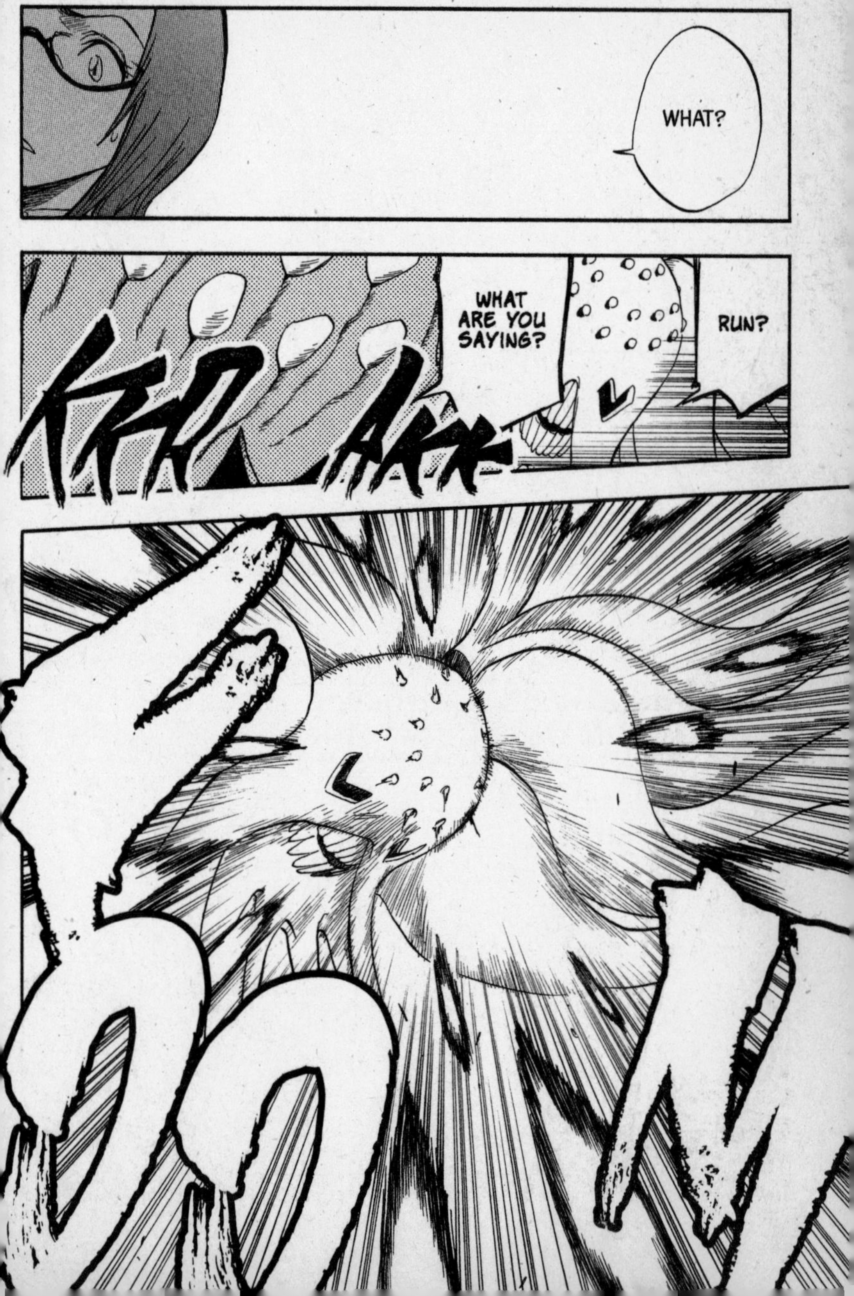
WHAT?
RUN?
WHAT ARE YOU SAYING?
KRRAKK

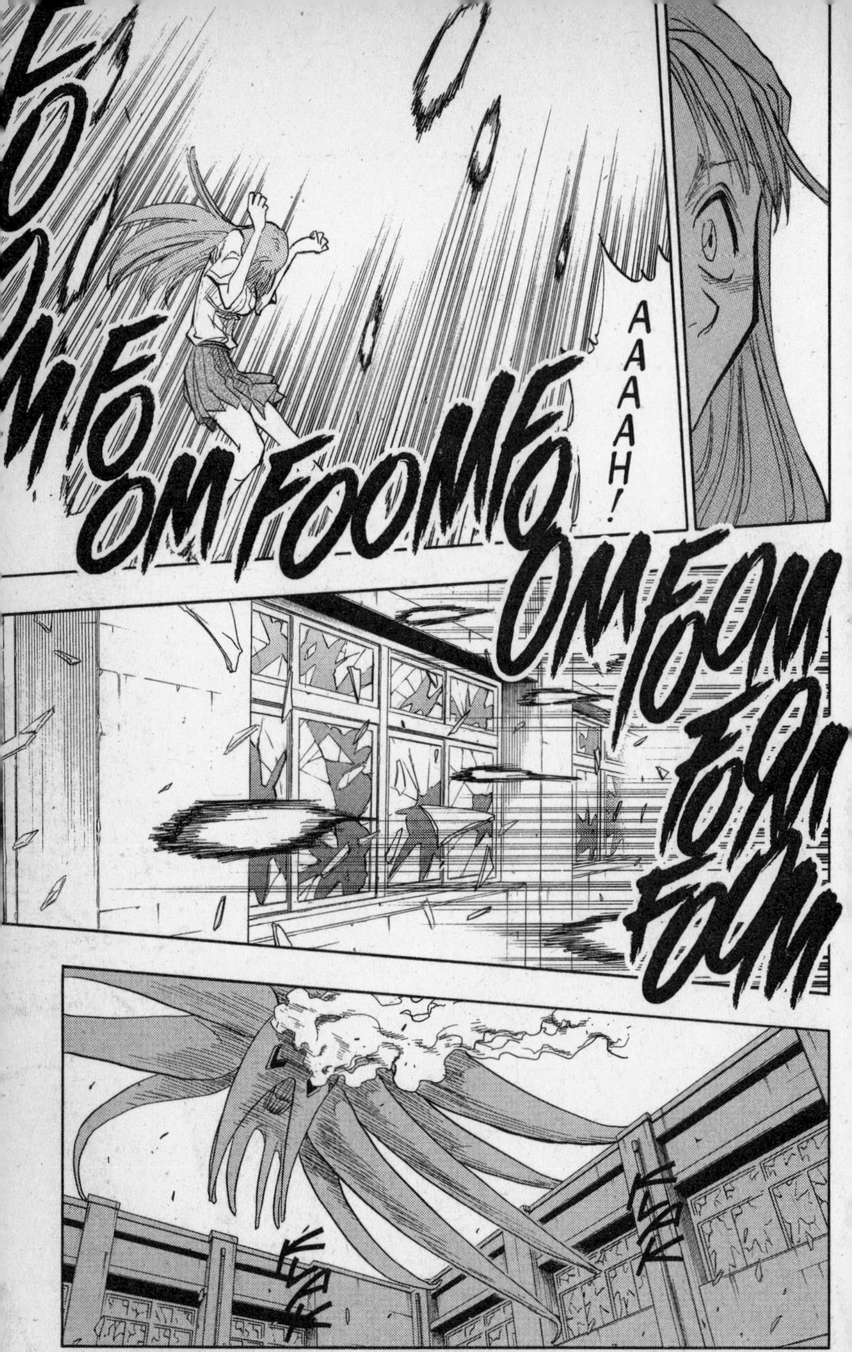
AAAAAH!

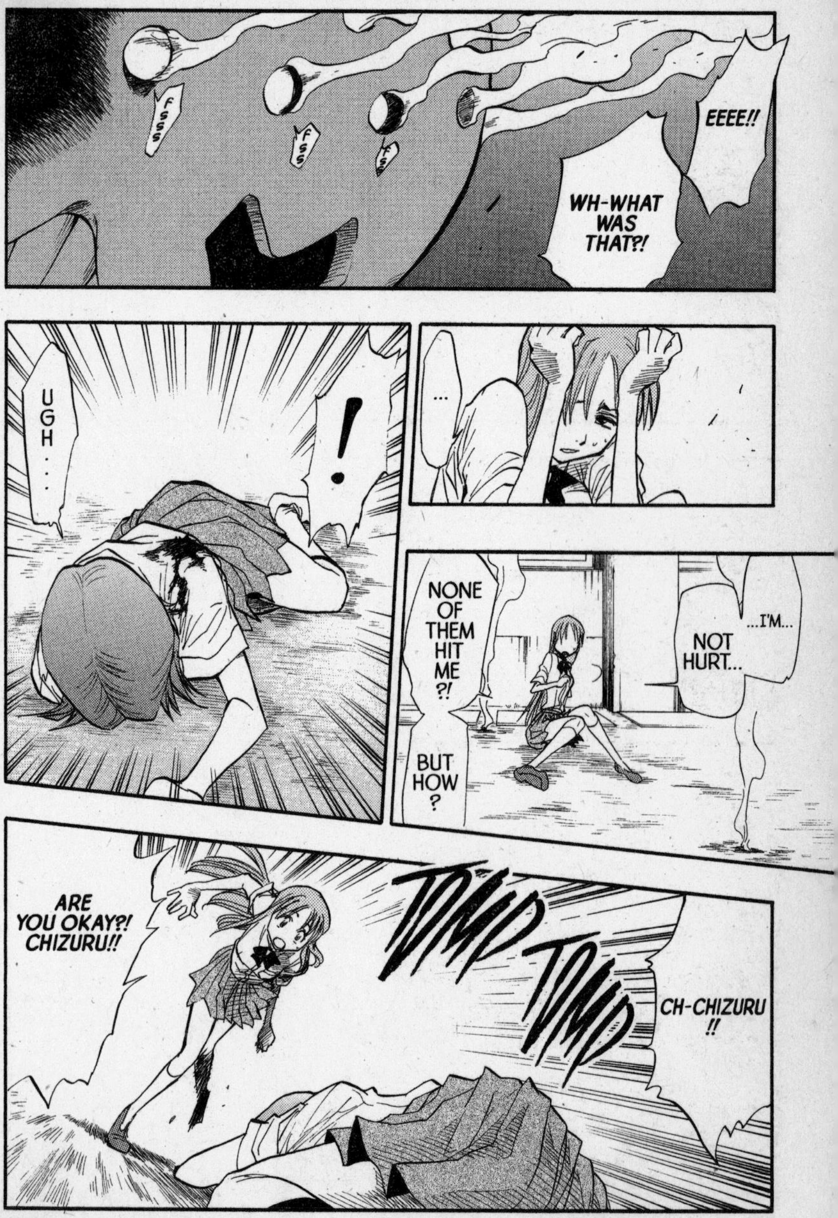
EEEE!!
fss
fss
fsss
WH-WHAT WAS THAT?!
...
...I'M... NOT HURT...
NONE OF THEM HIT ME?!
BUT HOW?
!
UGH...
CH-CHIZURU!!
TOMP TOMP TOMP
ARE YOU OKAY?! CHIZURU!!

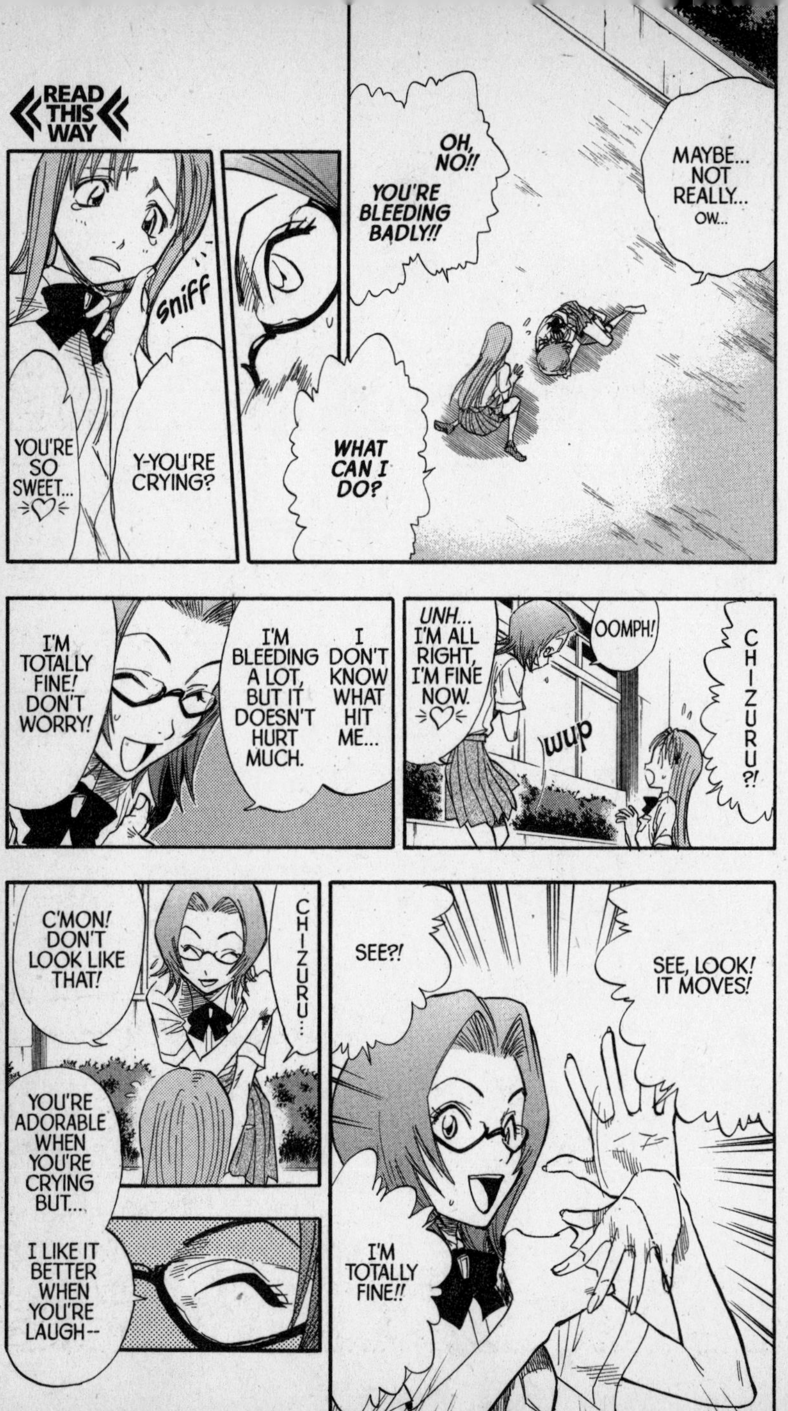
READ THIS WAY
MAYBE... NOT REALLY... OW...
OH, NO!!
YOU'RE BLEEDING BADLY!!
WHAT CAN I DO?
Sniff
Y-YOU'RE CRYING?
YOU'RE SO SWEET...
CHIZURU?!
OOMPH!
UNH... I'M ALL RIGHT, I'M FINE NOW.
wup
I DON'T KNOW WHAT HIT ME...
I'M BLEEDING A LOT, BUT IT DOESN'T HURT MUCH.
I'M TOTALLY FINE! DON'T WORRY!
SEE, LOOK! IT MOVES!
SEE?!
I'M TOTALLY FINE!!
CHIZURU...
C'MON! DON'T LOOK LIKE THAT!
YOU'RE ADORABLE WHEN YOU'RE CRYING BUT...
I LIKE IT BETTER WHEN YOU'RE LAUGH--

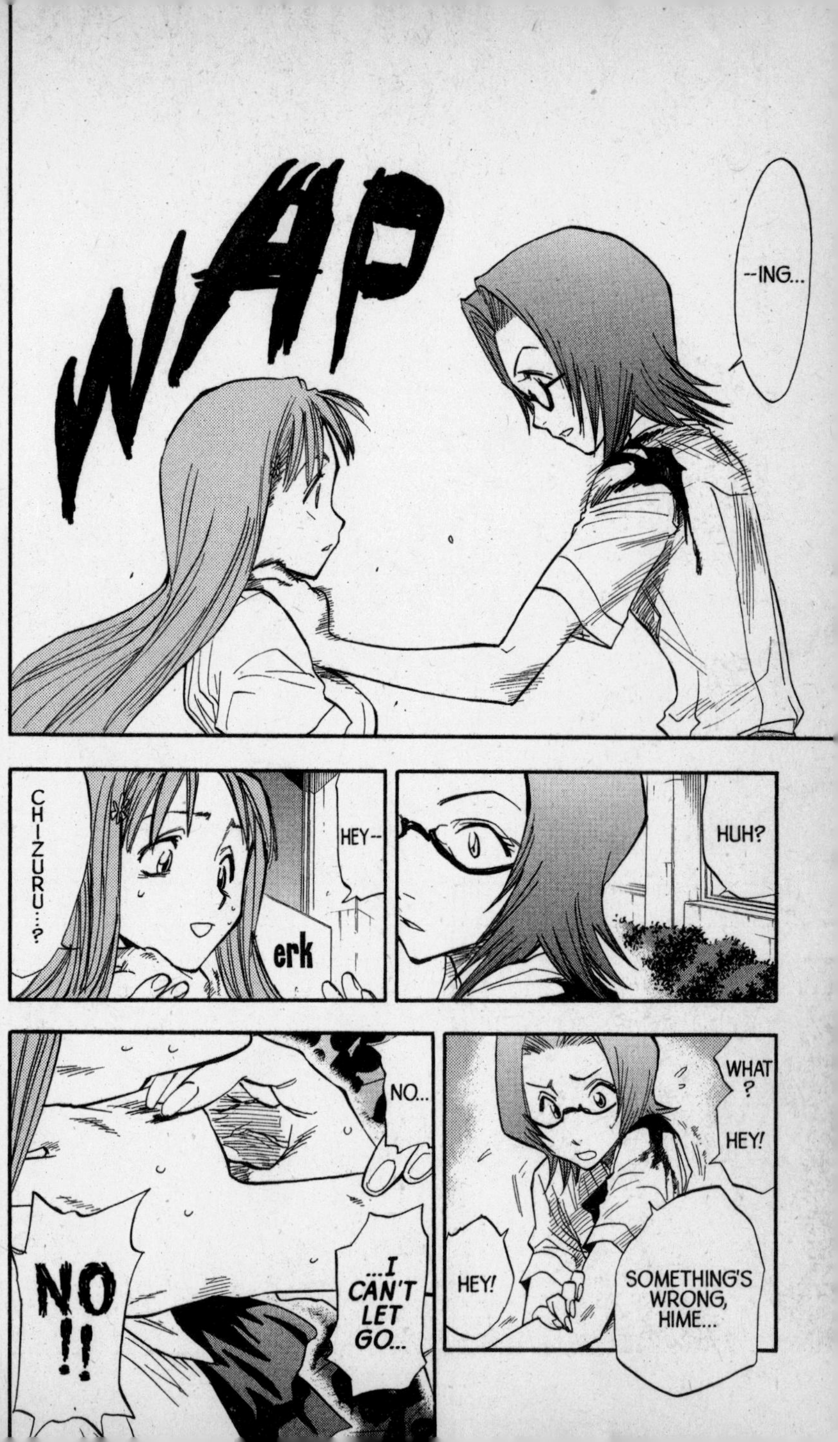
--ING...
WAP
HUH?
HEY--
erk
CHIZURU...?
WHAT?
HEY!
SOMETHING'S WRONG, HIME...
HEY!
NO...
...I CAN'T LET GO...
NO!!

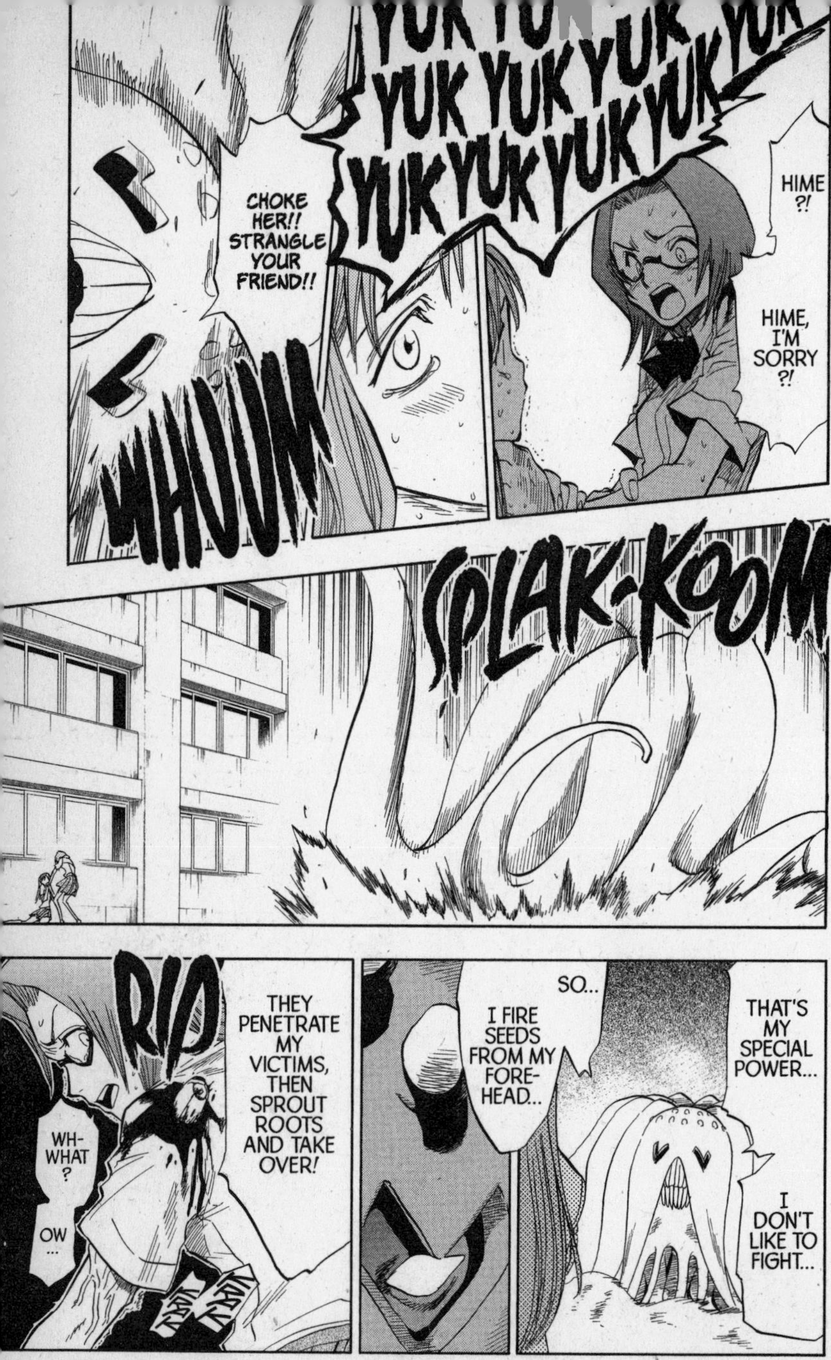
HIME ?!
HIME, I'M SORRY ?!
YUK YUK YUK YUK YUK YUK YUK YUK YUK YUK YUK YUK YUK
CHOKE HER!! STRANGLE YOUR FRIEND!!
WHUUM
SPLAK-KOOM
THAT'S MY SPECIAL POWER...
SO...
I DON'T LIKE TO FIGHT...
I FIRE SEEDS FROM MY FORE-HEAD...
RIP
THEY PENETRATE MY VICTIMS, THEN SPROUT ROOTS AND TAKE OVER!
WH-WHAT ?
OW ...

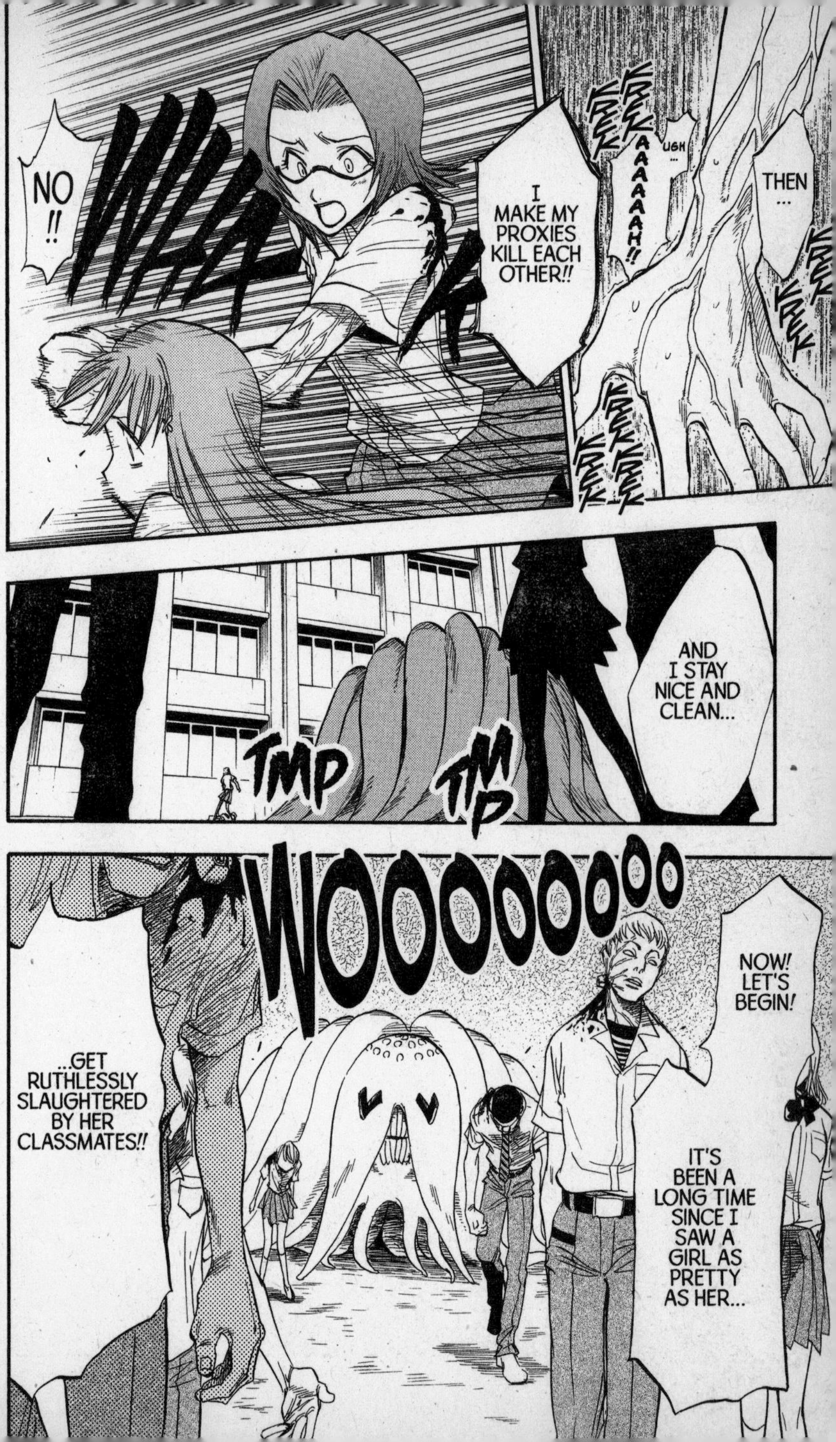
THEN ...
KREK KREK
UGH ...
AAAAAAAH!!
KREK KREK KREK
KREK KREK KREK KREK
I MAKE MY PROXIES KILL EACH OTHER!!
WHAK
NO !!
AND I STAY NICE AND CLEAN...
TMP
TMP
WOOOOOOOO
NOW! LET'S BEGIN!
IT'S BEEN A LONG TIME SINCE I SAW A GIRL AS PRETTY AS HER...
...GET RUTHLESSLY SLAUGHTERED BY HER CLASSMATES!!

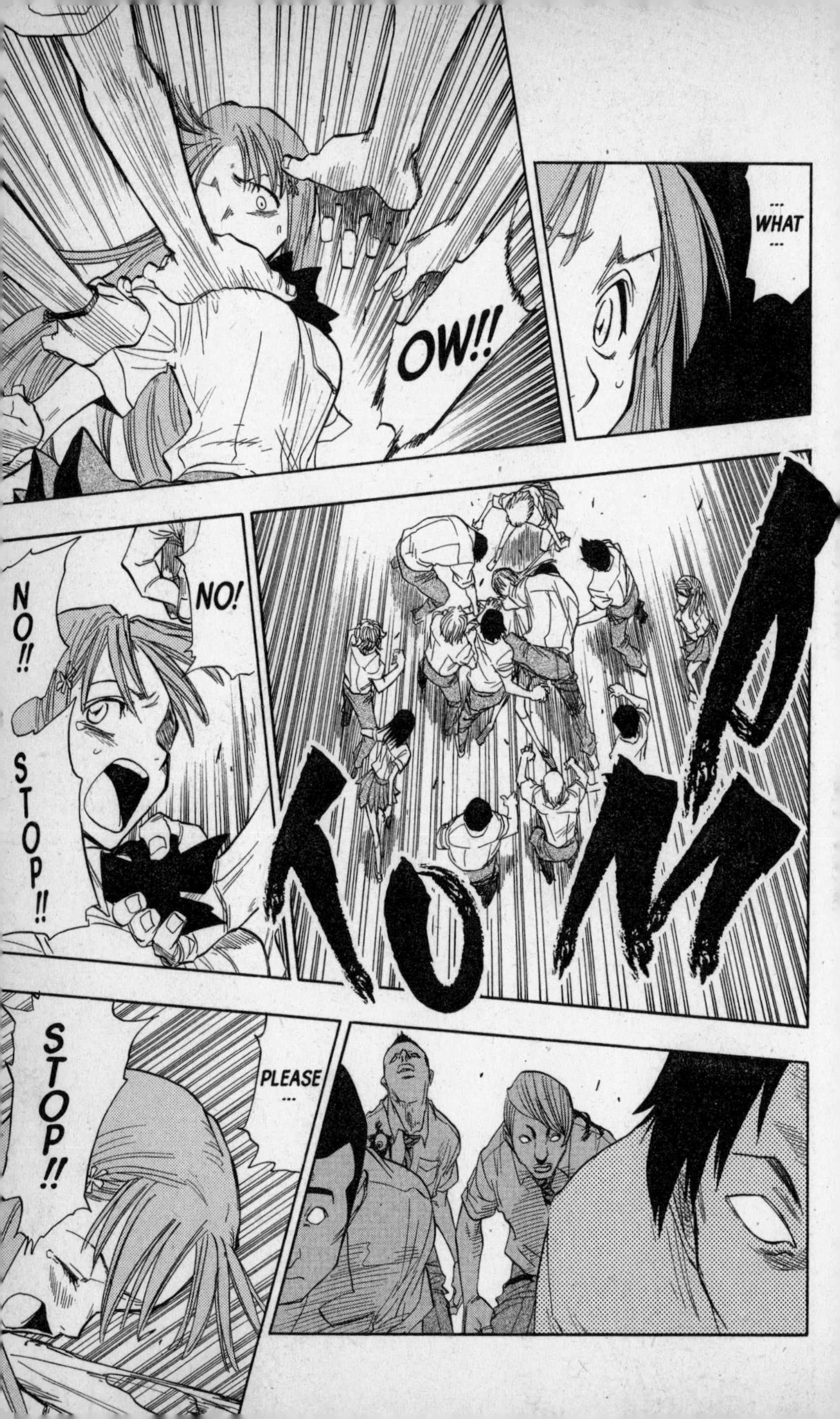

... WHAT ...
OW!!
NO!
NO!!
STOP!!
PLEASE ...
STOP!!

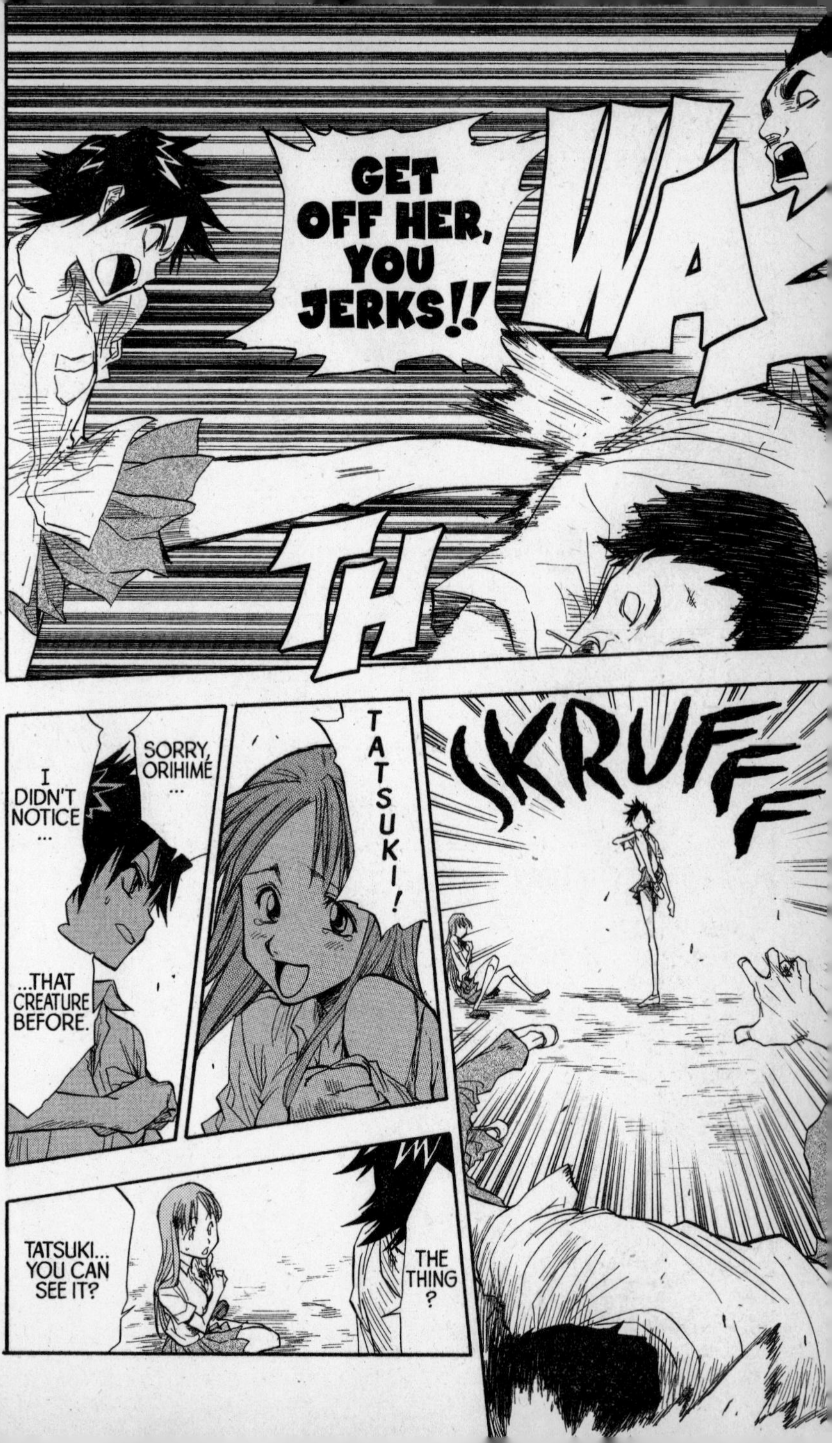
WA
GET OFF HER, YOU JERKS!!
TH
SKRUFFF
TATSUKI!
SORRY, ORIHIMÉ...
I DIDN'T NOTICE...
...THAT CREATURE BEFORE.
THE THING?
TATSUKI... YOU CAN SEE IT?

READ THIS WAY

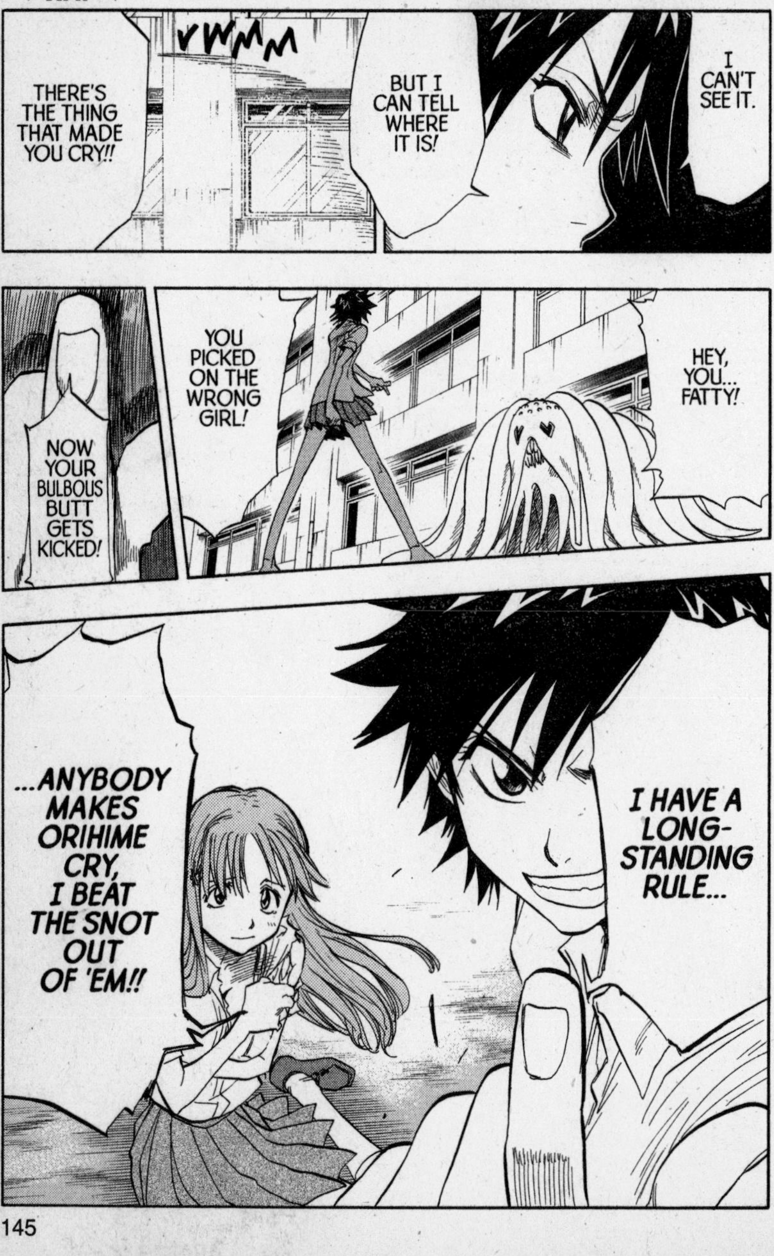
I CAN'T SEE IT.
BUT I CAN TELL WHERE IT IS!
VWMM
THERE'S THE THING THAT MADE YOU CRY!!
HEY, YOU... FATTY!
YOU PICKED ON THE WRONG GIRL!
NOW YOUR BULBOUS BUTT GETS KICKED!
I HAVE A LONG-STANDING RULE...
...ANYBODY MAKES ORIHIME CRY, I BEAT THE SNOT OUT OF 'EM!!

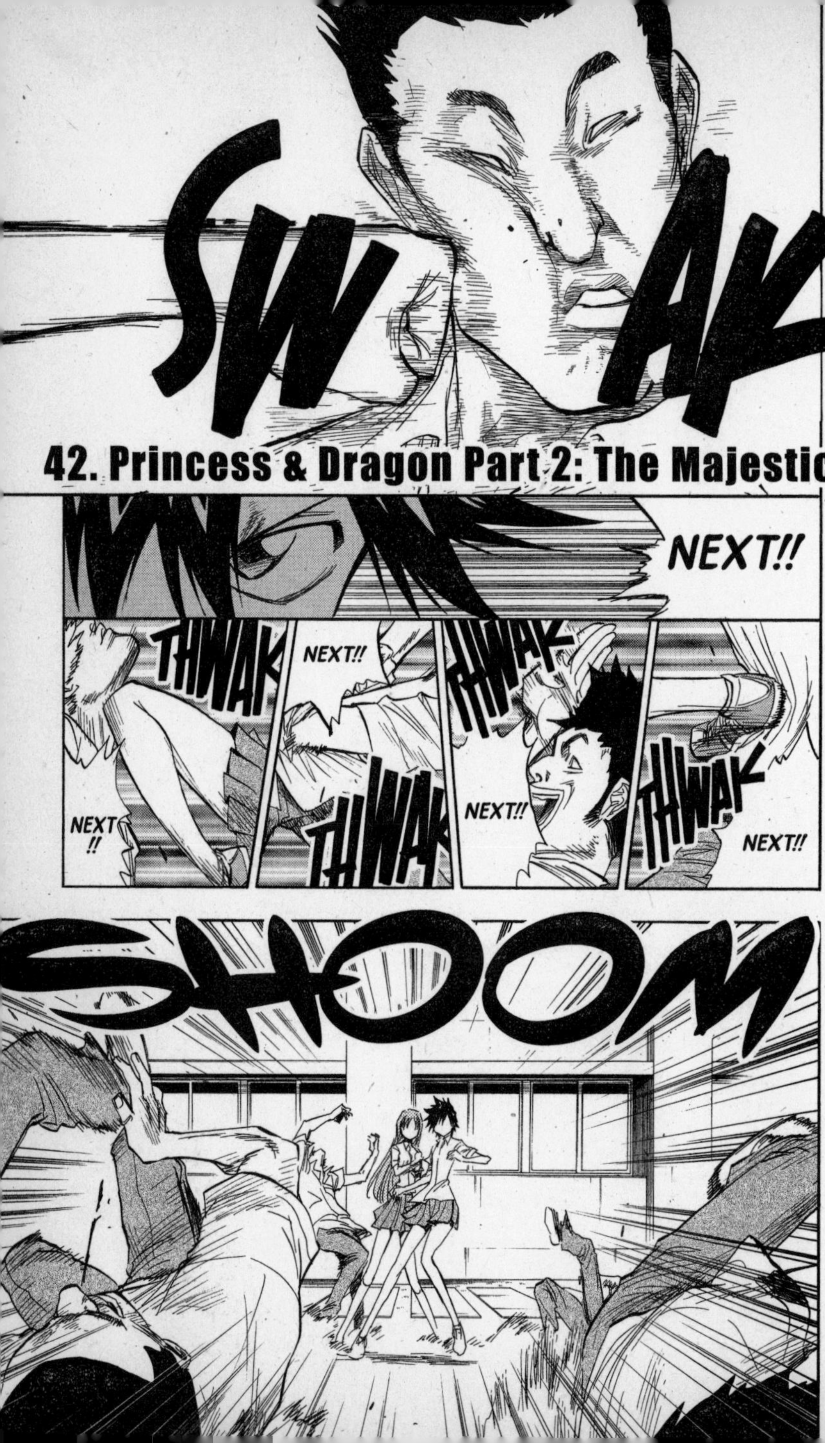
SWAK
42. Princess & Dragon Part 2: The Majestic
NEXT!!
THWAK
NEXT!!
THWAK
NEXT!!
THWAK
NEXT!!
THWAK
NEXT!!
SHOOM

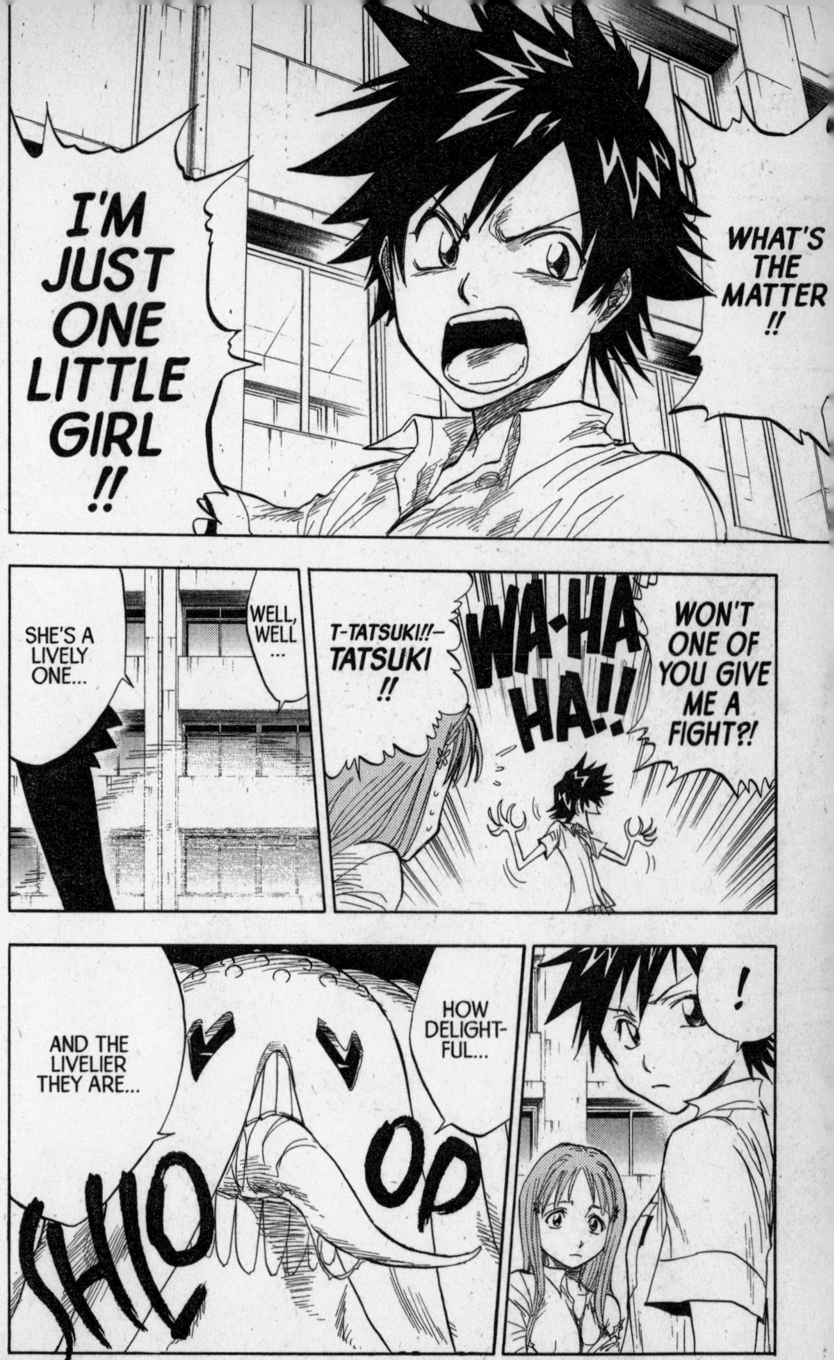
WHAT'S THE MATTER !!
I'M JUST ONE LITTLE GIRL !!
WON'T ONE OF YOU GIVE ME A FIGHT?!
WA-HA HA!!
T-TATSUKI!!- TATSUKI !!
WELL, WELL ...
SHE'S A LIVELY ONE...
!
HOW DELIGHT-FUL...
AND THE LIVELIER THEY ARE...
SHLO OP

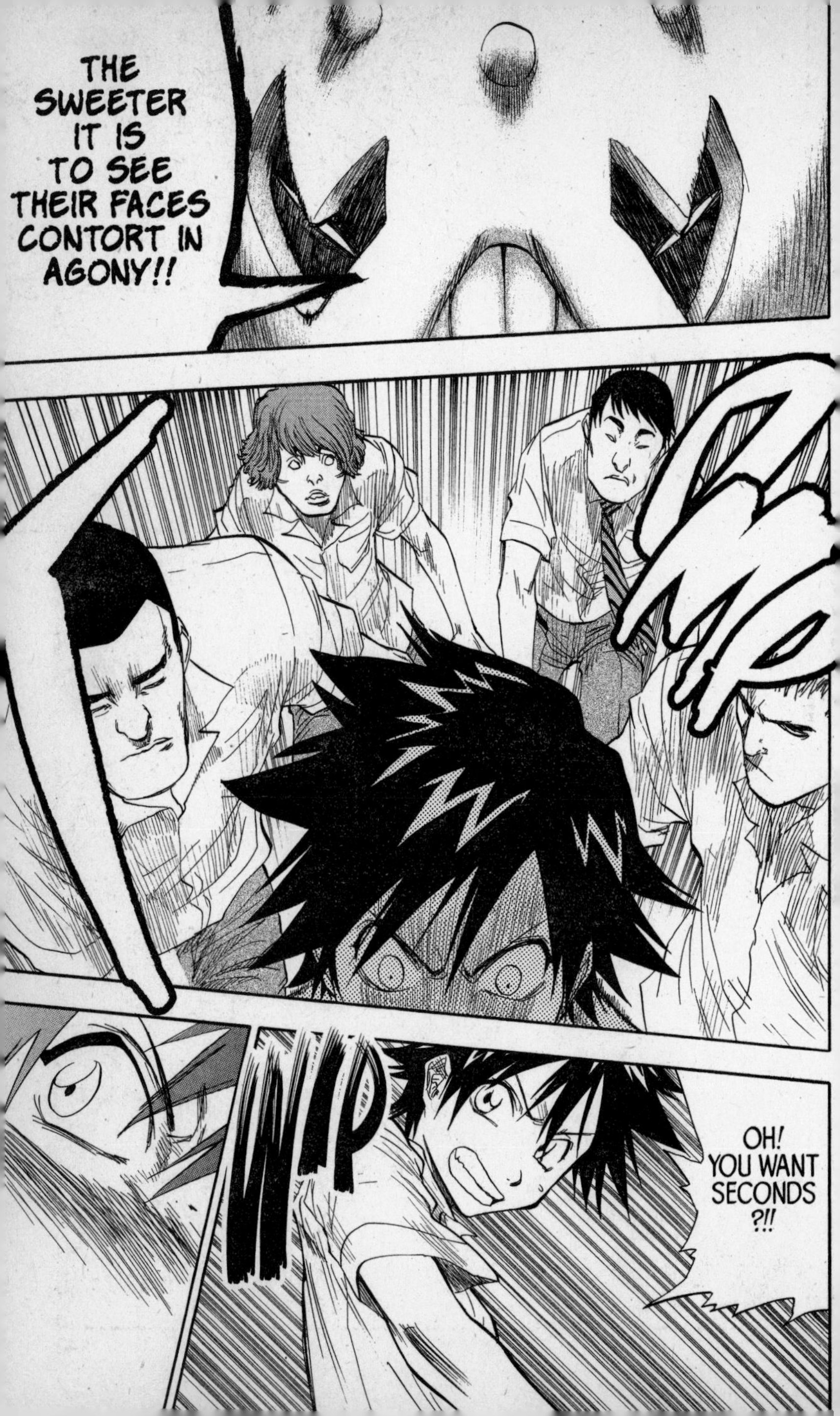
THE SWEETER IT IS TO SEE THEIR FACES CONTORT IN AGONY!!
OH! YOU WANT SECONDS ?!!

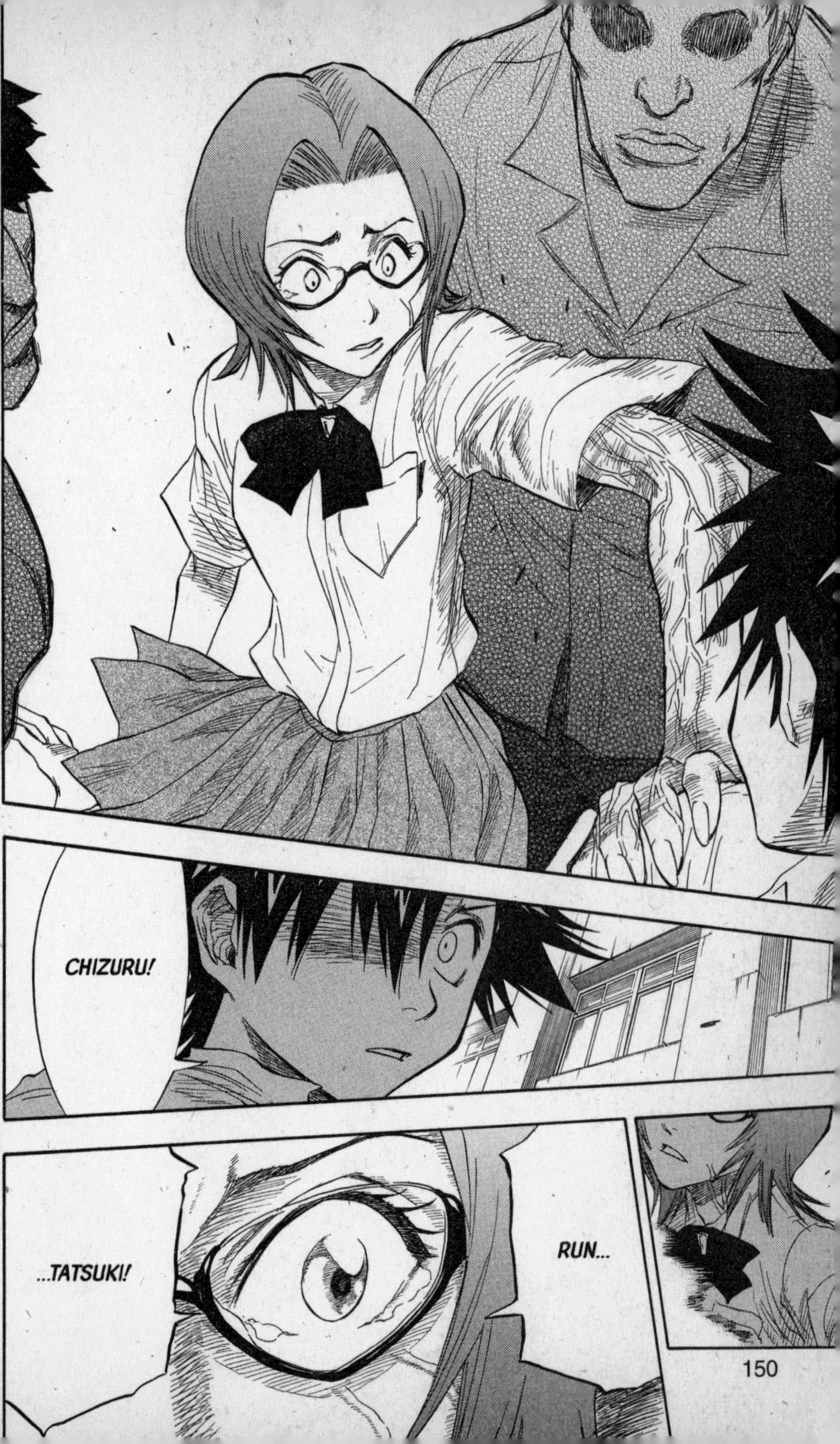
CHIZURU!
RUN...
...TATSUKI!

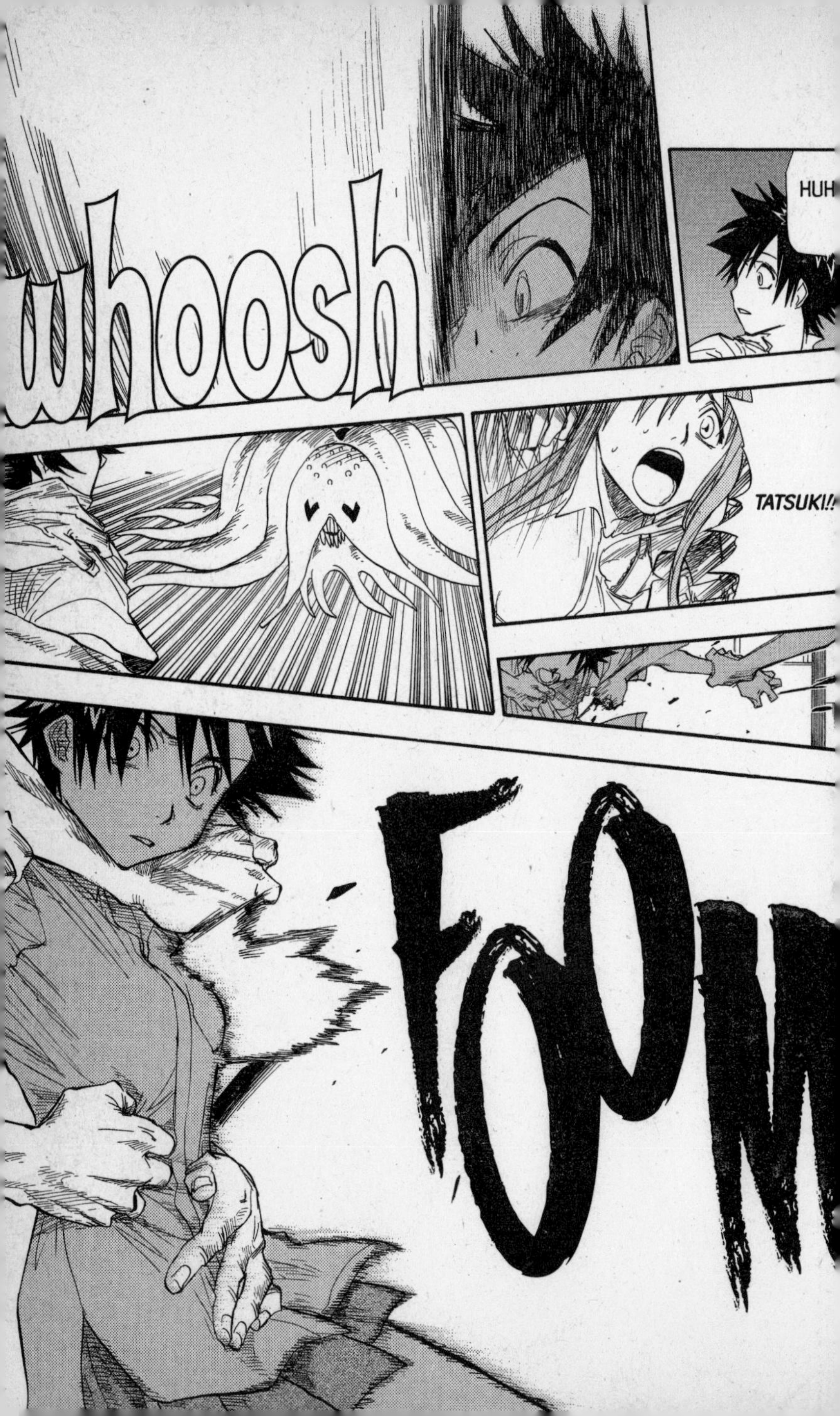
HUH
whoosh
TATSUKI!!
FOOM

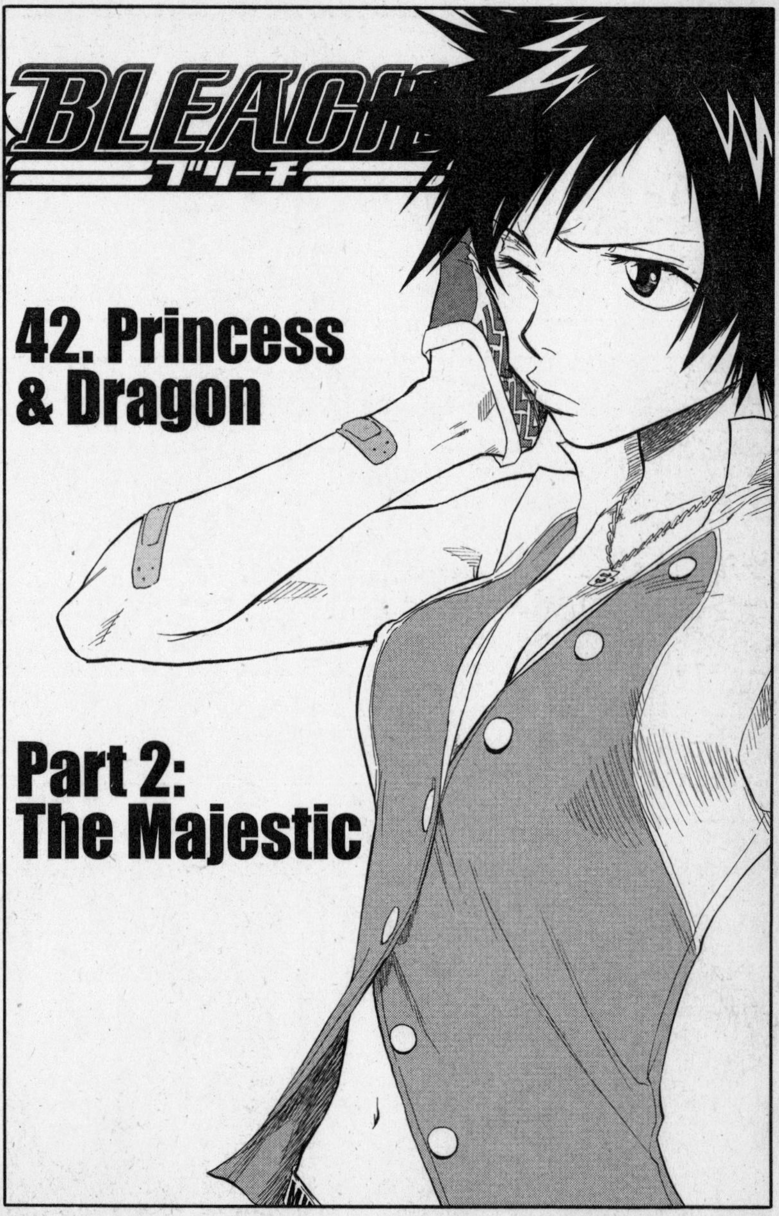
BLEACH
ブリーチ
42. Princess & Dragon
Part 2: The Majestic

READ THIS WAY

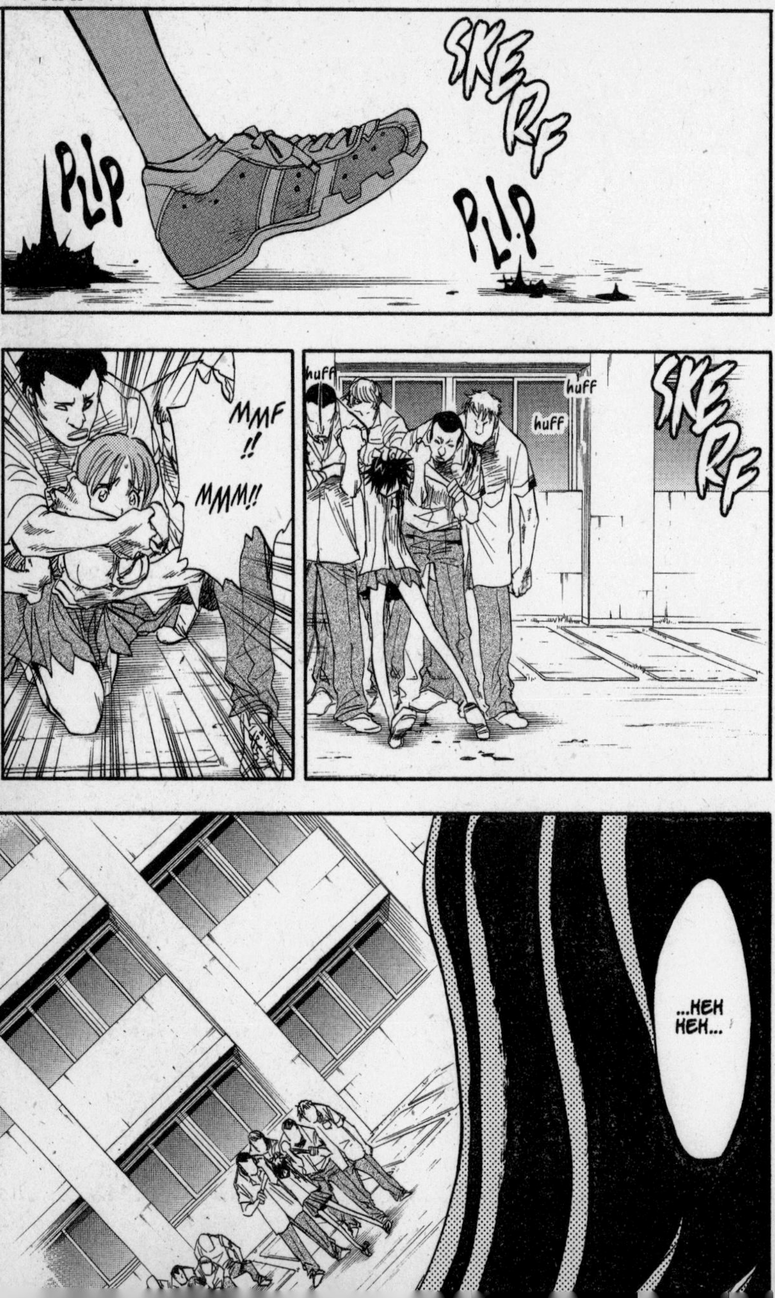
SKERF
PLIP
PLIP
SKERF
huff
huff
huff
MMF!!
MMM!!
...HEH HEH...

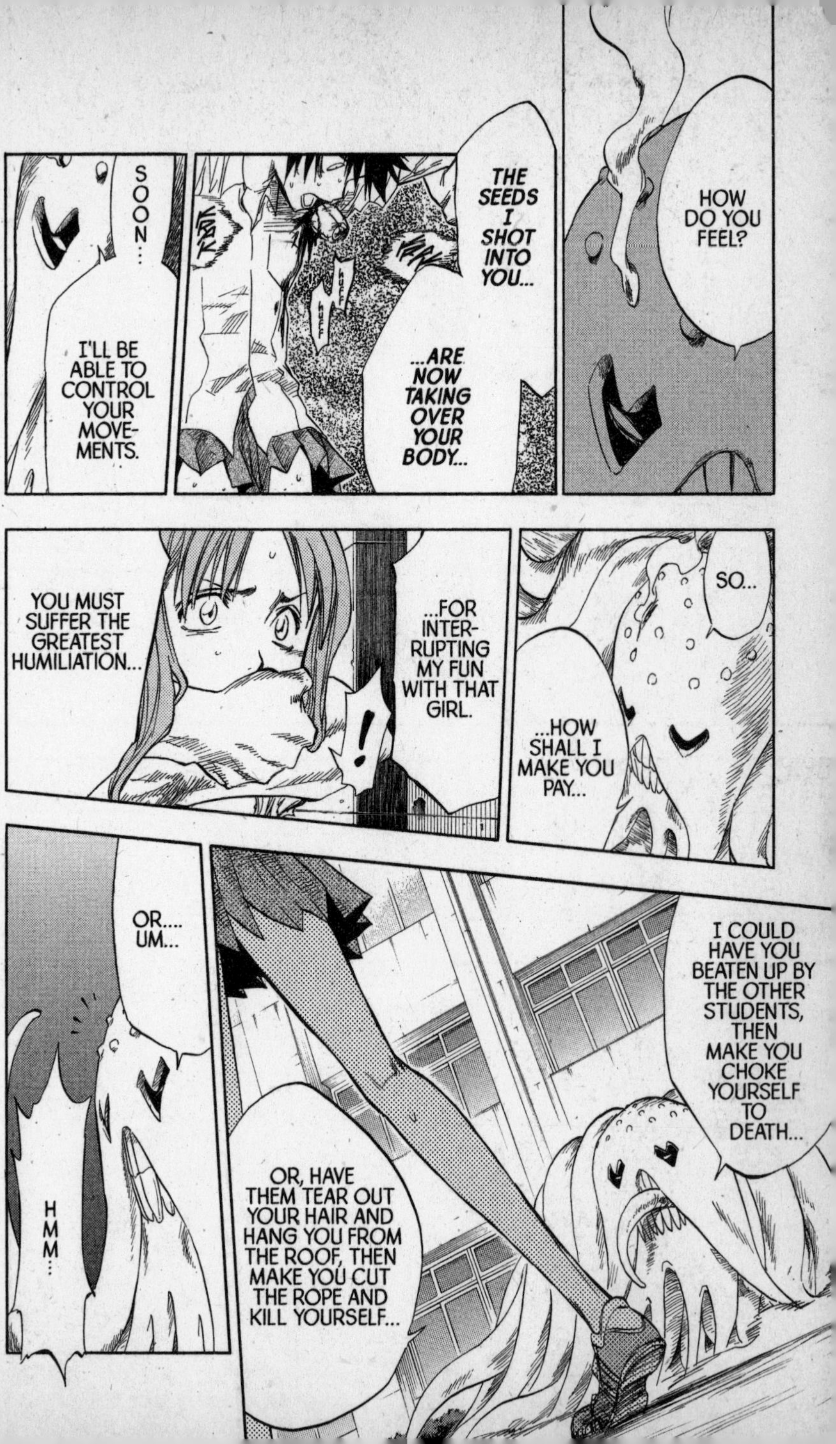
HOW DO YOU FEEL?
THE SEEDS I SHOT INTO YOU...
...ARE NOW TAKING OVER YOUR BODY...
SOON...
I'LL BE ABLE TO CONTROL YOUR MOVEMENTS.
SO...
...HOW SHALL I MAKE YOU PAY...
...FOR INTERRUPTING MY FUN WITH THAT GIRL.
!
YOU MUST SUFFER THE GREATEST HUMILIATION...
I COULD HAVE YOU BEATEN UP BY THE OTHER STUDENTS, THEN MAKE YOU CHOKE YOURSELF TO DEATH...
OR, HAVE THEM TEAR OUT YOUR HAIR AND HANG YOU FROM THE ROOF, THEN MAKE YOU CUT THE ROPE AND KILL YOURSELF...
OR.... UM...
HMM...

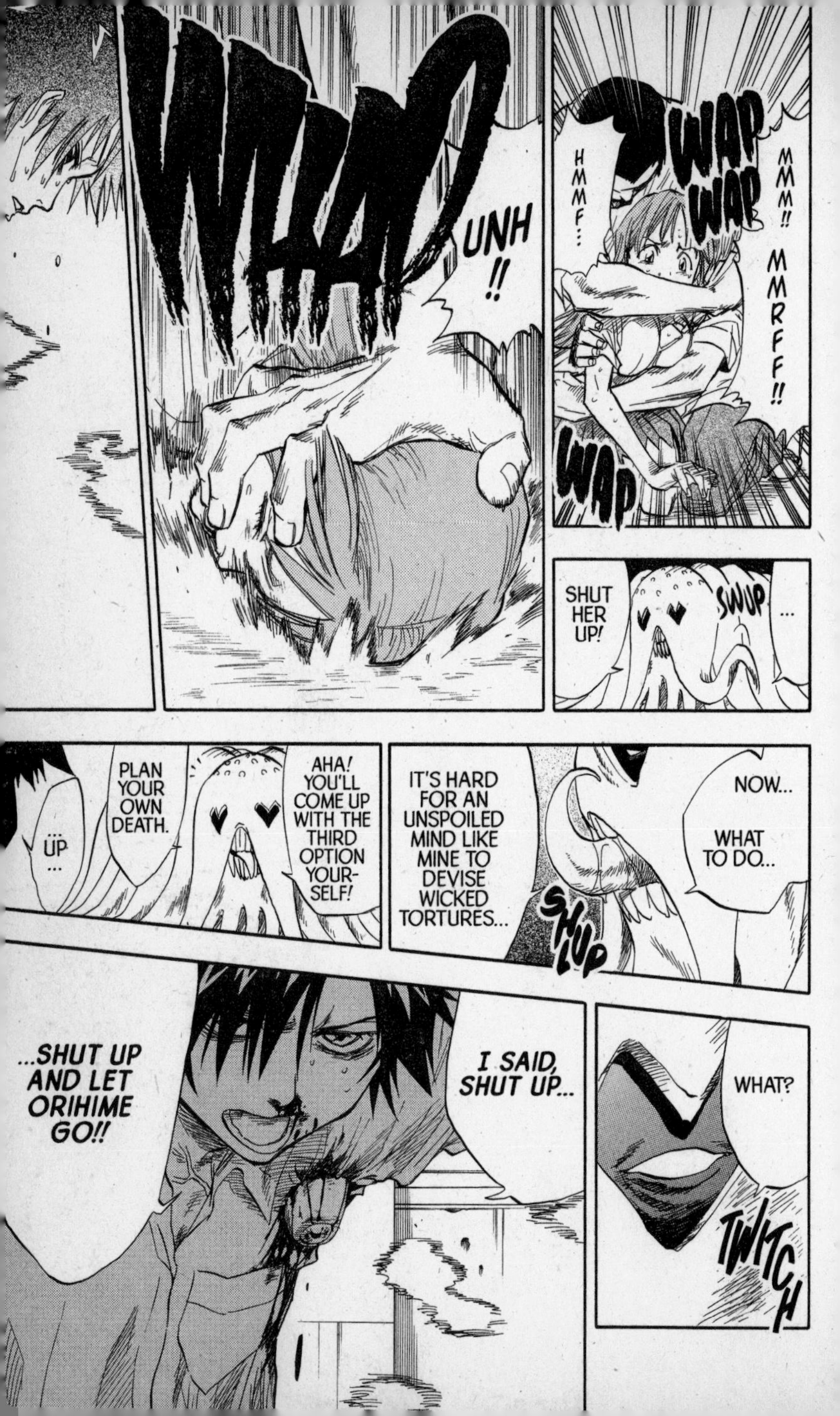
WAP WAP
MMMM!! MMRFF!!
HMMF...
WAP
...
SWUP
SHUT HER UP!
WHAP
UNH!!
NOW... WHAT TO DO...
SHLUP
IT'S HARD FOR AN UNSPOILED MIND LIKE MINE TO DEVISE WICKED TORTURES...
AHA! YOU'LL COME UP WITH THE THIRD OPTION YOUR-SELF!
PLAN YOUR OWN DEATH.
...UP...
WHAT?
TWITCH
I SAID, SHUT UP...
...SHUT UP AND LET ORIHIME GO!!

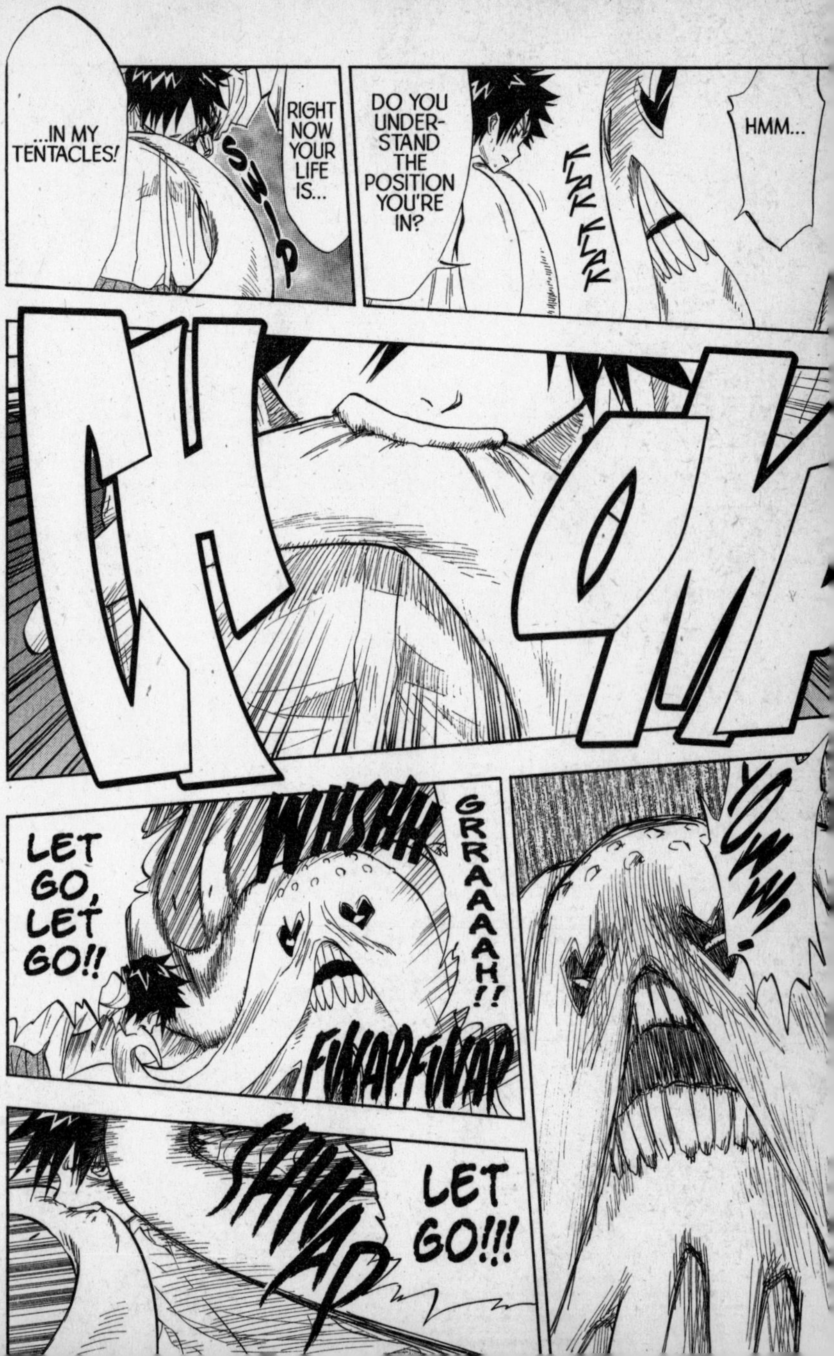
HMM...
KLAK KLAK
DO YOU UNDERSTAND THE POSITION YOU'RE IN?
RIGHT NOW YOUR LIFE IS...
SWIP
...IN MY TENTACLES!
CHOM
YOWW!
GRRAAAAAH!!
WHSHH
LET GO, LET GO!!
FWAPFWAP
LET GO!!!
SHWAP

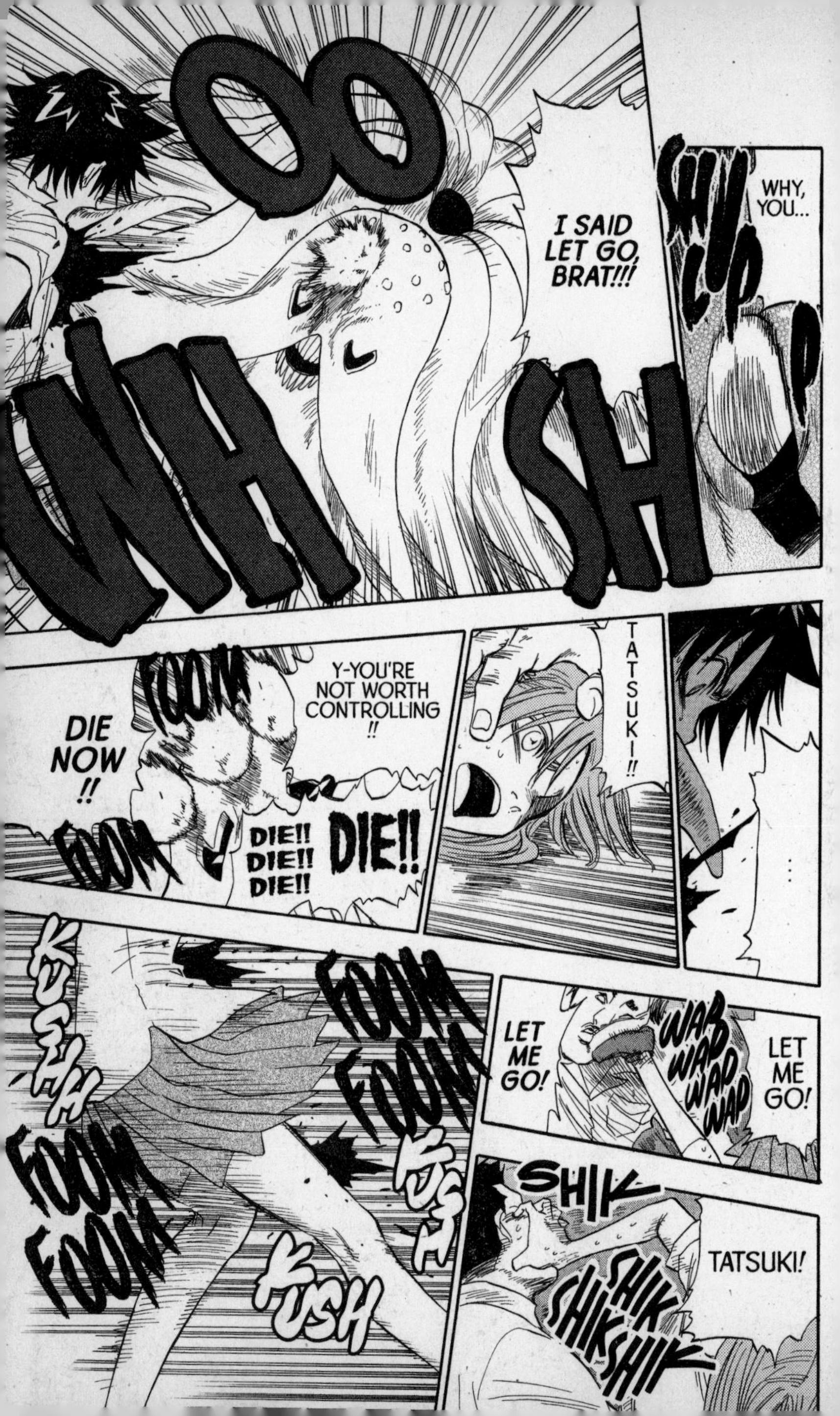
WHY, YOU...
I SAID LET GO, BRAT!!!
...
TATSUKI!!
Y-YOU'RE NOT WORTH CONTROLLING!!
DIE NOW!!
FOOM
FOOM
DIE!!
DIE!! DIE!! DIE!!
LET ME GO!
WAP WAP WAP WAP
LET ME GO!
SHIK
TATSUKI!
SHIK SHIKSHIK
FOOM FOOM
FOOM FOOM

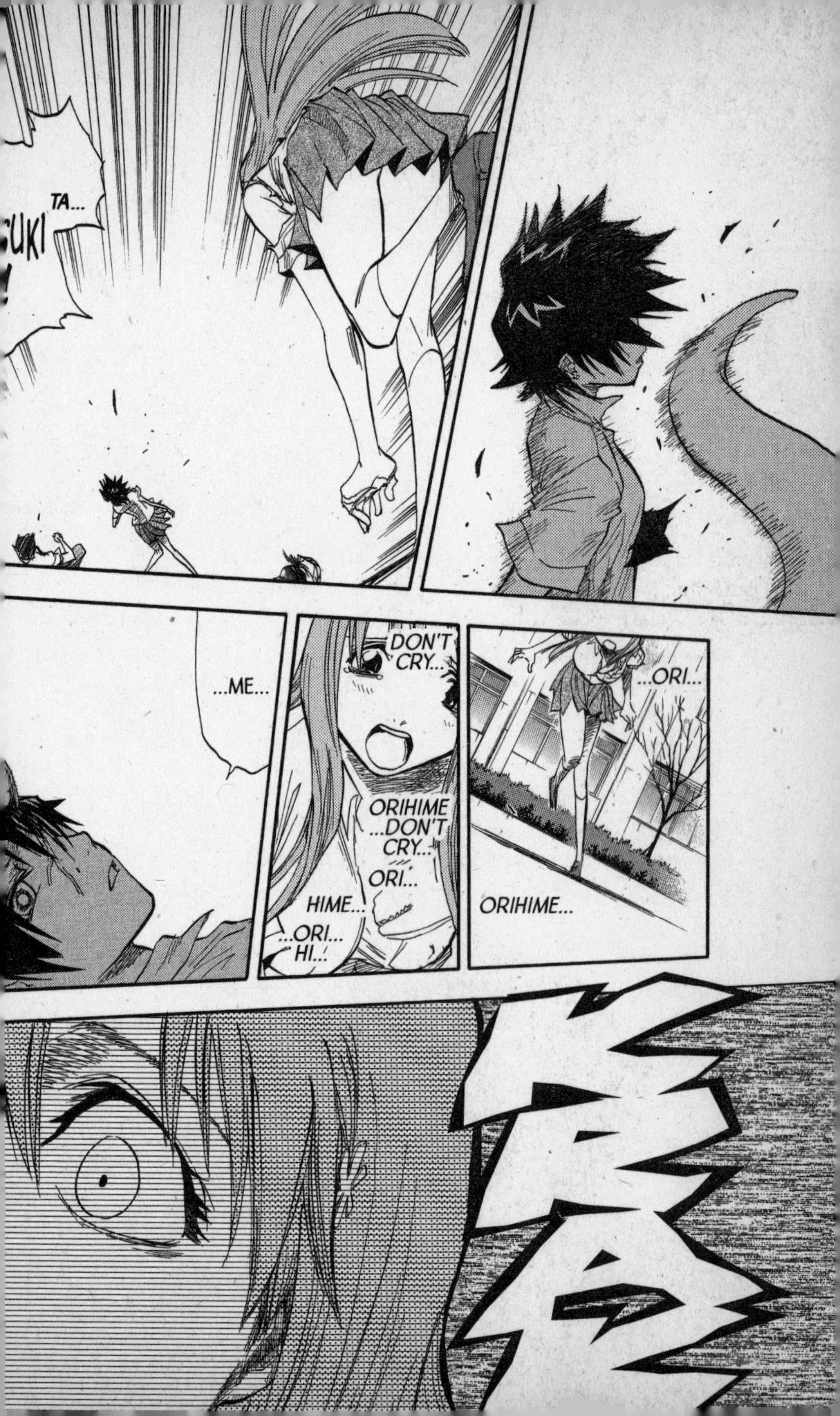
TA...
...UKI
...ORI...
ORIHIME...
DON'T CRY...
ORIHIME ...DON'T CRY...
ORI...
HIME...
...ORI... HI...!
...ME...

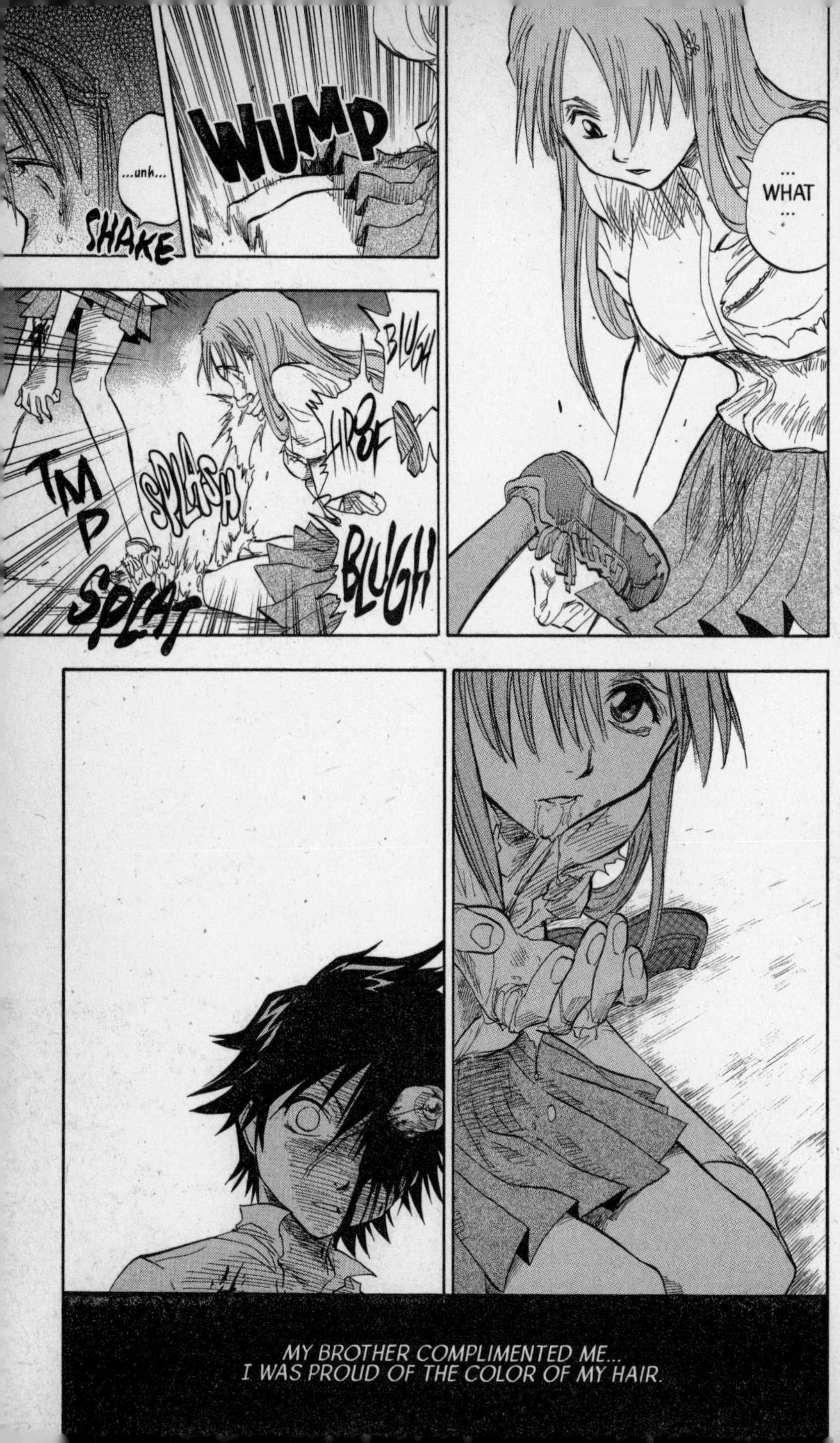
... WHAT ...
WUMP
...unh...
SHAKE
BLUGH
HRBOF
BLUGH
SPLASH
TMP
SPLAT
MY BROTHER COMPLIMENTED ME...
I WAS PROUD OF THE COLOR OF MY HAIR.

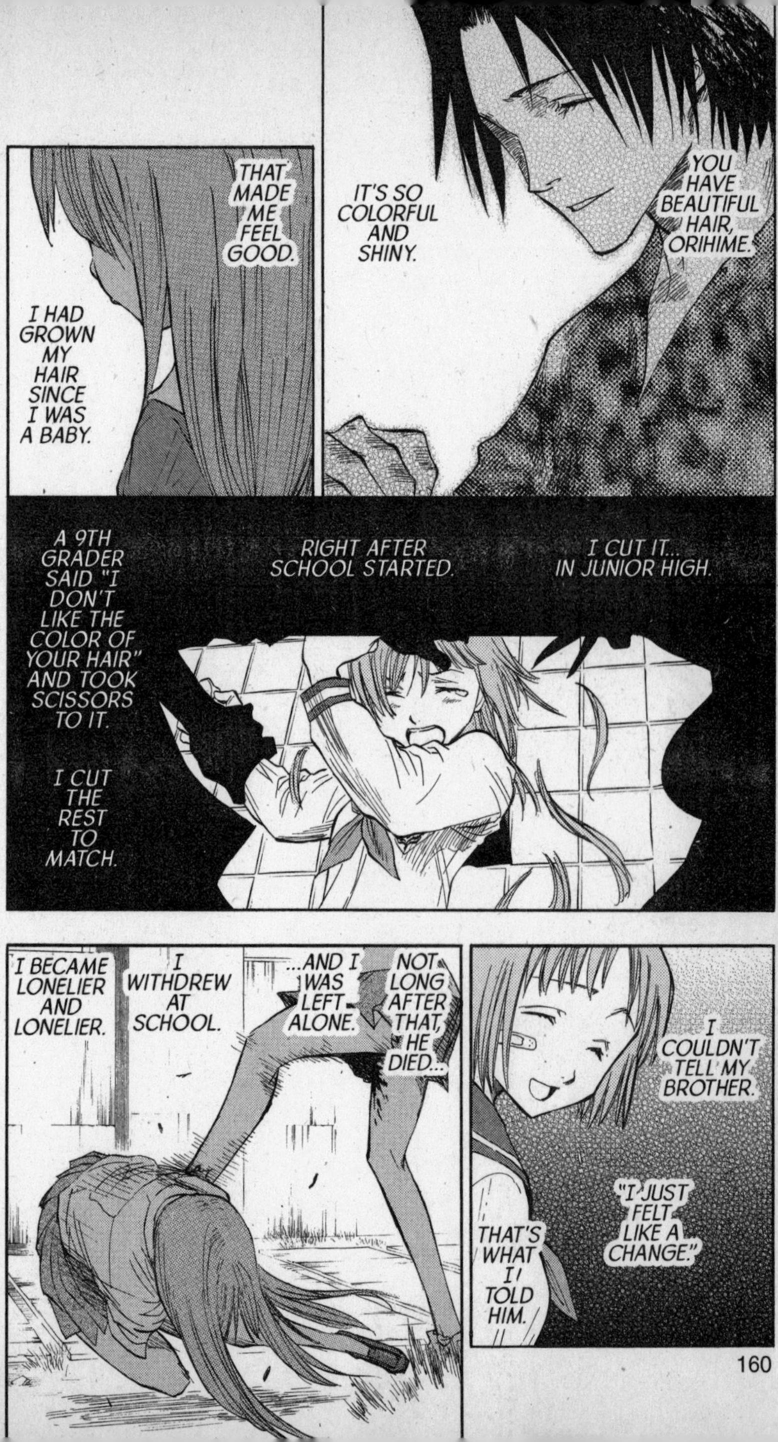
YOU HAVE BEAUTIFUL HAIR, ORIHIME.
IT'S SO COLORFUL AND SHINY.
THAT MADE ME FEEL GOOD.
I HAD GROWN MY HAIR SINCE I WAS A BABY.
I CUT IT... IN JUNIOR HIGH.
RIGHT AFTER SCHOOL STARTED.
A 9TH GRADER SAID "I DON'T LIKE THE COLOR OF YOUR HAIR" AND TOOK SCISSORS TO IT.
I CUT THE REST TO MATCH.
I COULDN'T TELL MY BROTHER.
"I JUST FELT LIKE A CHANGE."
THAT'S WHAT I TOLD HIM.
NOT LONG AFTER THAT, HE DIED...
...AND I WAS LEFT ALONE.
I WITHDREW AT SCHOOL.
I BECAME LONELIER AND LONELIER.

READ THIS WAY

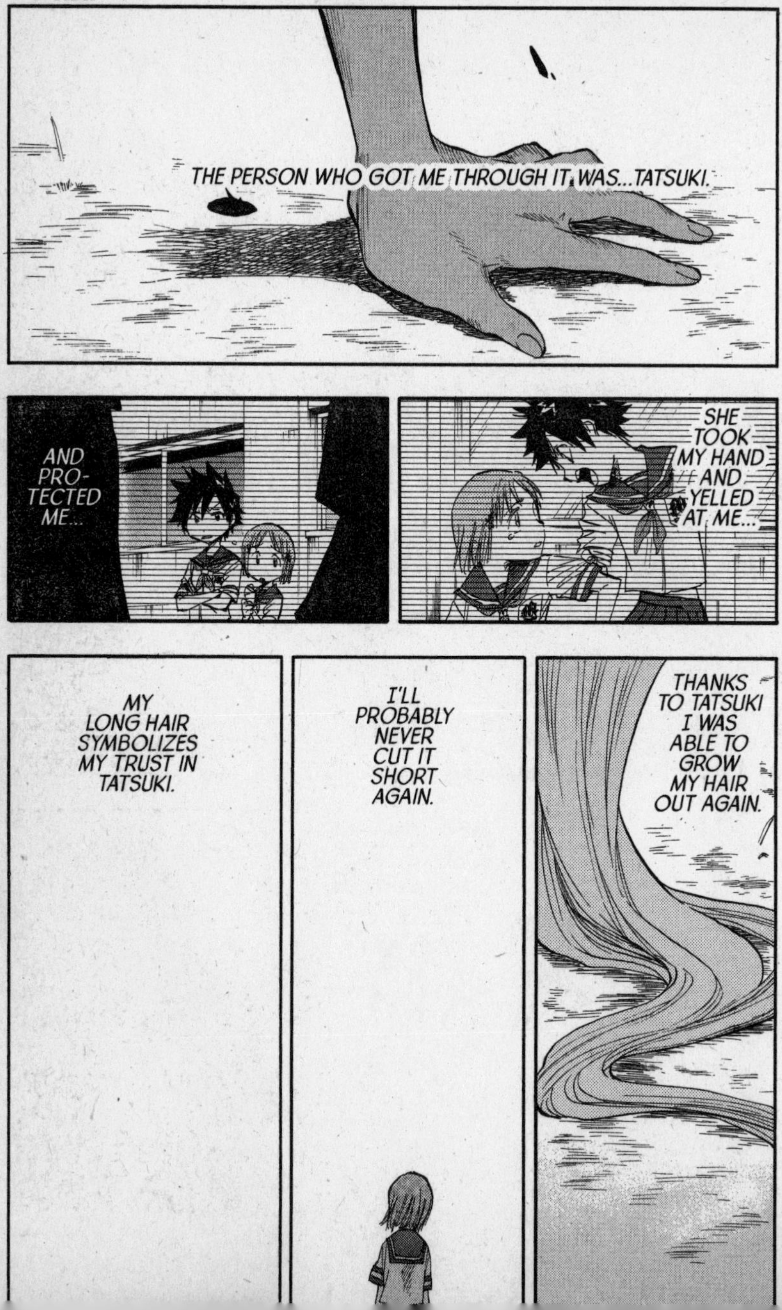
THE PERSON WHO GOT ME THROUGH IT WAS...TATSUKI.
SHE TOOK MY HAND AND YELLED AT ME...
AND PROTECTED ME...
THANKS TO TATSUKI I WAS ABLE TO GROW MY HAIR OUT AGAIN.
I'LL PROBABLY NEVER CUT IT SHORT AGAIN.
MY LONG HAIR SYMBOLIZES MY TRUST IN TATSUKI.

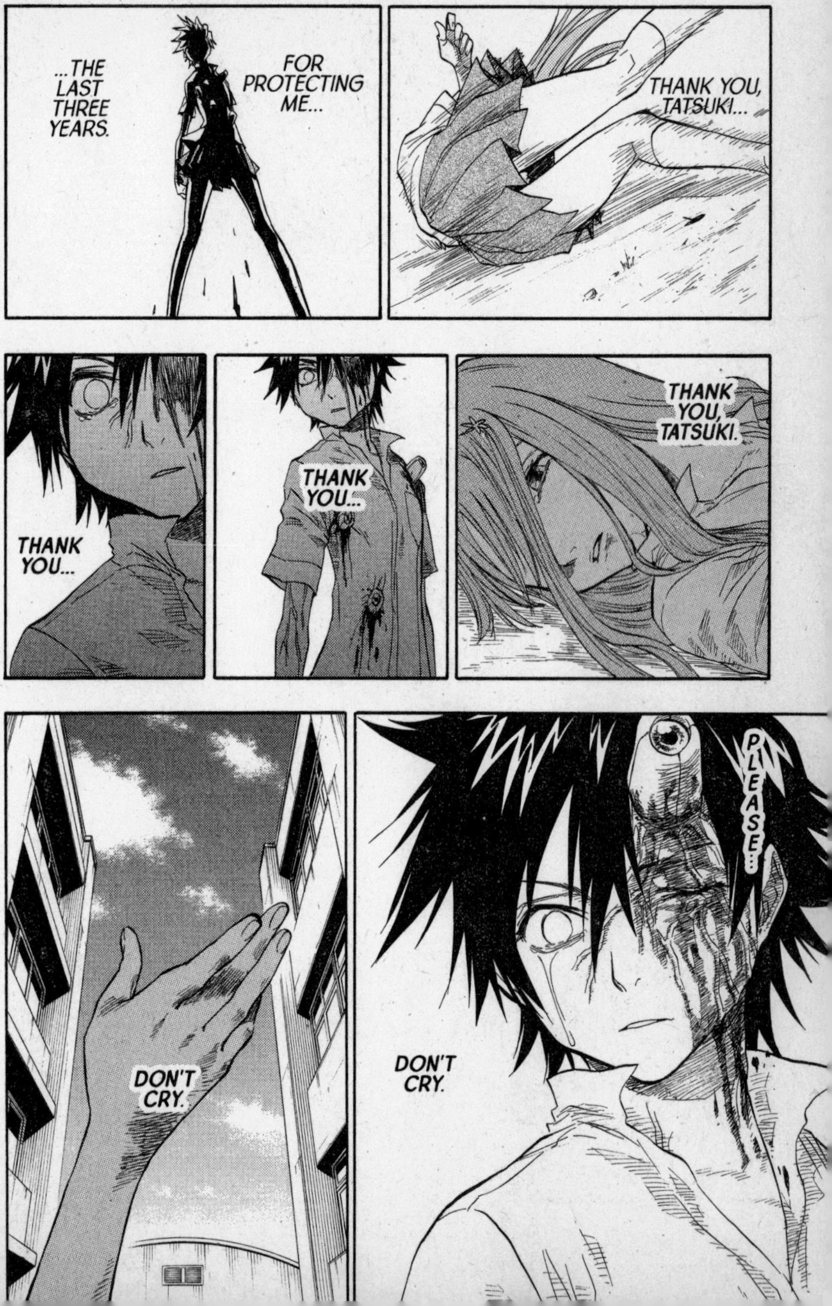
THANK YOU, TATSUKI...
FOR PROTECTING ME...
...THE LAST THREE YEARS.
THANK YOU, TATSUKI.
THANK YOU...
THANK YOU...
PLEASE...
DON'T CRY.
DON'T CRY.

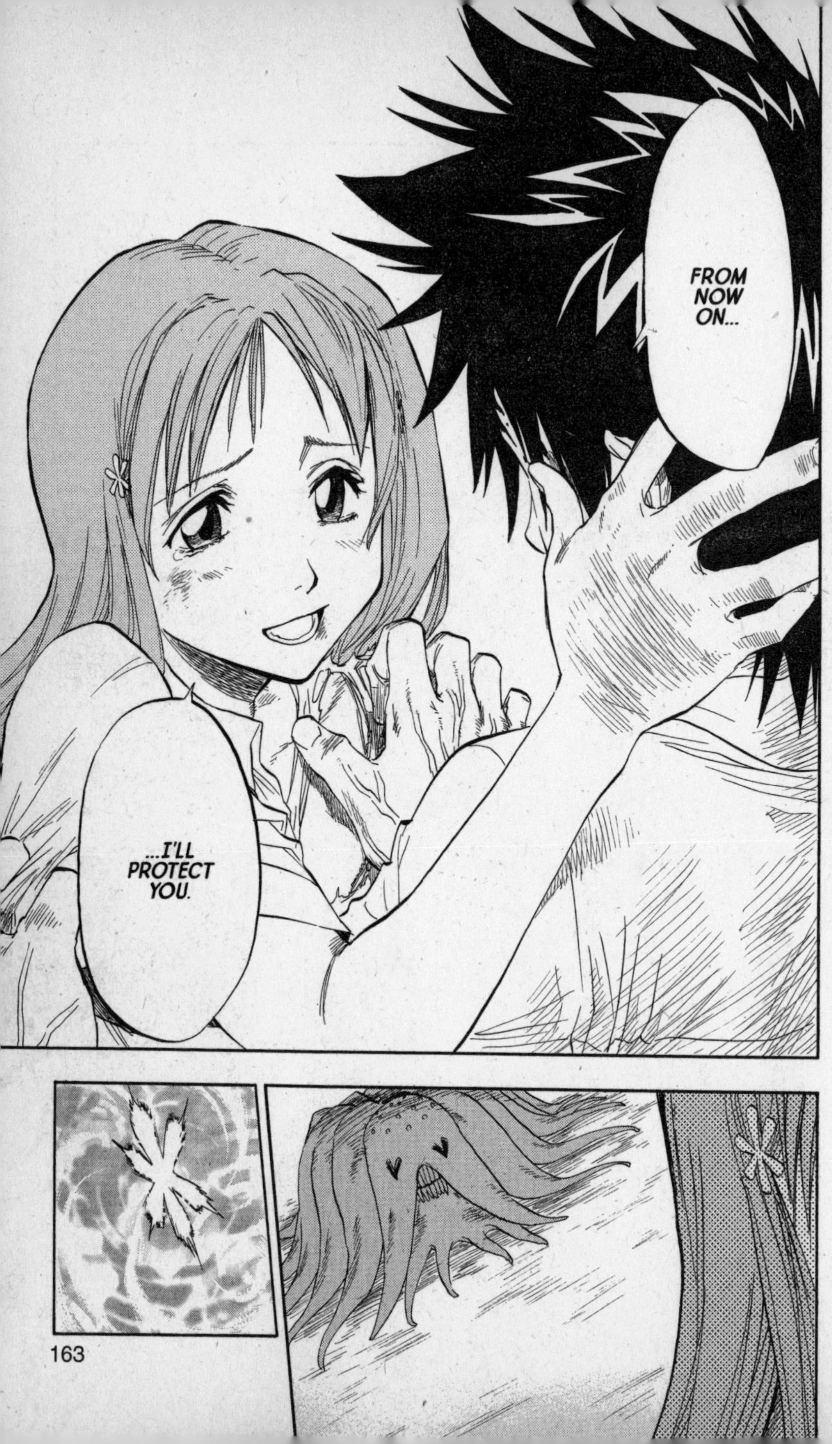
FROM NOW ON...
...I'LL PROTECT YOU.

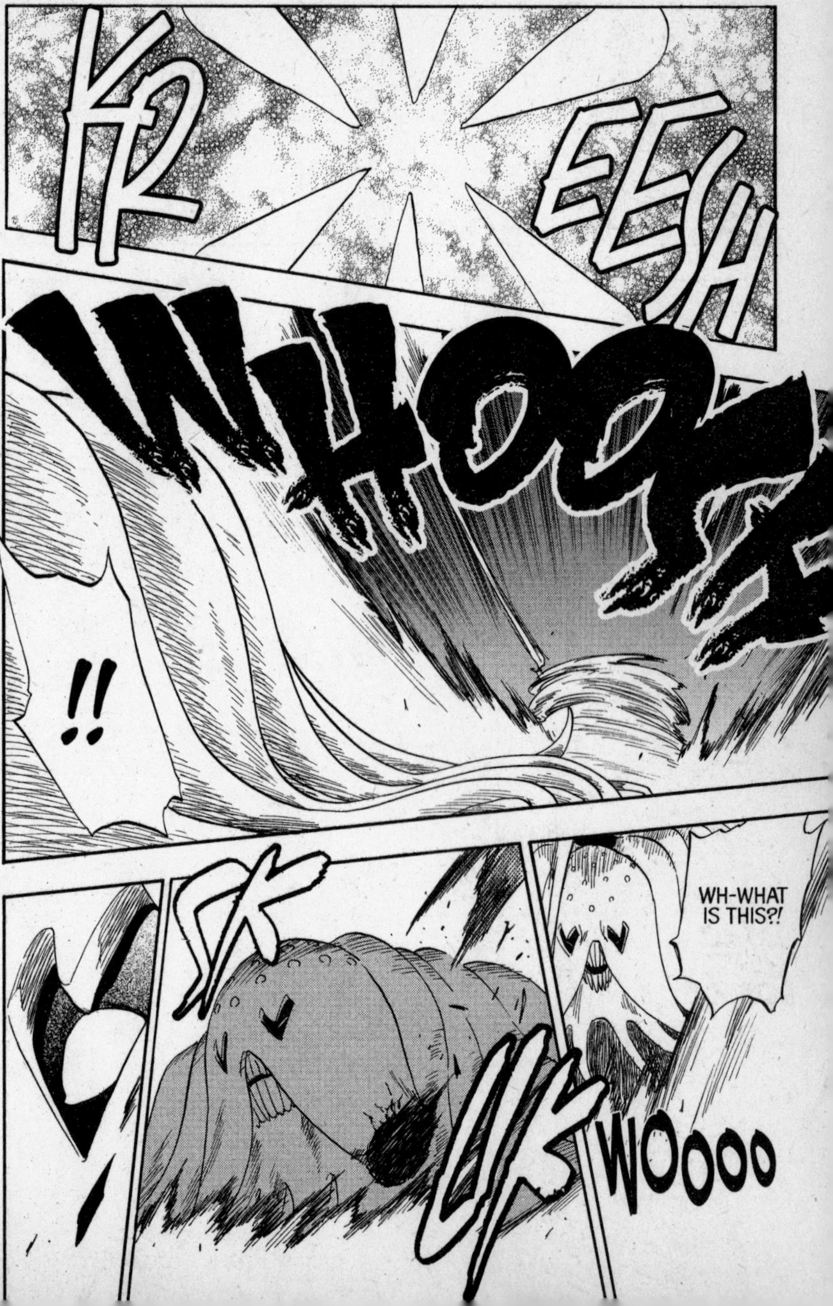
KR EESH
WHOOS
!!
WH-WHAT IS THIS?!
WOOOO

READ THIS WAY

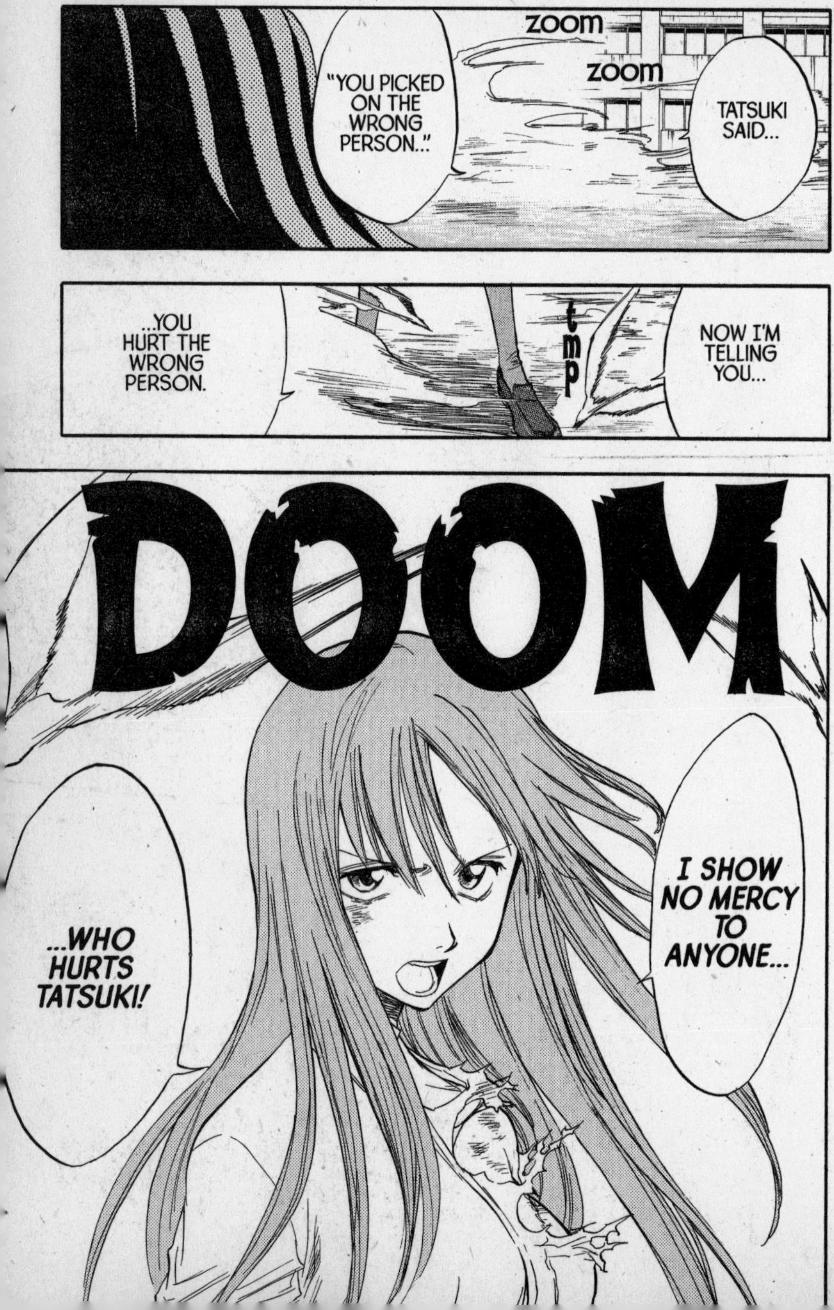

TATSUKI SAID...
ZOOM
ZOOM
"YOU PICKED ON THE WRONG PERSON.."
NOW I'M TELLING YOU...
tmp
...YOU HURT THE WRONG PERSON.
DOOM
I SHOW NO MERCY TO ANYONE...
...WHO HURTS TATSUKI!

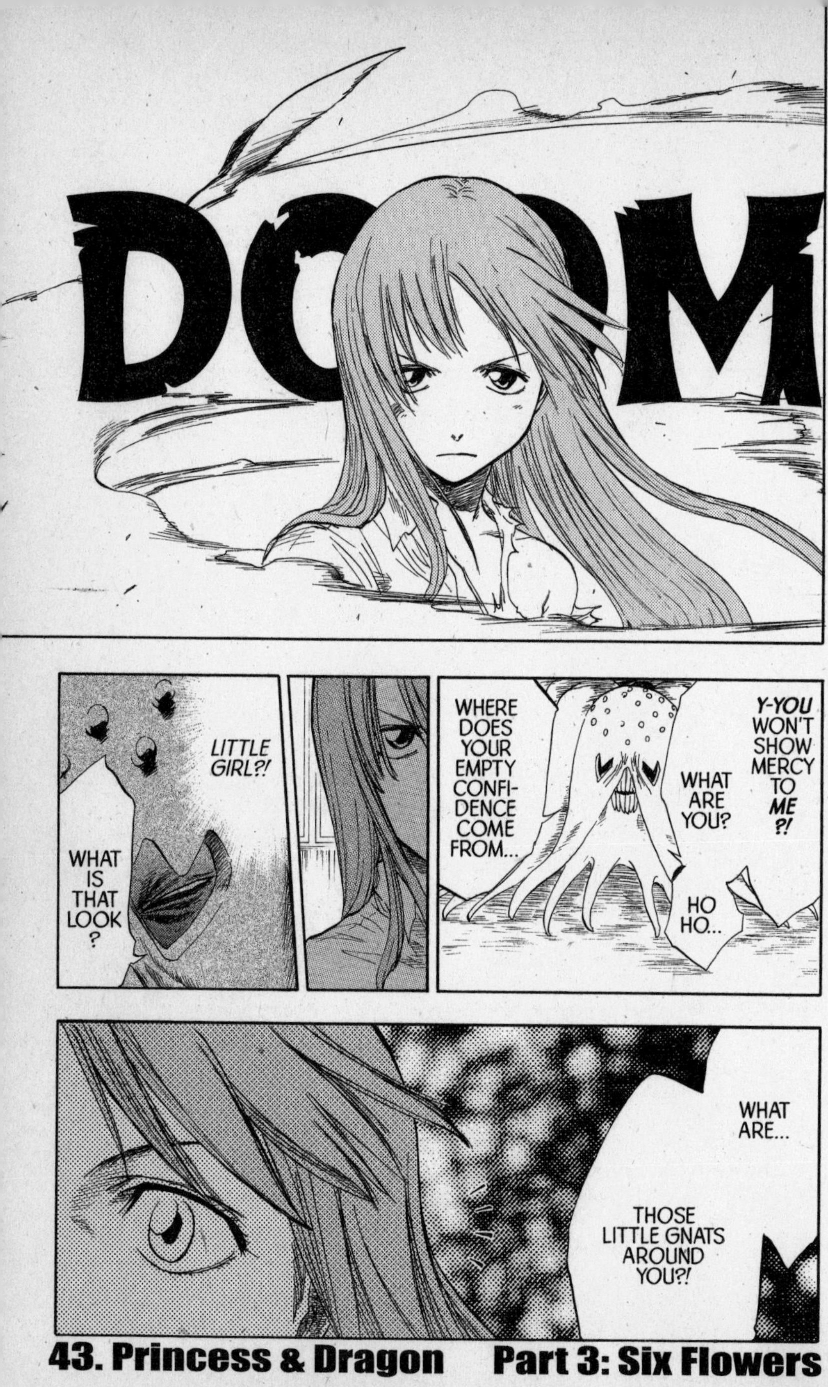
DOOM
Y-YOU WON'T SHOW MERCY TO ME?!
HO HO...
WHAT ARE YOU?
WHERE DOES YOUR EMPTY CONFIDENCE COME FROM...
LITTLE GIRL?!
WHAT IS THAT LOOK?
WHAT ARE...
THOSE LITTLE GNATS AROUND YOU?!

43. Princess & Dragon Part 3: Six Flowers

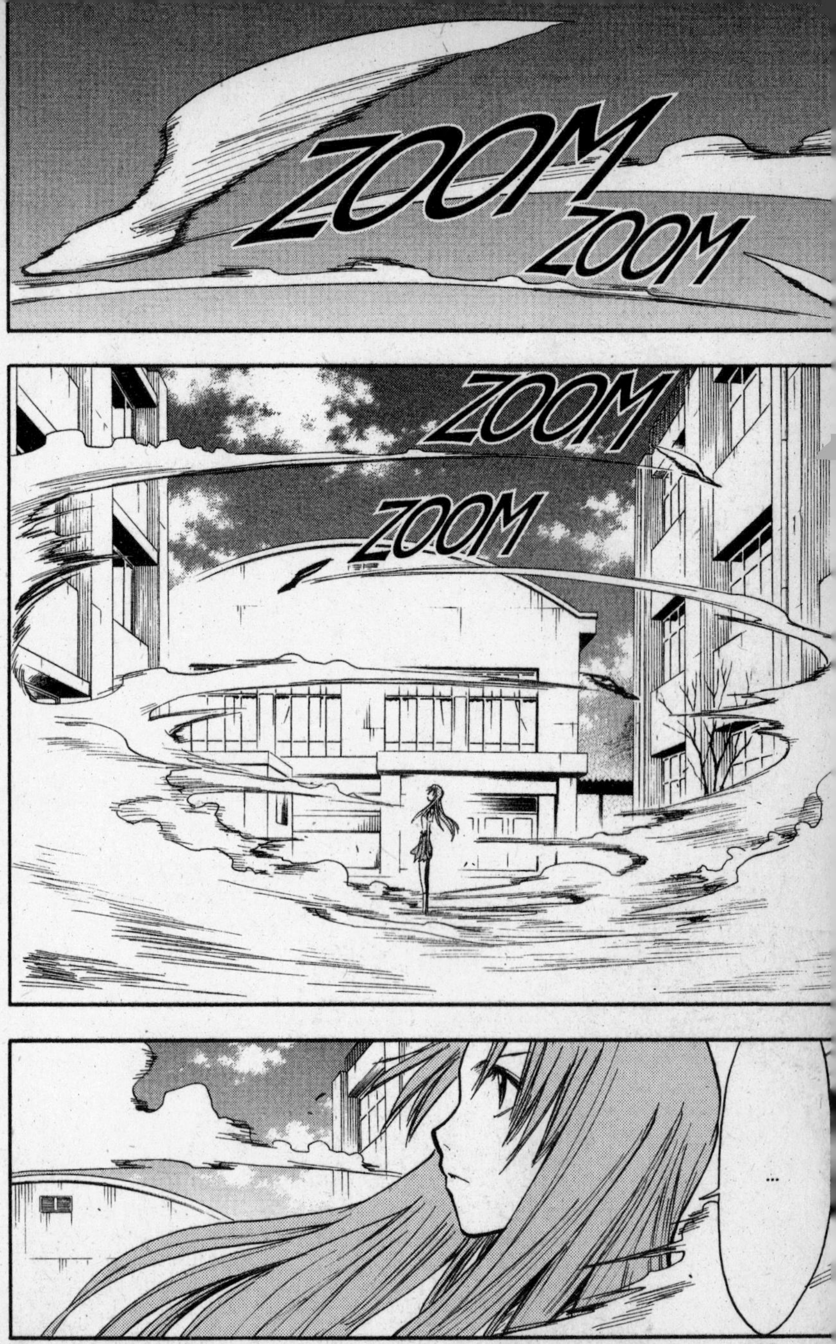
ZOOM
ZOOM
ZOOM
ZOOM
...

READ THIS WAY

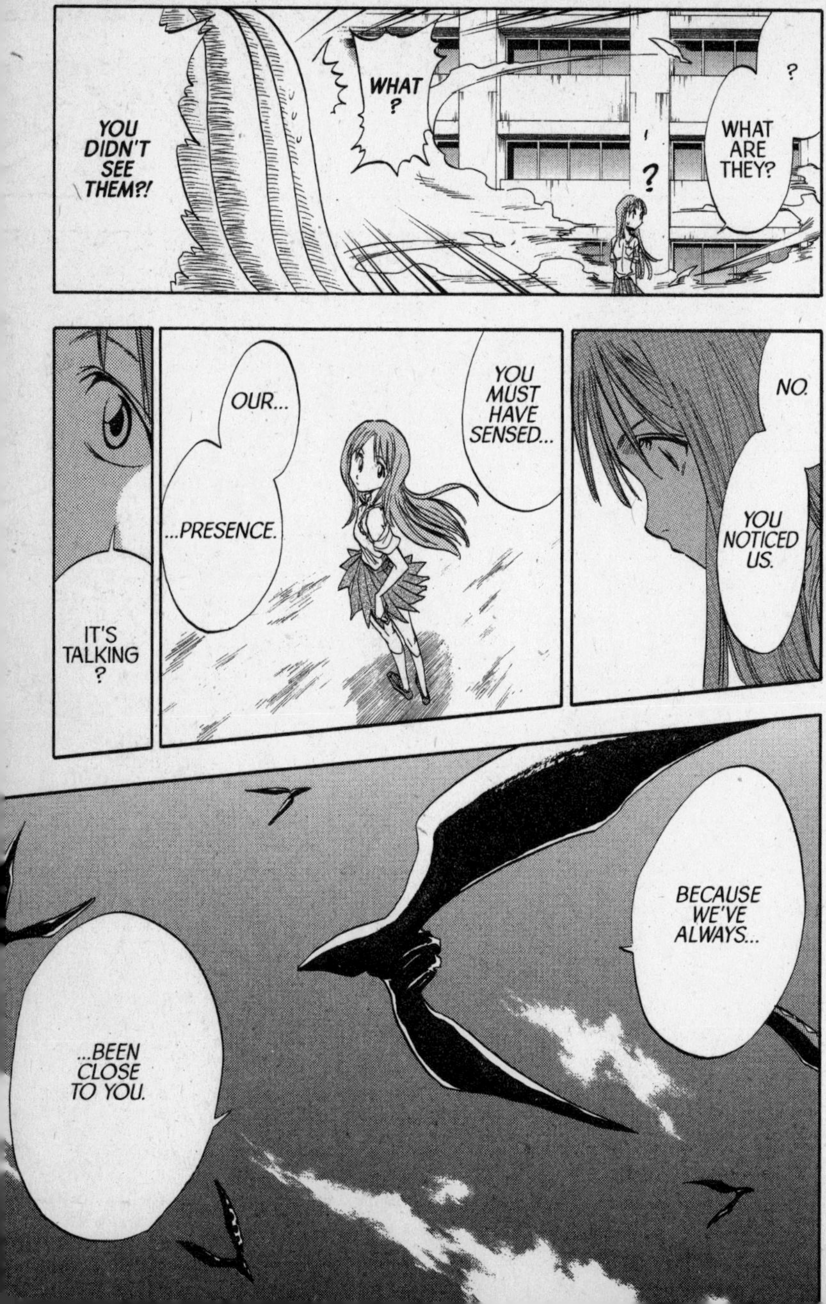
?
WHAT ARE THEY?
?
WHAT ?
YOU DIDN'T SEE THEM?!
NO.
YOU NOTICED US.
YOU MUST HAVE SENSED...
OUR...
...PRESENCE.
IT'S TALKING ?
BECAUSE WE'VE ALWAYS...
...BEEN CLOSE TO YOU.

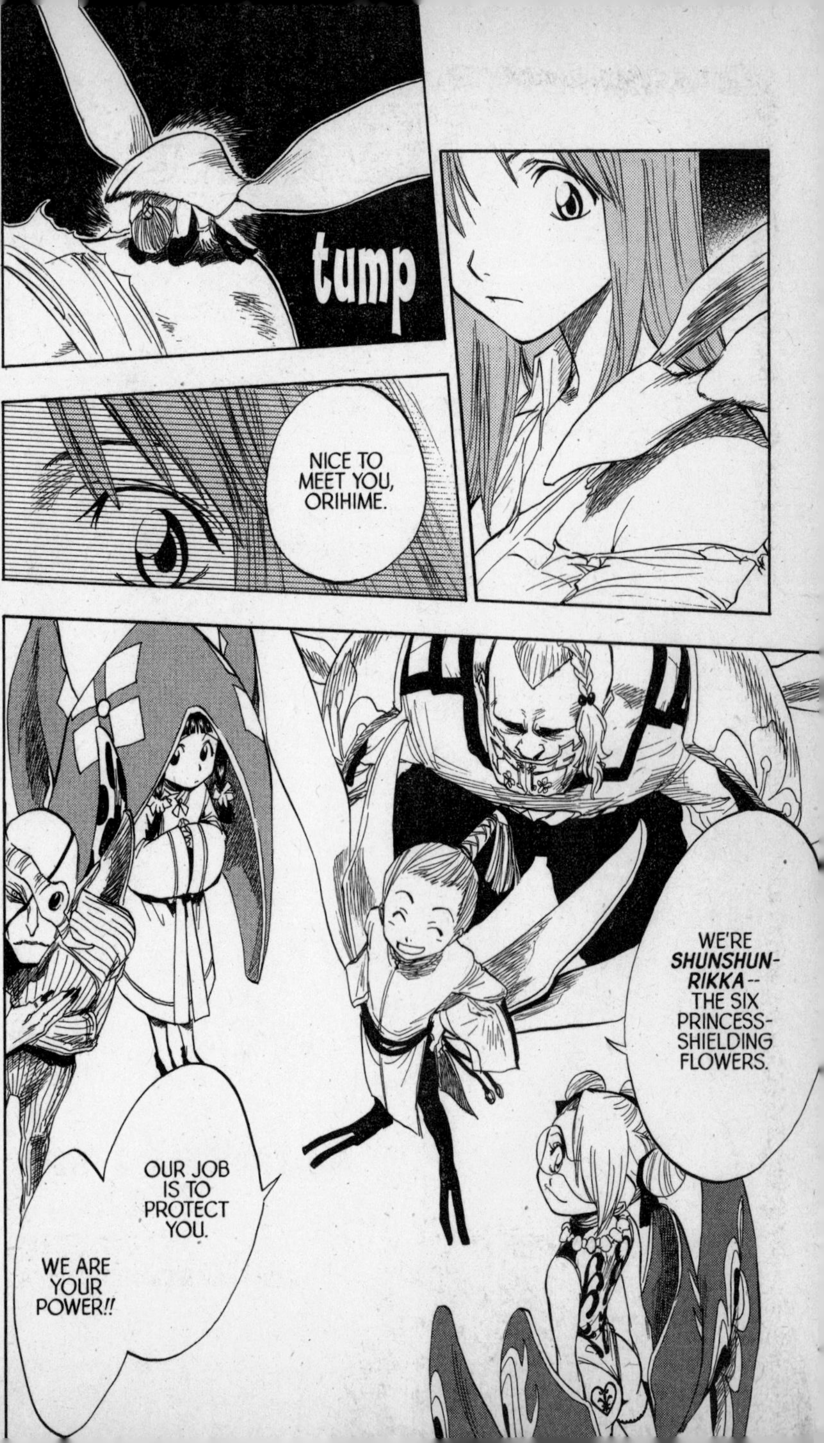
tump
NICE TO MEET YOU, ORIHIME.
WE'RE ***SHUNSHUN-RIKKA***-- THE SIX PRINCESS-SHIELDING FLOWERS.
OUR JOB IS TO PROTECT YOU.
WE ARE YOUR POWER!!

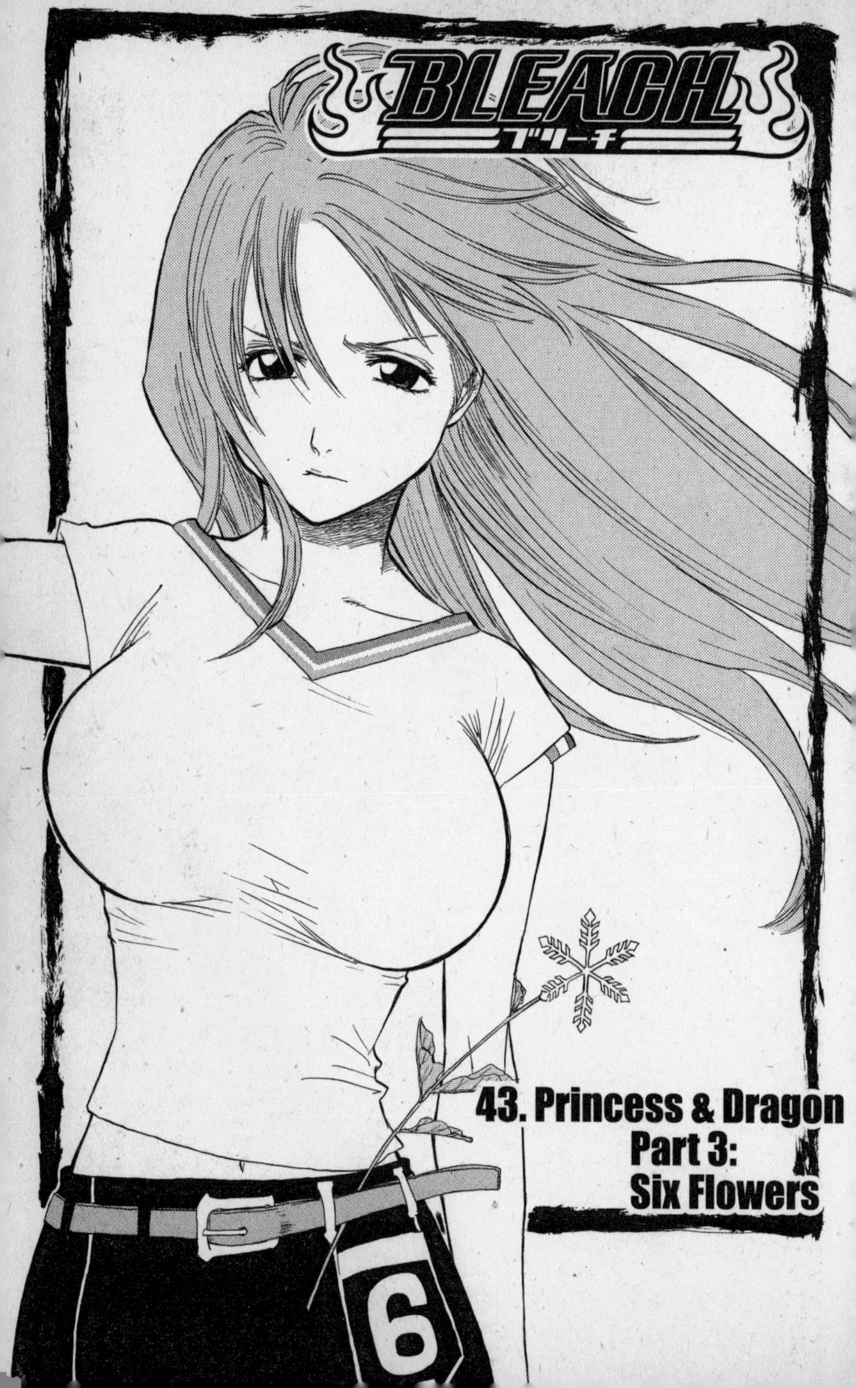
BLEACH
ブリーチ
43. Princess & Dragon
Part 3:
Six Flowers
6

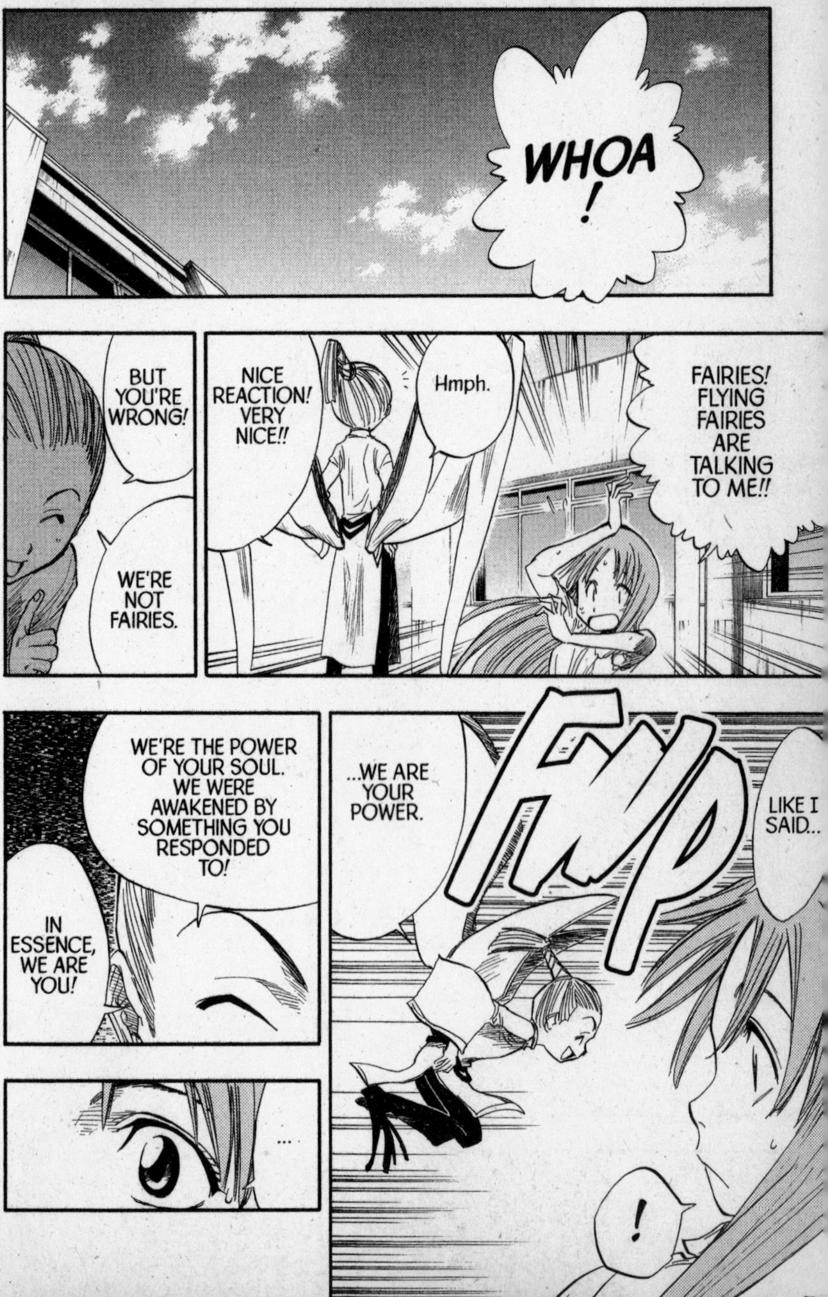
WHOA!
FAIRIES! FLYING FAIRIES ARE TALKING TO ME!!
Hmph.
NICE REACTION! VERY NICE!!
BUT YOU'RE WRONG!
WE'RE NOT FAIRIES.
FWP
LIKE I SAID...
...WE ARE YOUR POWER.
!
WE'RE THE POWER OF YOUR SOUL. WE WERE AWAKENED BY SOMETHING YOU RESPONDED TO!
IN ESSENCE, WE ARE YOU!
...

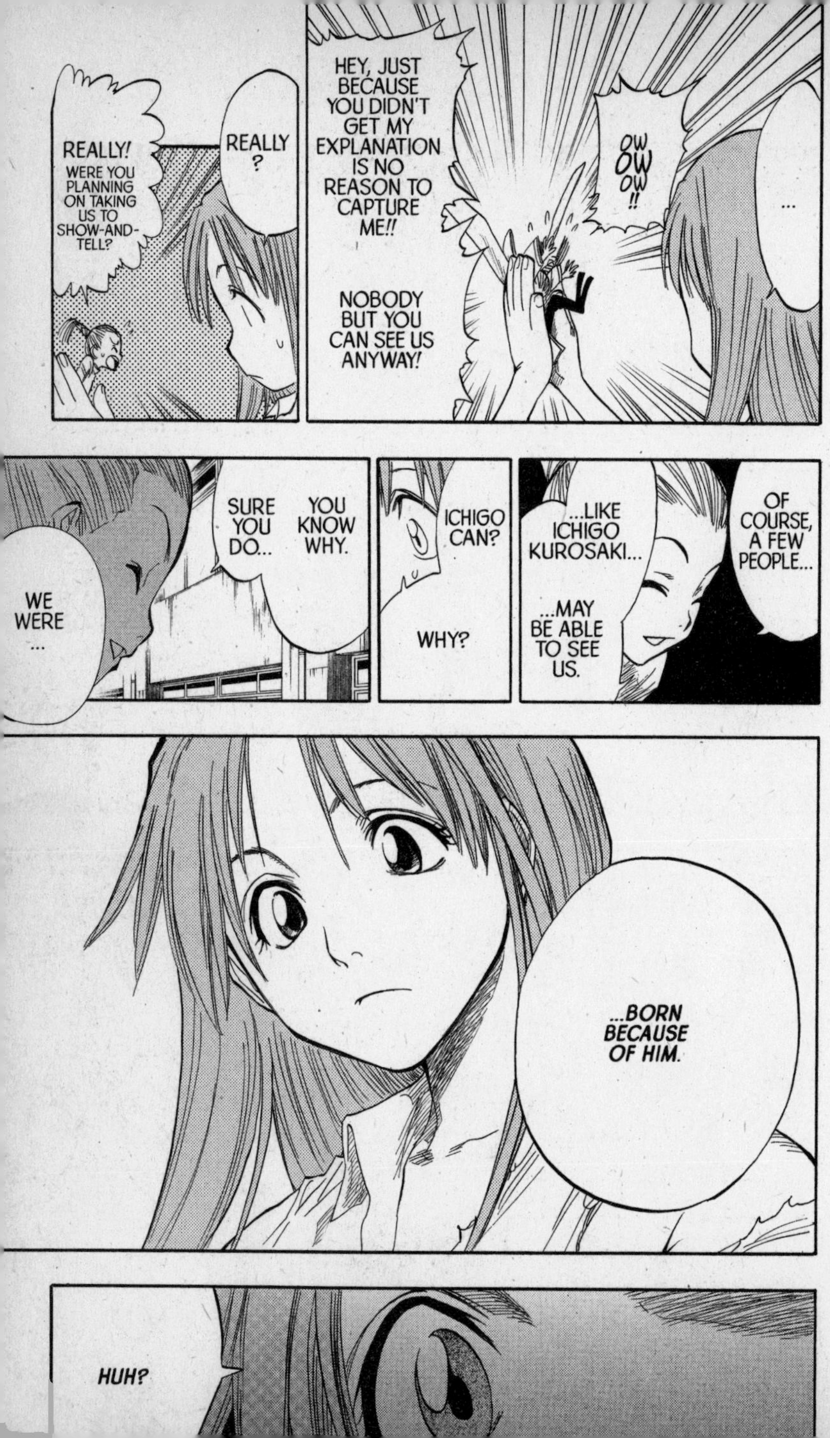
...
OW OW OW!!
HEY, JUST BECAUSE YOU DIDN'T GET MY EXPLANATION IS NO REASON TO CAPTURE ME!!
NOBODY BUT YOU CAN SEE US ANYWAY!
REALLY?
REALLY! WERE YOU PLANNING ON TAKING US TO SHOW-AND-TELL?
OF COURSE, A FEW PEOPLE...
...LIKE ICHIGO KUROSAKI...
...MAY BE ABLE TO SEE US.
ICHIGO CAN?
WHY?
YOU KNOW WHY.
SURE YOU DO...
WE WERE ...
...BORN BECAUSE OF HIM.
HUH?

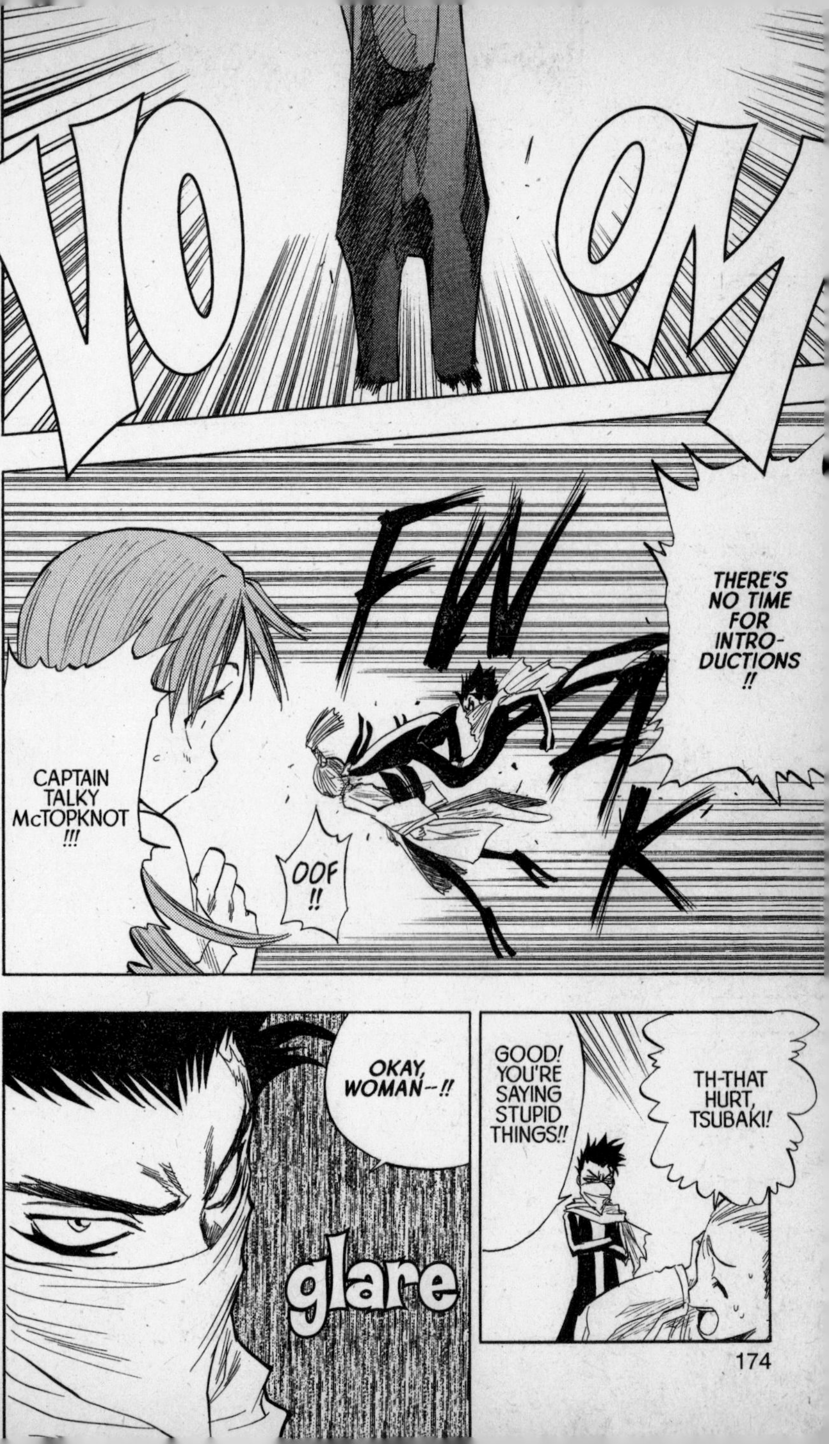
VO OM
THERE'S NO TIME FOR INTRO-DUCTIONS!!
FWAK
OOF!!
CAPTAIN TALKY McTOPKNOT!!!
TH-THAT HURT, TSUBAKI!
GOOD! YOU'RE SAYING STUPID THINGS!!
OKAY, WOMAN--!!
glare

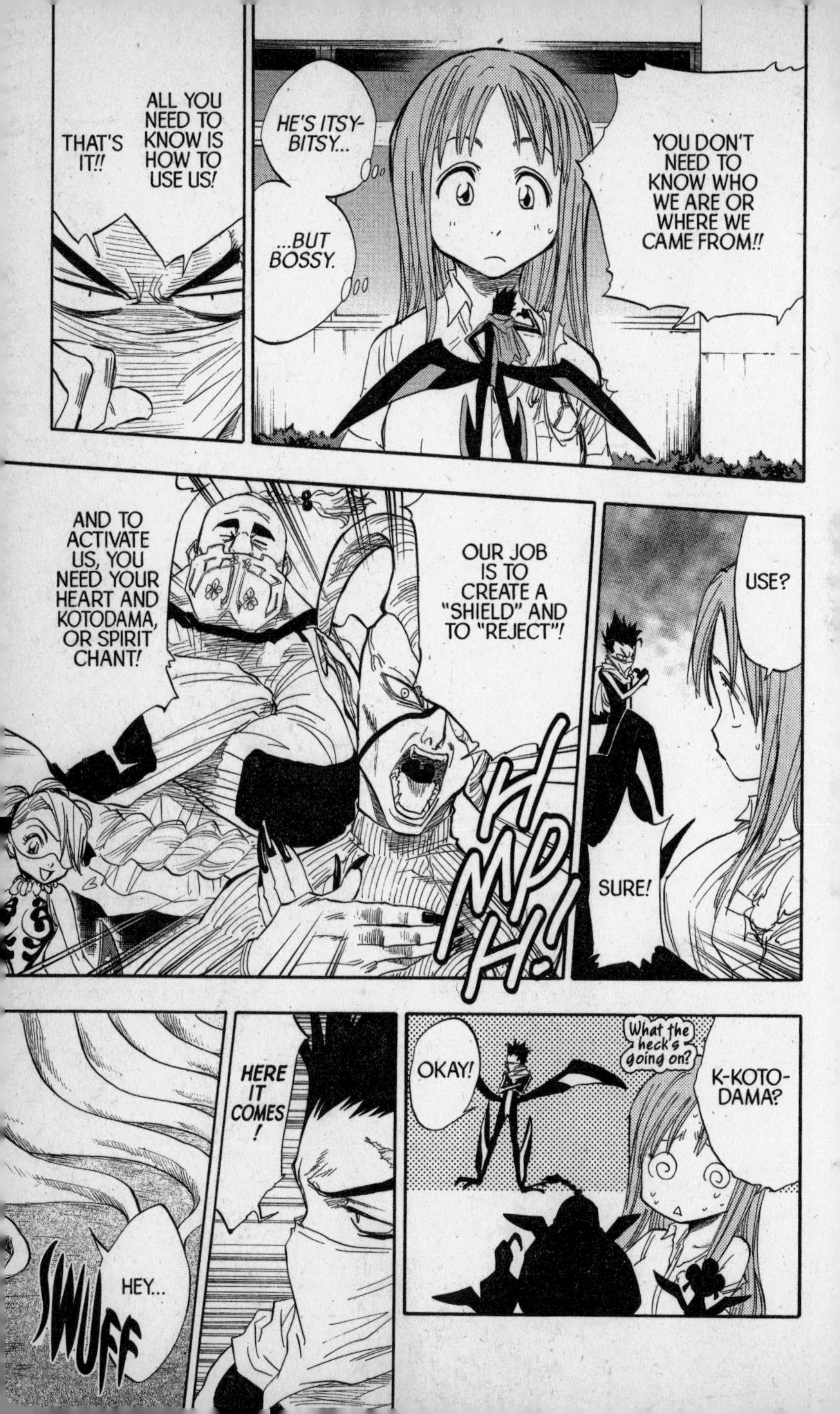
YOU DON'T NEED TO KNOW WHO WE ARE OR WHERE WE CAME FROM!!
HE'S ITSY-BITSY...
...BUT BOSSY.
ALL YOU NEED TO KNOW IS HOW TO USE US!
THAT'S IT!!
USE?
SURE!
OUR JOB IS TO CREATE A "SHIELD" AND TO "REJECT"!
AND TO ACTIVATE US, YOU NEED YOUR HEART AND KOTODAMA, OR SPIRIT CHANT!
HMPH!!
K-KOTO-DAMA?
What the heck's going on?
OKAY!
HERE IT COMES!
HEY...
SWUFF

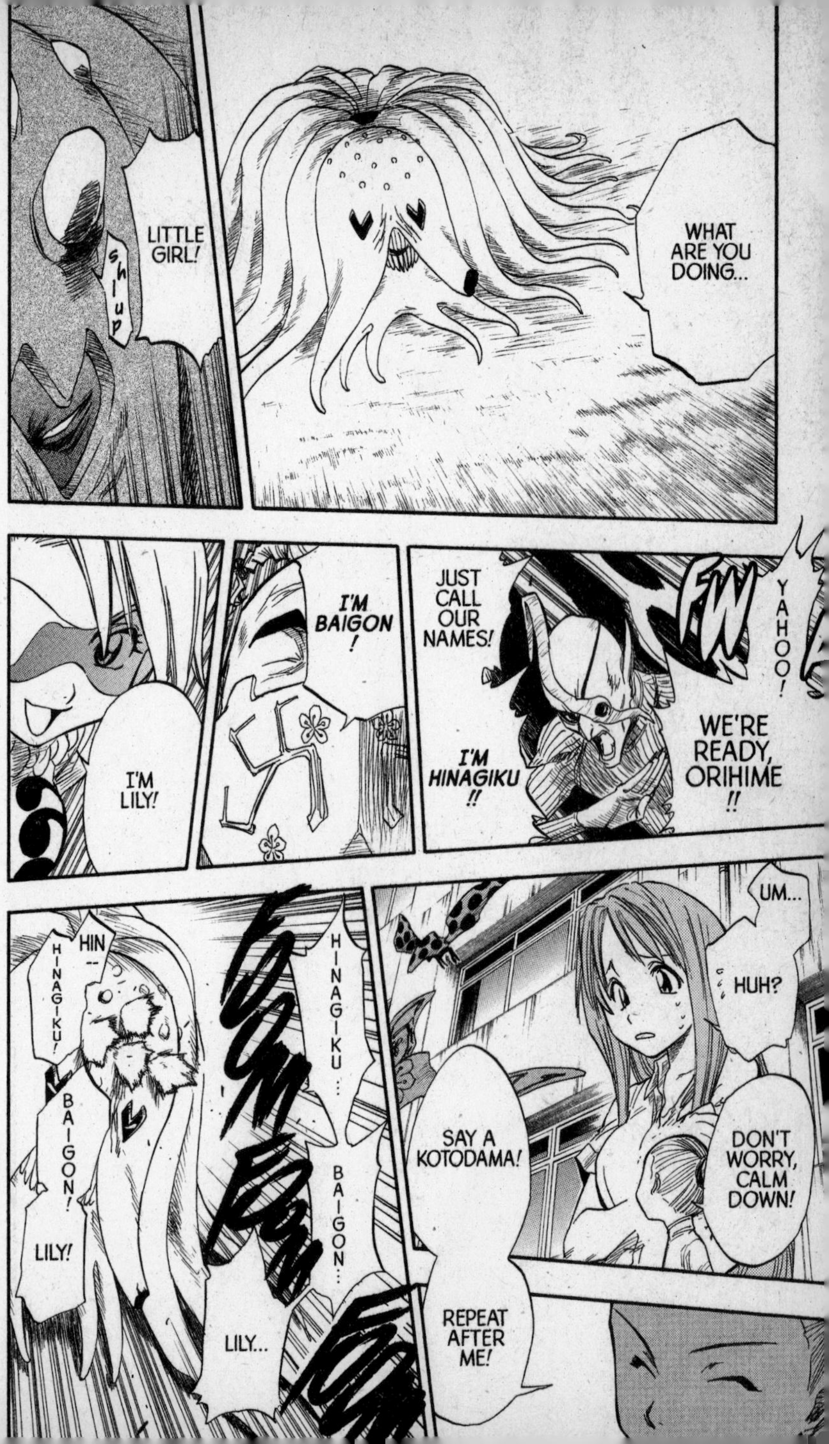
WHAT ARE YOU DOING...
LITTLE GIRL!
shlup
YAHOO!
FW
WE'RE READY, ORIHIME!!
I'M HINAGIKU!!
JUST CALL OUR NAMES!
I'M BAIGON!
I'M LILY!
UM...
HUH?
DON'T WORRY, CALM DOWN!
SAY A KOTODAMA!
REPEAT AFTER ME!
HINAGIKU...
BAIGON...
LILY...
HIN--
HINAGIKU!
BAIGON!
LILY!

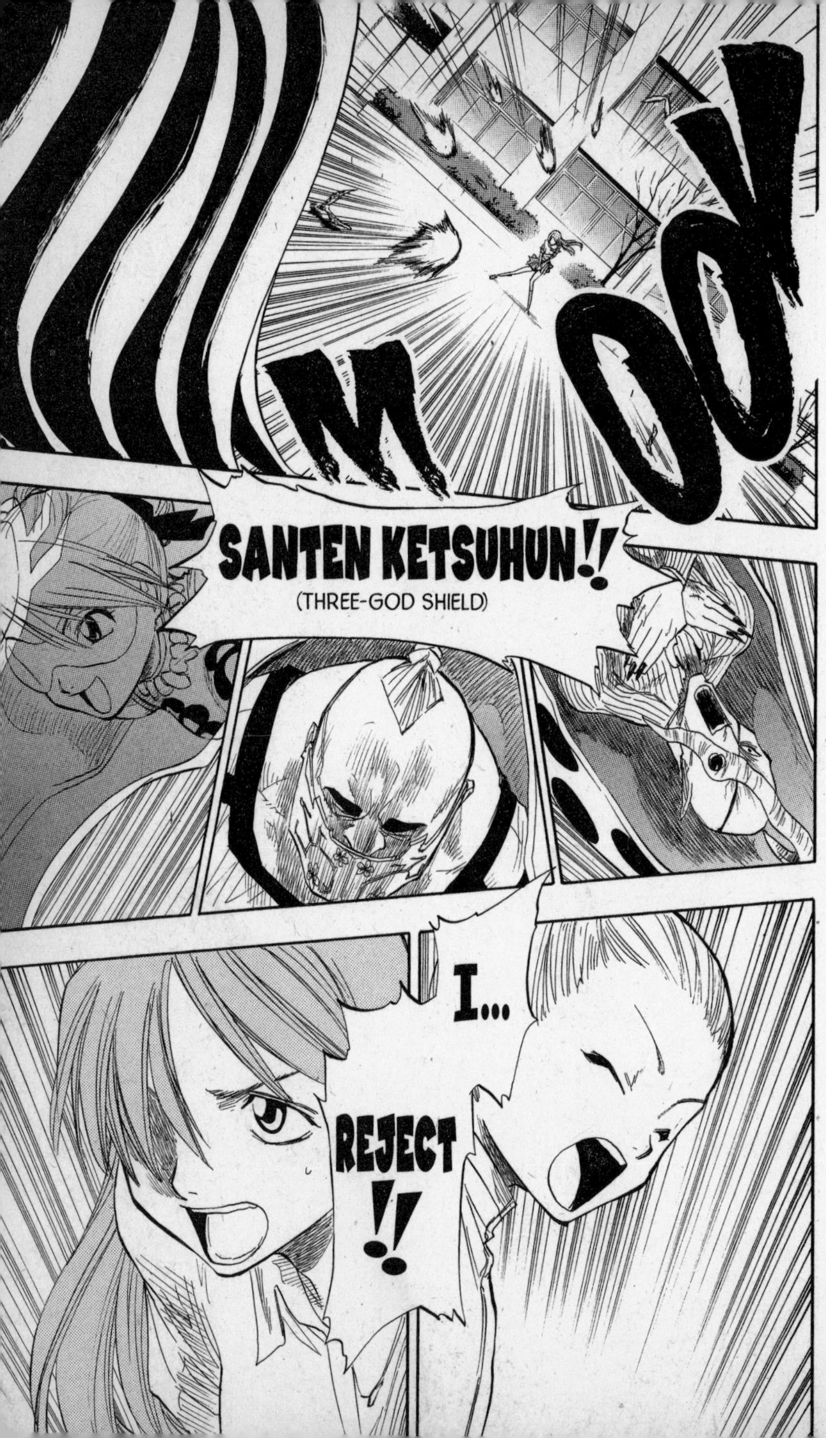
SANTEN KETSUHUN!!
(THREE-GOD SHIELD)
I...
REJECT
!!

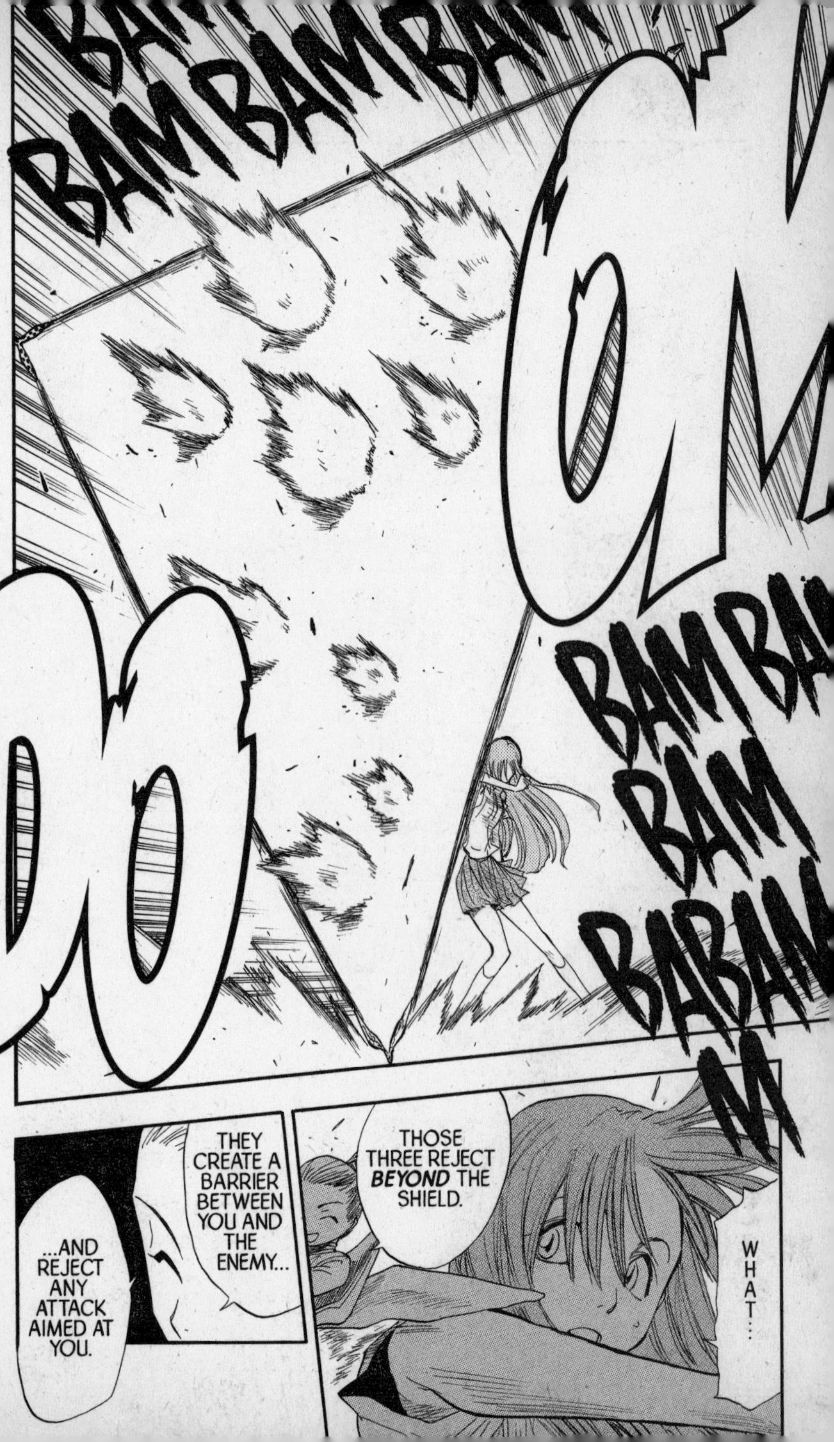
BAMBAMBAM
BAMBAM BAM BABAM
WHAT...
THOSE THREE REJECT *BEYOND* THE SHIELD.
THEY CREATE A BARRIER BETWEEN YOU AND THE ENEMY...
...AND REJECT ANY ATTACK AIMED AT YOU.

READ THIS WAY

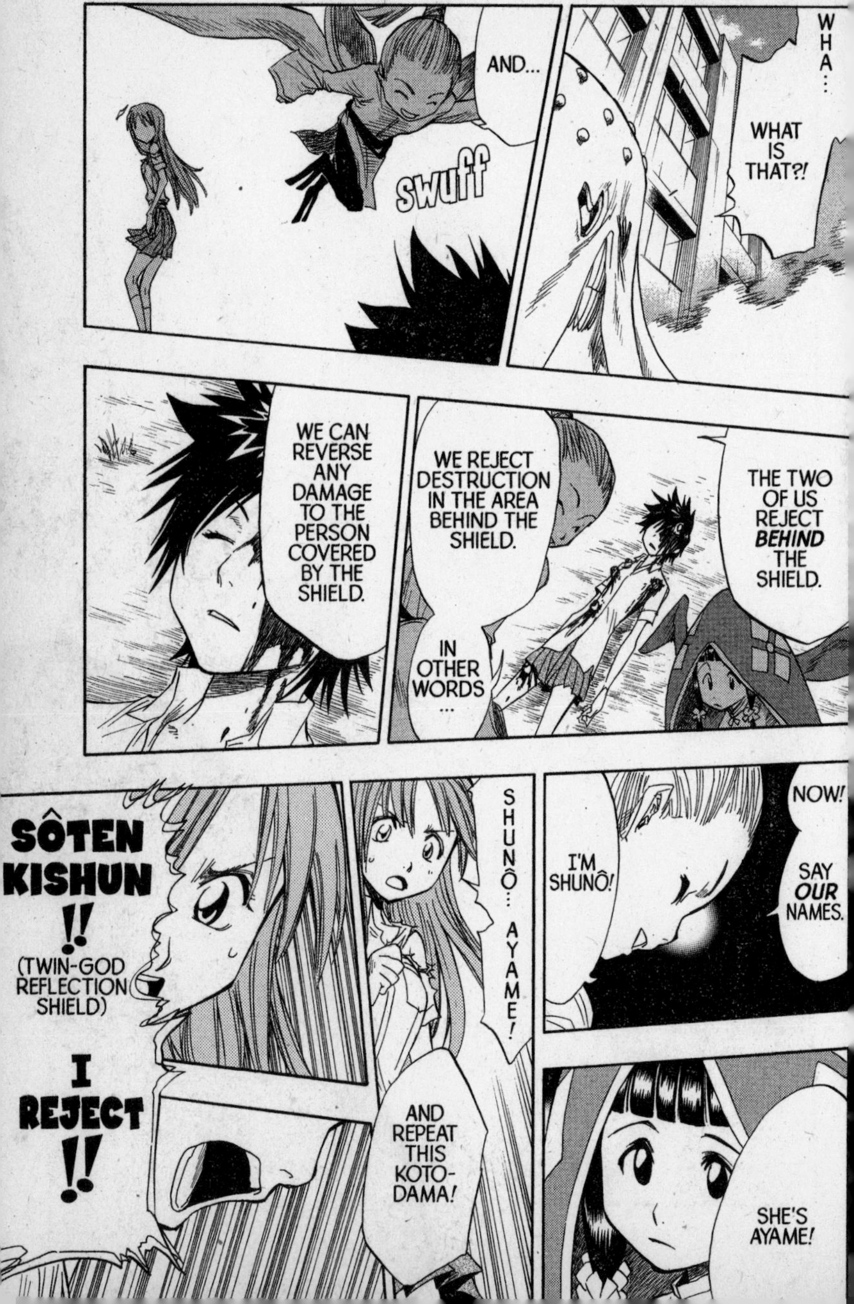
WHA...
WHAT IS THAT?!
AND...
swuff
THE TWO OF US REJECT *BEHIND* THE SHIELD.
WE REJECT DESTRUCTION IN THE AREA BEHIND THE SHIELD.
IN OTHER WORDS...
WE CAN REVERSE ANY DAMAGE TO THE PERSON COVERED BY THE SHIELD.
NOW!
SAY *OUR* NAMES.
I'M SHUNÔ!
SHE'S AYAME!
SHUNÔ... AYAME!
AND REPEAT THIS KOTO-DAMA!
SÔTEN KISHUN!! (TWIN-GOD REFLECTION SHIELD)
I REJECT!!

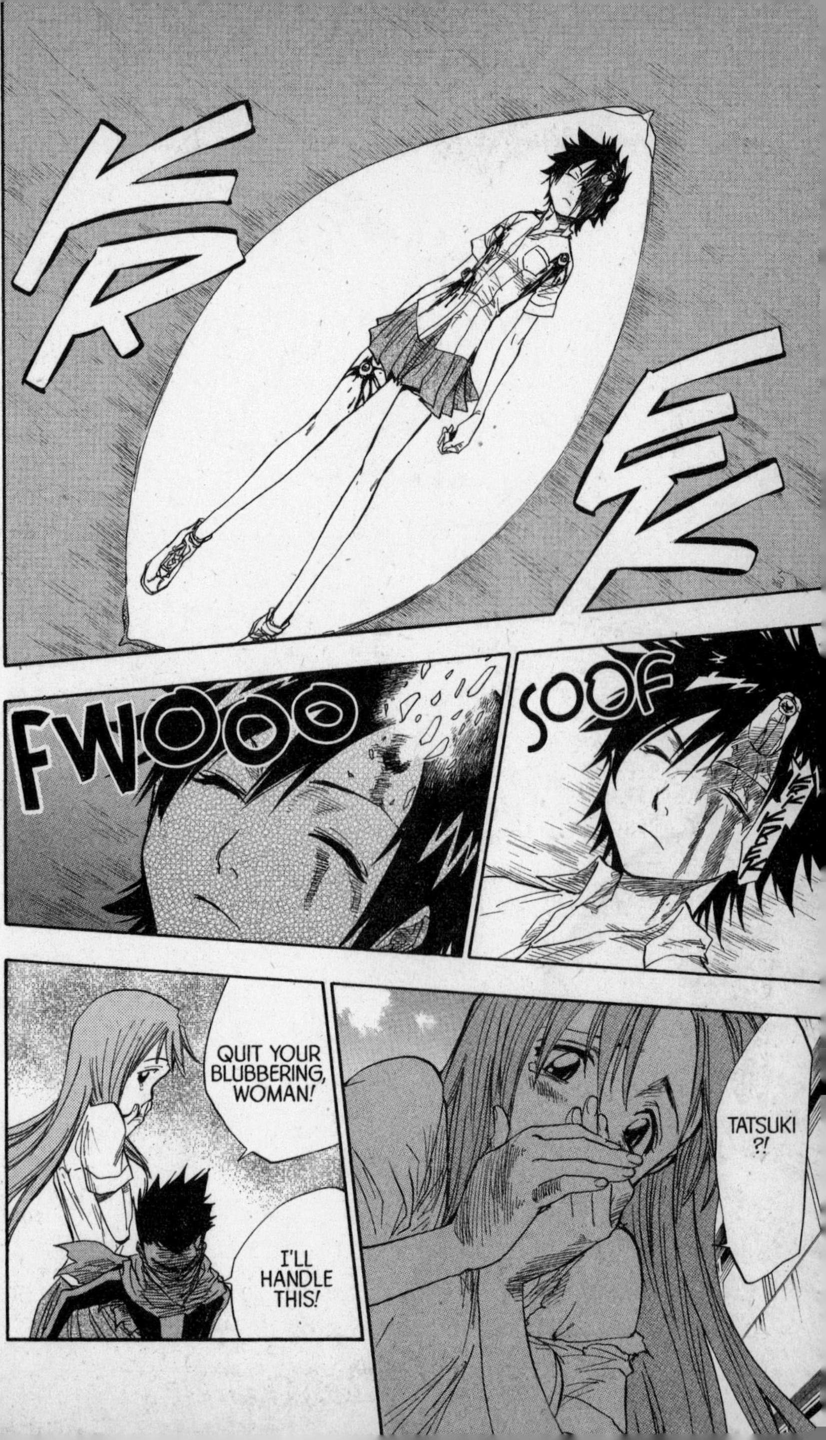
SOOF
FWOOOO
TATSUKI?!
QUIT YOUR BLUBBERING, WOMAN!
I'LL HANDLE THIS!

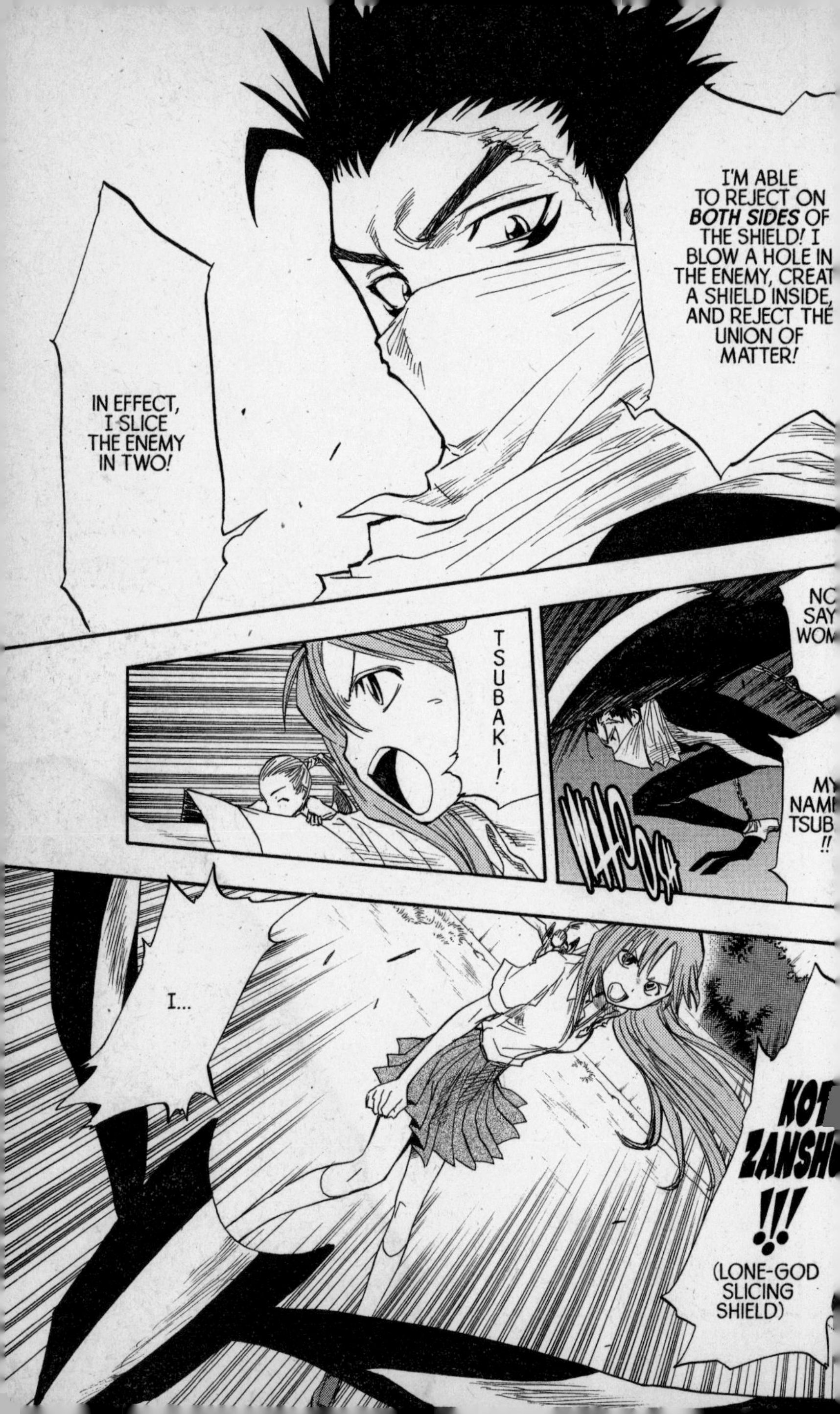

I'M ABLE TO REJECT ON ***BOTH SIDES*** OF THE SHIELD! I BLOW A HOLE IN THE ENEMY, CREAT A SHIELD INSIDE, AND REJECT THE UNION OF MATTER!
IN EFFECT, I SLICE THE ENEMY IN TWO!
NO SAY WOM
MY NAM TSUB !!
WHOOSH
TSUBAKI!
I...
KOT ZANSHU !!!
(LONE-GOD SLICING SHIELD)

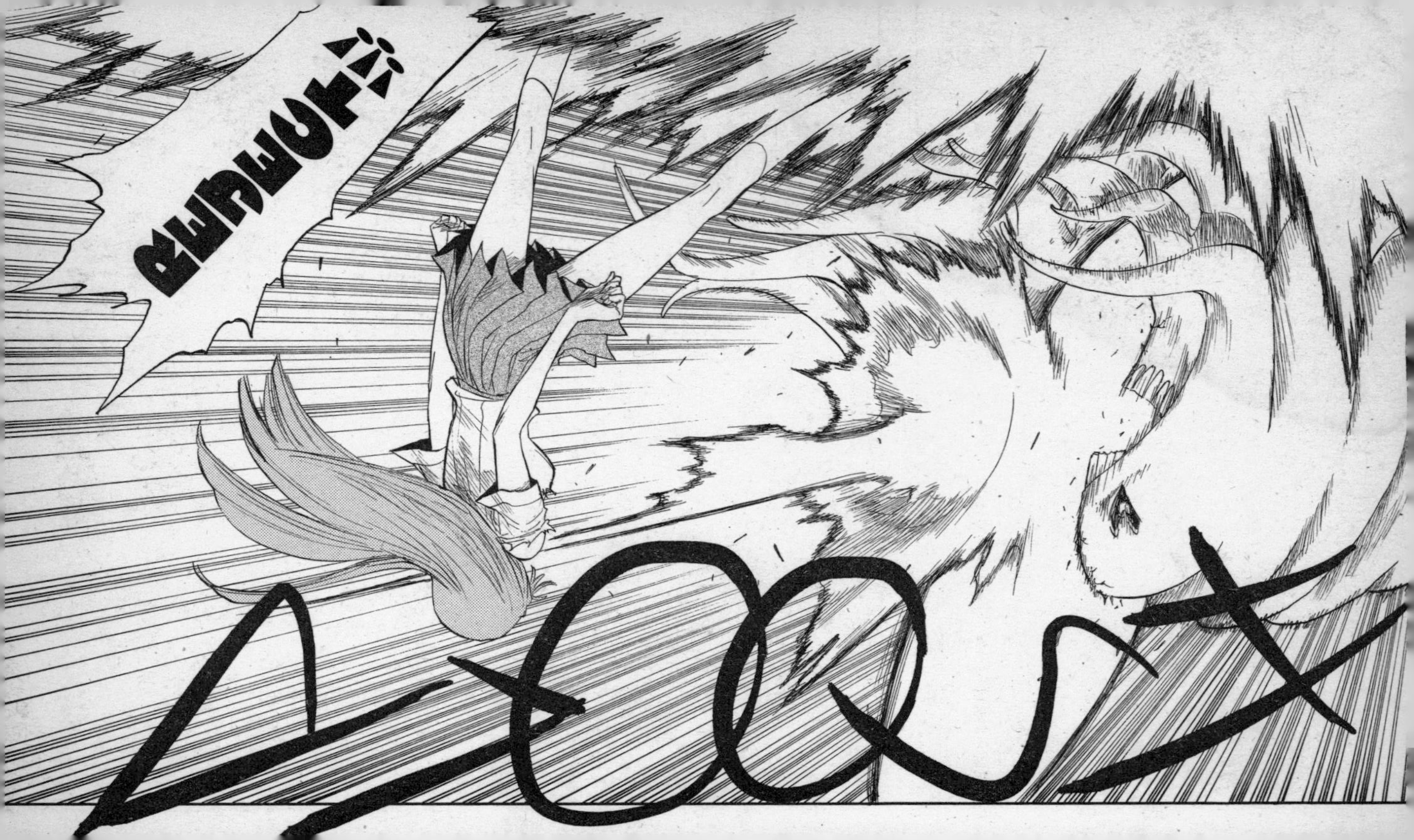

SKR... UKK

AA...

huff
huff
huff

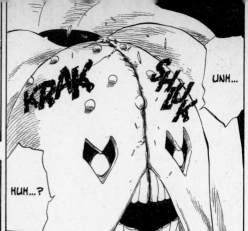

KRAK

SHLCK

UNK...

HUH...?

...I...

huff

...DID THAT?

huff

!

LOOKS LIKE ALL OF THIS WAS TOO MUCH FOR HER... BOY...

OH BOY...

HEY WOMAN?!

ORIHIME!!

ORIHIME?!

...YAY...

TUMP

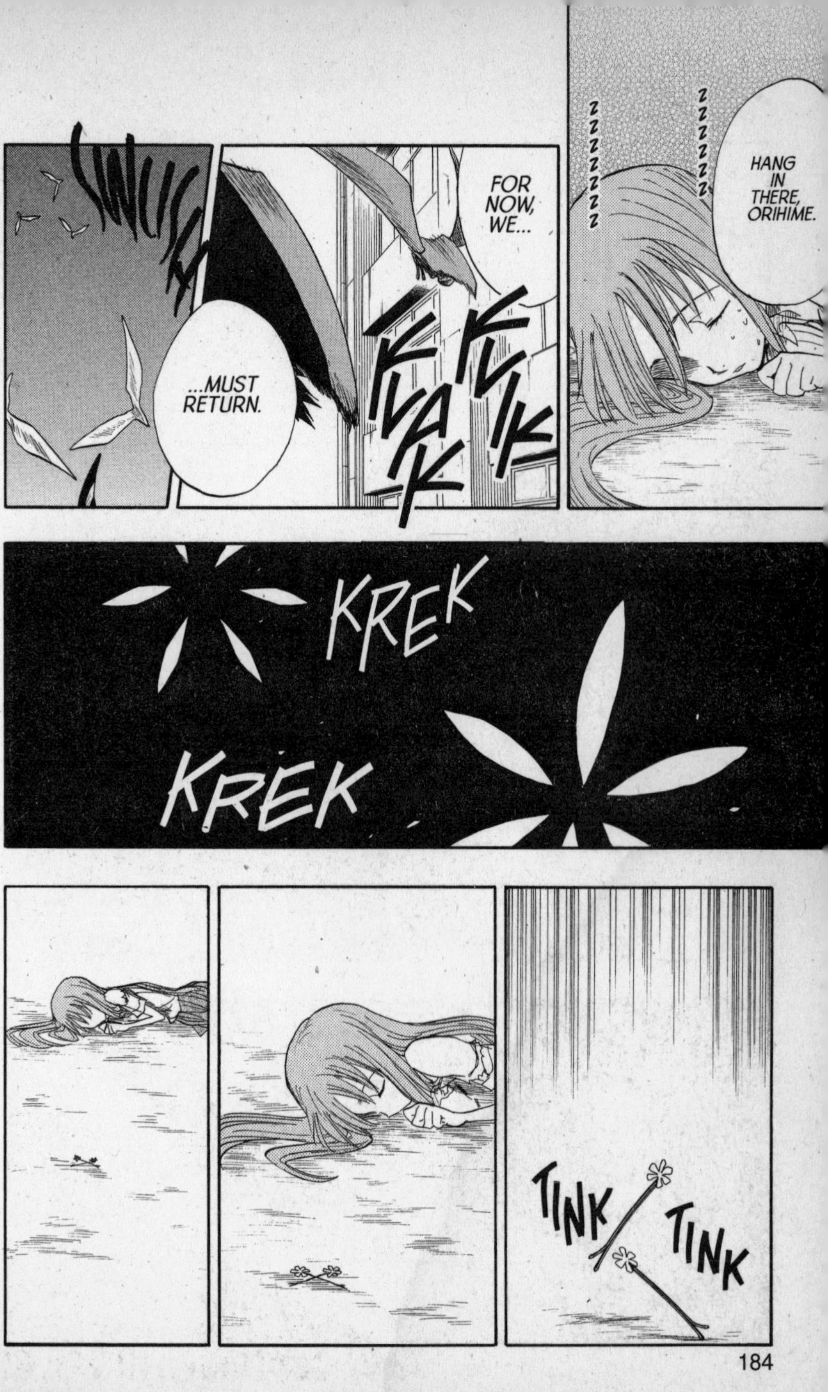
HANG IN THERE, ORIHIME.
FOR NOW, WE...
...MUST RETURN.
KREK
KREK
TINK
TINK

READ THIS WAY

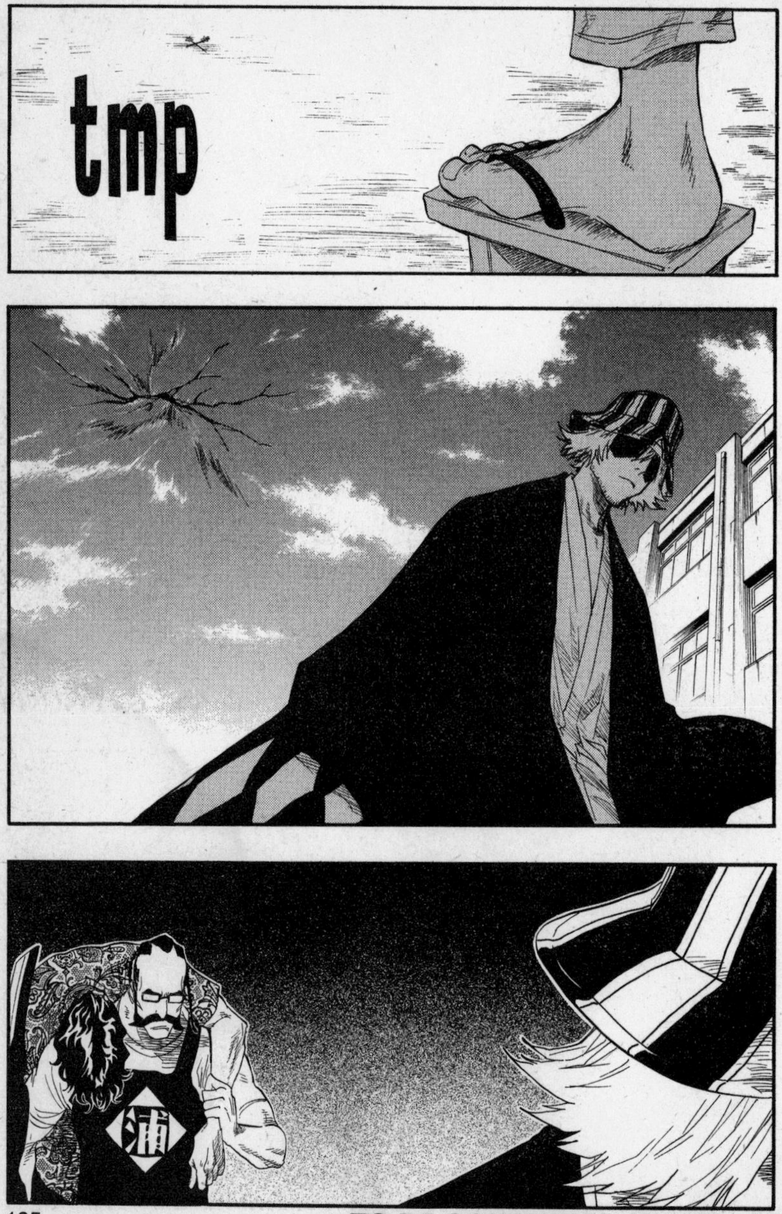
tmp

TO BE CONTINUED IN VOL. 6!

I will protect you.

Here is some important **BLEACH** data!!

Overall Attendance Number 4	URYÛ ISHIDA	イシダ・ウリュウ
Male Student 3		

171 CM

55 KG

BLOOD TYPE: AB

D.O.B. NOVEMBER 6TH

• MEMBER, HANDICRAFT CLUB

• HATES BUTTONS, PREFERS FASTENERS

• LOW BLOOD PRESSURE

• HATES PROCRASTINATION

• CHARACTERIZED BY DRAMATIC SPEECH. AT THE MOMENT, HE'S THE NO. 1 SHOWOFF. (NO. 2 IS ICHIGO, I THINK.)

• FAVORITE FOOD IS MACKEREL STEWED IN MISO (COOKED BY HIMSELF)

THEME SONG
RADIOHEAD
"Idioteque"
RECORDED IN
"Kid A"

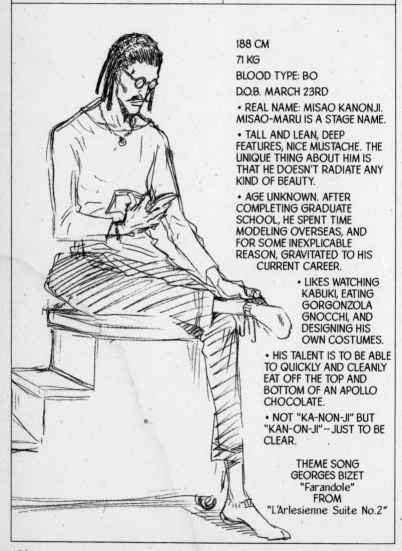

DON KANONJI
(MISAO-MARU KANONJI)

ドン・カンオンジ

188 CM

71 KG

BLOOD TYPE: BO

D.O.B. MARCH 23RD

• REAL NAME: MISAO KANONJI. MISAO-MARU IS A STAGE NAME.

• TALL AND LEAN, DEEP FEATURES, NICE MUSTACHE. THE UNIQUE THING ABOUT HIM IS THAT HE DOESN'T RADIATE ANY KIND OF BEAUTY.

• AGE UNKNOWN. AFTER COMPLETING GRADUATE SCHOOL, HE SPENT TIME MODELING OVERSEAS, AND FOR SOME INEXPLICABLE REASON, GRAVITATED TO HIS CURRENT CAREER.

• LIKES WATCHING KABUKI, EATING GORGONZOLA GNOCCHI, AND DESIGNING HIS OWN COSTUMES.

• HIS TALENT IS TO BE ABLE TO QUICKLY AND CLEANLY EAT OFF THE TOP AND BOTTOM OF AN APOLLO CHOCOLATE.

• NOT "KA-NON-JI" BUT "KAN-ON-JI"-- JUST TO BE CLEAR.

THEME SONG
GEORGES BIZET
"Farandole"
FROM
"L'Arlesienne Suite No.2"

Next Volume Preview

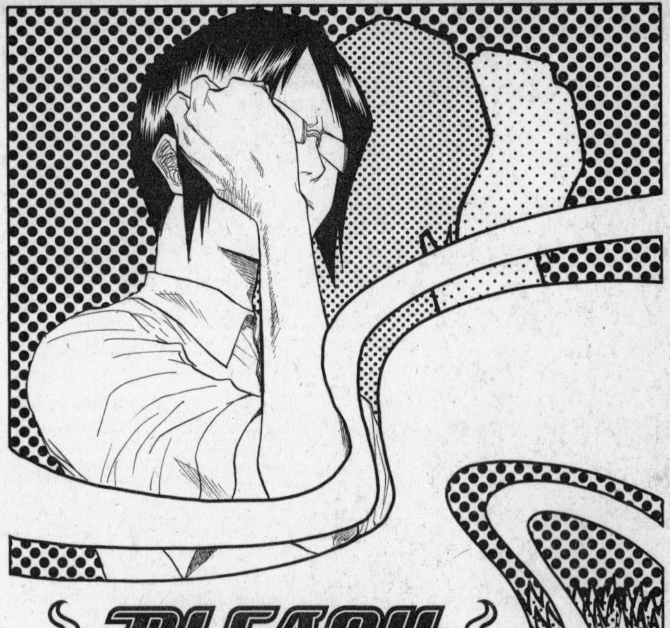
BLEACH
ブリーチ

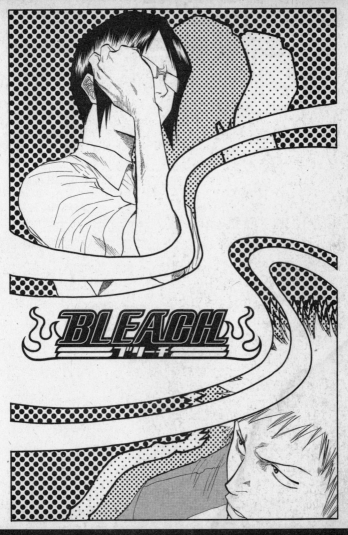

While Orihime and Chad recuperate at Urahara Shoten (and learn more about their own psychic capabilities), the contest between Ichigo and Uryû rages on. At stake—to decide whether a Quincy or a Soul Reaper is better at defeating Hollows. However, an inordinately huge number of malevolent spirits are popping up all over town, increasing the danger of the competition exponentially. And, to make matters worse, out of this conflagration is born Menos Grande, an enormous Hollow made of hundreds of lesser Hollows merged into one!

Available in April 2005

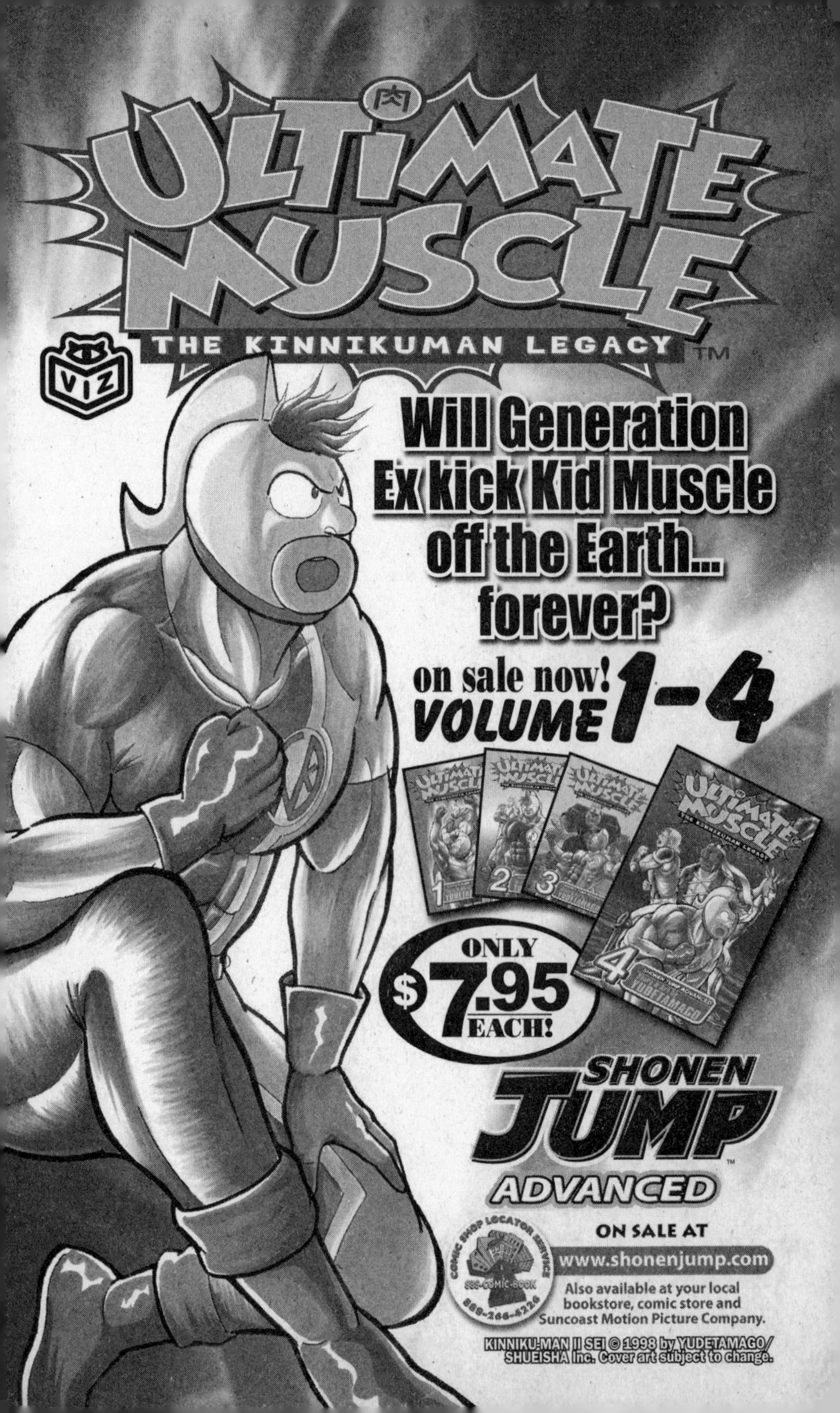
ULTIMATE MUSCLE
THE KINNIKUMAN LEGACY™
VIZ
Will Generation Ex kick Kid Muscle off the Earth... forever?
on sale now! VOLUME 1-4
ONLY $7.95 EACH!
SHONEN JUMP ADVANCED
ON SALE AT
www.shonenjump.com
Also available at your local bookstore, comic store and Suncoast Motion Picture Company.
COMIC SHOP LOCATOR SERVICE
888-COMIC-BOOK
888-266-4226
KINNIKU-MAN II SEI © 1998 by YUDETAMAGO/SHUEISHA Inc. Cover art subject to change.

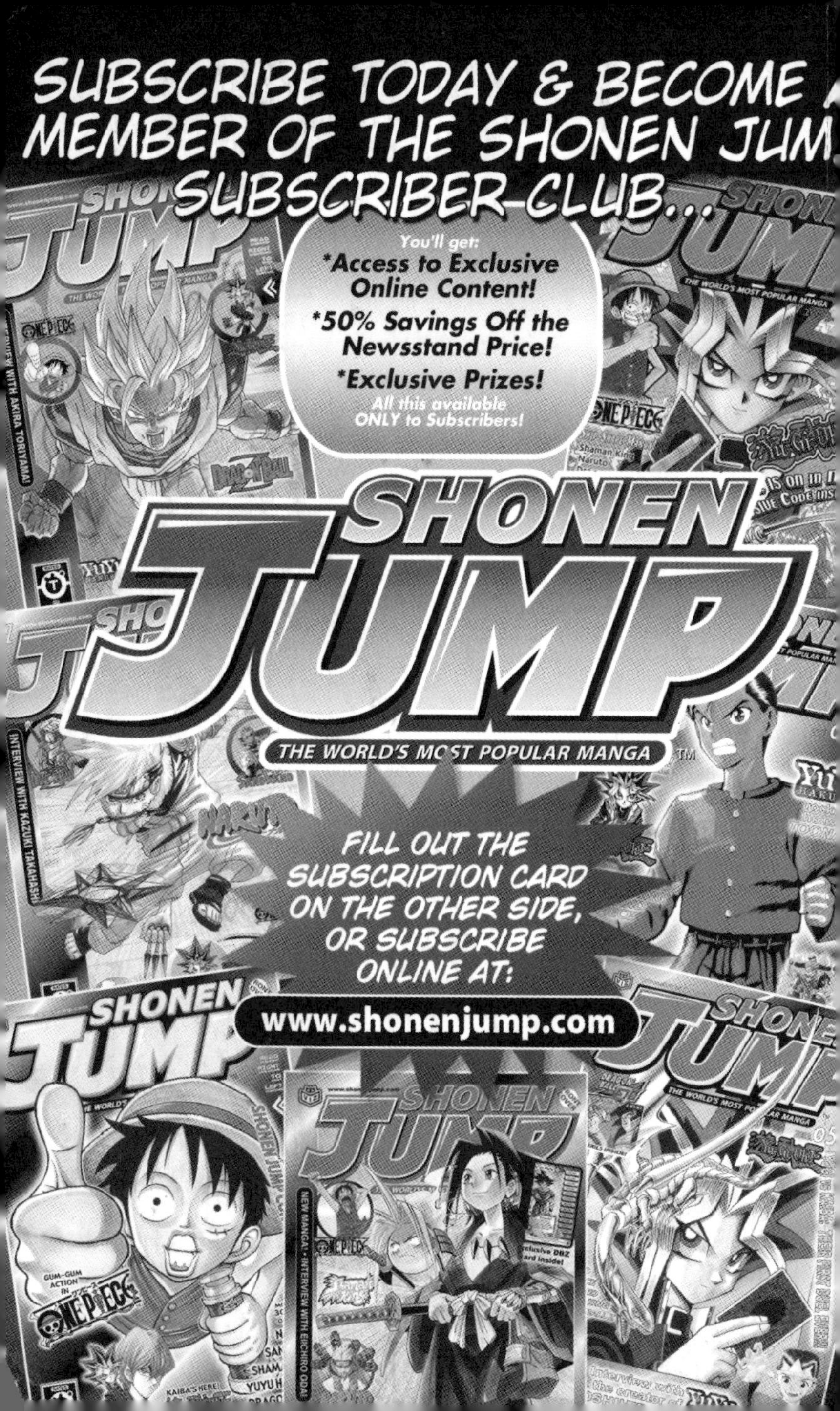
SUBSCRIBE TODAY & BECOME A MEMBER OF THE SHONEN JUMP SUBSCRIBER CLUB...
You'll get:
*Access to Exclusive Online Content!
*50% Savings Off the Newsstand Price!
*Exclusive Prizes!
All this available ONLY to Subscribers!
SHONEN JUMP
THE WORLD'S MOST POPULAR MANGA
TM
FILL OUT THE SUBSCRIPTION CARD ON THE OTHER SIDE, OR SUBSCRIBE ONLINE AT:
www.shonenjump.com

COMPLETE OUR SURVEY AND LET US KNOW WHAT YOU THINK!

☐ Please do NOT send me information about VIZ and SHONEN JUMP products, news and events, special offers, or other information.

☐ Please do NOT send me information from VIZ's trusted business partners.

Name: _____

Address: _____

City: _____ State: _____ Zip: _____

E-mail: _____

☐ Male ☐ Female Date of Birth (mm/dd/yyyy): ___ / ___ / ___ (Under 13? Parental consent required)

❶ Do you purchase SHONEN JUMP Magazine?

☐ Yes ☐ No (if no, skip the next two questions)

If **YES**, do you subscribe?

☐ Yes ☐ No

If **NO**, how often do you purchase SHONEN JUMP Magazine?

☐ 1-3 issues a year

☐ 4-6 issues a year

☐ more than 7 issues a year

❷ Which SHONEN JUMP Graphic Novel did you purchase? (please check one)

☐ Beet the Vandel Buster ☐ Bleach ☐ Dragon Ball

☐ Dragon Ball Z ☐ Hikaru no Go ☐ Knights of the Zodiac

☐ Naruto ☐ One Piece ☐ Rurouni Kenshin

☐ Shaman King ☐ The Prince of Tennis ☐ Ultimate Muscle

☐ Whistle! ☐ Yu-Gi-Oh! ☐ YuYu Hakusho

☐ Other _____

Will you purchase subsequent volumes?

☐ Yes ☐ No

❸ How did you learn about this title? (check all that apply)

☐ Favorite title ☐ Advertisement ☐ Article

☐ Gift ☐ Read excerpt in SHONEN JUMP Magazine

☐ Recommendation ☐ Special offer ☐ Through TV animation

☐ Website ☐ Other _____

4 Of the titles that are serialized in SHONEN JUMP Magazine, have you purchased the Graphic Novels?

☐ Yes ☐ No

If **YES**, which ones have you purchased? (check all that apply)

☐ Dragon Ball Z ☐ Hikaru no Go ☐ Naruto ☐ One Piece

☐ Shaman King ☐ Yu-Gi-Oh! ☐ YuYu Hakusho

If **YES**, what were your reasons for purchasing? (please pick up to 3)

☐ A favorite title ☐ A favorite creator/artist ☐ I want to read it in one go

☐ I want to read it over and over again ☐ There are extras that aren't in the magazine

☐ The quality of printing is better than the magazine ☐ Recommendation

☐ Special offer ☐ Other

If **NO**, why did/would you not purchase it?

☐ I'm happy just reading it in the magazine ☐ It's not worth buying the graphic novel

☐ All the manga pages are in black and white unlike the magazine

☐ There are other graphic novels that I prefer ☐ There are too many to collect for each title

☐ It's too small ☐ Other ______________________

5 Of the titles NOT serialized in the Magazine, which ones have you purchased?
(check all that apply)

☐ Beet the Vandel Buster ☐ Bleach ☐ Dragon Ball

☐ Knights of the Zodiac ☐ The Prince of Tennis ☐ Rurouni Kenshin

☐ Whistle! ☐ Other ____________ ☐ None

If you did purchase any of the above, what were your reasons for purchase?

☐ A favorite title ☐ A favorite creator/artist

☐ Read a preview in SHONEN JUMP Magazine and wanted to read the rest of the story

☐ Recommendation ☐ Other

Will you purchase subsequent volumes?

☐ Yes ☐ No

6 What race/ethnicity do you consider yourself? (please check one)

☐ Asian/Pacific Islander ☐ Black/African American ☐ Hispanic/Latino

☐ Native American/Alaskan Native ☐ White/Caucasian ☐ Other

THANK YOU! Please send the completed form to:

VIZ Survey
42 Catharine St.
Poughkeepsie, NY 12601

All information provided will be used for internal purposes only. We promise not to sell or otherwise divulge your information.